## PAGE 50 | ON THE ROAD

YOUR COMPLETE DESTINATION GUIDE
In-depth reviews, detailed listings
and insider tips

**Anegada**
p184

**Jost Van Dyke**
p175

**Virgin Gorda**
p162

**Tortola**
p136

**St Thomas**
p52

**St John**
p83

**Out Islands**
p191

**St Croix**
p108

## PAGE 227 | SURVIVAL GUIDE

VITAL PRACTICAL INFORMATION TO
HELP YOU HAVE A SMOOTH TRIP

THIS EDITION WRITTEN AND RESEARCHED BY

# Karla Zimmerman

# welcome to the US & British Virgin Islands

## Patches of Tropical Bliss

The Virgin Islands have the tropical thing down: consistently balmy weather, ridiculously white sandy shores, diving and snorkeling and calypso-wafting beach bars. But then they kick it up a notch. They float the Caribbean's most profuse and tightly packed group of islands, with more than 90 little landmasses bobbing in a 45-mile triangular patch of sea. Add steady trade winds, calm currents and hundreds of protected, salt-rimmed bays, and it's easy to see how the Virgins became a sailing fantasyland.

Exploring the archipelago is easy aboard the public ferries. Or hoist your own sail from the region's largest fleet of charter boats.

## Island by Island

Hmm, which island to choose for secluded beaches and conch fritters? Easy: any one, though each differs slightly in personality. The US Virgins hold the lion's share of population and development. St Thomas has more resorts and water sports than you can shake a beach towel at. St John takes a different tack: it cloaks two-thirds of its area in parkland – above ground and underwater. The largest Virgin, St Croix, pleases divers and drinkers with extraordinary scuba sites and rum factories.

*Prediction for your Virgin Islands arrival: it's sunny, 83°F (28°C). Soon you're on a boat gliding across the teal-blue sea. You sip a Painkiller and think of the suckers at home shoveling snow.*

(left) White Bay Beach, Jost Van Dyke.
(below) Diving at Lind Point, near Cruz Bay, St John.

If you're a US citizen and have a passport, you can hop onward to the British Virgins. These are officially territories of Her Majesty's land, but aside from scattered offerings of fish and chips, there's little that's overtly British. They're more like their US brethren, only quirkier and less developed.

Take Jost Van Dyke, population 200, where a man named Foxy is the island's main man. Chief island Tortola is known for its full-moon parties, fungi bands and fire jugglers. Virgin Gorda is beloved by movie stars and yachties; you'll understand the ardor once you've seen her national parks. And Anegada? It's so baked-in-the-sun mellow we can't be bothered to get out of our hammock to find better words for it.

## From Beach to Adventure

Believe it or not, a day will come during your Virgin stay when you decide enough with the beach lounging. Then it's time to slap on the mask and flippers and snorkel with turtles and spotted eagle rays. Or dive to explore a 19th-century shipwreck. Or hike to petroglyphs and sugar mill ruins. Or kayak through a bioluminescent bay. Or fork into garlic chicken and fried johnny-cakes at a West Indian snack shack. Or surf, bonefish, day-sail or eco-camp...

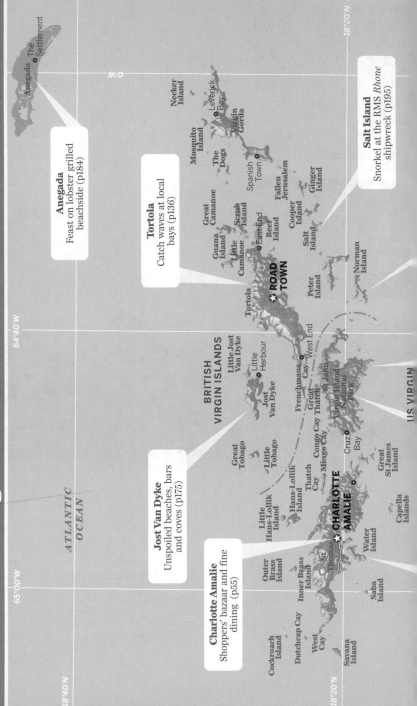

**Charlotte Amalie**
Shoppers' bazaar and fine dining (p55)

**Jost Van Dyke**
Unspoiled beaches, bars and coves (p175)

**Tortola**
Catch waves at local bays (p136)

**Anegada**
Feast on lobster grilled beachside (p184)

**Salt Island**
Snorkel at the RMS *Rhone* shipwreck (p195)

ATLANTIC OCEAN

BRITISH VIRGIN ISLANDS

US VIRGIN

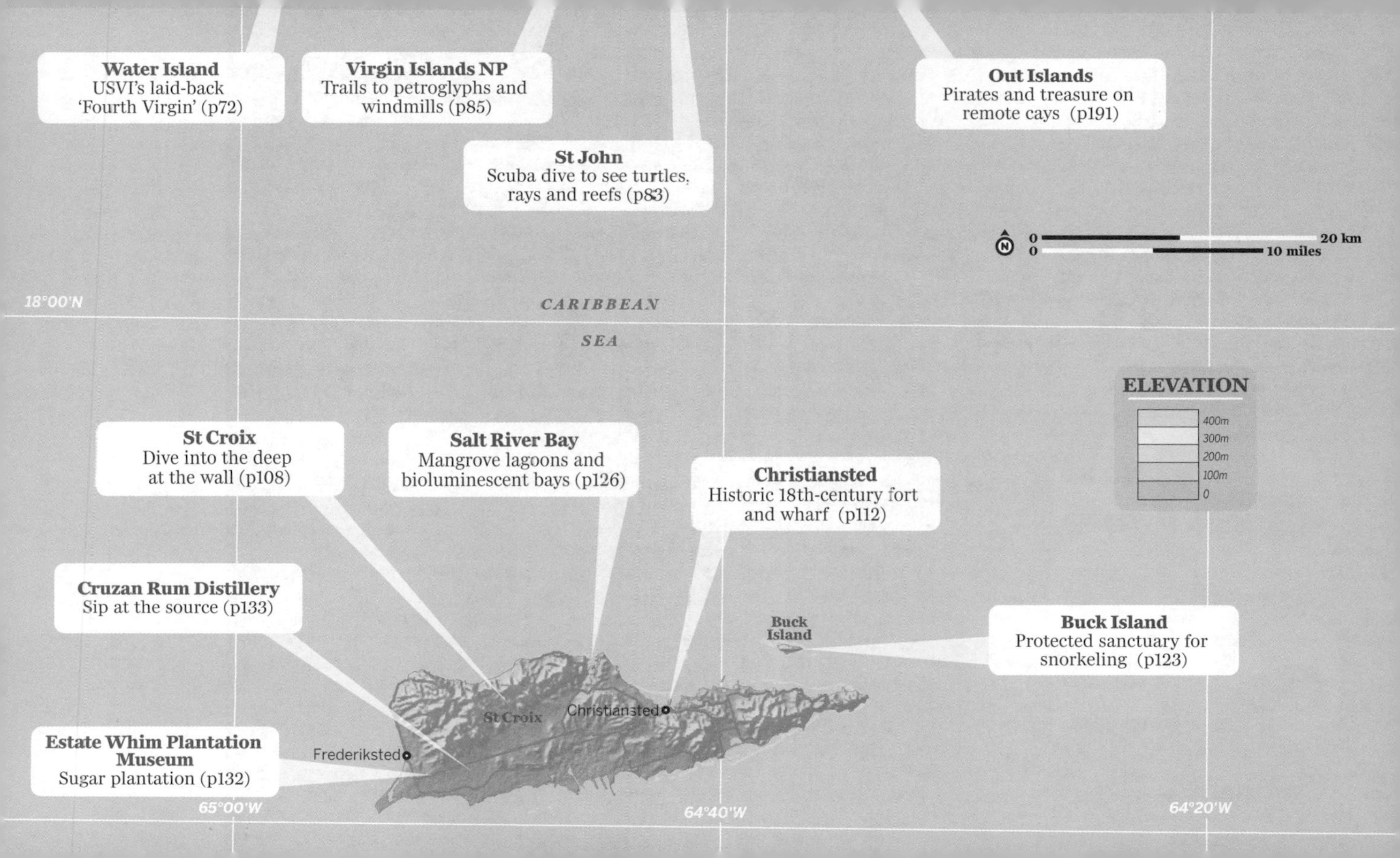

**Out Islands**
Pirates and treasure on remote cays (p191)

**Water Island**
USVI's laid-back 'Fourth Virgin' (p72)

**Virgin Islands NP**
Trails to petroglyphs and windmills (p85)

**St John**
Scuba dive to see turtles, rays and reefs (p83)

**Christiansted**
Historic 18th-century fort and wharf (p112)

**Buck Island**
Protected sanctuary for snorkeling (p123)

**Salt River Bay**
Mangrove lagoons and bioluminescent bays (p126)

**St Croix**
Dive into the deep at the wall (p108)

**Cruzan Rum Distillery**
Sip at the source (p133)

**Estate Whim Plantation Museum**
Sugar plantation (p132)

CARIBBEAN

SEA

ELEVATION

400m
300m
200m
100m
0

0    10 miles
0    20 km

N

18°00'N

65°00'W    64°40'W    64°20'W

Frederiksted

St Croix

Christiansted

Buck Island

# 20 TOP EXPERIENCES

## Hiking in Virgin Islands National Park

**1** This national park, with its gnarled trees and spiky cacti spilling over the edges, covers some three-quarters of St John (p85). Aside from awesome snorkeling, feral donkeys and eco-camps, the park's greatest gift to visitors is its hiking. Dozens of trails wind through the wild terrain, taking trekkers to cliff-top overlooks, petroglyphs and sugar-mill ruins. Several lead to beaches prime for swimming with turtles and spotted eagle rays. The paths are short and easy for the most part, so that any reasonably fit hiker can walk them and reap the rewards.

## Diving the RMS *Rhone*

**2** The RMS *Rhone* (p196) is one of the most famous shipwreck dives in the Caribbean. The twin-masted vessel sank off Salt Island's coast during a hurricane in 1867. Now a national park, the steamer's remains are extensive and have become an exotic habitat for marine life. Octopuses, eels and squid swim by a setting that couldn't be more classic – so classic, in fact, that Hollywood has used it as the backdrop for numerous films, such as *The Deep*. Snorkelers can access the wreck, too, since the ship's stern is in shallower water.

## Exploring the Out Islands

**3** The BVI's remote Out Islands (p191) are a wonderful mix of uninhabited wildlife sanctuaries, luxurious hideaways for the rich and famous, and provisioning stops for sailors. With more than 30 little landmasses to choose from, there's something for every taste. Cooper Island hosts affordable cottages. Norman Island holds buried treasure and a rowdy floating bar. Countless other isles – Ginger, the Dogs, Fallen Jerusalem – offer nothing but beaches and blue sea. If you're sans yacht yourself, climb aboard a day-sailing tour to reach them. Norman Island

## Beaches

**4** You don't have to be hit on the head with a coconut to know beaches are a major highlight of the Virgins. Secluded beaches, family beaches, snorkeling beaches and beaches unfurling miles of sand for sunset walks edge the islands. Loblolly Bay, Flash of Beauty, Smuggler's Cove – can you see the hammocks swinging from coconut trees? Famed White Bay on Jost Van Dyke gets its name from its crazy-white sand. Tortola has so many beaches it had to start repeating names (Long Bay on the east and west). White Bay Beach (p180), Jost Van Dyke

## Historic Christiansted

**5** This 18th-century town (p112) is a showcase of historic preservation. The cannon-covered fortress, flanked by West Indies neoclassical buildings in gold, pink and brown, evokes the days when Christiansted was the Danish colonies' capital and the St Croix plantocracy society was awash in gold. The district abuts Kings Wharf, the commercial landing where, for more than 250 years, ships landed with slaves and set off with sugar or molasses. Today it's fronted by a boardwalk of bars and dive-boat operators, with art galleries and court-yard bistros tucked into the town's laneways.

## The Baths

**6** The BVI's most popular tourist attraction, the Baths (p165) on Virgin Gorda are a sublime jumbled collection of sky-high granite boulders by the sea. The rocks — volcanic lava from up to 70 million years ago, according to some estimates — form a series of grottoes that fill with water and shafts of kaleidoscopic sunlight. You can snorkel around the otherworldly megaliths, or take the trail through them in which you'll slosh through tidal pools, squeeze into impossibly narrow passages, and then drop out onto a sugar-sand beach.

## Jost Van Dyke

**7** This island, northwest of Tortola, has developed a reputation that far exceeds its mere 4 sq miles of land – and a lot of that is due to a local calypso musician named Foxy Callwood and his legendary namesake bar. Even though folks such as Keith Richards drop by for a drink, Jost (p175) remains an unspoiled oasis of green hills edged by blinding white sand. There's a small clutch of restaurants, beach bars and guesthouses, but blissfully little else. In fact, Main St here is a beach.

## Estate Whim Plantation Museum

**8** One of St Croix's most striking reminders of its colonial sugarcane history, Whim Plantation (p132) rises out of the landscape a few miles from Frederiksted. Tour the atmospheric grounds to see windmills and steam engines used for grinding cane. Buildings such as the cookhouse (where they serve traditional snacks), bathhouse, watch house, caretaker's cottage and slave quarters also speckle the area. Some are restored to their vintage state; others function as exhibition spaces. The great house hosts intimate, candlelit classical music concerts.

STEVE SIMONSEN / LONELY PLANET IMAGES ©

## Snorkeling around St John

**9** More than 40% of Virgin Islands National Park (p88) is underwater, protecting the seagrass beds and reefs, as well as their many creatures. Strap on a mask and fins, swim from shore and behold: basketball-sized brain corals and a passing shark off one beach, squid and sea turtles at another, sting rays and starfish at the next one down the coast. Pick a beach as umbrella'ed or forlorn as you want. Even snorkeling beginners can pretend they're Jacques Cousteau.

## Charlotte Amalie

**10** To many travelers, the mere mention of the US Virgin Islands' capital spawns images of an exotic shopping bazaar. Indeed, it has the largest number of boutiques and jewelry shops in the Caribbean, with most floujut in architecturally rich, pastel-hued colonial buildings. It's convenient, too, that the USVI's busiest port also has the largest duty-free allowance in the Caribbean. If shopping isn't your thing, Charlotte Amalie (p55) remains a little town to sharpen your knife and fork on pungent West Indian fare such as fungi, callaloo and curried goat.

## Sailing

**11** Endowed with steady trade winds, tame currents and hundreds of protected bays, the Virgin Islands are a sailor's fantasyland. Many visitors come expressly to hoist a jib and dawdle among the 90-plus isles and cays, trying to determine which one serves the best rum-pineapple-and-coconut Painkiller. Tortola is the launching pad, known as the charter boat capital of the world, so it's easy to get geared up. Don't know how to sail? Learn on the job with a sailing school.
Sailing around St John

## Island Music

**12** The Virgins know how to throw a party, and that party has a soundtrack. Full moon celebrations rock Tortola. When the sun sets on the auspicious day each month, the fungi music begins at Aragorn's Studio (p158). Band members lay down a beat for stilt-walkers and fire jugglers. St Croix hosts 'jump ups', when steel pan bands take to the streets. And every island hosts a big carnival, usually around Easter or Christmas, with bands and calypso competitions. St Thomas Carnival Parade Celebrations

STEVE SIMONSEN / LONELY PLANET IMAGES ©

## Diving St Croix

**13** If you're a scuba enthusiast worth your sea salt, you'll be spending lots of time underwater around St Croix (p127). It is a divers' mecca thanks to two unique features: one, it's surrounded by a massive barrier reef, so turtles, rays and other sea creatures are prevalent; and, two, a spectacular wall runs along the island's north shore, dropping at a 60-degree slope to a depth of more than 12,000 feet. If you ever wanted to go over the edge, here's your big chance. Buck Island Reef National Monument, St Croix

## Kayaking in the USVI

**14** The US islands provide distinctive opportunities to dip a paddle. St Thomas has a mangrove preserve where you can glide through to a coral rubble beach. You can also steer to nearby Hassel Island, where old fort ruins and a fishy reef for snorkeling loom. On St Croix you can paddle Salt River Bay. This is the historic site where Columbus landed in 1493, but even more impressive come nighttime is the bioluminescent water. The algae spark like underwater fireflies when the moon is new. Magens Bay, St Thomas

LEE FOSTER / LONELY PLANET IMAGES ©

## Cruzan Rum Distillery

© DIGITAL FOCUS / ALAMY

**15** The Nelthropp family has been pumping out the Virgin Islands' favorite elixir since 1760. Stop by for a distillery tour in St Croix to see how it's done (p133). Journey through the gingerbread-smelling, oak-barrel-stacked warehouses, then belly up at the bar to sample the good stuff. The Callwood Rum Distillery (p150) on Tortola offers a similar atmospheric tour through its 300-year-old facility in the forest. Soon you'll be able to compare these oldies to the brand-new Captain Morgan Rum Factory (p134); it opens to visitors in 2012 on St Croix. Cruzan Rum Distillery

## Water Island

**16** Sometimes called the USVI's 'Fourth Virgin,' little Water Island (p72) drifts a mere quarter-mile from the urban frenzy of Charlotte Amalie, but with only about 100 residents and very few cars or shops, it feels far more remote. Take the ferry over for the afternoon and cycle around, joining the slowpoke lifestyle at Honeymoon Beach, prime for swimming, snorkeling and buying a slice from the pizza boat. Stay longer in one of the tent-cottages at the ecofriendly Virgin Islands Campground.

LEE FOSTER / LONELY PLANET IMAGES ©

## Anegada Lobster

**17** Every restaurant on the far-flung island of Anegada (p189) serves the massive crustaceans, usually grilled on the beach in a converted oil drum and spiced with the chef's secret seasonings. The critters are plucked fresh from the surrounding waters; many eateries let you go out to the traps and choose your own quarry. And when the dish arrives at your beachside table, as the sun wanes amber and yachts sway in the bay, you'll know you're living the good life.

© MELANIE ACEVEDO / IMAGE BANK / GETTY IMAGES

## Windsurfing Tortola

**18** While the windsurfing and surfing scenes on Tortola (p149) are no secret – the silly-blue water is always warm, and waves pack a notable punch – the beaches retain the feel of a lazy outpost. They're all dramatic strands at the foot of mountains, and you don't have to be a surfer yourself to appreciate them – just grab a cold drink, spread a towel on the sand, and watch the lineup as reggae music floats in from the inevitable beach bar. Trellis Bay, Josiah's Bay and Apple Bay are just a few of the island's hot spots.

GREG JOHNSTON / LONELY PLANET IMAGES ©

## Buck Island

**19** Tiny Buck Island (p123) floats a mile and a half off St Croix and dots an 18,800-acre marine sanctuary. On land, endangered hawksbill and green sea turtles come ashore to protected beaches. In the water, a complete Caribbean ecosystem is home to coral grottoes and flashy tropical fish. The National Park Service preserves the habitat. Several tour operators run trips to the island that include snorkeling on the reef and allow time to meander on shore, where picnicking and hiking opportunities await.

© BOB KRIST / CORBIS

## Eco-camping

**20** Eco-camps, aka tent resorts, have popped up throughout the USVI. Maho Bay Camps (p100) on St John leads the pack; each 'tent' (a permanent, canvas-sided structure) sits on a wooden platform that is propped up so far off the ground, and surrounded by vegetation so thick, it's like living in a tree house. Similar camps include Concordia Eco-Tents on St John, Mt Victory Campground on St Croix and Virgin Islands Campground on Water Island. Rainwater collection and solar-heated showers are common, as are reasonable costs. Maho Bay, St John

# need to know

## Currency
» US dollars ($) for both USVI and BVI

## Language
» English

## When to Go?

Mild to hot summers, cold winters

**Spanish Town** GO Feb–Apr

**Road Town** GO Mar–Jun

**Charlotte Amalie** GO Feb–Apr

**Cruz Bay** GO Jan–Mar

**Christiansted** GO Dec–Feb

### High Season
(Dec–Apr)

» Weather is at its best: dry and sunny, while trade winds keep humidity down

» Accommodation prices peak (30% up on average)

» Holidays and festivals ensure a fun ambience

### Shoulder
(May–Jul)

» Crowds and prices drop off

» Trade winds lessen and the sea calms, so snorkeling and sailing are smoother

» The pace is more relaxed, with a better chance to appreciate local culture

### Low Season
(Aug–Nov)

» Hurricane season peaks, along with rainfall

» Many attractions keep shorter hours

» Some businesses close altogether (especially during September)

## Your Daily Budget

### Budget less than
# $150
» Campsite or small room in a guesthouse: $35–$125

» Public bus and taxis: $5–30

» Supermarkets for self-catering

### Midrange
# $150– $350
» Double room at midrange hotel or resort: $150–$250

» Meal in a good local restaurant: from $25 plus drinks

» Rental car: $60–75 per day

» Day-sail tour: $50–90

### Top end over
# $350
» Four-star resort room: from $300

» Three-course meal in a top restaurant: from $45 plus drinks

» Two-tank dive: $110–$125

### Money

» ATMs available in main towns. Credit cards accepted in most hotels and restaurants.

### Visas

» US and Canadian citizens do not need a visa to enter the USVI or BVI. Visitors from most other Western countries also are exempt, but must get ESTA approval for USVI.

### Cell Phones

» Local SIM cards can be used in European and Australian phones. Other phones must be set to roaming.

### Driving/ Transportation

» Drive on the left; steering wheel is on the left side of the car.

## Websites

» **BVI Tourist Board** (www.bvitourism. com) Official site with comprehensive info.

» **BVI Welcome Magazine** (www. bviwelcome.com) Lists ferry schedules, beaches and diving sites.

» **USVI Department of Tourism** (www.visitusvi. com) Official site.

» **Virgin Islands Now** (www.vinow.com) USVI info from local residents.

» **Lonely Planet** (www. lonelyplanet.com/ us-virgin-islands and www.lonelyplanet.com/ british-virgin-islands) Destination information, hotel bookings, traveler forum.

## Exchange Rates

| Australia | A$1 | US$0.99 |
|---|---|---|
| Canada | C$1 | US$1 |
| Europe | €1 | US$1.37 |
| Japan | ¥100 | US$1.21 |
| New Zealand | NZ$1 | US$0.77 |
| UK | UK£1 | US$1.60 |

For current exchange rates see www.xe.com.

## Important Numbers

| Country code | ☑1 |
|---|---|
| International access code | ☑011 |
| Emergency USVI | ☑911 |
| Emergency BVI | ☑911 or 999 |
| BVI Search & Rescue | ☑767 |

## Arriving in the Virgin Islands

**Cyril E King Airport (St Thomas)**

Taxis $6-7 per person plus $2 per bag; 15 minutes to downtown

» **Havensight Dock (St Thomas)**

Taxis $5-6 per person; 10 minutes to downtown

» **Henry E Rohlsen Airport (St Croix)**

Taxis $9-16 per person plus $2 per bag; 20-25 minutes to Christiansted

» **Terrence B Lettsome Airport (Tortola)**

Taxis $12-27 per person; 25 minutes to Road Town

## Stormy Weather

Hurricane season officially runs from June 1 to November 30. August and September are the peak months, followed by October. If this is the only time you can visit, take heart: the chance of a major storm is small. What's more, a good watch system is in place with warnings that precede storms by several days, but do consider trip insurance during this period.

September, October and November are the wettest months, followed by May and August. Rain tends to fall in brief, heavy bursts rather than pouring all day. Most showers happen early in the morning or at night, so you can still get out and about with marginal impact on activities. Note that many businesses do shut down in September, the worst month for stormy weather.

# what's new

*For this new edition of Virgin Islands, our authors have hunted down the fresh, the transformed, the hot and the happening. These are some of our favorites. For up-to-the-minute recommendations, see lonelyplanet.com/us-virgin-islands and lonelyplanet.com/british-virgin-islands.*

## VI Ecotours, St Thomas

**1** Previously inaccessible Hassel Island, part of Virgin Islands National Park, can now be visited on a kayak, hike and snorkel trip to check out its ruins and reefs (p63).

## Night Ferry, St Thomas

**2** A service now runs between Red Hook (St Thomas) and Road Town (Tortola) four nights per week, enabling folks on late flights to get between territories (p79).

## BVI Kite Jam, BVI

**3** Sir Richard Branson cofounded this festival, which attracts kitesurfers for a week of big air around Virgin Gorda, Necker Island and Anegada (p22).

## Captain Morgan Rum Distillery, St Croix

**4** Captain Morgan Rum cranked up production at its new factory in 2010, and it's slated to open a LEED-certified visitors center with tours in 2012 (p134).

## Tap Room, St John

**5** St John Brewers pours its Mango Pale Ale and other sunny microbrews on site, plus house-made root beer, ginger beer and Green Flash energy drink (p95).

## Natural Livity, St Thomas

**6** This vegan cafe serving lentil burgers, bush tea and pumpkin soup attaches to the Kulcha Shop for buying incense, reggae CDs and peace-logoed jewelry (p64).

## Danny's Bonefishing, Anegada

**7** The Vanterpool family have long been the premier guides to Anegada's famed bonefishing grounds (just ask Jimmy Carter). Son Danny recently started his own company (p187).

## Comanche Mill Yacht-less Club, St Croix

**8** Set on Christiansted's scenic boardwalk, this old windmill has turned gin mill, serving rum and beer to a cast of local characters (p121).

## Frederiksted Pier & Waterfront Park, St Croix

**9** Frederiksted has revitalized its waterfront to welcome burgeoning cruise ship traffic. A spruced-up park, fountains and cobbled paths now stretch along the harbor (p130).

## Concordia Eco-Tents, St John

**10** Concordia has added several new ecofriendly 'tent-cottages' and amenity-laden studios to its resort on St John's remote south shore (p105).

## Old Stone Farmhouse, St Thomas

**11** This restaurant has been around for years, but the new chef who invites guests back to the kitchen for consultation has the island abuzz (p82).

# if you like...

## Beaches

Blue-lapped shores are why you're here, right? Each island has a bevy of beauties.

**White Bay, Jost Van Dyke** Wriggle your toes in the crazy-white sand, sip a Painkiller and watch people stumble in off yachts (p180)

**Isaac Bay & Jack Bay, St Croix** Hike to secluded strands that are eco-reserves for green and hawksbill turtles (p124)

**Lindquist Beach, St Thomas** Splash around this picture-perfect bay in an undeveloped, protected park (p74)

**Savannah Bay, Virgin Gorda** Walk the lengthy shore while gaping at sunsets (p171)

**Salt Pond Bay, St John** An ideal blend of cool hikes, groovy beachcombing and turtle-and-squid snorkeling (p104)

**Josiah's Bay, Tortola** It's all about big surf, cold drinks and the chilled vibe (p158)

**Cow Wreck Bay, Anegada** Snorkel and lounge where it will just be you and the wandering bovines (p187)

## Outdoor Adventures

When you've had enough lazing on the beach, the islands host a wide array of adventures.

**Sailing** One of the globe's premiere places to hoist a jib, the Virgins have steady trade winds, hundreds of protected bays and an abundance of charter boats to make it all possible (p37)

**Hiking** Trek the trails crisscrossing Virgin Islands National Park to cliff-top overlooks, petroglyphs and sugar mill ruins (p103)

**Kayaking** Dip a paddle in St Croix's luminescent Salt River Bay at night (p127)

**Bonefishing** Cast a line in the world-class flats that circle Anegada (p187)

**Surfing** Join the line-ups around Tortola's shores, or take a lesson if you're new to the waves (p151)

**Mountain Biking** Get pumped up on St Croix's spooky rainforest trails (p131)

## West Indian Food

Local dishes fuse West African, Caribbean and Indian ingredients. The restaurants are often holes-in-the-wall, but the chefs know how to cook a flavorsome plateful.

**Crandall's, Tortola** Known for its pates, in which warm spiced meat plumps a flaky-crust pocket. They come in chicken, beef, turkey or salt fish varieties (p150)

**Gladys' Cafe, St Thomas** She serves a spicy callaloo soup stirred with okra, various meats and hot peppers (p64)

**Vie's Snack Shack, St John** You can't beat the garlic chicken with johnnycakes (fried dough) – unless you get the coconut tarts (p106)

**Roti Palace, Tortola** Fiery chutney sets off the chicken, beef, conch or vegetable fillings in these burrito-like flatbread wraps (p146)

**Harvey's, St Croix** Fork into the fungi (okra and cornmeal), goat stew or conch in butter sauce, washed down with gingery bush tea (p119)

» Fort Christiansvaern (p113), Christiansted, St Croix

# Diving & Snorkeling

Coral-covered pinnacles, caverns, walls and ship-wrecks lie under Virgin seas. Whether you're a newbie or an old pro, there's plenty to explore.

**Wreck of the RMS Rhone** The famous shipwreck rests in just 20ft to 80ft of water off Salt Island, making it an accessible dive for all levels; snorkelers can access it, too (p195)

**Alice in Wonderland** This diving spot off Ginger Island has some of the region's best deepwater coral formations (p198)

**The Indians** These three cone-shaped pinnacles by Pelican Island are a popular fish-watching spot for snorkelers and divers (p199)

**Leinster Bay/Waterlemon Cay** Hike the trail on St John's north shore, then hit the water to snorkel with barracudas, turtles, spotted eagle rays and nurse sharks (p100)

**The Caves** Three large caves on Norman Island feature shallow waters with shrimp, tiny lobsters and glassy sweepers wriggling through (p192)

# Party Zones

Looking for a good-time gathering? Take your pick of classic bars.

**Foxy's Tamarind Bar, Jost Van Dyke** Sailors come from far and wide to hoist a drink with the namesake, calypso-crooning owner (p178)

**Bomba's Surfside Shack, Tortola** Drink with surfers who ride the waves curling out front, and howl at the infamous full-moon parties (p157)

**Duffy's Love Shack, St Thomas** Loud rock, Bathrobe Night and Dr Feelgood's Vile Foaming Liquid rock this frame shack the middle of a parking lot (p77)

**Woody's Seafood Saloon, St John** It spawns a literal party in the street every day for happy hour (p95)

**William Thornton, Norman Island** Patrons have been know to jump off the deck nude at this rowdy floating pirate bar (p193)

**Cane Garden Bay, Tortola** Locals and travelers alike groove to live music at the beach's throng of open-air bars (p154)

# Eco-Tourism

St John leads the pack in green facilities, but other islands hang their share of solar panels, too.

**Concordia Eco-Tents, St John** Here you'll find canvas-sided cottages on stilts, with compost-ing toilets, solar-generated electricity and killer sea views from a forested hillside (p105)

**Mt Victory Campground, St Croix** This small working farm has a handful of tents and cottages that are off the grid but near the beach (p134)

**Virgin Islands Campground, Water Island** Another small tent-cottage facility on an island off St Thomas, with rainwater running through the sinks and showers, and solar energy heat-ing it (p72)

**Virgin Islands Ecotours, St Thomas** There's only one way to access the centuries-old fort ruins on Hassel Island, and this national park–affiliated group is it; you'll kayak, hike and snorkel along the way (p63)

**Friends of the Park Store, St John** Virgin Islands National Park volunteers raise money by selling ecofriendly wares like paper made out of local donkey poo (p96)

**If you like... Impressionism**,
visit the home of Camille
Pissarro, the 'Father of
Impressionism.' He began
his brisk brushstrokes in
Charlotte Amalie before
sharing palettes with Cezanne
et al in France (p60).

# Tropical Cocktails

Hmm, what to have while swinging in the hammock? It's a tough choice.

**Painkiller** Jost Van Dyke's Soggy Dollar Bar supposedly invented this delicious-yet-lethal mix of rum, coconut, pineapple, orange juice and nutmeg (p182)

**Alcohol-spiked milkshake** How do you make a milkshake sweeter? Add a smidge of rum or liqueur, as they do to perfection at Udder Delite Dairy Bar (p81)

**Piña colada** OK, so it was invented in Puerto Rico, but Virgin Gorda's Mad Dog bar makes a revered, creamy glassful (p169)

**Mango Pale Ale** Little St John Brewers creates big flavor with its flagship suds, which you can sip at the Tap Room in Cruz Bay and elsewhere around the USVI (p95)

**Cruzan Rum** The St Croix distillery has been turning molasses into Caribbean happy juice since 1760, and you can sip it at the fragrant source (p133)

**Bushwhacker** Several island bars blend vodka, rum and five or so sweet, creamy liqueurs into a potent icy treat; the bartender mixes a fine one at Flash of Beauty on Anegada's East End (p190)

# Historical Sites

Forts, plantation ruins and other historical buildings fleck the landscape. Most are unspoiled sites sans bells and whistles.

**Christiansted National Historic Site, St Croix** The showpiece is the cannon-covered, 18th-century fort, flanked by gold, pink and brown West Indies neoclassical buildings preserved from Christiansted's days as a Caribbean power (p113)

**Annaberg Sugar Mill Ruins, St John** The most intact sugar plantation ruins in the Virgins, with national park experts on hand demonstrating traditional baking, crafting and gardening in the old facilities (p97)

**St Thomas Synagogue, Charlotte Amalie** The second-oldest temple in the western hemisphere has had worshippers on its sand floors for nearly 200 years (p60)

**Copper Mine National Park, Virgin Gorda** The ruins of a mid-1800s Cornish mine crumble atop a forlorn, wind-pounded bluff (p166)

**Estate Whim Plantation Museum, St Croix** This restored plantation great house with surrounding mills and slave quarters offers evocative exploration (p132)

# Romantic Getaways

All those honeymooners aren't coming to the Virgin Islands for nothing. Blue waters, white beaches and fiery sunsets spark love in the air.

**Biras Creek Resort, Virgin Gorda** An oasis on a remote isthmus between North Sound and the open Atlantic, you can hear the waves roar in your cottage amid the sea grape trees (p173)

**Caneel Bay Resort, St John** Lovebirds such as Angelina Jolie and Brad Pitt come to this plantation when they're in need of facilities such as seven beaches, 11 tennis courts and five restaurants, along with landscaped rolling hills, forests and rocky promontories (p101)

**Little Dix Bay, Virgin Gorda** When you're not in your swanky room at this upscale resort, you're on the perfectly manicured beach soaking up the elegant South Seas vibe (p168)

**Honeymoon Beach, Water Island** What better place to steal a kiss than this secluded strand of sand? It's Hollywood's go-to location for a romantic backdrop (p69)

# month by month

# January

The Christmas festivals are still wrapping up early in the month. Often there's a tourism lull in mid-January when savvy travelers can snag good bargains.

### ⭐ Bordeaux Farmers Rastafari Agricultural Fair

Rastafarians hold this weekend-long, mid-January festival at a community farm in Bordeaux, on St Thomas' western side. Vegan food, homegrown produce, crafts, African drumming groups and reggae bands are all part of the scene (www.facebook.com/wegrowfood).

### 🏃 Scenic 50 Ultra Distance Marathon

A small but mighty group of athletes runs 50 miles from Christiansted to Frederiksted and back through St Croix's wild, hilly terrain. The course follows the shoreline, providing lots of awesome scenery during the nine-plus-hour haul (www.stcroix50.com).

# February

This is the heart of high season, when the weather is at its dry and sunny best. Entertainment options are in full swing at local resorts and bars. Prices are at their peak.

### ⭐ USVI Agri-Fest

This three-day fair on St Croix features island crafters, food stalls with superb examples of West Indian and Puerto Rican cooking, flora exhibitions and livestock contests. Bands from around the Virgin Islands provide the soundtrack (www.viagrifest.org).

### 🏃 8 Tuff Miles

In late February, a crowd of tough runners and walkers lace up their shoes to cover the distance between Cruz Bay and Coral Bay on St John. The route follows Centerline Rd, which climbs 1400 feet along the way (www.8tuffmiles.com).

### 🏃 BVI Kite Jam

The weeklong, late-month event packed full of 'freestyle, sliders, big air and wave riding' takes place around Virgin Gorda, Necker Island and Anegada. Sir Richard Branson is the cofounder (www.bvikitejam.com).

# March

March is another prime-weather high-season month, when prices and crowds max out. Families from northern climes start to descend when schools go on spring break mid- to late-month.

### ⭐ St John Blues Festival

Musicians sing the blues all day long at this outdoor concert in Coral Bay. While the players aren't big names, they're all pros who've been around, bending frets in cities such as Memphis, Chicago and beyond (www.stjohnbluesfestival.com).

### ⭐ Virgin Gorda Easter Festival

The area around Spanish Town's yacht harbor fills with mocko jumbies (costumed stilt walkers representing spirits of the dead), fungi bands, a food fair and parades during this event, held Friday through Sunday during the Christian holiday, usually late March or April (www.bvitourism.com).

### International Rolex Cup Regatta

The fourth weekend in March brings world-class racing boats to St Thomas for the island's main regatta. The centerpiece for non-racers is a big reggae show at Yacht Haven Grande (www.rolexcupregatta.com).

# April

April is a festive month, full of regattas and carnivals. When Easter falls during the month the social calendar books up even more. Peak season winds down at the end of the month.

### BVI Spring Regatta

This is one of the Caribbean's biggest parties. It features seven days of small- and large-craft races and provides a time-honored excuse to swill beer, sip rum and listen to live music with sailors and crew from around the world (www.bvispringregatta.org).

### St Croix Food & Wine Experience

Celebrity chefs arrive for a week of gourmet feasting and drinking around St Croix. The mid-month event showcases local ingredients and includes special meals at restaurants, wine seminars and a cooking competition (www.stcroixfood andwine.com).

### St Thomas Carnival

Stemming from West African masquerading traditions, St Thomas' bash is the second-largest carnival in the Caribbean after the one at Port-of-Spain, Trinidad. It throws the island into nonstop party mode the last two weeks of April and first week of May (www.vi carnival.com).

# May

May sees a fair bit of rain, but it also hosts several parties. Businesses start to keep shorter hours as tourist season winds down. It's a good shoulder month for bargains.

### St Croix Half-Ironman Triathlon

Athletes strive for iron-man qualification in early May by swimming 1.2 miles, cycling 56 miles and running 13 miles over St Croix's varied topography. Heat, humidity and a hill nicknamed 'the beast' await (www.stcroix triathlon.com).

### Foxy's Woodenboat Regatta

Foxy hosts several sailing events, but none are bigger than this regatta, held off Jost Van Dyke in late May. It draws classic wooden yachts from all over the Caribbean for four days of light racing and heavy partying (www.foxysbar.com).

### BVI Music Festival

This fest brings big-name reggae, R&B and calypso acts such as Percy Sledge

and Wyclef Jean to wail on the beach at Cane Garden Bay, Tortola. It's held over a long weekend in late May (www.bvimusicfestival.com).

### Wreck Week

More than 300 shipwrecks speckle BVI waters, and during seven days in late May/early June, local dive companies put together a deal where you can explore 10 of them in a succession of morning and night dives (www.divebvi wreckweek.com).

# June

It's the official start of hurricane season, though there's not much action yet. The trade winds die down and humidity picks up. The plus side is that the sea calms for smoother snorkeling and sailing.

### Highland Spring HIHO

Windsurfers and stand-up paddleboarders converge for the weeklong Hook-In-Hold-On races, which zip around Tortola, Virgin Gorda and the Out Islands. A gaggle of cruisers follow the racers for the portable party, held in late June (www .go-hiho.com/hshiho).

### Mango Melee

The St George Village Botanical Garden celebrates St Croix's fruity bounty with a day of mango sips, salsas and sweets. The eating contest is the highlight – a wild frenzy of sticky orange excess. Held in late June (www.sgvbg.org).

# July

**July holds several holidays: Emancipation Day and Independence Day in the USVI, and Territory Day in the BVI. The US islands honor Hurricane Supplication Day on July's fourth Monday, as the winds begin to blow...**

 **St John Carnival**

St John's biggest celebration brings on the mocko jumbies, steel pan bands, parades and musical competitions. The party surrounds Emancipation Day (July 3) and US Independence Day (July 4).

# August

**August is peak hurricane season, along with September. But it's not all stormy weather. Several big events still rock the islands. Conch and lobster disappear from menus as stocks replenish during the annual fishing moratorium.**

 **BVI Emancipation Festival**

Held on Tortola, the BVI's premier cultural event features everything from beauty pageants to horse racing to 'rise and shine tramps' (3am parades led by reggae bands). The celebration marks the 1834 Emancipation Act that abolished slavery here (www.bvi tourism.com).

 **Texas Society Chili Cook-off**

More than 40 chefs stir the pot on the beach at Brewers Bay on St Thomas, while 4500 chili lovers brave the heat to eat. Crazy costumes, tug-of-war contests and steel pan bands are all part of package. The date varies.

 **USVI Atlantic Blue Marlin Tournament**

The tournament is a mega-lure for sportfishers worldwide, who unite on St Thomas in late August to participate in a tag-and-release event that benefits the islands' Boy Scouts (www.abmt.vi).

# October

**Businesses blow the dust off the hurricane shutters mid-to-late month and start to open up again (many close during September). The third Monday is Hurricane Thanksgiving Day in the USVI, and with that, the season's worst is over.**

 **Foxy's Cat Fight & Halloween Party**

Another of Foxy's good-time regattas on Jost Van Dyke, this one is for catamarans. It's held around Halloween weekend, and a wild costume party caps off the event (www.foxysbar.com).

# November

**It's a rainy month, but it comes in bursts. The cooling winds start to pick up. Other than the USVI Thanksgiving holiday at month's end, November offers value prices for activities and lodging.**

 **VI Fungi Fest**

Musicians from around the islands come to Road Town, Tortola, for a weekend of concerts celebrating the local folk music. Bands use homemade percussion such as washboards, ribbed gourds and conch shells to accompany a singer (www.vifungifest.com).

# December

**Christmas and New Year's are the busiest, most festive time to be on the islands. Markets, concerts, caroling and parades are all in abundant supply. Peak season rates officially start in mid-December.**

 **Cruzan Christmas Fiesta**

From early December to early January, St Croix lines up nonstop pageants, parades, food and craft bazaars, and calypso competitions that put a West Indies spin on the Christmas holidays (www.stxfestival.com).

 **Foxy's New Year's Eve Party**

Hundreds of boats show up in Jost Van Dyke's harbors on December 31. Party Central is Foxy's, which swings all night with live reggae and calypso. The other island beach bars are full of action as well (www.foxysbar.com).

# itineraries

*Whether you've got six days or 60, these itineraries provide a starting point for the trip of a lifetime. Want more inspiration? Head online to lonelyplanet. com/thorntree to chat with other travelers.*

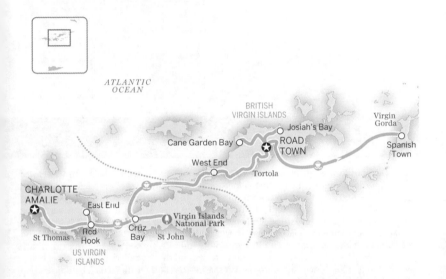

## Nine Days
## Essential Virgin Islands

> Hopscotch through the islands' greatest hits: St Thomas, St John, Tortola and Virgin Gorda huddle near each other, with frequent ferries connecting the dots.
>
> You'll likely arrive via **St Thomas**. Spend a day or two taking in the sights and shopping in **Charlotte Amalie**, the good-time bars and bistros of **Red Hook**, and the water sports and sea creatures of **East End**. Then zip over to **St John**, whose main town, **Cruz Bay**, serves up mango-tinged microbrews at party-hearty happy hour bars. Don't get too stuck to your bar stool: **Virgin Islands National Park** cloaks two-thirds of the island in forests and sublime beaches, ripe for hiking, snorkeling and eco-camping.
>
> Move onward to the BVI for the last five days, starting with **Tortola**. The ferry will drop you in **West End**, then wind your way around to **Road Town** for a good base from which to wine and dine with ease. Check out the music-fueled nightlife in **Cane Garden Bay** and surfers' favorite **Josiah's Bay** before journeying to **Spanish Town** on **Virgin Gorda**. The island is the BVI's rich, plump beauty and the quintessential, blue-sea-lapped retreat to round out your trip.

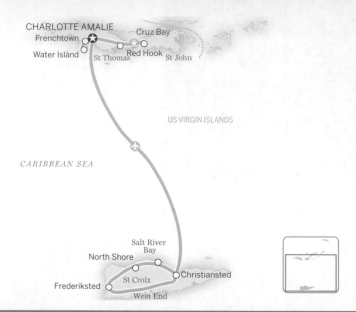

## Seven Days
# USVI in a Week

> Get your feet on the ground in **St Thomas**, starting out with two days in **Charlotte Amalie**. Spend the first day strolling the historic downtown and making a dent in your $1600 duty-free allowance in the shops. In the evening, swing by **Frenchtown** to check out the area's funky bistros and wine bars. The next day ferry over to the quiet fourth Virgin, **Water Island**, and walk to Honeymoon Beach to swim and snorkel.

Take the floatplane from downtown for the cool, 20-minute flight to **Christiansted**, on **St Croix**. Over the next three days drink at old windmills turned gin mills on the wharf, play like a pirate at the big yellow fort, and poke around the art galleries and colonial buildings scattered around town. Motor to the **West End** to visit the rum factory, botanic garden and evocative plantation museum. Drop by **Frederiksted** for a snorkel around the historic pier, or maybe a mountain bike ride into the spooky rainforest. Divers should set a course for the **North Shore** to immerse at the gaping coral-encrusted wall. Just east is **Salt River Bay**, where Christopher Columbus landed in 1493; modern-day explorers can rent a kayak and set off for a night-paddle through the glimmering bioluminescent waters.

From Christiansted, return to Charlotte Amalie via seaplane, then head to **Red Hook** to catch the ferry to **St John** for a couple of days. You can't beat it for snorkeling beaches with fish-frenzied reefs to explore, and for hiking trails that wind by petroglyphs, sugar mill ruins and feral donkeys. **Cruz Bay** makes a primo base thanks to its festive bars and restaurants, which plate up everything from Italian gnocchi to Mallorcan paella to West Indian barbecue.

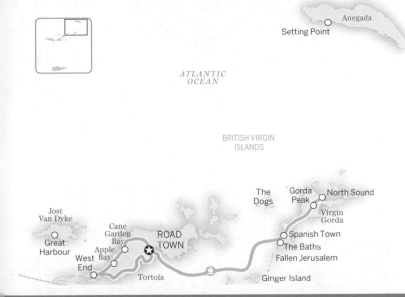

Seven Days
# Best of the BVI

Split your time between mountainous Tortola and prosperous Virgin Gorda, and day trip to the smaller isles by public ferry or charter boat.

**Road Town** makes a fine base for exploring **Tortola** if you want easy access to sophisticated cateries, gelato shops, pubs and boats. Fan out from there to inspect the island's beaches, such as **Apple Bay**, home to a world-famous, ramshackle surfers' bar, and **Cane Garden Bay**, the island's live music hot spot. To escape Tortola's 'crowds' head to **Jost Van Dyke** for a day. Fewer than 200 people live on the jovial little island, where yachters and rock stars like to drop by for drinks. Who can blame them? Jost is a rare, unspoiled oasis of green hills and blinding white sand. It even has a signature drink: the rum-bombed Painkiller. Ferries ply the route often from Tortola's **West End**.

From central Road Town, it's also easy to hop over to your next base on **Virgin Gorda**. **Spanish Town** is the gateway from which you can poke around the boulder-studded Baths, view-worthy Gorda Peak, and other national parks. Sea dogs can hail water taxis around **North Sound** to sail, kitesurf and drink with the yachtsfolk. It's also possible to day trip to **Anegada** from Spanish Town. The sleepy atoll might as well be from another planet compared to its BVI brethren. Flamingos ripple the salt ponds. Giant rock iguanas hide under blooming cacti. Hulking lobsters grill on beach barbecues. And hammocks lure around irresistible shores.

Spanish Town is also a great jumping off point for sailing expeditions to the Out Islands, too. Beauties such as **Ginger Island**, **The Dogs** and **Fallen Jerusalem** float nearby – uninhabited spots with just beaches and blue sea.

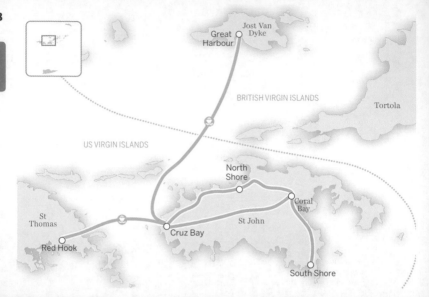

Four Days
# Quick Escape: St John

Short on time but still want the maximum Virgin experience? Hang your hat on **St John**. You can easily spend all four days hiking different trails and snorkeling off distinct beaches. What's more, St John floats near several other islands for day trips.

**Cruz Bay** is the main town and social hot spot. Nicknamed 'Love City,' it wafts a carefree, spring-break vibe, where hippies, sea captains and American retirees and reggae worshippers hoist happy hour drinks in equal measure. It's also the place to organize your active endeavors, and to fuel up in the surprisingly good restaurant mix.

Life's a beach on the **North Shore**, ripe for a day of adventure. Lengthy Cinnamon Bay has the most going on: an archaeological dig, stand up paddle boarding and trails through mill ruins. Families and snorkeling newbies may prefer shallow Maho Bay, where sea turtles swim. Experienced snorkelers can jump in amid rays and barracudas at Leinster Bay/Waterlemon Cay.

Next up: **Coral Bay**. Sure, it's a heckuva lot smaller than Cruz Bay, but it makes up for it in personality. Colorful characters run the handful of diners and taverns – and they like to dance, so shine up your shoes beforehand. From here head down to the **South Shore**, and spend some quality time at Salt Pond Bay partaking of cool hikes, groovy beachcombing and turtle-and-squid snorkeling. Don't forget to earmark a day for hiking the Reef Bay trail, kayaking along coastal reefs or another favorite activity.

Or go island hopping. With a passport you can ferry from Cruz Bay to **Jost Van Dyke**. Arrive in Great Harbour in the morning, people watch and sip microbrews at Foxy's in the afternoon, and return home before sunset. No passport? No problem. Whiz over to **Red Hook** on **St Thomas** and quaff a flaming drink at Duffy's.

## 14 Days
# Island Hopper

> With two weeks you can swoop through St Thomas and St John in US territory, the four main British islands, plus a scattering of pirate-spiced Out Islands.

Spend a day on **St Thomas** eating johnnycakes and browsing shops in **Charlotte Amalie**, then head to **Red Hook** on the island's East End for a few days of Margaritaville ambience. Both towns lie close to beaches where true-blue water worthy of Hollywood movies splashes ashore (indeed, St Thomas regularly hosts film crews around its coast).

Next up: **St John**. Scores of cafes and pubs await in **Cruz Bay** and scores of wild beaches and hiking trails await in Virgin Islands National Park. Get your snorkel mask ready, because this is the island to come face to face with sea turtles and mighty swimmers.

Spend week two in the BVI. Grab a ferry to **Great Harbour** on **Jost Van Dyke** and kick back on the 'barefoot island.' A calypso musician named Foxy Callwood is Jost's unofficial mayor, and he presides over a fun-loving clutch of beach bars and guesthouses. Ferry onward to **Tortola's West End** and its dandy collection of surfer hangouts and shores, particularly around **Cane Garden Bay**, where live music pumps nightly. **Road Town** is the island's restaurant and transport hub, so you'll wind up there eventually.

From Tortola, it's easy to charter a day-sail excursion, a DIY boat, or a crewed yacht and glide to barely inhabited **Norman**, **Peter** and **Cooper Islands**. Here, life is reduced to the pleasures of snorkeling, diving and sleeping under a shade tree. Spend a few days chilling with yachties on pretty **Virgin Gorda** (a half-hour ferry ride from Tortola). To really get away, sail on to **Anegada**, a magical and lonesome place to hang your hammock for a stretch.

# Diving & Snorkeling

## When to Go

In the USVI, 10- to 15-knot easterly trade winds in spring offer ideal diving conditions. Summer is the best time dive the north-shore sites, since these can be affected by strong swells and wind in winter.

In the BVI the strongest winds blow from November to April making some northwest dive sites inaccessible. The southwest, where many top sites are, is more pro-tected.

Water is generally clearest from April to August.

## Best Novice Dive

**The Indians** (p199) Pinnacles teeming with fish in the BVI's Out Islands

## Best Dive from Shore

**Cane Bay** (p127) Fall into the abyss on St Croix's north shore

## Best Snorkel from Shore

**Leinster Bay/Waterlemon Cay** (p100) Barracudas and turtles off St John's north shore

## Best Shipwreck

**RMS *Rhone*** (p195) An 1867 steamer for divers and snorkelers

Diving and snorkeling in the Virgin Islands are superb, with warm water temperatures and incredible visibility. To be specific: Virgin seas range from around 76°F (24°C) in the winter to 86°F (30°C) in the summer, while visibility averages between 60ft and 70ft, though it can well exceed 100ft. Coral-cov-ered pinnacles, walls, shipwrecks and plenty of tropical fish are in plain view underwater.

# Where to Dive: USVI

Near-shore reefs fringe St Thomas and St John and offer exploration amid arches, tun-nels and other eye-popping formations. St Croix is even more dramatic with vast can-yons and coral-encrusted walls that plunge into the deep. Marine life abounds wherever you go: more than 500 fish species swim in local waters, as well as three of the world's seven species of sea turtle.

## St Thomas & St John

Dozens of popular dive sites lie in Pills-bury Sound, the body of water that divides St Thomas and St John. A line of long, narrow cays fills the sea here. When the weather cooperates, divers can kick around caves, arches, tunnels and steep walls on the cays' windward north shores. The ac-tion moves to protected fringing reefs when the sea turns rough. Dive operators huddle

| NAME | DETAILS | EXPERIENCE LEVEL | DEPTH RANGE | LOCATION |
|------|---------|------------------|-------------|----------|
| Cow and Calf | Sailors used to mistake these above-water rocks for whales. Underneath, they're peppered with tunnels, arches and reeftops of swaying gorgonians and sponges. | Novice | Surface-45ft | St Thomas, just west of Great St James |
| Eagle Shoal | It's far from Cruz Bay, but the overhangs, tunnels, arches and an otherworldly cave are worth the trip. The latter has hosted underwater weddings. | Intermediate | 5-50ft | St John, between Ram Head and Leduck Island |
| Salt River Canyon | The canyon's east and west walls drop several hundred feet, harboring fish and coral in a wild mix of shapes and colors. | Intermediate | 30-130ft | St Croix, at mouth of Salt River Bay |
| Cane Bay | The site boasts a huge vertical drop and visibility that often exceeds 100ft, plus it's accessible from shore. Tropical fish, beautiful coral and anchors from ancient wrecks make for great for underwater photography. Further info: p127. | Intermediate | 25-130ft | St Croix, from Cane Bay Beach |
| Butler Bay Wrecks | There are five ships and an underwater habitat to explore in close proximity. Barracuda swim by the sponge-painted vessels. | Intermediate | 20-110ft | St Croix, 2.5mi north of Frederiksted |
| Frederiksted Pier | Easily accessible from shore or from the pier itself. Watch for anemones along with squirrel, trumpet and puffer fish. Further info: p130. | Novice | 15-50ft | St Croix, Frederiksted Harbor |

on St Thomas' East End and St John's West End to visit the sites; they're reachable via a 10- to 20-minute boat ride from either location.

Elsewhere on St Thomas, diving focuses on a handful of shipwrecks and craggy islands strung along the south shore, where dolphins, angelfish, lobsters and sharks patrol. On St John, diving also concentrates in the sheltered waters along its south shore. Dive boats can get to most sites in these regions within 20 minutes.

St Thomas' dive industry is the larger of the two, with about a dozen dive shops dotting the beaches between Lindbergh Bay near the airport and Coki Bay on the East End; many operators are resort-based. St John's small group of operators hub mostly in and around Cruz Bay.

## St Croix

The island's north shore is its claim to fame, thanks to the sheer wall that runs along the coast. This geological feature plummets more than 2 miles into the yawning Virgin Trough, offering divers a gasp-worthy glimpse into the abyss. From Christiansted, the best dive sites are 10 to 45 minutes away by boat. Travel times via the operators at Salt River Marina and Cane Bay are shorter; from Cane Bay, you can even dive from shore.

The calm waters on St Croix's west end are also a worthy descent. Several shipwrecks lie offshore, and the Frederiksted Pier makes a sweet night dive, teeming with fantastical sea creatures.

# Where to Dive: BVI

The BVI huddle to form a sheltered paradise of secluded coves, calm shores and crystal-clear water, which in turn provide outstanding underwater visibility, healthy coral and a wide variety of diving sites. The

# BEST BVI DIVING SITES

| NAME | DETAILS | EXPERIENCE LEVEL | DEPTH RANGE | LOCATION |
|---|---|---|---|---|
| RMS *Rhone* | The famous 310ft shipwreck has become an exotic habitat for octopuses, eels and squid; the stern lies in shallower water, making it an accessible dive for all levels. Further info: p195. | Novice to Intermediate | 20-80ft | West side of Salt Island |
| Blond Rock | This coral ledge has caves, crevices and deep holes, in which spiny lobsters like to hide. | Intermediate | 10-65ft | Salt Island passage, between Dead Chest Island and Salt Island |
| Alice in Wonderland | Alice has some of the best deepwater coral in the BVI, including bizarre 15ft mushroom-shaped formations (akin to what the storybook heroine encountered, hence the site's name). Further info: p198. | Intermediate | 40-80ft | South of Ginger Island |
| The Indians | The three cone-shaped rock formations rise from 36ft underwater to 30ft above water, featuring large sea fans, caves and lots o' fish. Further info: p199. | Novice | Surface-50ft | North of Norman Island |
| Angel Reef | This site is a crossroads for species from different habitats, with shallow canyons rising to the surface. | Intermediate | 20-65ft | Southwest peninsula of Norman Island |
| *Chikuzen* | The 250ft wreck is the BVI's most abundant for marine life, attracting big swimmers such as reef, bull and lemon sharks. | Advanced | 45-80ft | 5.5mi north of Great Camanoe Island |

Out Islands and cays south of Tortola hold the most sites, where divers will immerse to coral gardens and stunning arches, caverns and other geological formations. There are lots of shipwrecks to explore, too, thanks to the BVI's historic role as a pirate hideaway and trading route pit stop.

For marine life, it is common to see rays and dolphins. Between February and April humpback whales swim to the BVI to breed, and you're likely to hear them, if not see them, steaming through the water.

Most dive sites lie within 30 minutes of dive-operator bases.

Conservation is a big deal here, and there are lots of permanent mooring buoys.

# Equipment: Pack or Rent?

Well-maintained rental gear is available at most dive centers, as long as you're not picky about size. Some small, easy-to-carry items to bring from home include protective gloves and boots and spare straps. Here's a quick guide:

» **Mask, snorkel & fins** Many people bring these as they are not too huge to pack and you can be sure they will fit. Snorkeling gear rents at $7 to $10 per day.

» **Tanks & weight belt** Usually included with the cost of a dive.

» **Wetsuit** A lycra dive skin or 3mm shorty wetsuit is ample thermal protection in the summer, while a full 3mm suit will protect against coral scrapes and keep you toasty in winter. A wetsuit usually is included with the cost of a dive, but bring your own if you are worried about size.

» **Regulators & Buoyancy Control Devices** (BCDs) Most dive shops have them; rentals cost around $15.

# Dive Operators

Safe, professional dive operators are plentiful.

» Most offer at least three dives a day – a two-tank dive in the morning, followed by a one- or two-tank dive in the afternoon. Many also offer night dives.

» Most operate dive vessels, though a few in the USVI are shore-based and have specialized knowledge of the near-shore reefs.

» Expect to pay about $80 to $90 for a one-tank dive, $110 to $125 for two tanks.

» If you are in the USVI and the operator is going to a dive site in the BVI, you will need a passport and you will have to clear customs, which costs around $25.

» Most BVI operators offer rendezvous diving for visitors on yachts, which means the company will pick you up at your boat.

» Recommended operators include the following:

## St Thomas

**Blue Island Divers** (www.blueislanddivers. com; Crown Bay Marina) p69

**Coki Beach Dive Club** (www.cokidive.com; Coki Beach) p75

**Dive In!** (www.diveinusvi.com; Sapphire Beach Resort) p75

**Red Hook Dive Center** (www.redhook divecenter.com; Red Hook) p75

**St Thomas Dive Club** (www.stthomas divingclub.com; Bolongo Bay) p71

## St John

**Cruz Bay Watersports** (www.divestjohn. com; Cruz Bay) p88

**Low Key Watersports** (www.divelowkey.com; Cruz Bay) p88

## St Croix

For further information on all of the shops listed here, see p118.

**Anchor Dive Center** (www.anchordivestcroix. com; Salt River Marina)

**Cane Bay Dive Shop** (www.canebayscuba. com; Cane Bay)

**Dive Experience** (www.divexp.com; Christiansted)

**N2 The Blue** (www.n2theblue.com; Frederiksted)

**Scuba West** (www.divescubawest.com; Frederiksted)

**St Croix Ultimate Bluewater Adventures** (www.stcroixscuba.com; Christiansted)

## Tortola

**BVI Scuba Co** (www.bviscubaco.com; Road Town) p143

**We Be Divin'** (www.webedivinbvi.com; Road Town) p143

**Blue Water Divers** (www.bluewaterdiversbvi. com; Nanny Cay) p149

## Virgin Gorda

**Dive BVI** (www.divebvi.com; Spanish Town & Leverick Bay) p167

**Kilbride's Sunchaser Scuba** (www. sunchaserscuba.com; North Sound at Bitter End Yacht Club) p172

## Jost Van Dyke

**JVD Scuba** (www.jostvandykescuba.com) p177

## Anegada

**North Shore Divers** (www.diveanegada.com; Loblolly Bay) p190

---

### PRE-TRIP PREPARATION

» Make sure you possess a current diving-certification card (C-card) from a recognized scuba-diving instructional agency, and bring it with you. Dive operators will need to see it.

» Be sure you are healthy and feel comfortable diving.

» Choose sites within your realm of experience; if your skills are rusty consider taking a scuba review course.

» Bring a first-aid kit with decongestants, eardrops, antihistimines and seasickness tablets.

» Remember to allow 24 hours *after* diving before you fly.

## LEARN TO DIVE

| COURSE | DETAILS | DURATION | COST |
|---|---|---|---|
| Introductory/ orientation | Also known as a 'resort course,' this is a way for novices to see if diving is for them; usually entails a classroom session, followed by a pool session where you practice using scuba gear, then a guided open-water dive. | 1 day | $115-140 |
| Open-water referral | Do the class work and pool work at home, then do four open-water dives in the Virgins to complete certification. | 2 days | $270-300 |
| Open-water certification | The international PADI standard, recognized everywhere, which provides all facets of certification. | 4 or 5 days | $410-475 |

### Cooper Island

**Sail Caribbean** (www. sailcaribbeandivers. com) p194

# Evaluating a Dive Operator

Dive operators in the both the US and British Virgin Islands have an excellent standard of staff training and equipment maintenance. Since BVI operators depend on US divers, all equipment is maintained to US standards. Here are a few tips to help you select a well-set-up and safety-conscious dive shop.

» Dive boats range from small motor vessels for up to six passengers (aka six packs) to large pontoon boats that carry dozens of divers.

» Well-run dive boats have a radio and/or cell phone to communicate with onshore services. They also carry oxygen, a recall device and a first-aid kit. The bigger boats should have a shaded area and fresh drinking water.

» A well-prepared crew will give a detailed pre-dive briefing that explains how to handle emergencies in the water. The briefing will also explain how divers should enter the water and get back on board the boat. Crew also will collect everyone's name on the dive roster so they can know immediately if a diver is missing.

» Good dive operators explain that you should not touch corals or take shells from the reef.

# Dive Training & Certification

Whether you are a beginner or a seasoned veteran of the underwater realm, the Virgin Islands is a top-notch place for dive training. Most local operators provide a wide array of instruction, from introductory Open Water courses to specialty courses in wreck diving, underwater photography and buoyancy control. You can also take scuba refresher classes.

# Responsible Diving

Please bear in mind the following tips when diving and help preserve the ecology and beauty of reefs:

» Never use anchors on the reef and take care not to run boats aground on coral.

» Avoid touching or standing on living marine organisms or dragging equipment across the reef. Polyps can be damaged by even the gentlest contact.

» Be conscious of your fins. Even without contact, the surge from fin strokes near the reef can damage delicate organisms. Don't kick up clouds of sand, which can smother organisms.

» Practice and maintain proper buoyancy control. Major damage can occur from reef collisions.

» Do not collect or buy corals or shells or loot marine archaeological sites (mainly shipwrecks).

» Ensure that you take home all your garbage and any litter you find. Plastics in particular are a serious threat to marine life.

» Do not feed fish and minimize your disturbance of marine animals.

# Where to Snorkel: USVI

Snorkeling is mega-popular in the USVI, with St John leading the pack. Snorkelers can see tropical fish, sea turtles and even

## SNUBA & SEA TREKKING

For those who want to do more than snorkel but aren't quite ready to take the diving plunge, the USVI offers two options:

**VI Snuba Excursions** (www.visnuba.com) offers guided, half-hour underwater tours at Trunk Bay on St John and Coki Beach on St Thomas. The activity is a cross between snorkeling and scuba where participants use a standard scuba regulator, and a 20ft air hose connects the diver to the surface. Anyone in good health and older than age seven can participate. For details, see p75 and p100.

The **Sea Trek at Coral World Ocean Park** (www.coralworldvi.com) is another popular activity, where you walk on the floor of the sea wearing a special, astronaut-like helmet. A guide leads you along a trail equipped with a handrail 12ft to 30ft below the water. The helmet provides air and allows you to communicate with the guide while keeping your head dry. See p73 for further information.

nurse sharks within a quick swim from shore.

» If you're going DIY snorkeling, stop into a local dive shop beforehand and ask about area conditions. Staff can tell you where the fish and turtle hot spots are, as well as where hazards such as strong currents loom.

» On St John you can also ask park rangers for the lowdown, or pick up a copy of the brochure titled

*Where's the Best Snorkeling?* at the park visitors center.

» Snorkel gear is widely available for rental ($7 to $10 per day) at water-sports centers on beaches and at dive shops.

» If you plan on spending significant time in the water, a lycra skinsuit or thin wetsuit is recommended to protect from stings and scrapes, as well as the sun.

# Where to Snorkel: BVI

Shipwrecks and caves are among the cool features the BVI provides to snorkelers. The top spots are in the Out Islands, which you'll need a boat to reach. You can also explore from shore on the main islands. Water-sports vendors rent gear ($7 to $10 per day) at popular beaches such as the Baths on Virgin Gorda and Loblolly Bay on Anegada.

# Snorkel Tours

» Most day-sail operators that take visitors out sightseeing also include snorkeling stops as part of the itinerary. Gear typically is included in the rates, which hover around $70 for a half-day tour and $100 for a full-day one.

» Some diving boats also will bring snorkelers along for the ride.

» Several St Croix operators sail out to the **Buck Island** marine sanctuary for snorkeling on the underwater trail; see p123.

» There are heaps of operators around the islands, which we've listed in Activities sections

## BEST USVI SNORKELING SITES

| LOCATION | DETAILS | PAGE |
| --- | --- | --- |
| Salt Pond Bay | An ideal blend of cool hikes, groovy beachcombing and turtle-and-squid snorkeling on St John's south shore. | p104 |
| Leinster Bay/ Waterlemon Cay | Snorkel with barracudas, turtles, spotted eagle rays and nurse sharks on St John's north shore. | p100 |
| Francis Bay | Good snorkeling in shallow water with lots of little silvery fish, plus sea turtle sightings on St John's north shore. | p99 |
| Frederiksted Pier | The pier's pilings attract a fanciful collection of marine life such as schools of sea horses. | p130 |
| Isaac and Jack Bays | The reef at this St Croix eco-reserve hosts more than 400 fish species, including parrotfish, blue tangs and four-eyed butterfly fish. | p124 |

## BEST BVI SNORKELING SITES

| LOCATION | DETAILS | PAGE |
| --- | --- | --- |
| RMS *Rhone* – Stern | While the renowned shipwreck off Salt Island is best known as a dive site, its stern lies in water shallow enough for snorkelers to see the bronze propeller, rudder and aft mast from the surface. | p195 |
| The Caves | Three large caves dot Norman Island, where squid, coral and fish big and small like to hang out and feed. | p192 |
| Dry Rocks East | This shallow ridge by Cooper Island attracts sergeant majors, barracudas and other big fish, who flock to the surge created by the area's wind and currents. | p194 |
| Cistern Point | Coral-covered ledges and multi-hued fish surround this rocky point extending off Cooper Island. | p194 |
| The Indians | Several pinnacles rise near Pelican Island (north of Norman Island) and offer good viewing of glassy sweepers and other fish. | p193 |

throughout this book. Some of our favorites include the following:

**N2 The Blue** (www.n2theblue.com; St Croix) Trips around Frederiksted Pier and Sandy Point Wildlife Refuge; p131.

**St Croix Ultimate Bluewater Adventures** (www.stcroixscuba.com; St Croix) Frederiksted Pier excursions; p131.

**Homer's** (www.nightsnorkel.com; Hull Bay, St Thomas) Known for its night snorkel tours; p81.

**JVD Scuba** (www.jostvandykescuba.com; Jost Van Dyke) Tours that combine snorkeling, birdwatching and hiking; p177.

**Dive BVI** (www.divebvi.com; Virgin Gorda) Well-run snorkel trips aboard a catamaran; p167 .

# Resources

**BVI Scuba Organization** (www.bviscuba. org) Excellent website with BVI-specific information, with links to dive shops and lodgings.

**Sport Diver magazine** (www.sportdiver.com) PADI's official publication; the website has general destination information, photos and travel deals.

**USVI Department of Tourism** (www. visitusvi.com) Click 'Things to Do' and choose an island for information on dive sites and operators.

**Reef Environmental Education Foundation** (www.reef.org) This conservation group's website provides fish photos and sighting data for what divers will encounter in the region. Divers also can learn how to document marine life during their trip, which helps REEF monitor the environment's health.

# Chartering a Boat

## When to Go

Early December offers good weather and wind, and it's right before the peak-season crowds arrive, so there's plenty of room to drop anchor in the mooring fields.

April is the transition time from winter's big winds to spring's more gentles breezes, plus it's regatta season.

## Best Anchorages

**The Baths, Virgin Gorda** (p165) World-famous otherworldly rocks
**White Bay, Jost Van Dyke** (p180) Groovy beach bars and people-watching
**Norman Island** (p192) Pirates and scallywags at the local bars

## Websites

**BVI Charter Yacht Society** (www.bvicrewedyachts.com) Lists companies and prices.
**Virgin Islands Charter Yacht League** (www.vicl.org) The USVI equivalent.
**American Sailing Association** (www.american-sailing.com) Links to reputable sailing schools worldwide.

## Planning your Boat Trip

A felicitous combination of geography and geology has positioned the Virgin Islands as sailing's Magic Kingdom. Here you have a year-round balmy climate, steady trade winds, little to worry about in the way of tides or currents, a protected thoroughfare in the 35-mile-long Sir Francis Drake Channel, and hundreds of anchorages, each within sight of another. These factors make the Virgins one of the easiest places to sail – easy, that is, for capable sailors with piloting skills – and quite a bit lower on the seasickness scale than other Caribbean cruising grounds.

More than a third of visitors to the Virgins come to sail. In addition to the sandy beaches, waving palm trees and multihued waters, travelers find all the beach bars, ecologically sensitive moorings and purveyors of luxury groceries needed for a sailing sojourn lasting a week or two.

## Types of Charters

There are three basic options: a crewed boat, with skipper and cook; a 'bareboat' without staff that you operate on your own; or a sailing-school vessel.

### Equipment

Most boats available for charter range in size from 32ft to 52ft and have two to five cabins.

## SAILING RESOURCES

» **BVI Marine Guide** (www.bvimarineguide.com) This handy, free booklet lists everything a sailor needs: customs regulations, overnight moorings, chandlery locations, safety concerns. Much of the information is online, as well.

» **Yachtman's Guide to the Virgin Islands** (www.yachtsmansguide.com) For $16, you'll get a book that's updated annually and provides information on charting harbors, anchorages, channels and preparation for cruising the Virgins (Spanish Virgins included).

» **Marine Association of the BVI** (www.marinebvi.com) This is the website of a trade group with links to marinas, equipment suppliers and dive operators, in addition to charter companies.

» **Sail** (www.sailmag.com) Use this magazine's website for an up-to-date list of local services, prices and equipment.

» **BVI Yacht Magazine** (www.bviyachtguide.com) This monthly online publication offers articles about sailing in the BVI; while it's geared to those who want to buy a yacht, it has good general articles, too.

» **Cruising Guide to the Virgin Islands** (www.cruisingguides.com) This $32 guide features detailed charts of Virgin waters and anchorages.

Vessel types include the following:

» **Monohulls** These are heavier, tack more easily and typically cost less.

» **Catamarans** These are multihulled and provide greater stability (good for those prone to seasickness). They're also wider, providing more room on deck and below, but are also a little pricier.

» **Motor yachts (aka 'power yachts')** Companies sometimes offer these sail-free vessels as a third option. Motor yachts can cover a lot more ground than monohulls and catamarans, but cost more.

## Crewed Boat

Crewed boats – ie privately owned yachts with skipper, cook and any other crew needed for proper ship handling and your personal pampering – offer luxury accommodations that move from island to island. These can cost up to three times more than a bareboat charter, but for many visitors it's worth it to have a stress-free holiday with everything taken care of. Crew can also function as informal guides, since they're likely to know where the best anchorages, sunsets and snorkel spots are.

Meticulously maintained and often exquisitely decorated, these boats offer all the water toys (and electronic connections to your office) you might imagine, plus cuisine that tops most luxe resorts. In fact, the food served on board is the primary means by which the companies compete with one another, and the chefs often are culinary-school graduates.

Crewed boats are booked by brokers who get to know the boats and their crews at boat shows. They will get to know you, too, before making a recommendation based on your budget, the size of your party and your preferences for all those little things that make your vacation special.

## Bareboat

A 'bareboat' charter is bare of crew but fully equipped to sail, lodge and cook for two to eight people. Not surprisingly, you must meet certain qualifications before you're allowed to sail away in a $200,000 yacht. All bareboat charter companies require you to fill out a sailing résumé to demonstrate your ability to handle the boat and the sailing conditions. The company will need to see a physical demonstration of your skills upon arrival.

In practical terms, you should have a reasonable amount of recent coastal-cruising experience in an auxiliary sailboat more than 30ft long (this need not be a boat you own, however). You should be able not only to sail the boat, but to dock and anchor it, to run its systems and to deal with minor problems and routines (for example, checking battery and oil levels). You must also be competent in basic piloting and able to deal with passing squalls and winds.

Many charter companies consider the résumés of the group as a whole when deciding if you're qualified to take one of its boats. Be honest; feeling underprepared when you're under way can spoil your vacation. One option – one that the charter company may require – is to bring along an instructional skipper for a few days.

## Sailing Schools

Sailing schools can be a good option for rookies or those looking for a confidence boost, and offer a formal program of instruction leading to certification by a recognized sailing association – all while you live aboard and cruise the seas for five days or more. Many of the bareboat charter companies and a good number of the crewed boats also offer certification programs or instruction with the boat's skipper.

# When to Go

Weather and cost are the major considerations for when to set sail. If cost is your main factor, be aware that low-season rates drop by around 30% from the peak rates from January to April.

» **Winter** Winds average 15 to 22 knots from the northeast; the 'Christmas winds,' which have been known to extend into January and even February, are the strongest of the year. When the wind is northeast, northside anchorages,

including Tortola's popular Cane Garden Bay, are uncomfortable to impossible.

» **Spring & summer** The wind swings around through the east to the southeast and declines to an average of 10 to 18 knots. Many sailors prefer the milder and somewhat warmer conditions of spring. August can be dicey with big storms.

» **Fall** In September and October, when the trade winds are at their weakest, the weather tends to be more unsettled. September is also the most likely month for hurricanes, so it's probably the best month to avoid.

# Costs

Several factors influence charter boat costs, including the vessel's size, age, hull type and amenities.

## Charter Fees

January to April is the busy season when prices peak. Boats with a generator and air-conditioning drive up the fee. For crewed boats, add about $2500 per week to the price for catamarans, as they're the yacht type used most often. A live-aboard sailing school costs roughly $2200 per person for a five-day course.

Sample bareboat costs during high season:

» **Small monohull** (two to three cabins) $3000 to $5500 per week

» **Large monohull** (four to five cabins) $5000 to $8800 per week

---

### CHECKLIST WHEN CHOOSING A BOAT

Consider these things in the early stages of planning:

» **Monohull vs catamaran** A traditional, lower-priced monohull? Or a more stable and spacious catamaran?

» **Onboard amenities** Most boats come standard with satellite navigation systems, autopilots, motorized dinghies and entertainment systems, but do you also want wi-fi, air-conditioning, a generator, or toys such kayaks and windsurfers?

» **Boat size** How many cabins do you need for your group? In general, each cabin holds two people; the rooms typically are furnished with a double bed. Nicer boats have one 'head' (ie bathroom) per cabin.

» **Crew requirements** Are you certified and prepared to go it alone in true bareboat fashion? Do you want a skipper only? Do you want a fully crewed boat, where the cooking and cleaning are taken care of, too?

» **Sailing companions** Make sure you all have similar expectations about the trip. Are you looking to do serious sailing? Or do you want to use the boat as a base for shopping and partying? Can you agree on who will do the cooking, cleaning and other duties (if there's no crew)?

» **Small catamaran** (two to three cabins) $4500 to $7000 per week

» **Large catamaran** (four to five cabins) $6000 to $12,000 per week

## Extra Fees

While crewed boat costs are all-inclusive (except for tipping), bareboat charters have extra expenses to consider:

» **Food & drink** Charter companies in the Virgin Islands almost always offer provisioning packages, where they'll stock your boat. The most popular type includes all breakfasts, all lunches and three or four dinners, for an average of $25 per person per day. Doing your own provisioning (there are large markets in St Thomas, St John and Tortola) is always an option; it costs time but can save money.

» **Boat insurance** Ranges from $30 to $50 per day.

» **Crew** Maybe you don't need a full crew but would like a skipper for your journey. You can hire one for whatever length of time you desire for roughly $150 a day; add $25 a day for an instructional skipper. Cooks also work for hire for $125 to $150 per day. Note that whatever crew you take on, you'll have to provide their sleeping cabin and food, as well.

» **Tipping** It's customary to tip crew 10% to 15% in cash for good service. Base the amount on the charter fee, and give it to the captain for the entire crew's work.

» **Trip insurance** Though not compulsory, it's recommended. You may be responsible for the whole charter fee if you cancel less than 45 days before your booking.

» **Fuel** Figure on about $80 to $100 per week for a monohull, $100 to $125 per week for a catamaran.

» **BVI National Parks Permit** Ranges from $25 to $55 per week, depending on the number of passengers.

» **Mooring fees** Count on $25 to $65 per night.

» **Hotel** You may need to pay for a hotel on your first or last night. Check with your charter company. Many have arrangements with local innkeepers that provide discounts off the rack rate; sometimes companies allow you to pay a small fee and spend the night on board the docked boat before you start your sailing trip.

» **Other** Optional add-ons include rental equipment (a kayak or cruising spinnaker), a cell phone (often comes with larger boats) and a delivery fee for a one-way charter. Diving is usually arranged by rendezvous with a local dive company; they pick you up and return you to your boat. Snorkel gear often is included free as part of the boat package.

## Discounts

Many companies offer last-minute deals on their websites, and it never hurts to ask for available discounts when talking to a company agent.

# Choosing a Base: Tortola or St Thomas

» Tortola holds the greatest number of charter boat companies in the Virgins – more than anywhere else in the Caribbean – while St Thomas ranks a distant second.

» Tortola's pros include a wider selection of boats, and a shorter sailing time to reach the best cruising areas (most are in the BVI). If you decide to stay solely in the BVI you won't have to worry about going through customs.

» St Thomas' pros are that it's usually easier and cheaper to get to, and groceries and supplies are cheaper.

» In Tortola the main base is at Wickhams Cay 2 in Road Town. The marina is well located near a supermarket, liquor store, several accommodation options and other necessities.

» In St Thomas, the American Yacht Harbor marina at Red Hook serves as the primary base. It, too, has good provisioning options nearby.

# Choosing a Company

» Start by poking around on charter-company websites and looking at the photos and layout schematics for available boats.

» Call the companies that interest you. Ask for references from recent clients and spend some time talking with the company's representatives. They should be able to answer your questions about the charter area, the sailing conditions, their fleet, a suggested itinerary and whatever else you want to know. If you're not satisfied, call another company.

» Two trade groups provide information on crewed charters. **The BVI Charter Yacht Society** (www.bvicrewedyachts.com) and

## DAY-SAIL OPERATORS

If you don't have the time or inclination to charter a boat, you can always head out on a day sail. Most operators have a set schedule for visiting certain islands throughout the week. Costs hover around $70 for a half-day sail, to $100 or so for a full-day excursion. Prices usually include snorkeling gear and drinks.

### St Thomas
Several companies sail from Red Hook; see p75 for details:
» **Winifred** (www.sailwinifred.com)
» **Nate's Custom Charters** (www.natescustomcharters.com)

### St John
Boats launch from Cruz Bay; see p89 for details:
» **Low Key Watersports** (www.divelowkey.com)
» **Cruz Bay Watersports** (www.divestjohn.com)

### St Croix
Christiansted is the jump-off for the island's day sails; see p116 and p123:
» **World Ocean School** (www.worldoceanschool.org)
» **Big Beard's Adventures** (www.bigbeards.com)
» **Caribbean Sea Adventures** (www.caribbeanseaadventures.com)
» **Teroro II** (teroro@msn.com)

### Tortola
These boats depart from Road Town; see p143 for further information:
» **White Squall II** (www.whitesquall2.com)
» **Lionheart** (www.aristocatcharters.com)

### Virgin Gorda
Several companies depart from Yacht Harbour mall in Spanish Town; see p167 for details:
» **Dive BVI** (www.divebvi.com)
» **Spirit of Anegada** (www.spiritofanegada.com)
» **Double 'D'** (www.doubledbvi.com)

---

**Virgin Islands Charter Yacht League** (www.vicl.org) have the layman's lowdown on boat types, sizes and amenities to help you can make an informed decision. There are also links to reliable vessels and brokers.

## Charter Companies

The following is a list of respected charter services based in the Virgin Islands. Each can arrange bareboat charters, as well as a variety of crew options.

### Tortola

**BVI Yacht Charters** (www.bviyachtcharters.com) Longstanding company; located at Joma Marina at Port Purcell, Road Town.

**Barecat Charters** (www.barecat.com) Smaller company specializing in catamarans; located at Sea Cow Bay near Nanny Cay.

**Catamaran Company** (www.catamaranco.com) Another catamaran specialist; located at Village Cay Marina, Road Town.

**Conch Charters** (www.conchcharters.com) Smaller company; located at Fort Burt Marina, Road Town.

**Footloose Sailing Charters** (www.footloosecharters.com) Billed as a 'budget' company. It works in conjunction with the Moorings; located at Wickhams Cay 2, Road Town.

**Horizon Yacht Charters** (www.horizonyachtcharters.com) Smaller company; located at Nanny Cay Marina.

**Moorings** (www.moorings.com) This crew started the BVI bareboat business and remains the islands' largest yacht company. Many boats are less than two years old (they're the 'exclusive' boats vs 'club' boats). Located at Wickhams Cay 2, Road Town.

**Sunsail Yacht Charters** (www.sunsail.com) The BVI's second-largest company; also based at Wickhams Cay 2, Road Town.

**Tortola Marine Management** (www.sailtmm.com) Smaller company that provides free wi-fi aboard all its boats. Located at Road Reef Marina near Fort Burt.

## St Thomas

**CYOA Yacht Charters** (www.cyoayachtcharters.com) This smaller company is conveniently located at Frenchtown Marina, a stone's throw from the main airport.

**Island Yacht Charters** (www.iyc.vi) Smaller company offering environmentally aware touches such as solar panels and biodegradable toilet paper and cleansers as part of its packages; located at American Yacht Harbor, Red Hook.

**Virgin Island Power (VIP) Yacht Charters** (www.vipyachts.com) Has a fleet of motor yachts as well as sailboats; located at Benner Bay, near Red Hook.

## Sailing Schools

**Offshore Sailing School** (www.offshoresailing.com) Large, venerable company offering courses out of the Moorings in Road Town, Tortola.

**Rob Swain Sailing School** (www.swainsailing.com) Well-rated, smaller school operating out of Nanny Cay, Tortola.

**Sistership Sailing School** (www.sailsistership.com) Specializes in instruction for women, couples and families; based at Nanny Cay, Tortola.

# What to Expect Onboard

Your boat is, in essence, a floating hotel. You sleep aboard it nightly and eat most meals there. In general, you sail off in the morning and visit anchorages where you snorkel, dive or go ashore to explore the beaches by day. Before dark, you'll arrive at a final destination you've selected, where you'll tie up at one of the overnight buoys. It's best to arrive at your final destination each day before dark and with plenty of time to secure a mooring. They fill up fast in the most popular spots. In the BVI, the National Parks Trust has installed more than 200 mooring buoys (surface buoys attached to stainless steel pins set in bedrock) for daytime use at popular sites. These buoys protect the underwater marine ecology from physical damage by boat anchors. (Note they are different than the larger overnight buoys.)

# Itineraries

Most charterers head for the British Virgin Islands; a typical weeklong itinerary involves a sampling of the islands as part of a circumnavigation of Tortola, with a lunch stop at one anchorage and an overnight at another. There are about 90 islands, islets, rocks and cays in the 45 miles between St Thomas and Anegada. You won't be able to hit them all in a week.

If you're in the mood for a longer passage, many companies will let you sail to St Croix, about 40 miles from St Thomas or St John, and back. Another option is to arrange a one-way charter to the Spanish Virgins (Puerto Rico's Vieques and Culebra Islands and their surrounding cays). Going west from St Thomas to drop off in Fajardo (on the Puerto Rican mainland) avoids a nasty upwind slog going the other way. Anegada's reef-strewn approaches have claimed many boats, but if you can demonstrate appropriate experience or are willing to take a skipper, it's more than worth the effort.

# What to Bring
## Food & Provisions

If you're doing your own provisioning, there are good markets close to the main marinas.

» **Riteway Food Market** (p148) This fully stocked supermarket is near the Moorings in Road Town, Tortola.

» **Marina Market** (p79) Offers a good selection of produce, cheese and alcohol located by the marina in Red Hook, St Thomas.

## Clothing & Equipment

» Bring casual and breezy beach attire for on deck, and long pants or a sundress for evenings ashore.

## MOST POPULAR ANCHORAGES

» **Deadman's Bay, Peter Island** (p193) The first stop on many itineraries, as it is reachable from Road Town in an hour or two of sailing.

» **Salt Island** (p195) Once a regular stop for ships requiring salt for food preservation on trade routes, today it's home to the fascinating diving site at the RMS *Rhone* shipwreck.

» **Manchioneel Bay, Cooper Island** (p194) Makes a fine lunch stop for those sailing upwind to Virgin Gorda.

» **The Baths, Virgin Gorda** (p165) Home to the Virgins' beloved big boulders.

» **North Sound, Virgin Gorda** (p171) Lots of tall-masted mega-yachts and the yacht clubs to serve their thirsty sailors.

» **The Dogs** (p198) Good diving and snorkeling break halfway between Tortola and Virgin Gorda.

» **White Bay, Jost Van Dyke** (p180) Blinding white sand and good-time beach bars.

» **Norman Island** (p192) Home to a rowdy floating pirate bar moored in the bight.

» Rubber-soled shoes, such as boat shoes or tennis shoes, work best.

» Sun protection is vital. Bring lots of suntan lotion, wide-brimmed hats or sailing caps and loose-fitting cotton cover-ups.

» For cool or windy evenings, a windbreaker comes in handy.

» Bring an audio cable or iTrip (FM converter) to use iPods or MP3 players on board.

» Bring your passport or passport card.

# Travel with Children

## Best Regions for Kids

### North Shore, St John
At the heart of Virgin Islands National Park, with eco-camping opportunities, gentle hiking trails, ranger programs and great beaches for snorkeling.

### East End, St Thomas
Several resorts cluster here, as well as Coral World Ocean Park, the top spot for encounters with marine life, and a mangrove lagoon for kid-friendly kayak trips.

### Virgin Gorda
The Bitter End Yacht Club is the Virgins' best option for teaching kids sailing, windsurfing and other watersport lessons at its camps. The Baths are another splash-worthy locale.

### Christiansted, St Croix
A cannon-covered fort, a water-sport-laden beach, wharfside restaurants where fish swim up to nibble, and a bioluminescent bay come nighttime make St Croix's main town a well-provisioned base.

Waves to splash in, sand castles to build, sea turtles to visit, forts to explore – families will find activities throughout the islands, and you can bet the weather will oblige whatever you do. Add a boatload of resorts catering to children, along with casual beachside eateries, and you may find yourself (as many do) bringing the kids back year after year.

## Virgin Islands for Kids
Island culture welcomes children with open arms. St Thomas, St John and St Croix are the easiest for family travel, as they hold the majority of kid-friendly resorts (plus – for US visitors – there's no passport requirement). The British Virgins have family offerings too, just not quite to the extent of the USVI.

### Eating Out
The vast majority of restaurants are family friendly. Many offer special children's menus, but even without it, eateries typically have burgers and pizza as part of their line-up. The ambience tends to be informal and relaxed wherever you go.

## Children's Highlights
### Pint-Size Bites

» **Miss Lucy's, St John** – It's a great place to introduce young palates to West Indian food, and maybe even bottle feed the resident goats some milk.

» **Udder Delite Dairy Bar, St Thomas** – Milkshakes galore in every possible flavor at Magens Bay.

» **Rum Runners, St Croix** – Big fish and boats entertain kids while they munch here at Christiansted's wharf.

» **Cheeseburgers in Paradise, St Croix** – The setting is like being part of a giant picnic, complete with soft-serve ice cream.

## Hotels for Small Fry

» **Maho Bay Camps, St John** – Get the eco-camping experience, with all the gear provided. Children's craft classes with recycled bottles and paper add to the fun.

» **Westin Resort, St John** – This all-amenities property has a huge pool and supervised art and recreation activities to enroll in each day.

» **Bitter End Yacht Club, Virgin Gorda** – Youngsters learn to sail, windsurf, kayak and more at Kids Camp for ages five to 12 and the Junior Water Sports Program for ages 13 to 17.

» **Secret Harbour Beach Resort, St Thomas** – The spacious condo units here front a calm, shallow beach close to the East End's restaurants and attractions.

## Beachy Keen

» **Magens Bay, St Thomas** – The USVI's most popular beach has lifeguards, food vendors, paddle boats and plenty of little playmates.

» **Secret Harbour, St Thomas** – The secret here is calm water and a swimming platform to jump from.

» **Maho Bay, St John** – You might see a hawksbill or green turtle in the protected, shallow water.

» **Protestant Cay, St Croix** – A little boat tootles over to the wide beach in the shadow of the fort.

» **Cramer's Park, St Croix** – Meet local families who come here to picnic on weekends.

## Creature Features

» **Coral World Ocean Park, St Thomas** – Touch starfish, pet sharks, feed stingrays or swim with turtles.

» **St Croix Environmental Association** – Watch leatherback sea turtle hatchlings.

» **Butterfly Farm, St Thomas** – Learn about the fluttering beasties while walking among flowers.

» Spot fish, lizards and crabs everywhere on the islands.

## Adventures at Sea

» **Salt River Bay, St Croix** – Paddle through the bioluminescent water at night.

» **VI Ecotours, St Thomas** – Kayak through a mangrove sanctuary.

» **World Ocean School, St Croix** – Sail aboard the historic *Roseway* schooner.

» **The Baths, Virgin Gorda** – Explore grottoes and tidepools.

» **Sea Trek, St Thomas** – Kids over age eight can go deep and walk on the reef 15 feet underwater.

» **Bitter End Yacht Club, Virgin Gorda** – The top place to learn to sail.

## History Lessons

» **Fort Christiansvaern, St Croix** – Play pirates using the cannons and dungeon.

» **Fort Frederik, St Croix** – Red-brick battlements where slaves fought and got their freedom.

» **Salt River Bay, St Croix** – Columbus' 1493 landing site.

## Festivals

» **Aragorn's Fireball Full Moon Party, Tortola** – Fire jugglers and fungi bands.

» **Mango Melee, St Croix** – Fruitful celebration with eating contests for kids.

---

## BABYSITTING & GEAR RENTAL SERVICES

Many hotels and resorts provide babysitters. If you're not staying at such a place, you can call and ask for the children's program director; often they can refer you to a reliable sitter.

On Virgin Gorda, **Tropical Nannies** (☎284-495-6493; www.tropicalnannies.com) provides babysitting services by trained, professional nannies. They'll come to your hotel or take the kids off your hands starting at $20 per hour. The group also rents out cribs and high chairs.

On St John, **Island Baby VI** (www.islandbabyvi.com) rents out gear such as high chairs ($60 per week), baby hiking backpacks ($50 per week), baby monitors and much more, which can lighten your travel load considerably.

## WHAT TO PACK

Be prepared for lots of time in the sun and sea. Most lodgings provide beach towels, chairs and umbrellas. You can buy sand pails, snorkel masks or anything else you forget at local beach shops, though it'll be costly.

☐ Passport (US parents only need to bring their children's birth certificate for travel to USVI)

☐ Sun protection (sunscreen, hats, sunglasses, long-sleeved shirts)

☐ Snorkel gear (especially masks) that you've tested for leaks and proper fit

☐ Water wings and other flotation devices

☐ Pails and shovels

☐ Sturdy reef shoes

☐ Flip-flops

☐ Underwater camera

☐ Insect repellent

» **Jump Ups, St Croix** – Music-filled street carnivals.

## Planning

Traveling around the Virgin Islands with the tots can be child's play. Lonely Planet's *Travel with Children* offers a wealth of tips and tricks.

### When to Go

Mid-December through April is when children's activities are in full swing at the resorts. The water is calmest for sailing, swimming and snorkeling in spring.

### Accommodations

The islands offer a wide range of family accommodations, including campgrounds, condominiums, private villas and luxury resorts. We've identified kid-friendly places throughout this book with a 🔅. When making a reservation, be sure to mention that you're bringing the little ones.

Larger resort hotels offer supervised half- or full-day activity programs for kids up to age 12 (sometimes older).

The eco-campgrounds on St Thomas, St Croix and particularly St John offer opportunities to experience the islands' natural beauty; they're best for families with school-age kids.

Villa and condominium rentals offer an appealing alternative for larger families and longer stays, since the units have more space, kitchens for DIY meals and laundry facilities in some instances. However, the properties are not always child-proofed, and you might run into issues such as uncovered electrical outlets or glass tables and other sharp-edged decor. Always ask the rental agent for specifics.

### Driving

Renting a car is definitely the easiest way for families to get around. Both the US and British Virgin Islands require all passengers in private cars to wear seat belts, and children under age five must be in a car seat. In actuality, the law is rarely enforced. If you're not traveling with your own car seats, most car-rental firms provide them for about $10 per day. Supplies are limited, so reserve well in advance.

# regions at a glance

The Virgins are divided between the USA (St Thomas, St John, St Croix) and the UK (Tortola, Virgin Gorda, Jost Van Dyke, Anegada, Out Islands). St Thomas is the region's hub, jam-packed with cruise ships, resorts and jewelry shops. St John is the greenest island, literally and figuratively; it's mostly national parkland dotted with ecofriendly lodgings. St Croix floats out by its lonesome, offering a mix of rainforest, sugar plantations, old forts and great scuba diving. Tortola lets its hair down with sailing, surfing and full-moon parties, while plump Virgin Gorda offers boulder-studded beaches and billionaire yacht havens. For solitude there's the little guys – happy-go-lucky Jost Van Dyke and sleepy Anegada – each with fewer than 200 people. And on the Out Islands, it's really just golden beaches, blue sea and maybe a bar or two.

## St Thomas

**Shopping** ✓✓
**Cuisine** ✓✓✓
**Beaches** ✓✓

### Bauble Bazaar
Couple the highest duty-free allowance in the Caribbean with jewel-bedecked shops cloistered in exotic 18th-century buildings, and you've got Charlotte Amalie, the dream port of shopaholics worldwide.

### Feeding Frenzy
When the urge strikes to fork into fungi, callaloo, curried goat and other West Indian dishes, St Thomas' restaurants set a copious table. Wine and martini bars also await.

### Sand Boxes
Want to surf? Sorted. Secluded beach surrounded by nature? Check. Beach resort with water sports, drink vendors and volleyball? Yep, plenty. A beach pretty enough for Brad Pitt? Got that too. St Thomas has plenty of sand to choose from.

**p52**

## St John

**Parks** ✓✓✓
**Hiking** ✓✓✓
**Snorkeling** ✓✓✓

### Eco-Camps
Lush Virgin Islands National Park covers two-thirds of St John, keeping nature at a premium and development to a minimum. Tent-resorts let you sleep amid trees while keeping the environment intact.

### Paths of Least Resistance
The national park maintains 20 trails and any reasonably fit hiker can walk them. Paths lead to ancient petroglyphs, sugar mill ruins, mountain peaks and secluded shores.

### Snorkel the Day Away
Don your mask and flippers and swim offshore from Salt Pond Bay, Waterlemon Cay, Yawzi Point and myriad other beaches to commune (carefully!) with turtles, nurse sharks and spotted eagle rays.

**p83**

# St Croix

**Diving** ✓✓✓
**History** ✓✓
**Wildlife** ✓✓

### The Wall

Divers flock to Cane Bay's one-of-a-kind 'wall.' It drops at a 60-degree slope to a 12,000ft depth, offering a literal look into the deep a quick swim from shore.

### Forts & Windmills

Christiansted's yellow fort and Frederiksted's blood-red one let you time travel to the 18th century, when the towns traded in sugar, molasses and slaves. More than 100 windmill ruins hark back to when sugarcane plantations abounded.

### Meet the Turtles

Several isolated beaches are nesting grounds for turtles, including Jack and Isaac Bays, home to green and hawksbill slowpokes, and Sandy Point National Wildlife Refuge, where the mammoth 1500lb leatherback heaves ashore.

**p108**

# Tortola

**Festivals** ✓✓
**Sailing** ✓✓✓
**Surfing** ✓✓

### Moon Madness

Revelers flock in for Tortola's monthly full-moon parties. Fungi bands, stilt walkers and fire jugglers entertain families at Aragorn's Studio art center. The party skews more adult at Bomba's Surfside Shack, with reggae bands and mushroom tea.

### Set a Course

The BVI is a sailing hot spot, thanks to steady trade winds, calm tides and hundreds of protected anchorages. Tortola, with its charter-boat-filled marinas, is where the dream begins.

### Catch a Wave

Tortola has the requisite secluded beaches and party beaches, but it also has big-waved surfing beaches and breezy bays for wind sports that draw enthusiasts to its shores.

**p136**

# Virgin Gorda

**High Society** ✓✓
**Parks** ✓✓
**Beaches** ✓✓✓

### Yacht Clubbing

If ever there was a place where guys in white captain's hats sat around clinking ice in their drinks after coming ashore from tall-masted mega-yachts, it's Virgin Gorda's North Sound.

### Peaks & Mines

Gorda Peak and Copper Mine National Parks are worth the hike. The former is an easy climb amid orchids and hummingbirds to the island's high point. The latter offers wind-pounded ruins atop a forlorn bluff.

### Big-Bouldered Beauty

Visitors come to see the granite megaliths of the Baths. Boulders hulk over the beach and form sunlight-shafted grottoes prime for climbing and swimming in search of hidden 'rooms' and peaceful pools.

**p162**

# Jost Van Dyke

**Island Fun** ✓✓✓
**Music** ✓✓
**Beach Bars** ✓✓

### Barefoot Island

Yachters and glitterati (lookin' at you, Keith Richards) have long stopped by Jost, but fame hasn't spoiled the wee island. Main St is still a sandy path lined with hammocks and open-air bar-restaurants. In other words, it's a beach.

### Foxy Tunes

If you know anything about Jost, you know its most famous resident is cultural preservationist and calypsonian Foxy Callwood. Catch him crooning at his bar, or any of the other locals who strum here.

### Beach Bar Tales

White Bay holds mythic beach bars where boats anchor, crews swim ashore and plop down wet bills for a rum-soaked Painkiller. Or so the Soggy Dollar Bar story goes...

**p175**

# Anegada

**Cuisine** ✓✓
**Landscapes** ✓✓
**Beaches** ✓✓✓

## Lobster Dinners

Eating an Anegada lobster is a tourist rite of passage. Chefs grill them on the beach on old oil drums. When the hulking crustacean arrives at your table there's only one thing to do: get cracking.

## Odd Creatures

Anegada is steamrolled flat compared to its mountainous brethren. The odd landscape hosts an odd menagerie where pink flamingos wade in salt ponds and a lonely iguana roams in its final frontier.

## Quiet Shores

Snorkel, sip a frosty drink, swing in a hammock: that's how it happens at whimsically named beaches such as Loblolly Bay and Flash of Beauty. Add wandering bovines to the mix at Cow Wreck Bay.

**p184**

# Out Islands

**Pirate Lore** ✓✓✓
**Diving** ✓✓✓
**Beaches** ✓✓

## Tall Tales

Blackbeard left his men on Dead Chest Island with nothing but a saber and bottle of rum, while pirates buried chests of silver coins on Norman Island. Fiction? Sail over, and see for yourself.

## Underwater Sights

The wreck of the *Rhone* may be the most famous diving and snorkeling site, but you can also swim around treasure caves, 15ft mushroom-shaped coral, and reefs with fish so thick you're enveloped by them.

## Beach Parties

Norman Island is the biggest party pad, thanks to two beach bars. One shoots a cannon to launch happy hour, the other offers shots of a liquid kind aboard a pirate ship moored in the bight.

**p191**

**Look out for these icons:**

 **TOP** Our author's
CHOICE recommendation

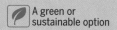 A green or
sustainable option

**FREE** No payment
required

# On the Road

# St Thomas

POP 52,200

## Best Places to Eat

» Old Stone Farmhouse (p82)

» Gladys' Cafe (p64)

» Pie Hole (p65)

» Craig & Sally's (p66)

» Toad & Tart (p77)

## Best Places to Stay

» Green Iguana (p62)

» Secret Harbour Beach Resort (p76)

» Miller Manor (p62)

» Crystal Palace B&B (p62)

» Bolongo Bay Beach Resort (p71)

## Why Go?

Most visitors arrive in the US Virgin Islands via St Thomas, and the place sure knows how to strike a positive first impression. Jungly cliffs poke high in the sky, red-hipped roofs blossom over the hills, and all around the turquoise, yacht-dotted sea laps. Dizzying cruise-ship traffic and big resorts nibbling its edges make St Thomas the most commercialized of the Virgins, but this is also a fine island to sharpen your knife and fork. Curried meats and hot-spiced callaloo soup fill local tables. Bars pour tropical drinks high and low, from coconut-cake martinis in a mountaintop bistro to cold beers in a parking lot tiki hut. Visitors who make the effort to move deeper into the island will find opportunities for surfing, kayaking through mangrove swamps and getting face-to-face with sea turtles.

## When to Go

Mid-December through April is the dry and sunny high season, when prices and crowds max out. Late March sees extra action courtesy of the Rolex Cup Regatta during the fourth weekend. The whopping, party-hearty St Thomas Carnival fills the streets from mid-April through early May. Stormy weather starts in August, though this month also hosts two notable shindigs: the Texas Society Chili Cook-off and the USVI Atlantic Blue Marlin Tournament, a mega-lure for sportfishers. May and early December are good shoulder season months for bargains and decent (if wet) weather.

## History

Christopher Columbus sailed by St Thomas in 1493. While he did not stop, the Spanish adventurers and colonists who followed shortly thereafter did, and by 1555 they had totally depopulated the island by kidnapping, murdering and driving off the indigenous Taíno and Caribs.

After 1625 the nations of Europe became hell-bent on acquiring colonies in the New World, yet while the English, Dutch and French fought over plums such as St Croix, the Danes staked a claim on a forgotten piece of fruit, St Thomas.

In the 1700s, St Thomas became a community of merchants and traders that included several nationalities and religions, with English, Dutch, Danes, Germans and Jews among the mix.

On July 4, 1848, the schooner *Vigilant* arrived at St Thomas from St Croix with the news that the Virgin Islands' Danish governor had proclaimed the emancipation of all slaves on Danish territory. In the decades that followed, the island's economy evolved to meet modern shipping needs, establishing itself as a major coaling station for steamships.

Maritime commerce was still bringing sailors to the shores when the US bought the Virgin Islands from the Danes in 1917. The Navy set up camp on St Thomas, and when it left in the 1950s, the naval port facilities and former air base became the crucial infrastructure for facilitating the flow of tourists to and from the island.

In 1989 Hurricane Hugo wreaked havoc on the island. Then, in 1995, Hurricanes Luis and Marilyn dealt a back-to-back blow.

### ⓘ Getting There & Around

**AIR**

St Thomas' **Cyril E King Airport** (STT; www.vi port.com) is the main hub for the Virgin Islands. Major operators from the US mainland include **American Airlines** (www.aa.com), **Continental** (www.continental.com), **Delta** (www.delta.com), **Spirit** (www.spiritair.com), **United** (www.united. com) and **US Airways** (www.usairways.com).

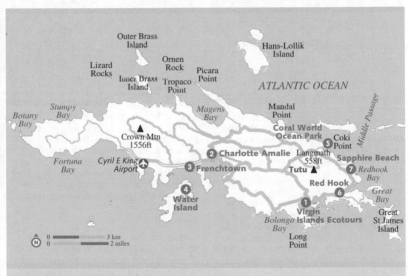

## St Thomas Highlights

❶ Kayak past twisted mangroves to a coral rubble beach with **Virgin Islands Ecotours** (p75)

❷ Shop for rum, pirate gear and fiery hot sauces in historic **Charlotte Amalie** (p67)

❸ Wine and dine in **Frenchtown** (p65)

❹ Slow to a leisurely pace on **Water Island** (p72)

❺ Pet sharks and feed stingrays at **Coral World Ocean Park** (p73)

❻ Quaff flaming drinks in funky bars in **Red Hook** (p78)

❼ Join the breezy fun and games at **Sapphire Beach** (p74)

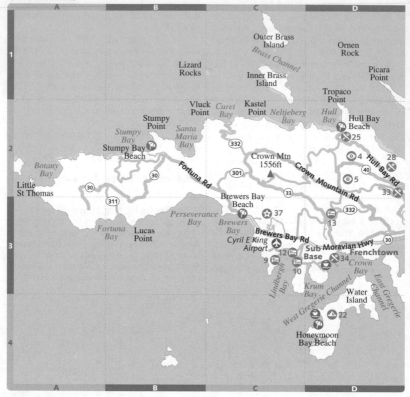

Between St Thomas and St Croix, **Seaborne Airlines** (www.seaborneairlines.com) flies cool floatplanes from wharves at Charlotte Amalie and Christiansted. The cost is around $80 each way.

### BOAT

St Thomas has excellent ferry connections to the rest of the Virgins. The two main marine terminals are at Charlotte Amalie and Red Hook. See the main ferry routes from St Thomas on p239. See **VI Now** (www.vinow.com) for cost and schedule details. St Thomas also has two cruise ship terminals:

**Havensight** The primary dock, located about a mile east of Charlotte Amalie.

**Crown Bay** The newer, secondary dock, located about a mile west of Charlotte Amalie.

### BUS

**Vitran** (fare $1) buses operate over the length of the island. Look for the bus stop signs on Rtes 30 and 38. Services run roughly once per hour.

'Dollar buses' (aka 'safaris' or 'gypsy cabs') also stop along the routes. These vehicles are open-air vans that hold 20 people. They look like taxis, except they're filled with locals instead of sunburned tourists. Flag them down by flapping your hand, and press the buzzer to stop them when you reach your destination. The fare is $2.

### CAR

Roads are narrow, steep, twisting and often pot-holed, making for slow travel times. Rte 30 follows the south shore and is the easiest route for getting around St Thomas; it has various names, including Waterfront Hwy, Veterans Dr and Frenchman Bay Rd. Rte 38 is a shortcut between the East End and Charlotte Amalie. This broad road (sometimes four lanes) scales the mountains and is the major commercial artery, lined with businesses and malls as it passes through the island's interior. A series of mountaintop roads, including Skyline Dr (Rte 40), lead to the north shore beaches. Rental cars are widely available at the airport and resort hotels.

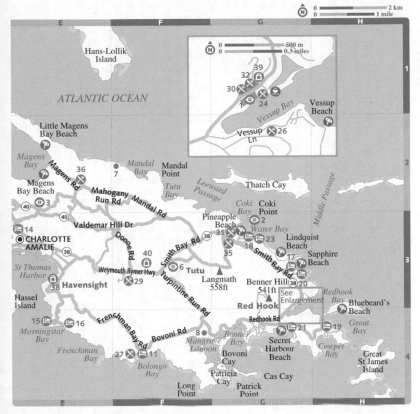

Prices start around $60 per day. Don't forget to drive on the left.

**Avis** (800-331-1084; www.avis.com)

**Budget** (340-776-5774, 800-626-4516; www.budgetstt.com)

**Dependable Car Rentals** (800-522-3076; www.dependablecar.com)

**Discount Car Rentals** (340-776-4858, 877-478-2833; www.discountcar.vi)

**Hertz** (800-654-3131; www.hertz.com)

**TAXI**

Territorial law requires taxi drivers to carry a government-set rate sheet, and prices are listed in the readily available free tourist guide *St Thomas/St John This Week*.

Many taxis are vans that carry up to 12 passengers. These service multiple destinations and may stop to pick up passengers along the way, so their rates are usually charged on a per-person basis. The following table shows current per-person rates for popular destinations from Charlotte Amalie. The price drops a few dollars when more than one passenger goes to the destination. Add $2 per piece of luggage.

| DESTINATION | COST |
| --- | --- |
| Airport | $7 |
| Magens Bay | $10 |
| Red Hook | $13 |

## Charlotte Amalie

With two to six Love Boats docking in town daily, Charlotte Amalie (a-*mall*-ya) is one of the most popular cruise ship destinations in the Caribbean. To many travelers, the mere mention of the town spawns images of an exotic shopping bazaar. Indeed, it has the largest number of boutiques, perfume vendors and jewelry shops in the Caribbean, with most housed in architecturally rich, pastel-hued colonial buildings.

Downtown buzzes with commerce by day, when the ships unload. The record to date is the arrival of 20,000 passengers one Wednesday in March 2010. By early evening, the masses clear out, the shops shut, and the narrow streets become shadowy.

Sure, the scene can overwhelm, but why not take a deep breath and focus on the town's lip-licking West Indian cuisine, Frenchtown wine bars and proximity to white-sand beaches?

### One Day

Stroll the downtown district of **Charlotte Amalie** and check out historic sites such as the sand-floored **St Thomas Synagogue** and **Emancipation Garden**, where the **Vendors' Plaza** now stands. Browse the town's famous shops for a Rolex or pirate eye patch. If you prefer shores to stores, grab a taxi to the beach at **Magens Bay**, the crowd favorite, unfurling a gorgeous stretch of sand with lifeguards, water-sports vendors and other amenities. Return to Charlotte Amalie for a late lunch of West Indian dishes at **Gladys' Cafe** or **Cuzzin's Caribbean Restaurant & Bar** or save your appetite for a big dinner later at one of the funky bistros in **Frenchtown**.

### Two Days

Head to St Thomas' **East End** and make the most of the activities on offer: windsurfing at **Vessup Beach**, diving at **Coki Beach**, kayaking through the mangrove lagoon with **Virgin Islands Ecotours**. Alternatively, just pick a beach and lounge – **Sapphire Beach** and **Lindquist Beach** are fine options. Hit happy hour in **Red Hook** at **Duffy's Love Shack** or one of the other gin joints, then book in for a lovingly prepared meal at the **Old Stone Farmhouse**.

## History

In 1666, a year after Denmark laid claim to St Thomas, the Danes began the construction of Fort Christian on St Thomas Harbor. Three years later, the colonists constructed four pubs near the water's edge on the western side of the fort, and in 1678, the Danes strengthened their military position here by building Blackbeard's and Bluebeard's Castles as lookout towers on the crests of two hills. People of the time called the colony Taphus, Danish for 'brew pub,' and the settlement outside the fort on St Thomas Harbor was, by all accounts, a rustic, free-spirited pirates' den.

A series of governors and investors tried to bring the port under control, turn a profit for the Danish West India and Guinea Company and get islanders to pay taxes. Their efforts met with only marginal success. One enterprise did take hold: slave trading.

In the late 1600s and early 1700s the town prospered as a slave market and a neutral port. During these years, the settlement gained the name of Charlotte Amalie in honor of Denmark's queen.

When the US bought the Danish West Indies in 1917, the Navy took control of the islands and made Charlotte Amalie its headquarters. Navy presence in the town truly overwhelmed Charlotte Amalie during WWII, when the harbor became a naval base to protect allied shipping to and from the Panama Canal.

##  Sights

Charlotte Amalie proper is all about shopping and checking out the historical buildings. For beaches and water sports, you'll have to head to the East End or North Side for the best options.

The red walls of Fort Christian and the open space of Emancipation Garden and its Vendors' Plaza are the old town's core. Many of the city's historic homes and businesses stand on the slopes of Government Hill just north of Emancipation Garden. This area is traditionally known as Kongens (Kings) Quarter.

Havensight (where cruise ships dock) anchors the east side of St Thomas Harbor, while Frenchtown anchors the west side. Around the peninsula from Frenchtown lies Crown Bay, another cruise-ship-filled marina. Many attractions are open only when cruise ships are in port.

### Emancipation Garden                                  PARK
(btwn Tolbod Gade & Fort Christian) This park, with its trees, benches and gazebo, is the center of Charlotte Amalie. Here, on July 3, 1848, town officials read the emancipation proclamation to the people of St Thomas after receiving word that Governor Peter von Scholten had freed the slaves on St Croix. A replica of the Philadelphia Liberty Bell stands in the corner.

Carnival celebrations and band concerts take place here, but most of the time it is a place for folks to kick back with a cold drink

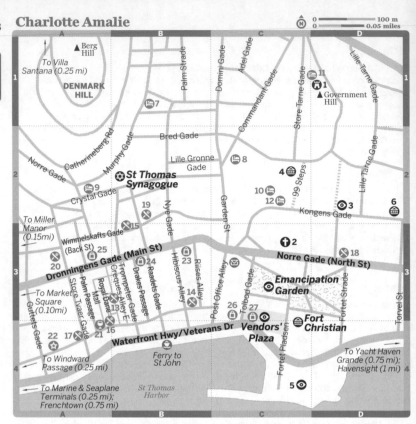

from the **Vendors' Plaza**, where sellers also hawk batik dresses, souvenir T-shirts and Prada knock-offs under blue-canopied stalls. Travelers will find this park a convenient rallying point and the easiest place to catch a cab. Vitran buses and safaris stop close by on Waterfront Hwy.

### Fort Christian
HISTORICAL SITE

(Waterfront Hwy; admission by donation; ☺8:30am-4:30pm Mon-Fri) Built with blood-red brick, Fort Christian, east of Emancipation Garden, is the oldest colonial building in the Virgin Islands. The core of the fort dates from 1666. Most of the ramparts were added in the 18th century. The clock tower came during an 1870s renovation of the fort to celebrate the colonial government returning to St Thomas. Over the years, the fort has functioned as a bastion, jail, governor's residence and a Lutheran church.

At press time, the fort and its artifact-rich museum were closed and undergoing reno-

vations. The reopening date for the multi-year project had not been determined.

### Kings Wharf &
### Legislature Building
HISTORICAL BUILDING

(Waterfront Hwy) This government compound, across from Fort Christian, is the original ship landing for the Danish colony. Today, the US Coast Guard shares the ground with the territorial legislature. The USVI governing body meets in the pale-green neoclassical building that dates from 1874.

Once a barracks for Danish and, subsequently, US troops, this building is where the Danes officially turned over the islands to the US. Island politicians have assembled here since the 1950s.

### Frederik Lutheran Church
CHURCH

(Norre Gade) One of Charlotte Amalie's architectural gems rises a few blocks behind the fort. Frederik Lutheran Church was mostly built between 1789 and 1793. The original structure was Georgian, but after two major reconstructions in the 19th century, the church now has Gothic Revival elements, including a gable roof and tower. The entrance has a West Indian 'welcoming arms' staircase (a reference to the way the staircase flares at the base). During the 19th century, the church had segregated congregations – one West Indian, the other Danish. The church is open sporadically during the week for a look-see. Services, which are open to the public, take place on Sunday at 9am and Wednesday at 12:15pm.

**Government House** HISTORICAL BUILDING
(21-22 Kongens Gade; ⊙9am-noon & 1-5pm Mon-Fri) Ascend the hill behind the church and you'll come to a grand white mansion, where the territorial governor has his offices. With three stories and a hipped roof, it is one of St Thomas' most famous structures. It was built between 1865 and 1867, and restored in 1994. You can walk around the first floor, though there's not much to see.

**Seven Arches Museum** MUSEUM
(☑340-774-9295; www.sevenarchesmuseum.com; Kongens Gade; suggested donation $5; ⊙by appt)

This 18th-century artisan's home sits in a tiny alley off Kongens Gade just to the east of Government House. The museum takes its name from the seven arches that support the welcoming arms staircase. You can admire the antiques in the great room and take in a view of the harbor before heading out back to the separate Danish kitchen, cistern and walled garden. Call to set up a visit.

**Blackbeard's Castle** HISTORICAL SITE
(www.blackbeardscastle.com; admission $12; ⊙9am-3pm when cruise ships in port) Blackbeard's Castle watches over town from atop Government Hill. In the 18th century this five-story masonry watchtower was said to be the lookout post of pirate Edward Teach, alias Blackbeard. Actually, historians don't lend much credence to the tale. What's known for certain is that colonial Danes built the tower as a military installation in 1678. You can climb up for good harbor views.

The admission fee includes use of the three pools on the grounds, photos with the myriad pirate statues that dot the property, and entrance to **Villa Notman**, **Britannia House** and **Haagensen House** – three colonial homes furnished with West Indian antiques and/or jewelry shops. It also includes entry to the **World Caribbean Amber Museum**, guarded by a hokey mechanical dinosaur; the **amber waterfall**, studded with 12,000 yellowy gems; and a **rum factory**, where a guide explains the distilling process, though there isn't much to see. The whole thing is kind of a hefty price without much payoff.

A better idea is to attack Government Hill from below and ascend the steep set of stairs – the so-called **99 Steps** – that lead from the commercial district near Kongens Gade up into a canopy of trees. These steps, of which there are actually 103 (though you'll be too out of breath to count), were constructed using ship-ballast brick in the mid-18th century. At the top of the 99 Steps, and about halfway up to the watchtower, you'll see **Haagensen House**, which you can sometimes peek in for free. Explore the area in the cool of the morning, before the crowds arrive.

FREE **St Thomas Synagogue**                    HISTORICAL BUILDING
(www.stthomassynagogue.com; 16A & B Crystal Gade; ☺10am-4pm Mon-Thu, to 3pm Fri) The second-oldest Hebrew temple in the western hemisphere (the oldest is on the island of Curaçao), peaceful St Thomas Synagogue is a National Historic Landmark. Its real name is Synagogue of Beracha V'Shalom V'Gimilath Chasidim, aka Synagogue of Blessing and Peace and Acts of Piety. The current building dates from 1833, but Jews have worshipped here since 1796, from Sephardic Jews from Denmark to today's 110-family Reform congregation. The temple floor is made of sand to symbolize the flight of the Israelites out of Egypt and across the desert. There's a tiny museum in the back room offering historical and cultural tidbits, such as a display on Jewish governors in the

USVI (lookin' at you, Morris de Castro). A gift shop sells mezuzahs and tchotchkes.

**Camille Pissarro Gallery**                    GALLERY
(14 Main St) Here in 1830, Jacob Pizarro was born as the son of Spanish Jews. As a young adult, Jacob became a very accomplished painter, moved to Paris, changed his name to Camille Pissarro and emerged as one of the founders of the French Impressionist movement in art. A display case at the building entrance summarizes the family's history. The gallery sells a few reproductions of Pissarro's St Thomas scenes, but mostly focuses on works by contemporary artists.

**Market Square**                    MARKET
(Main St at Strand Gade) The square and wrought-iron market shed a few blocks west along Main St is the site of Charlotte Amalie's renowned slave market. Possibly as many as 200,000 captive Africans arrived at this market to be sold as slaves during the 17th and 18th centuries. The actual auction block is difficult to find today because the square is usually covered with locals hanging out. If you're up at the crack of dawn Saturday, a **farmers market** (www.growvi.org; ☺4-7:30am Sat) takes over. The square is an intriguing place and worth a visit, but be aware it's in a bit of a sketchy area.

### FRENCHTOWN

Occupying a peninsula on the western side of St Thomas Harbor, this fishing village is now a hot restaurant quarter. The island's 'Frenchies,' aka Huguenots who immigrated to St Thomas from St-Barthélemy, populated the community of brightly painted frame houses during the mid-19th century. At one point, Frenchtown had about 1500 people who spoke a mix of 18th-century Breton French and West Indian Creole, but in recent years, many of the neighborhood's French citizens have assimilated or moved away.

There are still a number of fisherfolk here, and you can see them bring in their catch from the jetties and sell them at the **Quetel Fish Market** (☺5-9am Sat) on the waterfront.

To get to Frenchtown from downtown, take a taxi (per person $4), or walk west on Waterfront Hwy past the Seaplane Terminal and turn left just after the post office. The 1.25-mile walk takes about 25 minutes from Emancipation Garden. The neighborhood is compact, so everything is easy to find once you arrive.

## HAVE YOUR SAY

Found a fantastic restaurant that you're longing to share with the world? Disagree with our recommendations? Or just want to talk about your most recent trip?

Whatever your reason, head to lonelyplanet.com, where you can post a review, ask or answer a question on the Thorntree forum, comment on a blog, or share your photos and tips on Groups. Or you can simply spend time chatting with like-minded travelers. So go on, have your say.

**FREE** Frenchtown Heritage
Museum                                    MUSEUM
(www.frenchheritagemuseum.com; Rue de St-Barthélemy; ⊙9am-6pm Mon-Fri) The little yellow museum preserves the history of St Thomas' French inhabitants. Exhibits show old photographs of the community's first families and artifacts like fishing nets, musical instruments, French lace and mahogany furniture. It's located next to the Joseph Aubaine Ballpark.

### HAVENSIGHT

A hundred years ago, the area on the east side of St Thomas Harbor (known today as Havensight) was a bustling steamship wharf and coaling station. Today it's still busy, but with behemoth cruise ships that tie up to the West Indian Company Cruise Ship Dock.

When passengers disembark, they find **Havensight Mall** (www.havensightmall.com), a compound with row upon row of shops and restaurants. This mall, as well as the shops and restaurants across the street in the Al Cohen Mall and the Buccaneer Mall, constitute the largest shopping area on St Thomas outside the historic district of Charlotte Amalie. Jewelry shops, clothing boutiques, banks, a Hooters bar – you name it, it's here.

Taxis travel regularly to and from Havensight ($5 to $6 per person). It's about 1 mile east of downtown Charlotte Amalie following Waterfront Hwy.

**Butterfly Farm**                          GARDEN
(☑340-715-3366; adult/child $15/9; ⊙8:30am-4pm) The Butterfly Farm lies at the cruise-ship dock's far south end. Amid the garden full of fluttering beasties, you'll learn about metamorphosis during a 25-minute guided

tour. Wear bright colors and perfume if you want the butterflies land on you. A cheesy tropical bird show takes place in the front area. Coral World Ocean Park owns and operates the farm. Look for discount coupons in the free tourist guides.

**Paradise Point Skyride**              TRAMWAY
(☑340-774-9809; www.stthomasskyride.com; adult/child $21/10.50; ⊙9am-5pm when cruise ships in port) From a base station across the street from the Havensight Mall, gondolas whisk visitors 700 feet up Flag Hill to a scenic outlook; the ride takes seven minutes. At the top you'll find a restaurant, bar, gallery of shops and a short nature trail. The attraction stays open late twice per week: Tuesdays until 8pm, and Wednesdays until 9pm.

**Yacht Haven Grande**                   MARINA
This marina and chic shop complex is located east of downtown Charlotte Amalie, abutting Havensight. Gucci, Ferragamo and Louis Vuitton headline the tony roster, along with a hookah bar and several waterfront bistros where you can sip cosmos and watch mega-yachts drift in to the dock. A **farmers market** (www.growvi.org; ⊙10am-2pm) with

### THE ISLAND LOWDOWN

» **Virgin Islands Now** (www.vinow.com/stthomas) is a comprehensive website put together by locals. Useful facets include St Thomas ferry and cruise ship schedules, 'beaches at a glance' information, taxi rates and an active message board. The 'Colors of Paradise' videos and 'Podcasts from Paradise' audio clips are good for setting the mood pre-departure.

» **St Thomas/St John This Week** (www.virginislandsthisweek.com) is a free magazine widely available on the island. The website has links to restaurant menus, happy hour drink coupons, maps and a handy events schedule.

» Keep in mind that many attractions are only open when cruise ships are in port. Check VI Now to see how busy it'll be on the day you're visiting. Tuesdays and Wednesdays typically see the most traffic, Fridays the least. If it's an off day, consider heading to the beach instead.

**RENTAL ACCOMMODATIONS**

St Thomas has hundreds of time-share or individually owned vacation condos and villas that owners rent through property managers on the island. You will see advertisements for these rental agencies splattered throughout tourist brochures, newspapers and websites. Rentals are usually by the week. Most properties cluster on the East End.

**» Calypso Realty** (☏340-774-1620; www.calypsorealty.com) Manages a wide range of condos and villas all over the island.

**» McLaughlin Anderson Luxury Villas** (☏340-776-0635, 800-537-6246; www.mclaughlinanderson.com) A Charlotte Amalie–based company that represents swanky properties throughout the USVI and Tortola.

**» Vacation Rental by Owner** (www.vrbo.com) Say to heck with the management companies, and work out all the details with the property owners themselves; VRBO's website acts as a clearinghouse. Many visitors swear by this method.

produce and crafts sets up on the grounds the first and third Sunday of the month. If you're coming from Charlotte Amalie you'll pass the marina en route to Havensight, from which it is about a five-minute walk.

## 🛏 Sleeping

Small, simple, independently owned hotels and guesthouses comprise Charlotte Amalie's lodging scene. For chains and resorts, you'll have to motor outside of town. Lodgings add an 18% tax to your final bill.

TOP CHOICE **Green Iguana**  HOTEL **$$**
(☏340-776-7654; www.thegreeniguana.com; 1002 Blackbeard's Hill; r $140-170; ❄@⏾) Way the heck up the hill behind Blackbeard's Castle, this well-run establishment is set in lush gardens and overlooks St Thomas Harbor. The nine rooms come in several configurations, but all have free wi-fi, satellite TV, microwave, refrigerator and bright decor; some also have a fully equipped kitchen and private balcony. You can do laundry on-site

for a small fee, and the office has a little canteen where you can buy snacks and drinks. The Green Iguana is great value if you don't mind the steep walk.

**Miller Manor**  GUESTHOUSE **$$**
(☏340-774-1535, 888-229-0762; www.millermanor.com; 26 Prindsesse Gade, Frenchman's Hill; r $91-145; ❄⏾) Marge and Harry run this 26-room hillside establishment, which has been a guesthouse for more than half a century, and it has the feel of your Aunt Josie's summer place. A 150-year-old Danish townhouse anchors the complex, with a bar (with free wi-fi) overlooking the town and harbor. The manor offers a wide range of rooms, from singles with a shared bathroom to large rooms with balconies looking over the harbor. Some of the guests are long-term lodgers, ie local waiters and scholars, who sometimes can be found in the bar giving the lowdown on local hot spots. While Miller Manor is in a safe neighborhood, the dicey Savan district lies between here and the heart of town. Take a cab at night.

**Crystal Palace B&B**  B&B **$$**
(☏340-777-2277, 866-502-2277; www.crystalpalaceusvi.com; 12 Crystal Gade; r incl breakfast $119-149; ❄⏾) Ronnie Lockhart owns this five-room property in a colonial mansion that has been in his family for generations. Two rooms have private bathrooms; the other three share a bathroom. Antique West Indian decor pervades, and there's a viewtastic patio on which to eat the continental breakfast or swill a drink from the honor bar. While Crystal Palace is certainly not luxurious, it is mighty full of character. Ronnie is a fountain of local lore; he'll pick you up at the airport or ferry dock for free. The B&B is located up a steep hill by the synagogue. There's a $15 surcharge for stays of less than three nights.

**Hotel 1829**  HOTEL **$$**
(☏340-776-1829, 800-524-2002; www.hotel1829.com; 30 Kongens Gade; r incl breakfast $105-190; ❄⏾✷) Built in 1829, this seven-room inn blends the atmosphere of a Victorian gentlemen's club and a colonial villa. Exposed rubble walls, beamed ceilings and period West Indian furnishings characterize the rooms. The result is a romantic, Old World island vibe. Be aware the 'modest' rooms are tiny, and multiple flights of stairs will be your destiny. There is free in-room wi-fi, free continental breakfast and a small pool for guests, plus free access to Blackbeard's

Castle, to which the hotel is attached. The owners also operate the Inn at Blackbeard's Castle, higher up the hill, which has six additional units.

### Villa Santana
HOTEL **$$**
(☏340-776-1311; www.villasantana.com; 2602 Bjerge Gade No 2D; r $150-235; ◈🖥) Set on Denmark Hill overlooking Charlotte Amalie, Villa Santana was the 19th-century estate of Mexico's famous General Antonio López de Santa Anna. Guests can stay in one of six suites located around the property, in the villa's former wine cellar, kitchen, pump house and library. All rooms come with full amenities and Mexican decor. This is where you hear the Gypsy Kings on the stereo, rather than Bob Marley, while you're lounging poolside among well-traveled couples. You'll want a car if you're staying up here.

### Bellavista B&B
B&B **$$**
(☏340-714 5706, 888-333-3063; www.bellavista-bnb.com; 2713 Murphy Gade; r incl breakfast $195-265; ◈🖥) Bellavista is a classic B&B in the quilted, canopy bed, full cooked breakfast mold. Four bright-hued rooms each have their own bathroom. Three of the rooms face the harbor, offering great views since the property is atop Denmark Hill. A sunny pool and free wi-fi throughout add to the package. The owner is hands-on and happy to help with reservations and advice. Bellavista is located behind the synagogue and on up the hill. You can walk into town easily,

but you'll be huffing and puffing on the return trek.

### Galleon House
HOTEL **$$**
(☏340-774-6952, 800-524-2052; www.galleonhouse.com; 31 Kongens Gade; r incl breakfast $85-155; ◈@🖥) The 'harbor view' rooms are a winner at friendly Galleon House, with wood doors that open onto a balcony overlooking the waterfront. The 'shared bathroom' and 'interior private bathroom' rooms are confining and not recommended unless you're truly strapped for dough. Those units remind you Galleon House is not luxury lodging, but it does have its share of perks: it's located in the absolute heart of the town's historic district, and the veranda and pool are good for hanging out and munching the bountiful cooked breakfast. The property is located behind Hervé restaurant, up lots of stairs.

### Windward Passage
HOTEL **$$**
(☏340-774-5200, 800-524-7389; www.windwardpassage.com; Waterfront Hwy; r $210-275; ◈@🖥) The four-story Windward Passage (formerly a Holiday Inn) is primarily a business hotel. It's useful for those seeking free in-room wi-fi access, a fitness center, on-site eateries and quick taxi access. It's also right across from the Marine Terminal, and super convenient if you're catching an early morning ferry or seaplane. It's less beneficial to those seeking good value, since the peach-colored, cookie-cutter rooms are overpriced. However, when other hotels are

---

**WORTH A TRIP**

## HASSEL ISLAND

The 120-acre floater in the middle of St Thomas Harbor is **Hassel Island** (www.hasselisland.org), which was actually part of the main island until 1865. That year, the Danish dredged Haulover Cut to separate Frenchtown and Hassel Island in an attempt to help water flow more freely out of the harbor, thereby reducing the sewage buildup that promoted cholera epidemics.

Today, the entire mile-long island is on the National Register of Historic Places, and most of it is under National Park Service jurisdiction. During the late 19th century, Hassel Island was a coaling station and repair facility for the Royal Mail Steam Packet Company and several other shipping lines. Ruins from that era, and old forts from even earlier, lie disintegrating under island vegetation. While the NPS has been working to preserve the ruins and develop Hassel Island as a recreational facility, it is still a work in progress.

Currently, the only way to visit the island is with a guided tour. **Virgin Islands Ecotours** (☏340-779-2155, 877-845-2925; www.viecotours.com; 3hr tours $99) offers a kayaking/hiking/snorkeling excursion that departs from Frenchtown's marina. It involves a 20-minute paddle to reach Hassel Island, followed by a trek around the ruins and a snorkel along the surrounding reef. It concludes with the paddle back to Frenchtown. The tour runs on Monday, Thursday, Friday and Saturday mornings.

booked, there's usually room at the inn. The free shuttle to Magens Bay Beach is a nice bonus. The hotel is located at the edge of downtown, not far from Frenchtown; you'll have a 10-minute walk to reach either dining hub.

### Inn at Villa Olga    HOTEL $$

(☎340-715-0900, 800-524-4746; www.villa-olga-inn.com; Frenchtown; r $150-175; ❋@🈵🈂🈵) Villa Olga offers 12 motel-like rooms off the beaten path in Frenchtown. While the faded rooms have seen better days, they are spacious and scattered over pretty, palm-shaded grounds. The bonus here is free access to the beach and water-sports equipment at Bolongo Bay Beach Resort, Olga's sister property. The inn has poolside wi-fi access. It's on the waterfront, on a road that runs behind French-town's cluster of restaurants.

### Bunker Hill Hotel    HOTEL $$

(☎340-774-8056; www.bunkerhillhotel.com; 7A Commandant Gade; r incl breakfast $99-125; ❋@🈵🈂) You're gonna get what you pay for: the 16 rooms are cheap, but they're also relatively dark, shabby and mosquitoey. Each unit does have a big bathroom; some have patios, and the sunny deck and cooked breakfast are nice touches. Still, Bunker Hill is basic to the bone. The streets around the hotel become dubious at night.

## ✖ Eating

Charlotte Amalie is arguably the best place in the Virgin Islands to stuff your face given the large concentration of eateries and types of food on offer. Options cluster in four zones: downtown, which is good for breakfast and lunch, though dinner options are scarce (the area relies on cruise ship business, which dries up by late afternoon); Frenchtown, which is home to several great restaurants that buzz in the evening, all in a compact area; Havensight, which is more touristy and chain-oriented but in a fun, high-energy atmosphere; and Yacht Haven Grande, a complex of stylish bars and eateries that lies between downtown and Havensight.

### DOWNTOWN CHARLOTTE AMALIE

TOP
CHOICE Gladys' Cafe    WEST INDIAN $$

(☎340-774-6604; Royal Dane Mall; mains $13-21; ◷7am-5pm Mon-Sat, 8am-3pm Sun) With the stereo blaring beside her, Gladys belts out Tina Turner tunes while serving some of the best West Indian food around. Callaloo,

fungi, Ole Wife (triggerfish), fried plantains and sweet potatoes hit the tables along with Gladys' homemade hot sauce (for sale at the front, making a fine souvenir). There is no view here, but the bistro setting, art-covered walls and fun, breezy atmosphere make up for it. This is a great place to come for a full breakfast, too.

### Cuzzin's Caribbean
### Restaurant & Bar    WEST INDIAN $$

(☎340-777-4711; 7 Back St; mains $10-21; ◷11:30am-4:30pm Tue-Sat) With exposed-brick walls, burnished wood furnishings and red-clothed tables occupying a restored livery stable, classy-but-casual Cuzzin's is everybody's favorite stop for West Indian cuisine. The scent of onions, peppers and curry will draw you to this place from half a block away. Try the conch (curried, buttered or Creole style) or the Ole Wife fish alongside fungi, johnnycakes and a Blackbeard Ale.

### Green House    BURGERS, SEAFOOD $$

(☎340-774-7998; www.thegreenhouserestaurant.com; Waterfront Hwy at Store Tvaer Gade; mains $12-24; ◷lunch & dinner; 🈵) Green House has been an oasis for both locals and travelers for years. Raised a half-story above the surrounding sidewalks, the cavernous, open-air restaurant overlooks Hassel Island and the wharf where interisland trading boats tie up. The cuisine is predictable American pub fare, but the menu is extensive, with burgers, pizzas and seafood. Green House rocks hardest during happy hour (from 4:30pm to 7pm, when drinks are two for the price of one) and evenings after 10pm. Staff know how to work the scene: the host commonly places women by the window saying, 'Let me seat you here to showcase your beauty.'

### Natural Livity    VEGETARIAN $

(www.naturallivitykulchashop.com; 9A Norre Gade; mains $6-12; ◷8am-8pm Mon-Sat; 🈚) 'Your food is medicine' is Natural Livity's tagline. No surprise, then, that it is all healthy vegan fare. Lentil burgers, pumpkin soup and scrambled tofu are on the menu, or pick and mix a platter of daily specials (stewed eggplant, soy duck, veggie lasagna) from the glass case. Owner Jahleejah Love Peace also offers fruit smoothies, bush tea and vegan cakes and muffins at her little cafe, which is attached to her Kulcha Shop that stocks reggae CDs, books, jewelry and clothing. Only three tables sit in the steamy cafe, so it's best to carry out. Have a picnic at Veteran's Memorial Park, which offers shaded benches a block to the east.

**Petite Pump Room** WEST INDIAN **$$**
(www.petitepumproom.com; mains $10-20; Waterfront Hwy; ⌚breakfast & lunch Mon-Sat) The Pump Room sits above the Marine Terminal, but it's more than just a place to kill time while waiting for a ferry or seaplane. The family who operates it cooks delicious daily lunch specials like stewed mutton, callaloo, garlic-butter sautéed conch, and saltfish in sweet pepper sauce. They make their own hot sauce, as well as their own mango and soursop (a tropical fruit) ice cream. Omelets and pancakes emerge from the kitchen for breakfast.

**Virgilio's** ITALIAN **$$**
(☎340-776-4920; 18 Main St; mains $20-35; ⌚lunch & dinner Mon-Sat) Virgilio's has been heaping upscale northern Italian fare onto plates for many moons. The vaulted ceilings, 18th-century furnishings, opera music and scent of garlic and Chianti might remind you of a restaurant you would discover on an alley in Firenze. Pasta, veal parmesan, calamari, salmon and many more standards fill the menu. Several of the pasta dishes are meat-free. There's a carryout window fronting Back St (how's that for an oxymoron) where you can order salads and sandwiches ($10 to $14) piled with blackened tilapia and other ingredients.

**Hervé Restaurant & Wine Bar** FRENCH **$$$**
(☎340-777-9703; www.herverestaurant.com; mains $28-45; ⌚dinner) Longstanding Hervé focuses on French-Caribbean cuisine served in a candlelit, Old World ambience. The setting is a formal terrace in a historic townhouse with views of the downtown rooftops and the harbor. Nightly specials such as spinach flambé, seafood bouillabaisse and stuffed quail join standards like lamb chops and lots of buttery, spicy fish and shellfish options. Make reservations. Hervé's wife Paulette operates the adjoining patio which works well for a glass of wine.

**Trenchtown Rock** JAMAICAN **$$**
(☎340-774-1996; Back St at Raadets Gade; mains $10-20; ⌚11am-6pm Mon-Thu, to 8pm Fri & Sat; ✎) Trenchtown Rock serves Jamaican fare, mon. All the traditional dishes are here: brown stew, jerk chicken, curried goat, oxtail and saltfish. They go down well with a Red Stripe to a reggae beat (happy hour is from 4pm to 6pm). Vegetarians will find options, too, such as barbecue tofu and veggie pasta.

## BEST BITES FOR LOCAL FOOD

When the urge strikes to fork into fungi, callaloo, curried goat and other West Indian dishes, these restaurants cook a respected plateful:

» Gladys' Cafe

» Petite Pump Room

» Fungi's on the Beach (p77)

» Cuzzin's Caribbean Restaurant & Bar

**Beans, Bytes & Websites** CAFE **$**
(☎340-777-7089; 5600 Royal Dane Mall; sandwiches $6-8; ⌚breakfast & lunch; @📶) Join the queue of shop workers in the morning and cruise shippers in the afternoon for Charlotte Amalie's best java at this chic little cyber-bistro. Order a bagel and toasted sandwich to go with your drink, then sink into the couches to escape the surrounding mall hubbub. The back room holds an internet cafe with several terminals ($4.50 per 30 minutes) and wi-fi access ($3 per 30 minutes).

**Bumpa's** CAFE **$**
(☎340-776-5674; Waterfront Hwy; mains $9-14; ⌚breakfast & lunch) Climb the stairs to the second floor, order at the counter, then carry your plastic silverware and hearty oatmeal pancakes, pumpkin muffin, veggie burger, chicken pate or grilled fish wrap to the small patio overlooking the street. It's slow but friendly service.

### FRENCHTOWN

Frenchtown's restaurants huddle near the waterfront and around the main parking area. They're all within a few minutes' walk of each other, so you can check out the options. Dinner reservations are a good idea.

TOP CHOICE **Pie Hole** ITALIAN **$$**
(☎340-642-5074; mains $13-17; ⌚lunch Mon-Fri, dinner Mon-Sat) Six tables and nine bar stools comprise this cozy eatery next to Bella Blue. The 13-inch, crisp-crusted, brick-oven pizzas are the claim to fame. Super-fresh ingredients, ie spinach and ricotta or mozzarella and basil, top the white or wheat crust. You can even get wacky and order a beer-braised

chicken pie. Several house-made pasta dishes and a robust beer list raise Pie Hole to near perfection.

**Craig & Sally's** FUSION $$$
(☑340-777-9949; www.craigandsallys.com; mains $22-40; ☺lunch Wed-Fri, dinner Wed-Sun) Chef Sally Darash lives up to the claims that she is a 'kitchen witch.' Her fusion cooking draws a crowd every night to the limited seating in the open-air alcoves of this 'Frenchie' cottage. The menu changes according to Sally's whim, but expect elaborate mains such as pan-seared jumbo scallops with avocado slices, garlic and a lemony avocado sauce served with mozzarella mashed potatoes. Eclectic small plates are available too, such as lamb-burger sliders and barbecue eel. Reserve several days in advance, if possible.

**Epernay Wine & Champagne Bar** INTERNATIONAL $$
(☑340-774-5348; www.epernaystthomas.com; mains $16-28; ☺dinner Mon-Sat) Epernay, next to the Frenchtown Deli, is a favorite roost for the St Thomas in-crowd. The hip, the powerful and the beautiful come to hang at the bistro's bar, gnash appetizers like tuna tartare and steamed mussels, before they settle at a shadowy table for a main course of Kobe beef meatloaf or seared salmon with mustard dill aioli. At time of research, plans were afoot to open for lunch, too.

**Hook, Line & Sinker** BURGERS, SEAFOOD $$
(☑340-776-9708; www.hooklineandsinkervi.com; mains $13-25; ☺lunch & dinner Mon-Sat, brunch Sun) This open-air, mom-and-pop operation feels like a real sea shack, where you smell the salt water, feel the ocean breeze and see sailors unload their boats dockside. The menu mixes sandwiches, salads, pasta dishes and seafood mains, such as the jerk-seasoned swordfish, with plenty of beer to wash it down. The Sunday brunch draws a throng of locals. Look for a pack of cute iguanas patrolling the concrete by the water.

**Bella Blue** MEDITERRANEAN, AUSTRIAN $$
(☑340-774-4349; mains $18-30; ☺lunch & dinner Mon-Sat) Tagine and schnitzel aren't usually found on the same menu, but they are at this warm, inviting restaurant. Bella Blue's old chef was from Austria and earned a reputation for serving dishes from his homeland. He has since retired, but his greatest hits remain. The new chef focuses on dishes with a Mediterranean bent, such as hummus, lamb tagine and a variety of pasta options and grilled fish.

**Frenchtown Deli** DELI $
(☑340-776-7211; mains $5-12; ☺7am-8pm Mon-Fri, to 5pm Sat, to 4pm Sun) The deli is a popular stop for breakfast and lunch. Order at the counter, then plop down in a booth with an egg sandwich, bagel or good ole cup of coffee. Lunch is all about thick-cut sandwiches.

### HAVENSIGHT & YACHT HAVEN GRANDE

Several chain-style restaurants and bars, such as Hooters, line the malls at Havensight. Nearby Yacht Haven Grande harbors several trendy restaurants along the waterfront; they're better for happy-hour martinis than dinner, but at least they stay open late.

**Pizza Amore** ITALIAN $$
(☑340-774-2822; www.pizzaamorestthomas.com; 18 Estate Thomas; large pizzas from $22; ☺9am-8pm Mon-Thu, to 9pm Fri, 10am-9pm Sat) Pizza Amore is Charlotte Amalie's favorite independent pizza joint. The simple, congenial room packs locals of all stripes into its smattering of tables inside; many more tables spill onto the deck outside. You'll find it by following your nose to Al Cohen's Mall, across the street from Havensight Mall. Cash only.

🍃**Barefoot Buddha** CAFE $
(☑340-777-3668; 9715 Estate Thomas; mains $8-11; ☺breakfast & lunch; 🛜🍴) The island's yoga-philes hang out at yin-yang decorated wood tables, tucking into organic specials, such as the blackened tofu wrap, and the everyday list of toasted sandwiches (go for the hummus and rosemary goat cheese). The Buddha is also popular for breakfast, thanks to the long list of organic coffee drinks and egg sandwiches. Cash only. It's attached to an incense-wafting gift store located in the Guardian Building, a strip mall near the road that leads to Paradise Point.

## 🍷 Drinking & Entertainment

Most live music happens at the resorts and bars on the East End. Downtown Charlotte Amalie doesn't have much of a scene, except for a couple spots on Waterfront Hwy. Havensight and Yacht Haven Grande have bars where martinis swirl for happy hour and DJs take over as the evening progresses. Check **St Thomas/St John This Week** (www.virginislandsthisweek.com) to see what's on. The **Reichhold Center for the Arts** (www.reichholdcenter.com), west of town near the airport, is the main concert arena.

### Green House
BAR
(www.thegreenhouserestaurant.com; Waterfront Hwy, Charlotte Amalie; 🛜) Charlotte Amalie's long-time, go-to bar-restaurant attracts a big dance crowd on Tuesday nights when a DJ spins hip-hop, R&B and Caribbean rhythms and drink prices dive to two-for-one. The revelers are mostly under 30, West Indian and dressed in some fine threads. The party begins at 9:30pm.

### Tavern on the Waterfront
LIVE MUSIC
(www.tavernonthewaterfront.com; Waterfront Hwy, Charlotte Amalie) The Euro-tinged tavern hosts live jazz on Fridays from 7pm to 10pm. It's typically a piano-drums-vocal trio, but other musicians sometimes drop in. The room is also a fine-dining establishment that attracts an older crowd.

### Big Kahuna Rum Shack
BAR
(www.bigkahunausvi.com; Waterfront Hwy, Charlotte Amalie; 🛜) The Big Kahuna caters to 20-somethings smoking it up at the open-air bar, listening to rock and using the free wi-fi. It's a good setting to try a USVI-made Blackbeard Ale.

### Epernay Wine & Champagne Bar
BAR
(www.epernaystthomas.com; ⊘Mon-Sat) Guess what they pour here? Epernay is a popular hangout for St Thomian professionals, politicians and snowbirds. Friday evening's happy hour is the biggest scene. Cocktail dresses, slacks and collared shirts set the fashion.

### Le Petite Fenetre
BAR
(Frenchtown) 'The Little Window' sits across from the Frenchtown Heritage Museum, but you may learn more about the local lifestyle here, at this old-timers' bar where neighborhood fisherfolk sit, sip and chat on the front porch.

### Ship Wreck Tavern
BAR
(www.shipwreckstthomas.com; Al Cohen Mall, Havensight; 🛜) This place is your basic gin mill with pool tables, air hockey and a cast of the young and restless. Lots of cruise-ship crew members favor the bar. It also appeals to local continentals. DJs commandeer the turntable on Wednesday and Saturday nights, and dancing ensues.

### Fat Turtle Bar
BAR
(www.fat-turtle.com; Yacht Haven Grande) Fat Turtle is the stalwart in the Yacht Haven Grande complex. Play foosball or glue yourself to the plasma TVs for big games. A DJ and light show ratchet up the action on Friday nights.

## 🛍 Shopping

As a duty-free port with a long tradition of importing pretty things from all over the world, St Thomas is a shopper's paradise. Each US citizen can leave with up to $1600 worth of goods without paying the customs agent – the highest duty-free allowance in the Caribbean.

Jewelry is the big deal in town. Electronics can be a good buy as well. It's best to research what you want ahead of time to understand the market price; some shoppers claim they can get better bargains at home from big-box retailers, even though there's no sales tax to pay on St Thomas. You can haggle with shopkeepers, and often they'll bundle items (ie you might get a case, rechargeable batteries and an extra memory card to go with a new camera as part of the deal).

Vendors' Plaza, in front of Fort Christian, is a bazaar for crafts, costume jewelry, T-shirts and African imports. The area around Main St, Back St and the colonial warehouses that stretch down to the waterfront has been converted into what amounts to a large outdoor mall. Here, you will find more than 100 elegant shops and boutiques cloistered in historic 18th- and 19th-century buildings and tucked along narrow alleys scented with spices and echoing with jazz and West Indian rhythms. The best place to park is in the large lot on the east side of Fort Christian.

Havensight Mall is adjacent to the cruise ship wharf on the east side of St Thomas Harbor. It's a modern compound of buildings housing more than 50 businesses; there are more right across Rte 30 at the Buccaneer Mall, the Guardian Building and the Al Cohen Mall. All of these malls have plenty of parking.

Most stores are open from 9am to 5pm Monday to Saturday, and to 1pm Sunday if cruise ships are in town. If it is a day with low ship volume, many places don't bother to open.

### DOWNTOWN CHARLOTTE AMALIE

#### AH Riise
JEWELRY
(www.ahriise.com; 37 Main St) This is the famous store that most visitors beeline to, where you can buy everything from watches and

jewelry to tobacco and liquor. There's another outlet at Havensight.

### Boolchand's                    ELECTRONICS
(31 Main St) Boolchand's has been one of the Caribbean's largest retailers of cameras for more than 60 years. There's another outlet at Havensight.

### Pirates in Paradise             SOUVENIRS
(38A Waterfront Hwy) Argh! Here's your treasure trove of pirate gear, including eye patches, fake doubloons, kids' toys and party decorations. The shop is located underneath Bumpa's restaurant.

### Natural Livity Kulcha Shop   MUSIC, CLOTHING
(www.naturallivitykulchashop.com; 9A Norre Gade; ☺Mon-Sat) Attached to a vegetarian take-away restaurant, the Kulcha Shop features African clothing, herbs, incense, reggae CDs and funky peace-logoed jewelry.

### Native Arts & Crafts            SOUVENIRS
(Tolbod Gade) This is the place to buy local hot sauces, honey, straw dolls and painted gourd bowls made by island craftspeople, as well as books by local authors.

### Camille Pissarro Gallery        FINE ARTS
(14 Main St) Located in Pissarro's boyhood home (a display case outside summarizes the family's history), the gallery sells a few reproductions of the famous impressionist's St Thomas scenes, but mostly focuses on works by contemporary artists.

### HAVENSIGHT
### Dockside Bookshop              BOOKSTORE
(www.docksidebooks.com; Havensight Mall) The island's only real bookstore – and an impressive one at that – carries plenty of regional titles, kids' books and best-sellers.

### Urban Threadz                   CLOTHING
(Buccaneer Mall) It has all the Bob Marley shirts you ever dreamed of.

## ⓘ Information
### Dangers & Annoyances
Charlotte Amalie has some big-city issues including drugs, poverty, prostitution and street crime. Waterfront Hwy and Main St in the town center are fine at night, but move a few blocks away and the streets quickly get deserted. Avoid the Savan area, a red-light district that surrounds Main St west of Market Sq and north of the Windward Passage hotel; this is where the island's underworld takes root. In general, savvy travelers who take reasonable precautions should have no problems.

### Internet Access
Some restaurants and bars have free wi-fi, such as Green House.
**Beans, Bytes & Websites** (5600 Royal Dane Mall; per half hr $4.50; ☺7am-6pm Mon-Sat, to 1pm Sun) Connect with your electronic mailbox at the 12 or so terminals, plus wi-fi and data ports for laptops.

### Media
**St Thomas/St John This Week** (www.virgin islandsthisweek.com) Widely available free monthly magazine that has events listings and the cruise-ship schedule.
**VI Daily News** (www.virginislandsdailynews.com) The main newspaper.
**St Thomas Source** (www.stthomassource.com) Online news.

### Medical Services
**Roy Schneider Community Hospital** (☎340-776-8311; 48 Sugar Estate Rd at Rte 313; ☺24hr) On the east side of Charlotte Amalie, this full-service hospital has an emergency room, recompression chamber and doctors in all major disciplines.

### Money
FirstBank, Scotiabank, Banco Popular and other banks are on Waterfront Hwy.

### Post
**Main post office** (☎340-774-3750) It's on the west side of Emancipation Garden. There are several satellite post offices, including one west of the Marine Terminal (at Frenchtown's entrance), and one in the Havensight Mall. Most are open 7:30am to 4:30pm Monday to Friday and 8:30am to noon Saturday.

### Tourist Information
There is no official tourist office downtown, but the free *St Thomas/St John This Week* magazine has maps and everything else you'll need; it's available at most businesses.

### Websites
**USVI Department of Tourism** (www.visitusvi.com) Official tourism site.
**VI Now** (www.vinow.com/stthomas) Useful weather info and ferry and cruise-ship schedules.

## ⓘ Getting There & Around
### Air
The airport is 2.5 miles west of town. Taxis (ie multi-passenger vans) are readily available. The fare for one passenger going between the airport and Charlotte Amalie is $7; it's $15 to/from Red Hook. Luggage costs an additional $2 per piece.

### Boat

Charlotte Amalie is a hub for boat travel. It has two cruise ship terminals: one at **Havensight**, which is the primary dock, about 1 mile east of Charlotte Amalie; and the other at **Crown Bay**, the secondary dock, about 1 mile west of town. It holds the main **Marine Terminal** for ferries to Tortola, Virgin Gorda and St Croix; the terminal is west on Waterfront Hwy, about a 10-minute walk from downtown.

**TO TORTOLA (ROAD TOWN)** Between all the companies, ferries depart several times daily from 8am to 4pm (one way $30, 45 minutes direct):

**Road Town Fast Ferry** (☎340-777-2800; www. roadtownfastferry.com) Goes direct.

**Speedy's** (☎284-495-5240; www.speedysbvi. com) Goes direct.

**Smith's Ferry** (☎340-775-7292; www.smiths ferry.com) Goes via West End.

**Native Son** (☎340-774-8685; www.nativeson ferry.com) Goes via West End.

**TO VIRGIN GORDA (SPANISH TOWN)** There's direct service on Tuesday, Thursday and Saturday (one way $40, 90 minutes):

**Speedy's** (☎284-495-5240; www.speedysbvi. com)

**TO ST CROIX VI SEATRANS** (☎340-776-5494; www.goviseatrans.com) sails twice on Friday and Saturday, and once on Sunday and Monday (round trip $90, 90 minutes) to the Gallows Bay terminal in Christiansted. Look for humpback whales during winter crossings.

**TO ST JOHN** There's a ferry to Cruz Bay (one way $12, 45 minutes) that departs at the foot of Raadet's Gade (ie, not at the marine terminal) at 10am, 1pm and 5:30pm daily.

### Taxi

Following are costs to popular destinations from Charlotte Amalie (these are per one passenger; fares go down for multiple passengers):

| DESTINATION | COST |
| --- | --- |
| Frenchtown | $4 |
| Havensight | $6 |
| Crown Bay | $5 |
| Magens Bay | $10 |
| Coki Beach | $12 |
| Red Hook | $13 |

## Crown Bay & West End

Crown Bay is home to St Thomas' second cruise ship dock and its surrounding shopping complex. The airport lies a short distance east. The area holds no sights per se, but it does offer beaches and lodging options. Better yet, it is the jump-off to the demure fourth virgin – Water Island.

## Beaches

**Lindbergh Bay**                              RESORT BEACH

You reach this sheltered horseshoe beach by turning south off the airport access road. The Best Western Emerald Beach Resort and Island Beachcomber Hotel sit on the best bits; you can rent snorkels, masks and other water-sports gear at the Emerald Beach's shop. Amenities include a public change room and bathroom and a couple of restaurants. The beach is steep and a bit narrow. Lots of families with children frequent the resorts, but the depth of the water drops off pretty quickly and can be dangerous for kids. There is some good snorkeling among the rocks and coral heads along the arms of the bay.

**Brewers Bay**                                FAMILY BEACH

Located behind the University of the Virgin Islands on Rte 30, Brewers Bay is beloved by students, local families and shell collectors alike. The long strand has almost no shade but features very sheltered water and plenty of shallow areas for kids. On weekends, lots of West Indian families come here to cool off. There are no facilities other than snack vans serving pates and cold Heineken beers. Quietude can be in short supply because the airport's busy runway lies just across the bay. The area clears out fast come nighttime. Brewers is the one beach that can be reached easily by Vitran and safari buses, which make runs to the college campus.

**Honeymoon Bay Beach**           SECLUDED BEACH

When handsome Brad Pitt and Cate Blanchett needed a handsome beach as a backdrop for the film *The Curious Case of Benjamin Button*, Honeymoon won the role. See the Water Island boxed text, p72, for details on this gem.

## Activities

**Blue Island Divers** (☎340-774-2001; www. blueislanddivers.com; Crown Bay Marina) heads out to nearby sites for two-tank dives ($99) and night dives ($80).

## Sleeping & Eating

All the lodgings listed are near the airport. Other than the resort restaurants and the pubs and shops at Crown Bay Marina, you'll

Lindbergh Bay takes its name from Colonel Charles Lindbergh, who landed at a field here with his famous Spirit of St Louis in 1929. The 'Lone Eagle,' or 'Lucky Lindy,' was on a goodwill tour of the Caribbean and Latin America following his 1927 nonstop solo crossing of the Atlantic by airplane. Lindy definitely had luck with him when he plopped the Spirit down in a small open space between the sea and the mountains on the edge of the bay that now bears his name.

A year later, Lindbergh returned to the bay in a Sikorsky seaplane. Lindy became convinced that St Thomas was the perfect refueling stop for a commercial flight between the US and South America. And because of Lindbergh's visits, Pan American Airways' Flying Clippers began making regular stops at St Thomas in the 1930s. The Cyril E King Airport now has extended its runway to more safely accommodate modern jets. Of course, plenty of contemporary passengers may wish they were still landing aboard one of the Lone Eagle's graceful clippers after a brake-screeching, gut-in-the-mouth landing aboard a Boeing 757.

have to travel to Frenchtown or downtown Charlotte Amalie for more eating options.

**Best Western Emerald Beach Resort**          HOTEL $$
(☎340-777-8800, 800-233-4936; www.emerald beach.com; 8070 Lindbergh Bay; r from $260; ✳@🛜🏊) This 90-room resort is a step up from the Carib, its sibling down the road. The butter-and-coral-colored rooms are snazzier, with private beachfront balconies, flat-screen TVs and free in-room wi-fi. Staff is professional, and the place bustles with visitors hanging out at the beach and restaurant. It's a short distance down the road from the airport, so you'll hear noise from planes (they stop around 10pm). You'll need to take a cab ($6 to $7 per person) to get into town.

**Best Western Carib Beach Hotel**          HOTEL $$
(☎340-774-2525, 800-792-2742; www.carib beachresort.com; 70C Lindbergh Bay; r $159-179; ✳🛜🏊) It's as close as you'll get to the airport, barely 0.25 miles from the terminal. Rooms are fine, with balconies, but nothing special. They're usually a bit bigger than those at the Emerald Bay Resort. The trade-off is beach access. While the Carib is on the water, there's just a tiny man-made beach from which you cannot swim (for that you have to walk down to the sister resort). There is a park next door with swings and slides for children. Wi-fi is available in the bar and lobby only. Like the Emerald Beach Resort, you'll hear noise from planes and need a taxi to eat anywhere besides the on-site restaurant.

**Island Beachcomber Hotel**          HOTEL $$
(☎340-772-5250; www.islandbeachcomber.net; 8071 Lindbergh Bay; r $170-230; ✳🛜) The Island Beachcomber is right next to the Best Western Emerald Beach Resort and shares the shore. It is a much more humble property, but one of the least expensive hotels you'll find for a beachfront stay in the Caribbean. While there is nothing very remarkable about the flimsy motel-like structure, the rooms are decent-sized and equipped with air-con, TV, fridge and private patio. The beach, restaurant and festive bar are just steps away from the rooms. The departure end of the airport runway is only 300 yards away, so prepare for some noise by day.

**Island View Guesthouse**          GUESTHOUSE $$
(☎340-774-4270, 800-524-2023; Scott Free Rd; www.islandviewstthomas.com; r incl breakfast $115-175; 🛜🏊) You will find 12 clean but simple units here, all with private bathrooms. The higher-end rooms also have balconies overlooking the town and harbor, and catch the trade winds for ventilation (not all rooms have air-con). Rooms have a TV/DVD (and a library to choose from), some have kitchenettes, and all have access to the small pool and honor bar on the property. You will need a car or cab to get around from here. It is about a 10-minute drive west of Charlotte Amalie, halfway up the mountainside. Take Waterfront Hwy to Crown Mountain Rd; go right for a short distance, past the Old Mill, then veer right onto Scott Free Rd.

**Tickles Dockside Pub**          BURGERS, SEAFOOD $$
(☎340-776-1595; www.ticklesdocksidepub.com; 8168 Crown Bay Marina; mains $10-21; ⊙breakfast, lunch & dinner) Tickles appeals to wan-

nabe Jimmy Buffett types. The open-air, waterfront restaurant overlooks the harbor's maritime activities and serves up a selection of reasonably priced breakfasts, finger foods and sandwiches. Not hungry? It's a swell venue to sip a brew; there's live music several nights a week. Tickles is also where the ferry to Water Island departs.

## ☆ Entertainment

The restaurant at the Emerald Beach Resort hosts a steel pan band on Fridays from 6pm to 9:30pm. The Island Beachcomber Hotel's bar is a good time.

**Reichhold Center for the Arts**      LIVE MUSIC
(www.reichholdcenter.com; 2 Brewers Bay) The Reichhold Center, located at University of the Virgin Islands, is the island's active concert arena. The outdoor amphitheater has seating for 1200 people. Any list of current artistic events on St Thomas will include doings at Reichhold, including concerts by international celebrity artists like Itzhak Perlman, dance troupes and repertory theater groups.

# South Side

A couple of well-known resorts dot the shore between Charlotte Amalie and the East End, offering beaches, steel pan bands and cigar menus.

## 🏄 Beaches

**Bolongo Bay**      RESORT BEACH
A long, broad golden crescent in front of the hotel of the same name, this beach adjacent to Rte 30 has to be one of the most picturesque hotel beaches on the island. You have the hotel's beach bar and restaurant, Iggie's, and a water-sports operation to keep you in supplies. Nap under palm-frond umbrellas on the beach's left side, or hammocks on the right side. The water is pretty calm, with decent snorkeling. Some areas can be rocky. The people who frequent the beach are largely young couples and families on package vacations.

Those interested in diving should stop by well-regarded **St Thomas Dive Club** (340-776-2381; www.stthomasdivingclub.com) on the sand next door to Iggie's.

**Morningstar Bay**      RESORT BEACH
A thin, beige strand just east of the Marriott Frenchman's Reef resort, this site is a manicured hotel beach with all the trimmings. A water-sports vendor rents jet skis, kayaks and sailboats in a shop at the beach's east end, though they won't come cheap. Non-guests must pay for beach chair rentals ($10 per day). The water gets deep quickly and often has mild waves; it's great for a refreshing swim. If you're an early riser, it's fun to come here and watch the cruise ships glide into the harbor. Morningstar can be busy. While most of the people you meet here are hotel guests, some West Indians and expats sunbathe here.

## 🛏 Sleeping

**Bolongo Bay Beach Resort**      HOTEL **$$$**
(340-775-1800, 800-524-4746; www.bolongobay.com; 7150 Bolongo Bay; r $230-395; ✱⊛) Family-owned Bolongo is a casual, convivial resort with fewer than 100 rooms. Its public facilities are its strength: a beach with a full array of free water sports (kayaks, sailboats, snorkel gear etc), tennis courts, a pool and fitness center. Oceanview rooms are on the second and third floors, while Beachfront rooms are on the first floor – all have sea views and private patios. The Value rooms are in a building across the street. The interiors won't win any awards for size or decor, but who cares? You'll be outside enjoying fun in the sun, such as the weekly snorkel booze hunt (staff hide bottles of rum in the bay and if you find one, it's yours). You can opt for the meal plan, otherwise you'll need a car to access restaurants. Bolongo is about 3.5 miles east of Charlotte Amalie.

**Marriott Frenchman's Reef & Morning Star Beach Resorts**      HOTEL **$$$**
(340-776-8500, 800-524-2000; www.frenchmansreefmarriott.com; Rte 315, Estate Bakkeroe; r from $275; ✱@⊛) Added up, these two resorts offer more than 500 rooms. Seven-story Frenchman's Reef has most of them. It qualifies as a mega-resort, with three pools, five restaurants and buffets and bars galore. You'll find Jacuzzis, four lit tennis courts, diving instruction and sailing trips offered from the beach. Morning Star sits next door with fewer than 100 units in several cross-shaped villas tucked among shady palms. It's the more exclusive, upscale property. Rack rates are steep, but the Marriott almost always has some sort of promotional package going on; ask when you call. In-room wi-fi costs $17 per day. The resorts are 3 miles east of Charlotte Amalie's center on Flamboyant Pt. Marriott runs its own ferry (one way $6) to town hourly.

# WATER ISLAND

Do the Charlotte Amalie crowds have you seeking some peace and seclusion? Water Island is your answer. Sometimes called the 'Fourth Virgin,' it floats spitting distance from town, yet with only about 100 residents and very few cars or shops, it feels far more remote.

The 490-acre island takes its name from its freshwater pools. From WWI to WWII, Water Island was a US military reservation. Following WWII, the US government used the island as a chemical warfare test facility. After about 1951, US expats began to trickle onto the island to build homes. In 1996 Water Island was finally ceded to the territory.

The island has a low-key atmosphere in which most people travel by bike or golf cart, and community messages are posted on a bulletin board at the ferry dock. At 2.5 miles tip to tip, it doesn't take long to walk the whole thing.

**Honeymoon Beach** offers fine swimming and snorkeling (look for fish along the bay's southern shore). The water is shallow and calm, and so good for kids. Amenities include shade umbrellas, picnic tables and bathrooms (not always open). A boat sometimes drops by selling pizza, and Heidi's food truck sells snacks. The beach gets lively on weekends when locals join the scene. Honeymoon is a 10-minute walk from the ferry dock. Follow the road uphill from the landing; when the road forks, go right and down the hill to the sand.

**Water Island Adventures** (www.waterislandadventures.com; 3hr tours $60) offers bicycle tours of the island, including time to swim at the beach. Most bikes are Cannondales, and child-size bikes are available. Reserve in advance; the price includes the ferry ride over.

**Virgin Islands Campground** (☎340-776-5488, 877-502-7225; http://virginislandscampground.com; cottages $170; @☎⚒) is the only option if you want to spend the night, but it's an eco-winner. Each wood-frame-and-canvas cottage has beds, linens, electrical outlets and a table and chairs inside. Guests share the communal bathhouse, cooking facilities and hot tub, plus there's wi-fi access throughout the grounds. Captured rainwater runs through the sinks and showers; solar energy heats it. There's a three-night minimum stay requirement.

The **Water Island Ferry** (☎340-690-4159; one way $5) departs roughly every hour from outside Tickles Dockside Pub at Crown Bay Marina. The journey takes 10 minutes. Taxis from downtown to the marina cost $4 to $5 per person.

## 🍴 Eating & Drinking

**Iggie's**     BURGERS, SEAFOOD **$$**
(☎340-693-2600; www.iggiesbeachbar.com; 7150 Bolongo Bay; mains $13-22; ☺lunch & dinner; ⚒) At Bolongo Bay Beach Resort and set in a large, open-air pavilion overlooking the broad shore, good-time Iggie's is a cut above standard resort eateries. It serves top-notch sandwiches, burgers, salads and seafood mains, plus a kids' menu. Things kick up at night, when the place grooves to a festive bar atmosphere and there's live music almost every evening. Wednesday is 'Carnival Night' (adult/child $33/15) with a limbo show, fire-eaters, *mocko jumbies* (costumed stilt walkers) and a West Indian buffet; it's a kiddie crowd pleaser. Tuesday and Saturday are also big draws for the all you can eat crab legs special, perfect with a cold beer.

**Lobster Grille**     SEAFOOD **$$$**
(☎340-775-1800; 7150 Bolongo Bay; mains $25-40; ☺breakfast, lunch & dinner, closed Tue eve) This is Bolongo Bay Beach Resort's upscale eatery, serving the namesake crustacean, lamb chops, shrimp scampi and a couple of veggie options such as the goat-cheese-topped portobello mushroom tower. A steel pan band hits the metal on Saturday from 6pm to 9pm.

**Mim's Seaside Bistro**     SEAFOOD **$$$**
(☎340-775-2081; www.mimsseasidebistro.com; Bolongo Bay; mains $25-40; ☺dinner) Mim's has earned a loyal following among villa owners. House specialties include the coconut curry lobster, baked stuffed lobster, seafood bisque and butterscotch walnut bread pudding for dessert. King crab legs, chicken, fish and pasta dishes round out the menu. Thursday is popular for all you can eat shrimp. Choose

a table under the stars by the water, or undercover on the patio. The bistro is located in building 15 at Watergate Villas.

**Havana Blue** FUSION $$$
(☑340-715-2583; www.havanabluerestaurant. com; Marriott Morning Star Beach Resort; mains $32-40; ☺dinner) The Marriott goes Cuban at this clubby bar-restaurant. Swill a mojito or caipirinha while puffing a pick off the cigar menu. The cocktail list is extensive. Happy hour is from 5:30pm to 7pm. The drinks are our favorite reason to visit, but Havana Blue also serves Latin meets Pacific Rim dishes like lobster tacos and miso-glazed sea bass. Coco Blue is Havana's sister bar in Red Hook.

# Red Hook & East End

The East End has the bulk of the island's major resorts, an extensive collection of restaurants and entertainment options (particularly at Red Hook), the most popular tourist attraction (Coral World Ocean Park), well over a dozen beaches and easy access to neighboring St John. Here, the island has the feel of a vacation destination, rather than a multifaceted West Indian island.

## Sights

**Coral World Ocean Park** MARINE PARK
(☑340-775-1555; www.coralworldvi.com; 6450 Estate Smith Bay, adult/child $19/10; ☺9am-4pm; 🚶) This 4.5-acre marine park, at Coki Point, is the most popular tourist attraction on St Thomas. Pick up a schedule when entering – staff feed the sea creatures and give talks about marine biology and conservation throughout the day, and it's during these times that you'll engage in behaviors you never thought possible, such as petting baby nurse sharks, touching starfish and feeding raw fish right into a stingray's mouth. Many of the park's creatures have been rescued (ie the sea turtles were orphans and the sea lions were in harm's way in Uruguay, where fishers were shooting them as pests). Pay an extra $40 to $125, and you can swim with the sharks, turtles or sea lions.

The **Sea Trek** is another popular activity, where you walk on the floor of the Caribbean Sea wearing a special helmet. A guide leads you along a trail equipped with a handrail 12 to 30 feet below the water. The helmet provides air and allows you to communicate with the guide while keeping your head dry.

Coral World has restaurants and gift shops, along with changing rooms if you want to visit nearby Coki Beach. Look for Coral World discount coupons in the free tourist guides.

**Tillett Gardens** ARTS CENTER
(www.tillettgardens.com) This collection of artisan studios and shops off Rte 38 (Smith Bay Rd) in Tutu, between Charlotte Amalie and the East End, is several cuts above most of the island's tourist attractions. English silkscreen artist Jim Tillett started this artists' compound on a Danish farm in 1959 as a 'peaceful sanctuary of creativity and wonderment.' Fifty-plus years later, the compound is just that. You can stroll the grounds, eat in a cafe, meet working artists and buy handcrafted fabrics, jewelry and other objets d'art. The gardens sponsor an ongoing concert series (www.tillettfoundation. org) that features performances by superb jazz, blues and classical musicians, so try to time your visit to coincide with a concert.

## Beaches

The East End holds the bulk of St Thomas' popular resort beaches. Sapphire and Coki are the amenity-laden favorites. We've listed the following beaches starting from southeast and moving around the point to the northeast. Expect to pay between $12 and $15 per person for a taxi to reach them from Charlotte Amalie.

**Secret Harbour** RESORT BEACH
This west-facing beach in front of the eponymous resort could hardly be more tranquil. It is protected from breezes as well as waves, and the water remains shallow a long way offshore. The resort has a water-sports operation, and this is one of the best places to learn to windsurf. You will find great snorkeling off the rocks here. A platform floats in the middle of the bay that children enjoy swimming to and jumping off.

**Vessup Beach** WINDSURFING BEACH
To reach this long, broad strand overlooking St John and the BVI, follow a dirt road around the south side of the harbor at Red Hook until you reach Vessup Bay Marina. Park here and walk east. The beach is just 100 yards away. Serious windsurfers love this spot, as do a lot of continentals and travelers who have come to roost around Red

» **Sapphire Beach** Resort guests, continentals and West Indians mix it up on this family-friendly beach that's known for its snorkeling and volleyball games.

» **Lindquist Beach** This beach is located in an undeveloped, protected park where true-blue water laps the soft white sand, and you'll likely have it all to yourself.

» **Magens Bay** (p80) St Thomas' favorite beach is also a protected park, with a broad bay, calm water and a dairy farm with milkshakes nearby.

» **Honeymoon Bay Beach** (p72) Water Island's pretty patch is ripe for swimming, snorkeling and buying a slice from the pizza boat.

» **Brewers Bay** (p69) Where West Indian families and university students come to cool off with a pate and cold Heineken from the food trucks.

» **Hull Bay** (p81) Surfers, musicians and fishers hang out at this far-out, north-side shore.

Hook. The Latitude 18 bar and restaurant is at the marina, and one of the best sailboarding operations on the island – West Indies Windsurfing – works off the beach.

Vessup has been part of a land dispute, and the government recently gave the OK to let it be developed. Stay tuned for how this plays out.

**TOP CHOICE** **Sapphire Beach** RESORT BEACH

The Sapphire Beach Resort just off Smith Bay Rd is perhaps the most welcoming of all the island's resorts to transient beach visitors. On weekends, you will find a mix of resort guests (lots of families with young children), continentals and West Indians from the island. The beach volleyball games here can get spirited, as can the party scene on Sunday afternoon, when the resort brings in live bands. The beach affords a great view of St John, Jost Van Dyke and Tortola. An offshore reef slows the wave action and presents good snorkeling opportunities.

Virtually every conceivable type of watersports equipment is available for rent, from kayaks to jet skis to Sunfish sailboats (about $15 to $20 per hour). Drinks vendors add to the good-spirited ambience.

**Lindquist Beach** SECLUDED BEACH

(admission $2) This narrow strand along Smith Bay is probably the largest piece of undeveloped beach property on the island. In 2006 it became part of **Smith Bay Park**, comprising 21 acres of protected coast managed by the Magens Bay Authority. It's a beauty all right: calm, true-blue water laps the soft white sand. St John and several cays shimmer in the distance. A coconut grove and sea grape trees provide good shade.

There are lifeguards on duty, chairs for rent, portable toilets and security patrols, but no other amenities. On weekends, plenty of West Indian families and teens come here to picnic and party. At other times, Lindquist is mostly deserted. Access is via dirt road off Smith Bay Rd, north of Sapphire Beach. A paved upgrade reportedly is in the works.

**Pineapple Beach** SECLUDED BEACH

A short, broad beach at the head of Water Bay about a half-mile off Rte 38, Pineapple Beach (also known as Renaissance Beach or Water Bay) is adjacent to Point Pleasant Resort; take the short trail on the beach's right-hand side, where you'll find the cool beach bar Fungi's. Trade winds often make the water choppy and cloudy, but the beach itself is spacious and manicured, with lots of room for children to play. When the wind is calm, the snorkeling along the south shore of the bay is good.

**Coki Beach** SNORKELING BEACH

This beach is on a protected cove right at the entrance to Coral World Ocean Park, near the northeast tip of the island. The snorkeling here is excellent with lots of fish action, and you can dive from shore with the Coki Beach Dive Club. Coki is the one beach on St Thomas with touts – as soon as you arrive someone will quickly become your 'friend' and try to hook you up to a certain beach chair or snorkel-gear vendor. The touts aren't aggressive, but they come as a bit of a shock since it is so uncommon elsewhere in the Virgin Islands. There's an undeniable party atmosphere here: reggae-blasting bars line the sand, where locals hang out and shoot pool. Hair braiders, snack shacks and equipment vendors enhance the fun in the sun.

For years cruise ship passengers mobbed the place. Then, in early 2010, a young passenger was shot and killed at Coki. She wasn't the target, but a casualty of a stray bullet from a local fight. Many residents said this was the culmination of an unsavory group that had been hanging out at Coki in recent years. Authorities have taken the issue seriously. On our recent visit to Coki, police were on hand keeping an eye on things, and the beach seemed to be back to business as usual with visitors splashing around and enjoying themselves.

## 🏃 Activities

The East End is a prime spot for outdoor action.

### Kayaking

 **Virgin Islands Ecotours**

(☑340-779-2155, 877-845-2925; www.viecotours.com; 2½hr tours adult/child $77/43; ☺10am & 2pm) Offers a guided kayak-and-snorkeling expedition where you'll paddle through a mangrove lagoon to a coral rubble beach. Tours depart just east of the intersection of Rtes 30 and 32, at the entrance to the Mangrove Lagoon. There's also a three-hour tour (adult/child $88/54) that adds hiking to the mix.

### Diving & Snorkeling

St Thomas features several premier dive sites, and most island resort hotels have a dive service on the property. Dive centers charge about $90 for a one-tank dive, or $125 for two. They also rent snorkeling gear for about $15 per day. Recommended dive shops are listed:

**Red Hook Dive Center**

(☑340-777-3483; www.redhookdivecenter.com) The retail center is at American Yacht Harbor. It offers mostly boat dives out of the Wyndham Sugar Bay Resort, but also offers night dives and trips to the British Virgin Islands' wreck RMS *Rhone*.

**Coki Beach Dive Club**

(☑340-775-4220; www.cokidive.com; ☺Mon-Sat) Just steps away from Coki Beach, this place offers shore and night dives, plus Professional Association of Diving Instructors (PADI) courses.

**Dive In!**

(☑340-777-5255, 866-434-8346; www.diveinusvi.com; Sapphire Beach Resort) Mostly boat dives, plus PADI-certification courses.

**Snuba of St Thomas**

(☑340-693-8063; www.visnuba.com; Coki Point; adult/child $68/65) A cross between snorkeling and scuba diving; children older than age eight can participate. The fee includes admission to Coral World, which is where the snuba takes place.

### Boat Trips

Expect to pay $70 per person for a four-hour trip and about $125 for a full-day adventure bobbing around St Thomas and St John. The trips generally include a catered lunch, free drinks and snorkel gear, and depart from American Yacht Harbor in Red Hook. Try the **Winifred** (☑340-513-2690; www.sailwinifred.com) or **Nate's Custom Charters** (☑340-244-2497; www.natescustomcharters.com).

If you want to drive yourself:

**Nauti Nymph Power Boat Rentals**

(☑340-775-5066; www.nautinymph.com) Rents 25ft to 32ft speedboats with snorkel gear for $425 a day and up. You can hire a captain for an additional $115 per day.

**See & Ski Power Boat Rentals**

(☑340-775-6265; www.seeski.com) Has 26ft Prowler Cats for $380 per day; hire a captain for $130 more per day.

### Fishing

Troll for wahoo, or get the live bait ready for yellowfin tuna. Add blue marlin to the list May through October, when boats haul in 250lb fish and then some. Most trips depart from American Yacht Harbor in Red Hook. Expect to pay about $800 for a half-day excursion, and $1450 for a full day.

**Marlin Prince**

(☑340-779-5939; www.marlinprince.com) Captain John Prince operates this 45ft vessel. The boat and crew consistently place among the top spots in local tournaments for marlin, tuna, wahoo and mahimahi. Prince also offers saltwater fly-fishing for marlin.

**Nate's Custom Charters**

(☑340-244-2497; www.natescustomcharters.com) Hits the waves in a 27ft ProKat.

### Windsurfing

Most St Thomas resort hotels have windsurfing equipment for beginning and intermediate enthusiasts. The average rental price is $40 an hour. **West Indies Windsurfing** (☑340-775-6530; ☺10am-5pm Sat & Sun, by appt Mon-Fri) on Vessup Beach has advanced equipment (including kite boards) and instruction. Lessons start at $85 per hour.

# 🛏 Sleeping

Resorts and private villas are the East End's only options. **Antilles Resorts** (www.antilles resorts.com) manages six properties here, including Pavilions & Pools, Point Pleasant Resort, Sapphire Beach Resort, Anchorage Resort, Crystal Cove Resort and Sapphire Village Resort. Many units are privately owned condos, and they vary widely in quality. Savvy visitors say they have better luck booking through **VRBO** (www.vrbo.com), where they deal with the condo owners directly and can get more specifics about the unit they're renting. If you do book through Antilles, there are often discounts off the rack rates listed below.

### Secret Harbour Beach Resort
APARTMENTS **$$$**

(☎340-775-6550;       www.secretharbourvi.com; 6280 Estate Nazareth; apt $345-625; ✳@🛜🏊🍴) Secret Harbour is a family favorite. Of the 60 suites, 42 units sit on the beach and the rest are up a hill behind the beach with sea views. Suites come in three sizes – studio (600ft), one bedroom (900ft) and two bedroom (1300ft); all have a kitchen and a balcony or patio. You can get your exercise at the pool, fitness center and three tennis courts, but the calm, shallow beach is the main draw. Units have free wi-fi. You'll need a car or taxi to get around from here.

### Sapphire Beach Resort & Marina
APARTMENTS **$$$**

(☎340-775-6100,       800-874-7897;    www.antilles resorts.com; 6720 Estate Smith Bay; apt $335-495; ✳🏊) The draw for this condo resort is being on Sapphire Beach itself, a gorgeous half-mile stretch of teal-blue sea and watersports fun. It's also handy to be so close to Red Hook – a five-minute drive or a 15-minute walk (along the busy road) – where restaurants and bars abound. The condos themselves are studio-style suites that vary in quality. Some are more modern than others, but all have a kitchen and private balcony. This is one of those instances where you might fare best renting from individual owners through VRBO so you'll have more control over what you're getting. The suites spread out in a collection of large multistory buildings facing the beach and the resort's marina. Sapphire Beach Resort is not to be confused with Sapphire Village Resort, which comprises the green buildings on the hillside behind the beach and offers lower-priced, apartment-like accommodations.

Amenities such as wi-fi vary by unit at both resorts.

### Pavilions & Pools
APARTMENTS **$$$**

(☎340-775-6110, 800-524-2001; www.pavilionsand pools.com; 6400 Estate Smith Bay; apt incl breakfast $325-350; ✳@🛜🏊) The cool thing about this small hotel is that each of the 25 suites has its own pool – yeah, you read that right! Suites have full kitchens, wi-fi access and separate bedrooms with sliding doors that open to the pool. You can spend days here and never put on a stitch of clothing. When you're ready to get dressed, the friendly staff will shuttle you to nearby Sapphire Beach.

### Point Pleasant Resort
APARTMENTS **$$$**

(☎340-775-7200,       800-524-2300;    www.point pleasantresort.com; 6600 Estate Smith Bay; apt $300-550; ✳🏊) On a steep hill overlooking Water Bay, the property has lots of charm though the rooms are somewhat dated (in a flowery way, akin to your grandma's 1980 Florida condo). The 128 suites are in multi-unit cottages tucked into the hillside forest. Each unit has a full kitchen, separate bedroom and large porch. The grounds have walking trails, three pools and a beach. The property's two good restaurants – high-end Agavé Terrace and casual Fungi's – are an added attraction.

### Wyndham Sugar Bay Resort
HOTEL **$$$**

(☎340-777-7100,      877-999-3223;    www.wyndham sugarbayresort.com; 6500 Estate Smith Bay; d from $380; ✳🛜🏊🍴) The Wyndham is the island's only truly all-inclusive resort. This highrise hotel rises dramatically on a point of rock above a small sheltered beach, with 300 rooms, three interconnecting pools, a fitness center, tennis courts, water sports and a Kids Club program. The rooms are a bit cookie-cutter, but all have first-class amenities. The all-inclusive rate gets you three meals a day, booze, kayaks, Sunfish sailboats and much more. Wi-fi is free in the lobby. It you're willing to wing it, last-minute deals sometimes surface online. The property also offers a 'value package' that provides room and breakfast only, and you pay à la carte for everything else.

### Ritz-Carlton
HOTEL **$$$**

(☎340-775-3333;      www.ritzcarlton.com;     6900 Estate Great Bay; r from $600; ✳🛜🏊🍴) The 15-acre property with 180 guest quarters exudes a Mediterranean ambience with frescoed walls, imported pink marble and the continental accents of its concierge and front-desk staff. Accommodations are in multi-unit villas peppered around the property and surrounded by extensive tropical gardens. Rooms have private balconies and marble bathrooms; there's in-room internet access for a fee. The pools and sundecks are expansive, and the beach is broad and uncrowded. Children's programs are available for an extra fee.

## ✗ Eating

Red Hook has the biggest concentration of eating and drinking places. The commercial center is all of about two blocks long, so it's easy to wander around and take your pick. During the 1990s, this area developed the highest concentration of restaurants on St Thomas. Almost all are geared to continentals – those roosting in East End resorts, and those who have come to work on the island. Few West Indians frequent these establishments. Other eateries are scattered among the resorts.

**TOP CHOICE** Toad & Tart BRITISH $$
(☏340-775-1153; www.toadandtart.com; Estate Smith Bay; mains $14-21; ☉dinner Thu-Sun) Don't be put off by the humble exterior. Inside the squat, concrete building you'll find lovely, British pub food: bangers and mash, shepherd's pie, steak and onion pie and a curry dish, plus daily specials like fish and chips or pot roast. The owner Anna, aka the 'tart,' is quite a character and man, does she know how to cook. Books, board games, dart boards and draft beers from the motherland complete the experience. The pub is on Smith Bay Rd between Point Pleasant Resort and the road to Coki.

**Duffy's Love Shack** BURGERS $$
(☏340-779-2080; www.duffysloveshack.com; Red Hook; mains $9-16; ☉lunch & dinner) It may be a frame shack in the middle of a paved parking lot at Red Hook Plaza, but Duffy's creates its legendary atmosphere with high-volume rock and crowds in shorts and tank tops. The food is classic, burger-based pub fare with conch fritters and Pacific Rim skewers (satay) thrown in for good measure. The big attractions here are the people-watching and crazy cocktails. Consider the 64oz 'shark tank,' or Dr Feelgood's Vile Foaming Liquid. Hype? Yes. But fun, too. After dark, particularly on Friday, Duffy's turns into the biggest frat party on the island. Cash only.

**Randy's Wine Bar & Bistro** ITALIAN $$
(☏340-775-5001; 4002 Raphune Hill; mains $12-33; ☉lunch & dinner Mon-Fri) Randy's is probably the most unlikely restaurant on all of St Thomas. You will never find it unless you make the effort. Located mid-island off Rte 38, it is a secret hideaway tucked in a commercial storefront. The attraction is the scent of fresh basil, grilled mushrooms and the best wine list on the island. Tables in the bistro are spread among crates of wine. Sip reds and whites by the glass (or order a martini) to go with Randy's sandwiches like the chicken and Brie, or main dishes such as the pan-seared tuna with lentils and rice. The bistro is located in Al Cohen's Plaza, a few miles east of downtown Charlotte Amalie en route to the East End.

**Latitude 18** BURGERS, SEAFOOD $$
(☏340-779-2495; www.latitude18usvi.com; Vessup Bay Marina; mains $20-28; ☉lunch & dinner) Latitude 18 is Red Hook's funkiest bar and restaurant. The place is a patio protected by a roof of old sails and blue tarps that blow away in every hurricane. The decoration is a mix of marine flotsam, a huge plastic shark, Christmas lights and a pirate flag. Most of the clientele are world-cruiser types who come in off their boats and local continentals who are – or dream of being – seafaring ramblers. Locals rave about the flavorful dishes coming from the little kitchen, such as the scared tuna roll with papaya salad. Latitude brings in live entertainment most nights and the local buckos get fired up. It's located down a bumpy dirt road around the south side of Vessup Bay.

**Blue Moon Cafe** CAFE $$
(☏340-779-2262; www.bluemooncafevi.com; 6280 Estate Nazareth; mains $23-30; ☉breakfast, lunch & dinner) Set at the Secret Harbour Beach Resort, Blue Moon gets rave reviews from locals and travelers. This is not your average hotel restaurant. The attraction is the casual elegance of the waterfront setting overlooking the harbor and the care that goes into preparing dishes like the lemon-thyme roasted chicken, and pork chop topped with a crimini mushroom reduction. There is an extensive wine list with some reasonably priced grapes, and scotch, port and cognac for postmeal sips. Kids get their own menu.

**Fungi's on the Beach** BURGERS, WEST INDIAN $$
(☏340-775-4142; 6600 Estate Smith Bay; mains $9-18; ☉lunch & dinner) The rasta-colored beach bar at the Point Pleasant Resort wins big

points for its food and fun vibe. Rotis and platters of native dishes, such as conch fritters, snapper creole and the namesake fungi, are the specialties of the house, along with well-made burgers. The building is right on the water, so close you can dangle your feet in. The friendly bartenders crank the reggae and will offer you a spritz of insect repellent to fight off the mosquitoes.

### Agavé Terrace & Bar                 SEAFOOD $$$

(☎340-775-4142; www.agaveterrace.com; 6600 Estate Smith Bay; mains $22-38; ☺dinner) Located at the Point Pleasant Resort, Agavé is one of the island's most respected restaurants and one to dress up for. The deck hangs out in thin air over a steep slope, giving diners a breathtaking view of St John and the BVI. Expect candlelight, linen, crystal and professional waitstaff. Agavé specializes in fish, lobster and crab legs; vegetarians will find a couple of pastas and vegetable curry dishes. Make reservations early for weekend dining.

### Molly Malone's          BURGERS, SEAFOOD $$

(☎340-775-1270; www.mollymalonesstthomas. com; Red Hook; mains $13-27; ☺breakfast, lunch & dinner) A re-creation of a friendly Irish pub, Molly's has a huge menu, from omelets to shepherd's pie to veggie lasagna. It's a great place to chow down for breakfast, watch sports on overhead TVs, or cool off with a brew at the bar. It's on the lower level of the American Yacht Harbor complex.

### Romano's Restaurant                 ITALIAN $$$

(☎340-775-0045; www.romanosrestaurant.com; 6697 Estate Smith Bay; mains $25-40; ☺dinner Mon-Sat) Romano's gets many St Thomians' votes for the best Italian cuisine on the island. The setting is dark, with no view to speak of, but is rich with candlelight and violin music. Chef Tony's paintings hang on the walls, while his artful sweet clam and white wine linguini, four-cheese lasagna and braised veal fill the plates. The restaurant is located off Smith Bay Rd near Coki Point.

### Caribbean Saloon          BURGERS, SEAFOOD $$

(☎340-775-7060; www.caribbeansaloon.com; Red Hook; mains $13-27; ☺lunch & dinner) Caribbean Saloon is another longstanding player in Red Hook's pub-and-grub scene. Set on the top floor of the American Yacht Harbor complex, the venue is a contemporary rendering of a classic beer garden. Burgers and sandwiches scent the air at lunchtime, while the dinner menu revolves around steak, chops, seafood and pasta dishes. Like its rival saloons up and down the street, this place can rock with a young crowd on winter nights. It serves a late night menu until 4am.

### XO Bar & Bistro                 INTERNATIONAL $$

(☎340-779-2069; Red Hook; mains $15-25; ☺lunch & dinner) This narrow little hideaway in Red Hook Plaza has an exclusive, romantic feel. Patrons come dressed in cocktail dresses and long slacks to sample the hot artichoke dip or entrees like the *capellini pomodoro* (angel-hair pasta with garlic, basil, mushroom and tomatoes). The staff serves until midnight or later, when the bistro bar starts to hum.

### Coco Blue                 FUSION $$$

(☎340-774-7253; www.cocobluerestaurant.com; Red Hook; mains $29-39; ☺dinner) Swanky Coco Blue fuses Latin, island and Pacific Rim flavors in dishes like piña colada chicken and guava-glazed pork ribs. Chefs will substitute tofu for meat in many of the dishes. It's a good place to come for happy hour (5pm to 7pm) to hoist a posh mojito and nibble off the light bites menu on sushi rolls or coconut-chipotle ceviche. It's in the American Yacht Harbor building. Make reservations.

### Big Bambooz                 BURGERS $$

(☎340-714-7244; Red Hook; mains $7-16; ☺lunch & dinner) You know it's gonna be a good time when you walk into the thatched-roof, tiki-studded Big Bambooz. Bite into burgers, fish tacos, chicken curry or a mahimahi sandwich with a side of sweet-potato fries. It sits next to the American Yacht Harbor center.

### Burrito Bay Deli                 MEXICAN $

(☎340-775-2944; Red Hook; mains $8-12; ☺breakfast & lunch) Longing for healthy-leaning sandwiches, wraps or breakfast foods (including tofu and vegetarian options)? Or maybe a roasted pork burrito? Burrito Bay is your place. It's in the American Yacht Harbor complex.

### Señor Pizza                 PIZZA $

(☎340-775-3030; Red Hook; slice $3-4, large pizzas $16-24; ☺lunch & dinner) Across from the ferry dock, this little pizza joint can get very busy with takeout orders in the evening, when vacationers in East End condos decide they don't feel like cooking.

## Drinking & Entertainment

Several of the island's restaurants double as great bars. And don't forget: you can always zip over on the ferry to Cruz Bay in St John for the party scene there.

### Duffy's Love Shack                    BAR

(www.duffysloveshack.com; Red Hook) Almost every night of the week is a party scene here, but the crowd overflows into the parking lot on Ladies Night (Wednesday) and Friday. Saturday features themes like Bathrobe Night. Driving rock & roll fuels this crowd of under-30 continentals and travelers who pursue the rites of spring with bottomless gusto. Duffy's hosts a whopping party the Friday closest to the full moon each month. Happy hour sets the mood from 3pm to 6pm daily.

### Latitude 18                    LIVE MUSIC

(www.latitude18usvi.com; Vessup Bay Marina) Latitude 18 is a down-and-dirty sailors' bar. Most nights of the week there is live music, when island legends like Mighty Whitey, Dick Solberg (also called the Fiddler) and the Sun Mountain Band show up to play acoustic, rock, bluegrass, country and folk. Open-mike nights (usually Tuesday) with Mighty Whitey are a hoot – and so is the crowd. Just picture every character you have ever heard about in a Jimmy Buffett ballad.

### XO Bar & Bistro                    BAR

(Red Hook) XO gets going on weekends, when middle-aged continentals out for a night on the town stop in for cigars and martinis against a background of progressive jazz CDs. The crowd gets younger after midnight, when you find owners, managers and employees from other local businesses drifting in to stir up the party. Bands play Wednesday and Sunday.

### Caribbean Cinemas – Market
### Square                    CINEMA

(340-776-3666; www.caribbeancinemas.com) If it's first-run Hollywood films you are seeking, head for these cinemas between the East End and Charlotte Amalie, on Rte 38 in Tutu Park Mall.

##  Shopping

Since the development of the American Yacht Harbor complex, Red Hook has become the favorite shopping area for East Enders. The compound of multistory buildings is home to upscale shops and restaurants, and there are more shops across the street in Red Hook Plaza. You can park for a fee in a protected lot at American Yacht Harbor or for free at the shopping center.

### Marina Market                    FOOD

(www.marinamarket.com) The main supermarket on the East End, where self-caterers can stock up on produce, cheese, wine and spirits; it's across from the ferry dock.

### Tutu Park Mall                    MALL

(www.tutuparkmall.com) This is where most St Thomians do their everyday shopping. The complex includes supermarkets, discount stores, a theater and a Kmart. It's between the East End and Charlotte Amalie, on Rte 38 in Tutu.

## ℹ Getting There & Around

Red Hook is a busy hub for ferries to St John, Jost Van Dyke and Tortola's West End. You can park in the marine terminal's lot for $10 per day.

### To St John

Passenger ferries ($6 one way, 20 minutes) zip over to Cruz Bay at 6.30am, 7:30am and then on the hour between 8am and midnight. There's a $2.50 charge per bag for large pieces of luggage.

### To Jost Van Dyke

**Inter-Island** (☏340-776-6597; www.inter islandboatservices.vi; round trip $70) operates a passenger ferry twice daily to Jost at 8am and 2pm. No service Wednesday or Thursday. It takes about 45 minutes.

### To Tortola

A couple of companies alternate departures to the West End four or five times per day. The trip takes 35 minutes:
**Smith's Ferry** (☏340-775-7292; www.smiths ferry.com; one way $28)
**Native Son** (☏340-774-8685; www.nativeson ferry.com; one way $25)
**Road Town Fast Ferry** (☏284-494-2323; www. roadtownfastferry.com) This company differs from the others by offering a night service that departs Red Hook at 9pm Thursday through Sunday and goes to Road Town (one way $35).

### Car Ferries to St John

Three different companies run car ferries between Red Hook and Enighed Pond beside Cruz

Bay (round trip around $50, 20 minutes), with sailings almost every hour between 6am and 7pm. Note that most St Thomas car-rental companies do not allow you to take their vehicles to St John.

# North Side

The north side of St Thomas is the quieter section of the island. Steep-sloped mountains rise almost from the water's edge. Large coves such as Magens Bay have exquisite, secluded beaches at their heads. Largely residential, the north shore features a mix of undeveloped forests and fields with middle- and upper-class villas perched on the mountainside.

## ◎ Sights

**Drake's Seat**      SCENIC OVERLOOK
Legend has it that Sir Francis Drake came to this overlook, on a mountaintop just off Rte 40 south of Magens Bay, to plot the passage of his fleet through the British Virgin Islands east of here. Tour buses and street vendors flood the scene by day, but if you come late in the afternoon you'll have more elbow room.

**Mountain Top**      SCENIC OVERLOOK
(☎340-774-2400) This restaurant and shopping complex, off Rte 33 (Crown Mountain Rd) on St Peter Mountain, offers vistas from 1500ft above sea level. On a clear day, you can see almost all of the British Virgin Islands to the east and the Spanish Virgin Islands of Puerto Rico to the west. Mountain Top's bar specializes in banana daiquiris, which staff claim were invented here. A fire destroyed the complex in 2009, but the owners rebuilt and opened again in early 2011, so everything is shiny new.

You're likely to share the vista with a busload of folks on an island tour. The views you get by simply driving east from here on Crown Mountain Rd may not be quite as spectacular, but you will have them all to yourself.

**Estate St Peter Greathouse &**
**Botanical Garden**      GARDEN
(www.greathousevi.com; admission $15; ⊙8am-4pm) Like Mountain Top, this contemporary great house at the corner of Barrett Hill Rd and Rte 40 is a popular attraction for tour groups. The 11-acre property overlooking Magens Bay has been the retreat of a French consul, an island governor and the Johnson

& Johnson Corporation. Largely destroyed by Hurricane Hugo, the great house and botanical gardens have been restored. The house has photos of hurricane damage, a local art collection and views of the north-shore bays from an expansive deck. There are also a few shops, a bar and a cafe on the premises. The site is open only when cruise ships are in port.

## 🏖 Beaches

**Magens Bay**      FAMILY BEACH
(adult/child $4/2; ⊙6am-6pm; 🎟) The sugary mile that fringes heart-shaped Magens Bay, 3 miles north of Charlotte Amalie, makes almost every travel publication's list of beautiful beaches. The seas here are calm, the bay is broad, and the vista of the surrounding green hills is dramatic.

The beach and much of the surrounding land is protected as a territorial park (hence the admission fee). In a sense, Magens Bay is the public beach for St Thomas. It has lifeguards, picnic tables, changing facilities, a couple of food vendors and water-sports operators renting **kayaks and paddle boats** ($20 to 30 per hour). On weekends, when the locals come to party, and on days when the cruise ships bus in their passengers, you'll find mobs of people here, but the beach is so long that you may not feel claustrophobic. If you do, head for the west end, which is always sparsely populated.

Snorkeling is not very good at Magens, but **swimming** and **walking** are. Children will do well here since the water is calm and shallow. There's a **nature trail** about midway down the bay that takes off into the bush, but be prepared for attack by biting insects if you decide to venture forth.

No regularly scheduled public transportation stops here, but there's a taxi stand on-site with bountiful cabs. A taxi to/from Charlotte Amalie costs $10 (it goes down to $8 per person in a multi-passenger vehicle). If you drive, parking costs $2. Don't forget to stop at Udder Delite Dairy Bar for a milkshake on the road down.

**Little Magens Bay**      SECLUDED BEACH
This is the only nude beach on the island, and it is beautiful. To reach it, start at Magens Bay and, as you face the water, head right along the beach to the end. Then wade along the rocky shore around the point. It is about a quarter-mile trek. It can be tricky when the tide is high, as then you'll be sloshing in water up to your chest; early morning

When you've had enough lazing on the beach, pick up a paddle (or golf club or fishing pole…)

» **Virgin Islands Ecotours** (p63 and p75) Kayak to the ruins around Hassel Island, or through the mangrove swamp on the East End.

» **Marlin Prince** (p75) You'll have a mighty-fine fishing tale to tell after reeling in a mighty blue marlin.

» **Mahogany Run Golf Course** Tee off on the Devil's Triangle seaside holes.

» **Water Island Adventures** (p72) Cycle around the fourth Virgin's beaches and old plantations.

» **Coki Beach Dive Club** (p75) Swim from shore to active coral reefs.

is usually the best time to go. The beach has no amenities and most of the time it's empty.

**Hull Bay**  SURFING BEACH

Lying to the west around Tropaco Point from Magens Bay, Hull Bay is the island's most popular surfing beach and usually a gem of solitude when Magens Bay is overrun with people. The strand lies at the base of a steep valley and features excellent shade along its entire length.

Amenities include a boat ramp, which the 'Frenchie' fisherfolk use; the Hull Bay Hideaway beach bar; and changing facilities. The surf is at its best during the winter, when the swells roll in from the northeast and you get a 4ft point break. On days when the surf is up, Hull Bay can be a major surf scene with youths from all over the island abandoning jobs and schools to catch a wave.

**Homer's** (☑340-774-7606, 866-719-1856; www.nightsnorkel.com; ◌10am-5pm) has a water-sports shack on site and rents surfboards ($50 per half day) and kayaks ($40 per half day) and conducts raved-about night snorkel tours ($38 per person). Taxis are scarce, so you'll need a car to get here.

**Stumpy Bay**  SECLUDED BEACH

If solitude is what you're seeking, head for Stumpy Bay near the northwest end of St Thomas. Look for the dirt road that leads off Rte 30 and down a steep hill. The road ends after a half-mile, and beachgoers must park their cars here and then walk another half-mile down a trail to the beach. The beach features shade trees, brown sand and calm water within the arms of this northwest-facing bay. Some people risk nudism here, but they are a definite minority. The car park at Stumpy Bay is not secure, so take precautions with your valuables.

🏃 **Activities**

**Mahogany Run Golf Course**  GOLF

(☑340-777-6006; www.mahoganyrungolf.com) East of Magens Bay is the island's only option for golf – but what an option it is. The 18-hole championship course owes its design to George and Tom Fazio and features the famous 'Devil's Triangle' seaside holes. Greens and half-cart fees are $165. Club rentals cost $60.

🛏️ **Sleeping & Eating**

**Mafolie Hotel**  HOTEL $$

(☑340-774-2790, 800-225-7035; www.mafolie. com; 7091 Estate Mafolie; r incl breakfast $150-200; ❋ 🛜 ❄) On Mafolie Hill, 850 feet above Charlotte Amalie, the eponymous hotel has the feel of a Danish colonial villa, and offers a dramatic vista and popular alfresco restaurant. The good points: killer harbor views considering the relatively low prices. The not-so-good points: room furnishings are reminiscent of a budget motel chain in the US, and Mafolie's location is far from town, making wheels necessary. Try to avoid the rooms above the restaurant, which are tiny and can be noisy. If the free wi-fi is important to you, be sure to ask for a room with good reception.

**TOP CHOICE** **Udder Delite Dairy Bar**  ICE CREAM $

(☑340-777-6050; milkshakes $5; ◌1-6:30pm Mon, 10am-6:30pm Tue-Sat, 11:30am-6:30pm Sun; ⊞) It doesn't get any sweeter than this working dairy farm that swirls its own ice cream, blends it into milkshakes and then spikes the treats with alcohol. The flavor board provides plenty to choose from, but the crowd pleaser is the coffee-chocolate Jamocha shake blended with Bailey's, usually served up by a smiling gentleman named Bailey.

You can order without booze, of course, so no need to worry about the kids lined up at the window. Udder Delite is about 1 mile from Magens Bay beach, up a steep hill.

### Old Stone Farmhouse CARIBBEAN $$$

(☎340-777-6277; www.oldstonefarmhouse.com; Mahogany Run Golf Course; mains $24-36; ☺dinner Wed-Mon) The 200-year-old farmhouse sits high on a hill overlooking St Thomas' only golf course. The rustic, low-lit room impresses with its arched stone walls and mahogany ceiling. The chef invites guests back to the kitchen to select their own meat and fish and discuss their preferences; he then prepares the dish accordingly. The menu changes, but local fish (snapper, wahoo, mahimahi, live lobster) are always available, as well as a vegetarian option. A robust wine list accompanies the fare. The stellar service, setting and chef make this a one-of-a-kind evening.

### Hull Bay Hideaway BURGERS $

(☎340-777-1898; www.hullbayhideaway.com; mains $9-14; ☺lunch & dinner Wed-Mon) Beckoning next to the entrance to Hull Bay beach, the Hideaway looks like a cross between a campground and a Mexican cantina. The basic 'Arthur burger' has fans worldwide, and the Presidente burger (seared in the namesake beer, then topped with pepperjack cheese) runs a close second. Other house favorites include gyros, chicken sandwiches and beer-battered onion rings. Lots of locals hang out for the live music on Sunday afternoons and the Monday night blues jam.

### Northside Bistro CAFE $$

(☎340-775-5098; www.northsidebistro.com; 15 Hull Bay Rd; mains $15-26; ☺dinner Mon-Sat)

Northside's offerings include meatloaf, seafood ravioli, apple-and-pear-stuffed pork chops and baby back ribs among its arsenal. Several vegetarian options (veggie lasagna, hummus and couscous) also make appearances. There's a nice selection of wine by the glass. Musicians play piano or strum guitar most nights. This is the rare place where you can have your cake and drink it too, compliments of the coconut-cake martini. So if nothing else, stop in for a drink. After you pass Drake's Seat veer right onto Hull Bay Rd. The bistro is 2 miles from there.

### Mafolie Restaurant CARIBBEAN $$

(☎340-774-2790; www.mafolie.com; 7091 Estate Mafolie; mains $19-25; ☺dinner Wed-Mon) Sitting high above the bay at the Mafolie Hotel, the dining patio here offers incredible alfresco dining. Cool breezes, candlelight and striking vistas complement the Caribbean and Creole-infused seafood, such as seared tuna, crab and lobster, and coconut-crusted chicken and BBQ ribs. An extensive wine list offers choices in all budgets, and the friendly staff can help you pick the perfect meal.

### Sib's Mountain Bar & Restaurant AMERICAN $$

(☎340-774-8967; Mafolie Rd; mains $17-27; ☺dinner) Sib's is a small roadhouse with a huge local following. Some folks come to drink and shoot pool. Others claim you can't get better red snapper anywhere on the island. Meatloaf, baby back ribs, chicken-fried steak and prime rib form the core of the meaty menu.

# St John

POP 4300

## Best Places to Eat

» Rhumb Lines (p93)

» Jake's (p93)

» Vie's Snack Shack (p106)

» Skinny Legs (p106)

» La Tapa (p94)

## Best Places to Stay

» St John Inn (p90)

» Garden by the Sea B&B (p90)

» Concordia Eco-Tents (p105)

» Maho Bay Camps (p100)

## Why Go?

Outdoor enthusiasts and ecotravelers: welcome to your island. Two-thirds of St John is a protected national park, with gnarled trees and spiky cacti spilling over its edges. There are no airports or cruise ship docks, and the usual Caribbean resorts are few and far between. Instead, the island hosts several tent-resorts (aka campgrounds with permanent canvas structures), keeping costs reasonable and the environment intact.

Hiking and snorkeling are the main must-dos. Trails wind by petroglyphs and sugar mill ruins, and several drop out onto beaches prime for swimming with turtles and spotted eagle rays. Scuba trips, kayaking voyages and cycling trail rides add to the adventure.

All that action can make a visitor thirsty, so it's a good thing St John knows how to host a happy hour, where the party often spills out into the street.

## When to Go

Mid-December through April is the perfect-weather high season, when prices and crowds max out. Events that bring bunches include 8 Tuff Miles, an island-spanning road race in late February, and the Blues Festival around the third weekend in March. The St John Carnival in early July is biggest blowout of all. May and early December are good shoulder season months for bargains and decent (if wet) weather. Thursdays and Fridays are the best days to be on the island for live music.

## History

Columbus did not stop at St John in 1493 on his sail along the south coast of the island. However, most scholars credit him with naming St John (San Juan) and putting the island on the map for Spanish adventurers, whose slave raids drove the indigenous population off the island by the 1650s.

Starting in the late 1600s, the English and Danes battled over St John. The Danes won out and put down roots. By 1739 St John's population stood at more than 200 white settlers and 1400 slaves. The island's cane and cotton plantations began to mature.

In 1733 a slave revolt broke out, resulting in several deaths and widespread destruction around the island. The Moravian Mission built its first church at Coral Bay in the late 1750s. In 1760 the settlement at Cruz Bay became an official town, and a ferry began service between St Thomas and Cruz Bay.

Economic conditions worsened after the emancipation of slaves in 1848. When the US took possession of St John in 1917, the island's plantations had been abandoned, the island depopulated, and the landscape turned wild again. The last operating sugar mill, at Reef Bay, closed in 1918.

### ✯ Festivals & Events

**8 Tuff Miles**                    ROAD RACE
(www.8tuffmiles.com; late Feb) Popular foot race from Cruz Bay to Coral Bay.

**St John Blues Festival**             MUSIC
(www.stjohnbluesfestival.com; mid-Mar) Music bash in Coral Bay over a weekend; tickets cost $30 per night.

**St John Carnival**               CULTURAL
(www.visitusvi.com; early Jul) The island's biggest celebration, with mocko jumbies (stilts walkers), steel pan bands, parades and musical competitions; surrounds Emancipation Day (July 3) and US Independence Day (July 4).

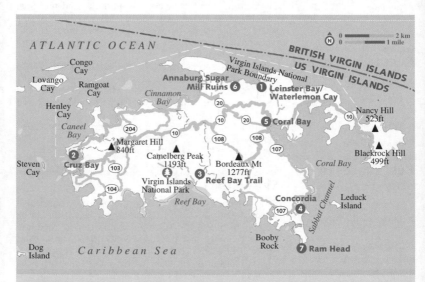

## St John Highlights

❶ Snorkel with barracudas, turtles and nurse sharks at **Leinster Bay/Waterlemon Cay** (p100)

❷ Raise a glass to happy hour in **Cruz Bay** (p95)

❸ Hike the **Reef Bay Trail** past ancient petroglyphs (p103)

❹ Eco-camp up in the hills at **Concordia** (p105)

❺ Slow down to local speed at the restaurant-bars in **Coral Bay** (p105)

❻ Explore the impressive **Annaberg Sugar Mill Ruins** (p97)

❼ Climb to the worth-every-drop-of-sweat clifftop view at **Ram Head** (p103)

## ℹ Getting There & Around

### BOAT

There's only one way to reach St John: boat. All ferries arrive in Cruz Bay. Ferries from St Thomas and the British Virgin Islands arrive at separate docks, though they are within steps of each other. Check **See St John** (www.seestjohn. com) for schedules. Main routes:

**FROM ST THOMAS (RED HOOK)** Passenger ferries ($6 one way, 20 minutes) run almost every hour, starting at 6:30am until midnight. Three different companies run car ferries between Red Hook and Enighed Pond beside Cruz Bay (round trip around $50, 20 minutes), with sailings almost every hour between 6am and 7pm.

**FROM ST THOMAS (CHARLOTTE AMALIE)** Passenger ferries ($12 one way, 45 minutes) run three times a day from Charlotte Amalie's waterfront, departing at 10am, 1pm and 5:30pm.

**FROM JOST VAN DYKE**
**Inter-Island** (☑340-776-6597; www.inter Islandboatservices.vi; round trip $70) operates a passenger ferry twice daily from Jost at 9:15am and 3pm. No service Wednesday or Thursday. It takes about 45 minutes.

**FROM TORTOLA (WEST END)**
**Inter-Island** (☑340-776-6597; www.inter islandboat services.vi; round trip $45) operates a passenger ferry three times daily from West End at 9:15am, 12:15pm and 4:15pm (later on Friday and Sunday). It takes about 30 minutes.

### BUS

**Vitran** (fare $1) operates air-conditioned buses over the length of the island via Centerline Rd. Buses leave Cruz Bay in front of the ferry terminal at 6am and 7am, then every hour at 25 minutes after the hour until 7:25pm. They arrive at Coral Bay about 40 minutes later. In reality, the schedule can be erratic.

### CAR

St John has a handful of rental agencies. Most provide Jeeps and SUVs to handle the steep, rugged, twisted roads. Costs hover near $80 per day. The following agencies have outlets in Cruz Bay near the ferry terminals. Whatever agency you use, be sure to ask if you can park in their lot when in Cruz Bay, since parking is notoriously difficult in town. Remember to drive on the left and fill up in Cruz Bay, where the only gas station is.

**Cool Breeze Jeep/Car Rental** (☑340-776-6588; www.coolbreezecarrental.com)
**Denzil Clyne Car Rental** (☑340-776-6715)
**St John Car Rental** (☑340-776-6103; www. stjohncarrental.com)

### HITCHHIKING

Although Lonely Planet does not recommend hitchhiking, quite a few people use this method for traveling around St John. If you hitchhike, don't travel alone and always exercise caution.

### TAXI

Some taxis are passenger vans that carry eight to 10 passengers. Many are open-air safaris like the ones on St Thomas. Territorial law sets the island's rates for all taxis. They're listed in *St Thomas/St John This Week* magazine. Call the **St John Taxi Commission** (☑340-774-3130) for pick-ups.

The following table shows current per-person rates for popular destinations from Cruz Bay. The price drops a few dollars when more than one passenger goes to the destination. There's also an additional $2-per-bag luggage fee.

| DESTINATION | COST |
| --- | --- |
| Annaberg Sugar Mill Ruins | $13 |
| Caneel Bay | $6 |
| Cinnamon Bay | $9 |
| Coral Bay | $16 |
| Maho Bay Campground | $13 |
| Reef Bay Trail | $9 |
| Trunk Bay | $8 |
| Westin Resort | $6 |

# Cruz Bay

Nicknamed 'Love City,' St John's main town indeed wafts a carefree, spring-break party vibe. Hippies, sea captains, American retirees and reggae worshippers hoist happy-hour drinks in equal measure, and everyone wears a silly grin at their great good fortune for being here. Cruz Bay is also the place to organize your hiking, snorkeling, kayaking and other island activities, and to fuel up in the surprisingly good restaurant mix. Everything grooves within walking distance of the ferry docks. About half of the island's population lives here.

## ⊙ Sights

FREE **Virgin Islands National Park**   PARK
(www.nps.gov/viis) The park is the most popular single attraction in all of the Virgin Islands, offering miles of shoreline, pristine reefs and 20 hiking trails (see p103 for details).

In the early 1950s, US millionaire Laurance Rockefeller discovered and fell in love with St John, which was nearly abandoned at the

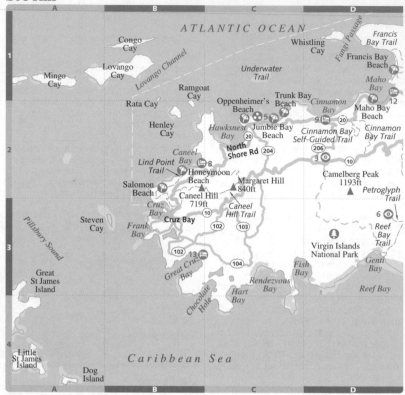

time. He purchased large tracts of the land, built the Caneel Bay resort, and then donated more than 5000 acres to the US government. The land became a national park in 1956, and over the years the government added a couple of thousand more acres. Today Virgin Islands National Park covers two-thirds of the island, plus 5650 acres underwater.

Among the attractions are the Cinnamon Bay Campground and the underwater snorkeling trail at Trunk Bay. Beaches, including Francis Bay, Hawksnest Bay and Salt Pond Bay, are prime for lounging, swimming and sea turtle encounters. The Annaberg Sugar Mill Ruins and Reef Bay petroglyphs are also intriguing draws.

### Park Visitors Center

(☎340-776-6201; www.nps.gov/viis/parkmgmt/index.htm; ◷8am-4:30pm) The park visitors center sits on the dock across from the Mongoose Junction shopping arcade in Cruz Bay. It's an essential first stop to obtain free guides on hiking trails, snorkeling spots, bird-watching lists and schedules of daily ranger-led activities, such as the Reef Bay Hike.

### Flora & Fauna

More than 30 species of tropical birds, including the bananaquit (or 'yellow bird', the official bird of the Virgin Islands), hummingbirds and smooth-billed ani, nest in the park. Lizards such as the green iguana and gecko, hawksbill turtles and an assortment of feral animals and introduced species inhabit the park. Reef fish bring the island alive below the water.

Largely regenerated after 18th-century logging and clearing, the island flora is a mix of introduced species and native plants like the bay rum tree, whose aromatic leaves were a principal ingredient in the Virgin Islands' cologne industry. Another curious native plant is the night-blooming cereus; its vanilla scent attracts bats and moths to

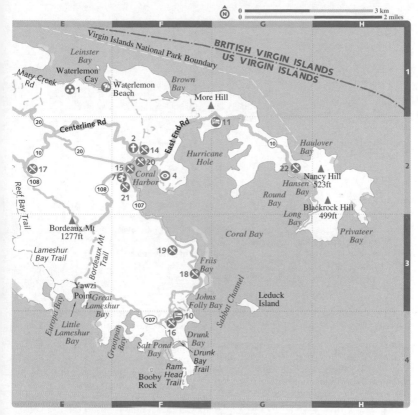

pollinate it by starlight. The South Shore and East End are magnificent tropical dry forest; the Uplands and West End get more rain.

*Volunteering Programs*
(☺8am-1pm Tue & Thu, Nov-Apr) A great way to give back to the park is by volunteering for trail or beach clean-ups; meet at the maintenance parking lot (it's well marked) by the visitors center. Clean-ups also take place at Maho Bay and Cinnamon Bay beaches during the same time frame on Thursdays.

**The Battery**                    HISTORICAL BUILDING
On the small peninsula to the left of the ferry dock stands a large Georgian building, rising on the foundation of an 18th-century fort that the Danes built to protect the island. Today, the battery houses government offices and is also the residence the governor uses when visiting St John.

## 🏖 Beaches

Your real selection starts about 1 mile north of town on the North Shore; see p98 for details.

**Frank Bay (Cruz Bay Beach)** ACTIVITIES BEACH
True, the beach hardly compares to those on the North Shore, but it's an easy walk from town and a pretty place to watch the sun set. There's decent snorkeling off the point near the desalination plant. To avoid the coral, enter the water at the beach's less-rocky south end, near the pipes that go to the plant. Be careful of speedboats and the wake from passing ferries.

To get here, head south of town past Wharfside Village and the Gallows Point Resort and down the hill. Along the road, you will see a thin beach with a few coconut palms. Beach houses line the other side of the street, and the island's desalination plant chugs along at the far end of the beach. There's also an open-air restaurant cooking up traditional West Indian fare at the south end.

**Great Cruz Bay**                    RESORT BEACH
(Map p86) Broad but short, Great Cruz Bay fronts the Westin Resort. The water is calm and great for swimming; it's not so great for snorkeling due to cloudiness. Non-resort guests are welcome to use the beach and its water-sport rentals, restaurants and bar by the pool, though the lounge chairs are for guests only. The beach is about 1.5 hilly miles south of Cruz Bay via Rte 104 (Southside Rd); look for the Westin sign and park in the resort lot.

## ⚡ Activities

### Diving & Snorkeling
St John has cool dive sites, all of which are accessed by boat, including wreck dives on the *General Rogers* and RMS *Rhone*. A two-tank trip including gear costs around $95 (about $160 to the *Rhone*, plus a $25 British Virgin Islands customs fee). The following shops in Cruz Bay also offer dive certification, as well as snorkel-gear rental ($8 to $10 per day for a full set) and snorkeling boat trips (half/full day including gear around $65/125) that cruise to offshore reefs by St John. They arrange longer trips that go to the BVI (passport required), too.

**Low Key Watersports** (☎340-693-8999 www.divelowkey.com; Wharfside Village; ⊗8am-6pm) This is a great dive-training facility and has some of the most experienced instructors in the islands. It offers wreck dives to the *General Rogers* and the RMS *Rhone,* as well as night dives and dive packages. It also has dinghy rentals and powerboat rentals. Trips to the BVI go to either the Baths ($135 plus customs fee) or Jost Van Dyke ($110 plus customs fee).

**Cruz Bay Watersports** (☎340-776-6234; www.divestjohn.com; Lumberyard; ⊗8am-6pm) It's located behind the Lumberyard, with another outlet at the Westin Resort. The half-day snorkel trips visit two different cays ($60 per person). Full-day trips go to Jost Van Dyke ($99, plus $25 BVI customs fee) or the Baths on Virgin Gorda ($130, plus $25 customs fee). These folk likewise rent dinghies.

### Kayaking
Even though some of these guided paddling expeditions do not depart from Cruz Bay, we're listing them here so you can see the island's best options at a glance.

**Arawak Expeditions** (☎340-693-8312, 800-238-8687; www.arawakexp.com; Mongoose Junction; half/full day tours $65/110) Offers tours that depart from Cruz Bay and paddle over to Henley Cay and Lovango Cay for snorkeling; you must supply your own snorkel gear.

**Hidden Reef Eco-Tours** (Map p86; ☑877-529-2575; www.hiddenreefecotours.com; 3hr/5hr tours $65/115) Departs from Haulover Bay at the island's more remote East End; snorkel gear is included. Also offers night paddles.

**VI Eco-Tours** (Map p86; ☑340-779-2155, 877-845-2925; www.viecotours.com; 3hr tours $99) Offers a tour that combines paddling with snorkeling and hiking around Caneel Bay, and another tour that includes photography lessons with a paddling-snorkeling trip at Coral Bay on the East End.

### Boat Trips

Given St John's proximity to the BVI, many trips jump the border, though it still involves going through customs (and paying around $25 in extra fees). For a nice sunset sail, where you swap snorkeling gear for champagne and a cheese tray, head out on **Wayward Sailor** (☑340-473-9705; www.waywardsailor.net; 2-hour trip $65), a classic 30-foot sloop.

If you want to drive yourself, try:

**Low Key Watersports** (☑340-693-8999; www.divelowkey.com; Wharfside Village) This dive operator also has dinghy rentals and powerboat rentals (without/with captain from $470/525).

**Cruz Bay Watersports** (☑340-776-6234; www.divestjohn.com; Lumberyard) The dive operator has dinghy rentals ($150 per day).

**Ocean Runner Powerboat Rentals** (☑340-693-8809; www.oceanrunnerusvi.com;

Wharfside Village) On the beach at Wharfside Village, it rents larger speedboats.

### Hiking

The Lind Point and Caneel Hill Trails are the main ones accessible from Cruz Bay. For trail details, see the 'These Trails Are Made for Walking' boxed text, p103.

Park rangers provide guided walks several days per week. Check with the **visitors center** (www.nps.gov/viis) for the schedule.

The nonprofit group **Friends of the Virgin Islands National Park** (www.friendsvinp. org) also provides occasional guided hiking trips around the island. It offers a slew of other activities, too, including sailing and snorkel trips, cooking, painting, jewelry-making and West African drumming workshops. Activities occur two or three times weekly; costs range from $25 to $85.

### Cycling

Kayak operator **Arawak Expeditions** (☑340-693-8312, 800-238-8687; www.arawakexp. com; Mongoose Junction; half/full day $50/90) also provides guided cycling tours of remote areas of the national park, with swimming breaks at the beach built in.

### Fishing

For information on casting a line, see the St Thomas chapter. The boats listed there will arrange to meet you on St John.

## ☞ Tours

The street in front of the Cruz Bay ferry dock swarms with cabs offering island tours. A two-hour circuit of the island costs $50 for one passenger; it's $25 each for two or more.

---

## ST JOHN IN...

### One Day

Let's set our priorities: beach, hike, happy hour. Luckily, the island is filled with beach/hike combos. The low-key option is to take the **Lind Point Trail**, which departs around Cruz Bay from the ferry dock, and walk to secluded **Honeymoon Beach**. For more pizzazz, grab a cab to **Cinnamon Bay** for windsurfing, paddleboarding and trails to sugar mill ruins. Hoist a happy-hour beverage back in Cruz Bay at **Woody's** or **Joe's Rum Shack**. Soak it up with dinner at **Rhumb Lines** or **Lime Inn**.

### Two Days

Devote the day to a favorite activity: go hiking with a national park ranger, diving on a shipwreck or kayaking along coastal reefs. Tour operators can set you up. DIY types can rent a 4WD and head to **Coral Bay** and the South Shore for trekking, snorkeling and dancing at **Skinny Legs**.

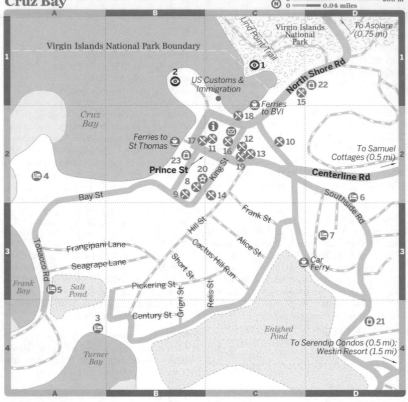

## 🛏 Sleeping

St John's accommodations appeal to two groups: one group is upper-middle-class vacationers fond of villas and resorts, the other adventure travelers keen on camping and ecotourism (for which they must head to the North Shore). There's not much in the middle range. Properties add an 8% hotel tax to your bill, and many also charge a 10% service fee (sometimes called an 'energy surcharge') on top.

**TOP CHOICE St John Inn** INN **$$**
(☑340-693-8688, 800-666-7688; www.stjohn inn.com; r incl breakfast $175-225; ❄🤶❄) Located near competitor the Tamarind Inn (from which it's a step up in value), the St John Inn has rooms decked out with tiled floors, handcrafted pine furniture and iron beds. Many also have water views or a kitchen. A homey atmosphere pervades, as guests grill fresh fish on the communal barbecue,

laze on the sun deck or dip in the small pool. It's located off Rte 104 (Southside Rd), down a quiet side road that leads to Enighed Pond.

**Garden by the Sea B&B** B&B **$$**
(☑340-779-4731; www.gardenbythesea.com; r incl breakfast $250-275; ❄🤶) Fans of B&Bs swoon over this place. The owners live on site and have splashed the three rooms in bright hues of sea green, lavender and blueberry, each with a sturdy, four-post canopy bed and private bathroom. Rid your mind of luxury – it's more about good, honest comfort here. Solar panels provide the electricity. They serve the hot breakfast on the veranda, where birds flit by from the nearby salt pond. The B&B is located a block and a half from Frank Bay beach, and is an easy 10-minute walk into town. Cash or traveler's checks only.

**Samuel Cottages** COTTAGES **$$**
(✆340-776-6643; www.samuelcottages.com; 4-person apt $125; ❊) These three peach-colored cottages are a stiff 10-minute walk uphill from the ferry dock, but you'll be hard-pressed to beat the value. They're sort of like state park cabins – nothing fancy, but clean and spacious enough, with a fully equipped kitchen and deck for sitting and contemplating how much cash you're saving. A $25 per night surcharge applies for stays of three nights or less.

**Inn at Tamarind Court** INN **$$**
(✆340-776-6378, 800-221-1637; www.innattamarindcourt.com; s/d/q $75/148/240; ❊❊) The rooms are small, thin-walled and lack frills such as private decks and water views, but Tamarind Inn does try hard with its friendly staff, bamboo-and-tiki decor and jumpin' courtyard bar-restaurant. A separate building holds six single rooms sharing two bathrooms. The central location and economical rates makes Tamarind popular with budget travelers. It's located along busy Rte 104 (aka Southside Rd), a short walk from the town center. The free wi-fi is available in the courtyard only (no in-room access).

**Serendip Condos** APARTMENTS **$$**
(✆340-776-6646, 888-800-6445; www.serendipstjohn.com; apt $225-295; ❊❊❊) On the hill above Cruz Bay, Serendip offers a lot for a moderate price. But you must have transportation, or not mind the 0.75-mile hike along Rte 104 (Southside Rd) to town. There are 10 studios and one-bedroom units in three-story concrete buildings. Each unit has a private balcony with sea view, a full kitchen, TV, wi-fi and beach chairs and a cooler you can take to the beach. Furnishings have a Pier 1 Imports flare. The on-site laundry facilities are handy. Prices and the seven-day stay requirement may be negotiable if you call at the last minute and there is space available.

**Westin Resort** HOTEL **$$$**
(✆340-693-8000, 800-808-5020; www.westinresortstjohn.com; r from $650; ❊@❊❊❊) The 321-room Westin is St John's biggest property by far, and it has all the hallmarks of a

**LOCAL KNOWLEDGE**

## DON NEAR: INTERPRETIVE RANGER

Near has worked at Virgin Islands National Park for 26 years.

### Best trails for beginners

The Peace Hill Trail (p103) goes to an old windmill with panoramic views. The Cinnamon Bay Loop Trail (p103) circles on a gentle grade through a bay rum forest, starting and ending at sugar factory ruins.

### Best trails for experienced hikers

The Reef Bay Trail (p103) has mill ruins and a side trip to pre-Columbian petroglyphs. The 0.7-mile Tektite Trail climbs to cliffs overlooking a 1970s underwater laboratory. It's on Cabritte Horn Point, a remote South Shore peninsula between Grootpan and Great Lameshur Bays.

### Best snorkel spot for beginners

Maho Point, from the end of Maho Bay Beach (p99), is a short swim in relatively shallow water where you'll see good quantities and diversity of fish.

### Best spots for experienced snorkelers

Waterlemon Cay (p100) for the extensive corals, numerous fish and frequent turtles. Yawzi Point (p104) affords excellent snorkeling above canyons formed by large boulders and ridges.

### Best spots to snorkel with sea turtles

Waterlemon, Francis and Maho Bays, especially early in the morning or late afternoon.

### If you only have one day at the park

Beach it. Go snorkeling and hiking. All three can be experienced at many locations, including Honeymoon and Salomon Beaches, Cinnamon Bay, Francis Bay, Salt Pond Bay and Lameshur Bays.

contemporary five-star resort: a quarter-acre pool, a palm-shaded beach on Great Cruz Bay, a fitness center, spa, lit tennis courts and four restaurants. You even get a 'boat butler' to help arrange your water sports. Guests can choose between the cedar-roof villas at seaside or the lower-priced condo units on the hill across the road. Rooms feature all the first-class amenities, private decks and contemporary furnishings, but no cooking facilities. The resort caters for kids as well, with a program of supervised art and recreation activities. The Westin is 1.5 miles south of Cruz Bay via Rte 104 (Southside Rd), so you'll need wheels to get to town.

**Coconut Coast Villas** APARTMENTS **$$$**
(☏340-693-9100, 800-858-7989; www.coconut coast.com; apt from $289; ✳🛜🏊) The nine units in this compound, including studios and townhouses, stand right on the cobblestone beach at Turner Bay. Each villa comes with local art, a kitchen, private deck and

wi-fi. There's a communal swimming pool, hot tub and barbecue grill. Cruz Bay is a 10-minute walk over the hill. Four-night minimum stay required.

**Gallows Point Resort** HOTEL **$$$**
(☏340-776-6434, 800-323-7229; www.gallows pointresort.com; r $495-575; ✳@🛜🏊) It stands out for being small (only 15 suites), independently owned and a three-minute walk from the shops, restaurants and nightlife in town. The suites are set amid lushly landscaped grounds, and each has a full kitchen, a private deck, free wi-fi and French doors that open onto water views. The beach isn't that great, but the setting overall is pretty dang awesome.

### Rental Accommodations

St John has loads of privately owned condos and villas. These rentals can be a reasonable option, especially if you're accommodating more than two people. One-, two- and three-

## CRUISE SHIP CROWDS

St Thomas' cruise ship traffic spills over to St John. Many passengers make a quick trip over when they're in port, which can impact St John's car rental capacity and beach crowds (especially at Trunk Bay). Tuesdays and Wednesdays typically see the most cruise traffic. Check **VI Now** (www.vinow.com) for the daily ship schedule to know what to expect during your visit.

bedroom properties are all common. Most require a week-long stay in high season. A typical one-bedroom villa costs $1600 to $2700 per week. To be near Cruz Bay, look for listings in the Chocolate Hole or Great Cruz Bay areas. In addition to **VRBO** (www.vrbo.com), browse offerings from the following St John-focused companies:

**Carefree Get-Aways** (☑340-779-4070, 888-643-6002; www.carefreegetaways.com)

**Caribbean Villas** (☑340-776-6152, 800-338-0987; www.caribbeanvilla.com) Has Tortola rentals, too.

**Catered To** (☑340-776-6641, 800-424-6641; www.cateredto.com)

## Eating

Cruz Bay offers the traveler an unexpected range of distinctive eateries. They are all within an easy walk of each other, which makes window-shopping for a place to eat one of the joys of dining out on St John. Because of the easy and frequent ferry service between St Thomas and St John, a lot of people from St Thomas come to Cruz Bay for a night of restaurant- and bar-hopping.

The road that fronts the BVI ferry dock hosts several stalls that sell gingery bush tea in the morning and fruit smoothies in the afternoon.

**TOP CHOICE Jake's**     BREAKFAST, BURGERS **$$**
(☑340-777-7115; Lumberyard; mains $10-17; ⊙7am-4am) Jake's will fill your belly no matter what time you roll out of bed. All-day breakfast is its forte, including well-stuffed omelets, crispy home fries (with Sriracha hot sauce as a dipping condiment) and strong coffee. Ceiling fans whir, newspapers rustle and reggae drifts from the speakers...then the couple next to you orders a triple shot of

Jack Daniel's to accompany their pancakes! Jake's is that kind of place. The open-air, 24-seat cafe is up the hill across from the BVI ferry dock, on the second floor, with views of the busy harbor scene.

**Shela's Pot**     WEST INDIAN **$$**
(cnr Prince St & Strand St; mains $10-15; ⊙lunch Tue-Sat) This is home cookin' where the locals go. Shela opens around noon when the fisherfolk return with the daily catch. Then she takes the shrimp, conch, fish and chicken, stirs them up in her big pots, and scoops them into takeaway boxes along with side dishes like mashed sweet potato, fried plantains and mac and cheese. Dig in at the shaded picnic tables. Shela is in a small shack across from the St Thomas ferry landing; look for the spot where all the taxi drivers are hanging out. Cash only.

**Rhumb Lines**     ASIAN FUSION **$$**
(☑340-776-0303; www.rhumblinesstjohn.com; Meada's Plaza; mains $16-30; ⊙dinner Wed-Mon; ☑) Tucked in a lush courtyard, this little restaurant has superb salads, sandwiches and fresh, healthy tropical cuisine served by happy, friendly hippies. Try selections from the 'pu pu' menu, a mix of tapas-like treats. There's air-conditioned indoor seating, or outdoor seating under palms and umbrellas.

**Joe's Diner**     BREAKFAST **$**
(☑340-777-7115; cnr Prince St & King St; mains $5-10; ⊙6am-6pm) This hole-in-the-wall, with about six street-side tables, is a Cruz Bay institution. It's a favorite place for locals and travelers to catch a fast bite, especially at breakfast. You will see a steady queue of folks lined up at the window after 7am ordering juices, coffees, beers, bagels or egg sandwiches to start their day. Joe's percolates with a wealth of island gossip, and there are local papers for news junkies.

**DON'T MISS**

## WEST INDIAN FOOD

Johnnycakes, garlic chicken, conch fritters, pigeon peas and rice – hungry yet? Get in line for the home cookin' these ladies stir up at their eateries:

» Vie's Snack Shack (p106)
» Shela's Pot
» Sweet Plantains (p106)
» Miss Lucy's (p106)

**Lime Inn**  SEAFOOD **$$**
(☎340-776-6425; www.limeinn.com; King St;
mains $20-30; ☺lunch Mon-Fri, dinner Mon-Sat)
Lime Inn is a travelers' favorite for quality
cuisine, ambience and service at moderate
prices. Owner Rich Mayer has filled his ter-
race restaurant with a mix of plants, wicker
and tropical fabrics and hired some of the
friendliest waitstaff in town. The New Eng-
land clam chowder and the shrimp dijon get
rave reviews. Reservations are a good idea.

**Morgan's Mango**  CARIBBEAN **$$**
(☎340-693-8141; www.morgansmango.com; Mon-
goose Junction; mains $15-28; ☺dinner) Take in
a view of the harbor while dining on imaginative Caribbean recipes for dishes such as
Haitian voodoo snapper or Cuban citrus
chicken. The owners often bring in live
acoustic acts (usually on Tuesday and Friday), making Morgan's a good choice for a
fun or romantic night out.

**Uncle Joe's BBQ**  BARBECUE **$$**
(☎340-693-8806; mains $10-14; ☺lunch & dinner)
Locals and visitors go wild, tearing into the
barbecue chicken, ribs and corn on the cob
at this open-air restaurant across from the
post office. The chef grills the meats outside,
perfuming the entire harbor-front with their
tangy goodness. Cash only.

**La Tapa**  MEDITERRANEAN **$$$**
(☎340-693-7755; www.latapastjohn.com; small
plates $11-18, mains $35-41; ☺dinner) Next door
to Woody's and across the street from First-
Bank, La Tapa has the look and smell of a
sangria well you may have visited in Ibiza
or Mallorca. The menu and wine list change
daily, but expect some sort of paella and
maybe grilled langostinos with chipotle-
lime aioli and organic greens grown on the
island. Reservations are essential.

**Fish Trap**  SEAFOOD **$$**
(☎340-693-9994; www.thefishtrap.com; Raintree
Court; mains $15-32; ☺dinner Tue-Sun) The Fish
Trap has been a popular travelers' stop for
years for its fish, shellfish and pastas. The
restaurant stands on a sheltered deck. Con-
sider the fish chowder or the vegetarian pri-
mavera pasta with a garlic Parmesan sauce
over fettuccine. Lighter appetites can opt for
the fish-and-chips basket.

**Asolare**  ASIAN FUSION **$$$**
(☎340-779-4747; Estate Lindholm; mains $30-45;
☺dinner) Perched on a hill overlooking Cruz
Bay, Asolare offers the most exotic view and

cuisine on St John – it's the place people go
for a romantic splurge. The chef constantly
rotates menu items, frequently drawn from
the Pacific Rim, such as Kampuchea shrimp
ravioli and Indochine bouillabaisse. It's a
short drive north of town; take North Shore
Rd and look for Asolare's sign pointing left.
You'll need reservations.

**Woody's Seafood Saloon**  SEAFOOD **$$**
(☎340-779-4625; www.woodysseafood.com; mains
$8-17; ☺lunch & dinner) A block and a half up
the road from the ferry dock, Woody's cheap
beer is legendary. While lots of folks show
up at the little place just to whoop it up with
fellow tanned bodies, you can actually get
some reasonable pub food, such as grilled
fish or corn-crusted scallops.

**Inn at Tamarind Court
Restaurant**  INTERNATIONAL **$$**
(☎340-776-6378; www.innattamarindcourt.com;
Southside Rd; breakfast $5-9, dinner mains $10-19;
☺breakfast & dinner, closed Sat eve) Each night
brings a different-themed menu to this
jovial courtyard eatery. Monday is for Greek
dishes, Tuesday and Thursday are Mexican
food, Wednesday is bistro night, and Friday
is for chowing down on prime rib. Fruit-
filled pancakes, omelets and French toast fill
breakfast plates.

**Da Livio**  ITALIAN **$$**
(☎340-779-8900; King St; mains $17-32; ☺dinner
Mon-Sat) Fork into authentic northern Ital-
ian food lovingly cooked by a chef-transplant
from the motherland. The staff make all the
pasta, gnocchi and bread from scratch, and
it goes down nicely with the hearty wines.
Corks dot the ceiling, and the black-and-
white decor gives the trattoria a sleek-casual
ambiance.

**Sun Dog Cafe**  CAFE **$$**
(☎340-693-8340; www.sundogcafe.com; Mongoose
Junction; mains $10-20; ☺lunch daily, dinner Mon-Fri)
Little Sun Dog serves an eclectic menu that
ranges from fish tacos to spinach quesadillas to pulled-pork sandwiches. It's an odd set
up, with tables sprinkled in the courtyard of
the Mongoose Junction mall, but the myriad
ex-pats chomping down don't seem to mind.
Wednesday night is a local musician open-
jam session.

**Mojo Cafe**  CAFE **$**
(☎340-776-8399; Wharfside Village; mains $7-14;
☺breakfast, lunch & dinner) Mojo is a good
stop for breakfast or lunch. The tiny kitchen

cranks out American fare such as egg sandwiches, burgers and turkey clubs. Eat at the handful of outdoor tables, or order as takeaway and walk a few steps to the beach for a picnic. Cash only.

### JJ's Texas Coast Cafe TEX-MEX $

(☑340-776-6908; mains $7-14; ⊘breakfast & lunch) The town's party animals often rejoin the world here to munch on steak and eggs or the breakfast burrito after a night of reggae and calypso.

### Happy Fish JAPANESE $$

(☑340-776-1717; Marketplace Bldg; mains $10-20; ⊘lunch & dinner) Happy Fish slices the island's only sushi. Many city slickers find it's not quite the quality they get at home, but it'll do. Sit at the eight tables or so sprinkled around the room, at the sushi bar, or do what most folks do – carry out.

### ZoZo's ITALIAN $$$

(☑340-693-9200; www.zozos.net; Gallows Point Resort; mains $35-40; ⊘dinner Mon-Sat) ZoZo's plates high-end northern Italian fare, like osso bucco (veal shank simmered in red wine, tomato and veal stock) and shrimp on white truffle risotto, accompanied by million-dollar views.

## 🍷 Drinking

Most places stay open until 2am on Friday and Saturday, and until 1am the rest of the week.

### Woody's Seafood Saloon BAR

(www.woodysseafood.com; ⊘from 11am) St John's daily party starts at Woody's at 3pm, when the price on domestic beers drops precipitously. By 4pm the crowd in this tiny place has spilled over onto the street. Bartenders pass beers out a street-side window. Meanwhile, the crowd basks in the glow of the tropical sun and listens to The Rolling Stones or Merle Haggard blasting from the sound system. Over the course of the night, the gang ebbs and flows, but by 11pm, Woody's has a crowd inside and out. The result is part frat party, part college reunion. And while you probably won't meet the love of your life at Woody's, you may well meet somebody to love.

### Joe's Rum Hut BAR

(Wharfside Village; ⊘from 11am) Around 11am, a bartender materializes with rum and a whopping bowl of limes at this beachfront boozer. After that, it's all about sitting at the open-air counter, clinking the ice in your

---

**DON'T MISS**

## ST JOHN'S CLASSIC CAFES & BARS

Known to sailors and beach bums far and wide for a good-time scene:

» **Woody's Seafood Saloon** The party-in-the-street joint to ring in happy hour.

» **Joe's Diner** (p93) Coffee, eggs, newspapers and gossip to start the day off right.

» **Skinny Legs** (p107) Burgers, beer and dancing at Coral Bay's 'town hall'.

---

mojito and watching the boats bob in the bay out front. Grab a slice of pie at the adjoining pizza joint if hunger strikes. To find Joe's, head through the Wharfside Village mall in the opposite direction of the ferry dock; it's on the first floor fronting the water. It's a swell place to kill time before or after a ferry.

### Tap Room MICROBREWERY

(www.stjohnbrewers.com/taproom.html; Mongoose Junction; ⊘noon-9pm Mon-Sat, 2-9pm Sun; 🛜) St John Brewers taps its sunny, citrusy suds here (the actual brewing takes place stateside). Sip a flagship Mango Pale Ale, play some Trivial Pursuit with the cards on your table, or surf using the free wi-fi. They serve a small menu of pizzas and sandwiches, but you're welcome to bring in your own food, too. Alcohol-free options include house-made root beer, ginger beer and Green Flash energy drink. The aircon blows inside, or you can take your drink outdoors to the patio.

### Quiet Mon Pub PUB

(www.quietmon.com; ⊘12:30pm-4am; @🛜) Situated above La Tapa restaurant, this tchotchke-laden Irish pub is one of the few places you'll stay indoors (thanks to the air-con) and pound pints into the wee hours. The tables on the 2nd-floor deck make for the best people-watching in town because you can see the crowds flowing in and out of Woody's next door, as well as the neighboring gin joints. You can surf the web ($5 per half hour), and meet other travelers while checking email.

## ☆ Entertainment

Several bars and restaurants host bands throughout the week. Click the 'live music' link at **See St John** (www.seestjohn.com) for a daily schedule.

**Fred's Bar Disco & Restaurant** NIGHTCLUB
(King St; cover charge $10) Across the street from the Lime Inn, Fred's has been a gathering spot forever. This is the place to be if you crave reggae and calypso, or if you want to party with a mix of euphoric West Indians and continentals. Bands usually play Saturday; at time of research it was country music, but you never know who will take the stage.

**St John Film Society** CINEMA
(www.stjohnfilm.com) A group of local filmmakers and film enthusiasts screen free, Caribbean-focused art films and documentaries in Cruz Bay and Coral Bay. Check the website for times and places.

## Shopping
St John's shopping district is, to a large extent, Cruz Bay. Here you will find a collection of boutiques, galleries, studio shops and salons mostly located in two attractive shopping arcades. **Wharfside Village** is on the waterfront just to the south of the ferry dock. The larger **Mongoose Junction** is a place that looks like a collection of Italian palaces on the North Shore Rd near the national park visitors center. A third collection of shops is in the **Marketplace building**, on Southside Rd (aka Rte 104) about a 15-minute walk southeast from the ferry dock. Most shops have long hours, usually 10am to 8pm Monday to Saturday and to 6pm Sunday.

**Starfish Market** FOOD
(Marketplace Bldg; 7:30am-9pm) Self-caterers can head to this full-service supermarket that offers good produce and a deli. In a separate shop, across the hall from the main market's front door, you'll find a wide selection of beer, wine and cheese in the gourmet market.

**Papaya Cafe** BOOKSTORE
(Marketplace Bldg) The island's only true bookstore is stacked to the rafters with new and used tomes and local art. It doubles as a cafe, and makes a sturdy Vietnamese coffee.

**Friends of the Park Store** SOUVENIRS
(Mongoose Junction) Looking for paper made out of local donkey poo? Thought so. It's here, along with shelves of other ecofriendly wares, such as purses made out of aluminum-can pull tabs, and lots of local nature books. Proceeds go to Virgin Islands National Park.

**Bamboula** ACCESSORIES
(Mongoose Junction) Vibrant Bamboula sells all manner of Caribbean art, fabrics, crafts and furniture.

**St John Spice Company** SOUVENIRS
(Wharfside Village) It carries your requisite fiery Caribbean hot sauces, barbecue spice rubs and rum ball candies.

**Bougainvillea** CLOTHING
(Mongoose Junction) Upscale island shirts, dresses and straw hats fill the racks.

## Information
To find out about current events on the island, go to the bulletin board in front of Connections (corner of Prince St and King St), at the center of town.

**Internet Access**
There's free wi-fi in some of the popular drinking establishments. Also, if you sit in the park behind Connections, you can usually pick up free wi-fi from Computer Express, which makes its signal available to the public.
**Connections** (www.connectionsstjohn.com; cnr Prince St and King St; per 30min $5; 8:30am-5:30pm Mon-Sat) An all-purpose communications center where you can use the internet terminals, print, send packages etc.

**Media**
**See St John** (www.seestjohn.com) Excellent resource by local author Gerald Singer, with detailed hiking trail directions and beach guides.
**St John Source** (www.stjohnsource.com) Online local news source.
**St John Sun Times** (www.facebook.com/suntimesmag) Free biweekly magazine with restaurant and event listings.
**VI Now** (www.vinow.com/stjohn) The lowdown on beaches, ferry schedules, taxi rates and more.

**Medical Services**
**Myrah Keating Smith Community Health Center** (340-693-8900; 8am-8pm Mon-Fri) About 2 miles east of Cruz Bay on Centerline Rd, this is the place to come for routine medical attention.

**Money**
**FirstBank** Branch with ATM near Woody's Seafood Saloon.
**Scotiabank** Located at the edge of town in the Marketplace Building.

**Post**
**Post office** (340-779-4227) Across the street from the British Virgin Islands ferry dock.

Whether you are camping, hiking or driving on St John, it won't be long before you have a close encounter with the island's odd menagerie of feral animals. According to National Park Service estimates, 500 goats, 400 donkeys, 200 pigs and hundreds of cats roam the island, descendants of domestic animals abandoned to the jungle eons ago. White-tailed deer and mongooses are two other introduced species that multiplied in unexpected numbers.

Park rangers are most concerned with the goats and pigs, whose foraging wipes out underbrush and leaves hillsides prone to erosion. Many of the animals have grown adept at raiding garbage cans and food supplies in the camping areas, and the donkeys meandering on island roads pose a serious hazard to drivers.

Do not tempt these animals by offering them food or leaving food or garbage where they can get at it. And do not approach them for petting or taking a snapshot. While most have a live-and-let-live attitude and don't mind you stepping around them on the trails, they are all capable of aggression if provoked.

## Tourist Information

Most businesses offer free island maps.

**Visitors center** (⊘8am-4:30pm) A small building next to the post office with brochures and whatnot.

**US Customs & Immigration** (☑340-776-6741; ⊘8am-noon & 1-5pm) Adjoins the British Virgin Islands ferry dock. If you arrive on a ferry or on a yacht from the BVI, you must clear immigration here (typically a no-hassle process) before you head into town.

## North Shore

Life's a beach on the tranquil North Shore, where most of the national park's major attractions, trailheads and campgrounds lie. A rental car is the easiest way to see the area via North Shore Rd (Rte 20) and Centerline Rd (Rte 10), but taxis also will drop you at the beaches.

## ◎ Sights

FREE **Annaberg Sugar Mill Ruins** HISTORICAL SITE

(www.nps.gov/viis; North Shore Rd; ⊘9am-4pm) Part of the national park, these ruins near Leinster Bay at the far end of North Shore Rd are the most intact sugar plantation ruins in the Virgin Islands. A 30-minute, self-directed walking tour leads you through the slave quarters, village, windmill, horse mill, rum still and dungeon.

The schooner drawings on the dungeon wall may date back more than 100 years. Park experts offer **demonstrations** (⊘10am-2pm Tue-Fri) in traditional island baking, gardening, weaving and crafting.

When you're finished milling around, hop on the **Leinster Bay Trail** that starts near the picnic area and ends at, yep, Leinster Bay (see p98). It's a 1.6-mile round trip.

**Estate Catherineburg Sugar Mill** HISTORICAL SITE

(Centerline Rd; ⊘sunrise-sunset) In 1986 the National Park Service restored this atmospheric old windmill. It dates from the mid-18th century and is an excellent example of barrel-vaulting construction techniques. Just imagine the talent of the slave masons who built the tower and the lust for money that drove their masters. It's a quiet place with no restricted visiting hours, guards or tours.

**Cinnamon Bay Archaeological Dig** HISTORICAL SITE

(www.friendsvinparch.blogspot.com; ⊘9am-4pm) The beach at Cinnamon Bay Campground holds an excavation site where scientists have unearthed a Taíno presence that dates back 1000 years. The Taíno were a peaceful group of farmers and fishers, and the site is thought to be a chief's ceremonial temple. Workers also have dug up remnants of a plantation slave village that stood on the site a couple of centuries after the Taíno mysteriously disappeared. The plantation burned down during St John's 1733 slave revolt.

A small **museum** (admission free) displays some of the artifacts found. It's at the end of the road that leads to the beach, on the east side (the building's other half is the Beach Shop). The excavation site itself is a short distance beyond. You can ask at either place about volunteering at the dig. Time is of the essence, as erosion is eating away at the site, and artifacts are at risk of being washed away.

## Beaches

The North Shore holds St John's most popular patches of sand. Trunk and Cinnamon Bays are the amenity-laden tourist favorites. We've listed the following beaches starting from Cruz Bay and moving eastward. Expect to pay between $6 and $13 per person for a taxi to reach them. Vendors (on the beaches that have them) usually open around 8:30am and close around 4pm.

### Salomon Beach      SECLUDED BEACH

Salomon is the closest wild beach to Cruz Bay and one of the few you can walk to from town. To get here, follow the Lind Point Trail (see p103), which departs from behind the national park visitors center. After about 1 mile, the trail descends to this secluded beach. It's on national park land, where nude sunbathing is prohibited. Nevertheless, it is popular with nudists and gays, who slip into something when the 'Ranger call' echoes up the beach, announcing the arrival of a Park Service patrol. You will find good snorkeling at each end of the beach, but no facilities at Salomon.

### Honeymoon Beach      SECLUDED BEACH

If you follow the Lind Point trail from Salomon Beach past a pile of rocks, you reach Honeymoon Beach, a long thin strand. It has no facilities, other than shady sea-grape trees to hang your towel on. It's often empty and quiet – except when tour boats dinghy in big groups to soak up the scene from mid-morning to mid-afternoon. Snorkeling is good off the rocks to the west and from the end of Honeymoon east to Caneel Bay. For a shorter walk, drive to the Caneel Bay Resort and park in the visitors' lot ($10 fee), then follow the shoreline west away from the buildings.

### Caneel Bay      RESORT BEACH

This is the main beach in front of the dining terrace at the Caneel Bay Resort. The resort has seven beaches, but this is the one it permits visitors to use. It's a lovely place, with fair snorkeling off the east point. You must sign in at the guardhouse when you enter the resort property, and pay $10 if you're parking.

Travelers can use the hotel's restaurants and bars. Joggers sometimes come to the beach, then jog the resort grounds and trails before returning for a dip. Because the resort has so many beaches and the grounds are so expansive, all the beaches are tranquil. Beach chairs are for resort guests only.

### Hawksnest Bay      FAMILY BEACH

The bay here is dazzling to behold, a deep circular indentation between hills with a broken ring of sand on the fringe. Because the main beach lies right along North Shore Rd and is the closest public beach you can reach by car from Cruz Bay, it can get busy, particularly after school when young St Johnians come to cool off. On winter mornings, Hawksnest is at its quietest and shadiest.

There are changing facilities, picnic tables and barbecue pits. Snorkelers will find the reef just a few strokes off the central beach. If you prefer to be alone, swim around the rocks at the west end of the beach to a secluded strand tucked under a cliff. You can make a similar swim at the east end of the main beach to Oppenheimer's Beach.

### Oppenheimer's Beach      SECLUDED BEACH

Also called Little Hawksnest and Gibney's, this strand lies on the eastern edge of Hawksnest Bay. To get here, take the dirt road to the left just after you pass the public beach at Hawksnest (it'll be about 530 yards, or the third driveway). Go through the gate and down the driveway to reach the shore. This is not a National Park Service beach. The

---

## BEST BEACHES

» **Honeymoon Beach** An easy, mile-long trail from Cruz Bay drops you at this secluded beauty.

» **Cinnamon Bay** The island's longest beach also has the most going on: there's an archaeological dig, stand-up paddleboarding and trails through mill ruins – and that's just for starters.

» **Salt Pond Bay** (p104) A perfect blend of cool hikes, groovy beachcombing and turtle-and-squid snorkeling.

» **Maho Bay** A big sandy crescent kissed by shallow water that's good for families and snorkeling newbies.

WORTH A TRIP

## PEACE HILL

Pull over when you see the Peace Hill sign shortly after driving past Hawksnest Bay. If you're willing to walk about 200 yards you'll be rewarded with moody ruins of an old windmill and superb views out to sea. A statue of Jesus once 'lorded' over the hill, but Hurricane Marilyn in 1995 proved to be the stronger force. Look for the plaque marking his former post.

land and house on the property belonged to Dr Robert Oppenheimer, one of the inventors of the atomic bomb. His daughter committed suicide and left the land and beach house to the children of St John.

Longtime expats favor the beach because they can bring their dogs (illegal on park land). Islanders also use the beach for communal parties to benefit social and environmental causes. There's very limited parking.

### Jumbie Bay
SECLUDED BEACH

Jumbie is the word for ghost in the Creole dialect, and this beach east of Oppenheimer's has a plethora of ghost stories. Look for the parking lot on North Shore Rd that holds only three cars. From here, take the wooden stairs and a short trail down to the sand. The remote, compact location, lack of facilities and associated ghost stories keep crowds at bay. Snorkeling is best along a shallow reef on the beach's right side, though be careful on windy days when the water can be choppy.

While you are here, consider stories of how, during the revolt of 1733, rampaging slaves cut up the local plantation owners and stuffed them down a well. The murders were in retaliation against a slave master who allegedly buried slaves in the sand up to their necks on the beach and used the exposed heads as bowling pins.

### Trunk Bay
ACTIVITIES BEACH

(adult/child $4/free; ⊘8am-4pm) This long, gently arching beach is the most popular strand on the island and the only one to charge an admission fee. The beach has lifeguards, showers, toilets, picnic facilities, snorkel rental, a snack bar and taxi stand. No question, the sandy stretch is scenic, but it often gets packed. Everyone comes here

to swim the underwater snorkeling trail, which features plaques on the ocean bottom describing the local marine life. Experienced snorkelers will not be impressed by the murkiness or quality of what's on offer beneath the surface.

### Cinnamon Bay
ACTIVITIES BEACH

You can easily spend a day at this exposed sweeping cove. The mile-long beach – St John's biggest – is home to the Cinnamon Bay Campground and has showers, toilets, a restaurant, grocery store and taxi stand. It also offers a full slate of activities through its **Water Sports Center** (see p100). Two cool hiking trails cross the grounds (see p103), and there's an active archaeology dig site to poke around (see p97).

The one thing Cinnamon is not great for is snorkeling, since the area lost much of its underwater life in recent storms. Still, many visitors enjoy flippering around, and you can rent snorkel gear ($7 per day) at the Beach Shop, just east from the Water Sports Center.

A small island – Cinnamon Cay – that you can swim to for sunbathing floats offshore. Be careful during winter months, when wind and swells can roll in from the northeast.

### Maho Bay
SNORKELING BEACH

Don't confuse Maho Bay beach with the small beach servicing Stanley Selengut's eco-tent campground (see p100); that beach is Little Maho Bay and it's around the point to the east. Maho Bay beach stretches along North Shore Rd east of Cinnamon Bay. Come here for protected waters when other North Shore beaches are taking a beating from the northeasterly winds and swells in winter. The calm and shallow water makes it a popular place for families with young children. The snorkeling is over turtle-grass beds, where you might see hawksbill and green turtles feeding in the early morning. Alas, the sand fleas are brutal at Maho.

There are no facilities and no parking lot; just pull over at the side of the road and voilà – you're at the beach.

### Francis Bay
SECLUDED BEACH

A popular yacht anchorage because of the calm seas, this bay also boasts a long arch of broad sand around its fringe. There are bathrooms, picnic tables and barbecue facilities here, but few people. Francis Bay is a great beach for walking or embarking on a bird-rich trail hike, and don't be surprised if you run into a clutch of wild donkeys, goats or even a horse, which hang around to scavenge in the garbage cans. The southern end of the beach toward Maho provides good snorkeling in shallow water with lots of little silvery fish. The bay is also prime for sea turtle sightings.

To get here follow North Shore Rd (aka Rte 20) as it veers inland at Maho. After a short stretch you'll come to a fork in the road. Veer left, and continue left when you come to the shoreline road.

### Leinster Bay
SNORKELING BEACH

This bay adjoins the grounds of the Annaberg Sugar Mill ruins, and the beach has been named Waterlemon Beach after an island in the bay. To get here, park in the plantation's lot and follow the dirt road/trail around Leinster Bay. The sandy part of the beach is about 880 yards along the shore to the east.

To reach the best snorkeling, continue past the beach on the trail until you are adjacent to the offshore islet, Waterlemon Cay. If you are a strong swimmer, head out to the island and explore the cay's reef fringe. You will probably not be alone here – Leinster Bay is a popular anchorage for yachts. Dive operators bring snorkeling tours here as well, so watch out for moving boats. Turtles, spotted eagle rays, barracudas and nurse sharks swim in the waters. Some folks claim this is the best snorkeling on St John, but the East End is arguably better. Be aware the current can be quite strong, especially on the Tortola (northeast) side of the cay.

## 🏃 Activities

### Cinnamon Bay Water Sports Center
MULTI-SPORT

(Cinnamon Bay; ⏰8:30am-4:30pm) Situated at the campground's beach and stocked with a good selection of sailboats, windsurf boards, stand-up paddleboards and kayaks (each ranging from $20 to $35 per hour). Lessons cost around $65 per hour. Snorkeling gear ($7 per day) is available a few steps away at the Beach Shop.

### VI Snuba Excursions
SNUBA

(☎340-693-8063; www.visnuba.com; Trunk Bay; 1.5hr tours $65; ⏰11am & 1pm Mon-Fri, 11am Sat & Sun) Get underwater using special equipment that fuses snorkeling with scuba diving. No experience necessary; accessible to kids aged eight and older. Tours (including a short training session) depart from the Trunk Bay gift shop. Reserve in advance.

### VI Eco-Tours
KAYAKING

(☎340-779-2155, 877-845-2925; www.viecotours.com; Caneel Bay; 3hr tours $99; ⏰10am & 2pm) This operator combines paddling with snorkeling and hiking around Caneel Bay. Reserve in advance.

## 🛏 Sleeping

Travelers unenthused by big swanky resorts will love the two ecofriendly options here. Maho is more remote, quiet and regimented; Cinnamon is a bit creakier but easier to get around. Bring insect repellent for both.

### 🌿 Maho Bay Camps
ECO-TENTS $$

(☎340-776-6226, 800-392-9004; www.maho.org; tents $135; @🍴🛏) Stanley Selengut's popular, eco-sensitive tent resort lies 8 miles east of Cruz Bay on North Shore Rd. The complex offers 114 units spread up a sheer, forested hillside overlooking the water. Each 'tent' sits on a wooden platform that is propped up far off the ground, and surrounded by vegetation so thick it's like living in a tree house. To access the beach, other tents, the toilet/shower buildings or on-site outdoor restaurant and store, you follow a maze of boardwalks and stairs through the jungle. The hillside is steep and the complex vast, so be prepared for a lot of climbing.

The 16ft by 16ft tents look like canvas cottages with airy, screened walls. Each tent has a private deck, table and chairs, two twin beds, a futon mattress, propane stove, cooler, water container, cooking and eating utensils, towels and bedding. They're electrically equipped, with lights and fans. Barbecue grills are built along the boardwalks for communal use.

Maho's green philosophy includes water conservation: community toilets are low-flush, and solar-heated (frequently cold) showers have pull-chains for brief dousing. The resort also recycles glass and other trash into crafts sold in its Arts Center; guests can take part in classes or watch free nightly glass-blowing demonstrations. The beach offers water-sports rentals for snorkeling, sailing, windsurfing and kayaking.

While all of this sounds great, keep in mind the tents and bathroom facilities are very basic.

Now for the sad news: Maho sits on leased land, and the lease runs out in 2012. Everyone is bracing for the landowners to sell out to big developers, and Maho will cease to be after 30-plus years. At time of research, it was taking reservations only through May 2012. But the **Trust for Public Land** (www.tpl.org) is fighting hard to acquire the property; check the website for updates.

Mr Frett runs the official safari taxi ($9 per person) to Maho every other hour in sync with ferry arrivals. Look for him at the back of Cruz Bay's taxi stand, and hold on tight for Maho's insanely bumpy access road.

**Harmony Studios**                    APARTMENTS **$$**
(☑340-776-6226, 800-392-9004; www.maho.org; apt $225-250; @✿✕♿) For those who want to stay at Maho but prefer higher-grade amenities, these 12 multistory units pepper the hillside above the tent camps. Here, you get a private bath, kitchen and deck in an eco-sensitive building with solar-generated electricity, rainwater-collection and wind scoops on the roof for cooling. A lot of the construction materials come from recycled trash.

As with the Maho tents, be prepared for climbing lots of stairs up the hillside. And be prepared for the location's remoteness: other than the restaurant and commissary on site, there are no food and drink options nearby, cell phone service is patchy, and internet access at Maho's cyber-hut can be slow. Checkout procedures are similar to Maho: guests are required to strip their beds, take out their trash and clean their dishes to get their security deposit back.

**Cinnamon Bay Campground**   CAMPGROUND **$**
(☑340-776-6330, 800-539-9998; www.cinnamonbay.com; campsites/equipped tents $32/93, cottages $126-163; ⊙closed Sep) About 6 miles east of Cruz Bay on North Shore Rd, Cinnamon Bay Campground has close to 130 campsites in the national park. The setting is a mile-long crescent of sand at the base of forested hills. This operation is really a campers' village with a general store, snack bar and a restaurant. But the grounds are so expansive, and the vegetation so thick, that you have more privacy than you might expect at a place that often has 400 to 500 guests.

There are three accommodation options at Cinnamon Bay:

» **Cottages** are 15ft by 15ft concrete shelters with two screened sides, electric lights, a propane stove, cooking and eating utensils, a water container, ice chest and ceiling fan. Outside is a picnic table and charcoal grill. The cottages have four twin beds and may be equipped with two extra cots or a crib. You can get a beachfront, water view or forest location.

» **Equipped tents** are all 10ft by 14ft on a solid wood platform. Each tent comes with four cots, a propane lantern, propane stove, ice chest, water container, cooking and eating utensils. A charcoal grill and picnic table are outdoors. You get a change of bed linens here twice a week, just as you do with a cottage rental.

» **Bare sites**, for those who have their own equipment and want to rough it, fit one large tent or two small ones. Each spot has a picnic table and charcoal grill.

The best bets are using your own tent or the cottages; the equipped tents are a bit gloomy. All guests use the public toilet facilities and cold-water showers.

**Caneel Bay Resort**                    HOTEL **$$$**
(☑340-776-6111, 888-767-3966; www.caneelbay.com; r from $550; ✿@✿✕♿) For a sense of old-school casual elegance, Caneel Bay is still the reigning queen of USVI accommodations. Built in 1955 around the ruins of an old sugar plantation, the resort covers 170 acres of national park land. It's where folks such as Angelina Jolie and Brad Pitt come when they need seven beaches, 11 tennis courts and five restaurants, along with landscaped rolling hills, miles of hiking and jogging trails, forests and rocky promontories. Cars are restricted to a satellite parking lot, and guests travel by foot or golf cart. Only 166 guest quarters are spread around the property in units that are masked by the surrounding trees. Rooms are elegant with plantation-style furnishings from Indonesia, but without TVs or cooking facilities. It's a favorite of honeymooners and well-heeled families. Parking costs $10. Located 2 miles northeast of Cruz Bay via North Shore Rd.

## ✗ Eating

**Le Chateau de Bordeaux** BURGERS, SEAFOOD **$$**
(☑340-776-6611; Centerline Rd; lunch $10-20, dinner mains $29-36; ⊙lunch Mon-Sat, dinner Tue-Thu) Drive to the top of Bordeaux Mountain and munch well-made burgers, soups, sandwiches and grilled fish on the deck while sublime sea views unfurl around you. Lunch is the favorite meal here, or you can just pop in for a frozen daiquiri or cold beer. Dinner is by reservation only.

**T'ree Lizard Restaurant** BURGERS, SEAFOOD **$$**
(☑340-776-6330; Cinnamon Bay Campground; breakfast & lunch $7-10, dinner mains $15-22; ⊙breakfast, lunch & dinner) Cinnamon Bay Campground's casual restaurant dishes up

# THESE TRAILS ARE MADE FOR WALKING

St John's greatest gift to visitors (aside from the awesome snorkeling, feral donkeys, eco-camps and happy-hour booze) is its hiking trails. The national park maintains 20 paths, and any reasonably fit hiker can walk them safely without a local guide. The park visitors center provides trail details in the helpful free *Trail Guide for Safe Hiking* brochure. Uber-enthusiasts should also buy the **Trail Bandit map** (www.trailbandit.org; $4) that lists several additional footpaths; it's available at the park visitors center, Maho Bay Camps store or online. Perhaps the best resource of all, with free step-by-step directions for each trail, is **See St John** (www.seestjohn.com); click the 'hiking trails' link on the page's left side.

If you prefer guided hikes, the National Park Service sponsors several free ones, including birding expeditions and shore hikes. Its best-known offering is the **Reef Bay Hike** (☑340-776-6201, reservations ext 238; $21; ☺9:30am-3pm Mon & Thu year-round, plus Fri Dec-Apr). This begins at the Reef Bay trailhead, 4.75 miles from Cruz Bay on Centerline Rd. The hike is a 3-mile downhill trek through tropical forests, leading past petroglyphs and plantation ruins to a swimming beach at Reef Bay, where a boat runs you back to Cruz Bay (hence the fee). It's very popular, and the park recommends reserving at least two weeks in advance.

The various trails lead to ruins, archeological sites, mountain peaks and secluded shores. All have identifying signs at the trailheads. The following are some of our favorite treks (mileage is one way).

## North Shore Trails

**Lind Point Trail** (1.1 miles, moderate) This is one of the most accessible trails. It departs from behind the national park visitors center in Cruz Bay and moseys through cactus and dry forest, past the occasional donkey and bananaquit, to Honeymoon Beach. A scenic, 700-yard upper track goes to Lind Battery, once a British gun emplacement, 160ft above the sea. The lower track goes directly to the beach. If you don't want to hike back, you can walk onward to the Caneel Bay Resort and catch a taxi.

**Caneel Hill Trail** (2.4 miles, rugged) It links Cruz Bay with the Caneel Bay Resort entrance on North Shore Rd. The hike starts with an almost one-mile schlep to the top of Caneel Hill (719ft), where there's a viewing platform and vistas all the way to Puerto Rico. It then climbs further to the top of Margaret Hill (840ft) before making a steep descent through the forest to the coast.

**Peace Hill Trail** (170 yards, easy) It takes just 10 minutes to walk to the old windmill on this grassy promontory with eye-popping land and sea views. It's 2.8 miles from Cruz Bay, signposted off the North Shore Rd.

**Cinnamon Bay Loop Trail** (900 yards, easy) Pick up the trailhead a few yards east of the Cinnamon Bay Campground entrance road, and follow a shady trail among native tropical trees to the ruins of a sugar factory. Placards along the way identify relevant vegetation and explain local history. Takes about one hour.

**Cinnamon Bay Trail** (1.1 miles, rugged) No question about it, this hike through tropical wet forest on an old plantation road is a challenging hill climb (unless you walk it one way downhill from Centerline Rd). You join the trail 100 yards east

eggs and nutmeg-battered French toast for breakfast, standard burgers and wraps for lunch and a handful of mains such as jerk chicken, shrimp scampi and pasta primavera for dinner.

**Maho Pavilion Restaurant**   INTERNATIONAL **$$**
(☑340-776-6226; Maho Bay Camps; mains $17-25; ☺7:30-9:30am & 5:30-7:30pm) Maho Bay Camps' open-air restaurant is cafeteria style. Walk to the cashier, place your order from among the evening's four or so mains (like lasagna, grilled fish or Thai curry tofu), and pick it up when your name is called. Salad bar and iced tea are included. Diners bus their own tables after eating. Entertainment – usually an environmental presentation, live music or movie – begins at 7:30pm.

of the campground entrance and start your climb to the top of the island's spine, where the trail hits Centerline Rd. Serious trekkers continue east along the road for about a mile, where they join the Reef Bay Trail.

**Francis Bay Trail** (900 yards, easy) Pick up the path at the west end of the Mary Creek paved road, where an old stone sugar mill stands sentry. The trail follows the rim of a salt pond that usually harbors a good collection of wading birds. It continues through a mangrove forest before reaching the broad crescent beach at Francis Bay.

### South Shore Trails

**Reef Bay Trail** (2.2 miles, rugged) The most famous of all the island trails, it starts on Centerline Rd about 4.75 miles east of Cruz Bay and makes a steep descent around Bordeaux Mountain (1277ft), the highest point on St John. Along the way, you pass the ruins of four sugar plantations before reaching the South Shore at Reef Bay. Take the park's guided hike and you won't have to make the slog back up.

**Petroglyph Trail** (530 yards, moderate) This is a spur that veers west 1.5 miles down the Reef Bay Trail. It leads to waterfalls and mysterious rock carvings attributed to pre-Columbian Taíno people.

**Lameshur Bay Trail** (1.5 miles, moderate) If you want a sandy beach at the end or beginning of your assault on Bordeaux Mountain, follow this spur that breaks off the Reef Bay Trail at the Petroglyph Trail intersection and heads east. Near the base, another spur breaks off to the coral rubble beach on Europa Bay.

**Bordeaux Mountain Trail** (1.2 miles, rugged) This trail leaves from Little Lameshur Bay and climbs to an elevation of 1000ft, where it joins the dirt Bordeaux Mountain Rd that continues north, 1.7 miles to Centerline Rd. The vistas and the challenge of this trail make it well worthwhile.

**Yawzi Point Trail** (530 yards, moderate) It begins on the east side of Little Lameshur Bay Beach and winds through thorny scrub to isolated coves. Years ago people afflicted with yaws (a contagious skin lesion disease) had to live on this narrow peninsula, hence the name

**Drunk Bay Trail** (530 yards, easy) The trail leaves the south end of Salt Pond Bay Beach and follows the rim of the salt pond to the extremely wild and rocky beach that faces east to Sir Francis Drake Channel and the BVI. Swimming is dangerous here, as the trade-wind-driven seas pile up on this shore. The waves carry all manner of flotsam and jetsam, including wrecked yachts. Beachcombing here can be fascinating.

**Ram Head Trail** (1 mile, moderate) The trailhead is also at the south end of Salt Pond Bay Beach. You follow an exposed trail over switchbacks to the Ram Head, a promontory 200ft above the seas at the southernmost tip of St John, a grandly lonesome and windswept place.

# Coral Bay, East End & South Shore

Coral Bay, St John's second town, is really just a handful of shops, restaurants and pubs clustered around the 1733 hilltop Emmaus Moravian Church. Two hundred years ago, it was the largest settlement on the island. Known then as 'Crawl Bay', presumably because there were pens or 'crawls' for sea turtles here, the settlement owes its early good fortune to being the largest and best-protected harbor in the Virgin Islands. Today it serves as the gateway to the island's most remote beaches and coastal wilderness, ripe for hiking, snorkeling and eco-camping.

## SNORKELING ST JOHN

St John offers loads of snorkel hot spots accessible from shore. The park service publishes an oft-photocopied but useful brochure called *Where's the Best Snorkeling?*, which you can pick up at the park visitors center. You'll pretty much see the same fish, turtles and coral whether you swim on the north or south side of the island; the main difference is that it's warmer on the Caribbean south side versus the Atlantic north side. Gold stars go to the following:

» Salt Pond Bay
» Leinster Bay/Waterlemon Cay (p100)
» Francis Bay (p99)
» Yawzi Point

## ◉ Sights

**Emmaus Moravian Church**          CHURCH
(cnr Rtes 10 & 107; no tourist entry hours, but open for Sunday services) Built in 1783 as the second of two missions at Coral Bay, this large yellow church with its red roof is on the National Registry of Historic Places. It sits on land once known as Caroline Estate, the plantation where the 1733 slave revolt broke out, resulting in the murder of the judge who owned the plantation and his 12-year-old daughter.

The Moravians arrived on the island in the 1750s. Once Coral Bay managed to prosper again after the slave revolt, the Moravian missionaries bent to the single-minded purpose of ministering to the slaves and teaching them to read. This building was a cornerstone of that dedication and continues to serve descendants of those slaves today. The church is not normally open to visitors, but you can come to Sunday morning services. Contemporary parishioners call their congregation Bethany Moravian Church.

**Fort Berg**          HISTORICAL BUILDING
The ruins of this fort lie in the brush atop Fort Berg Hill on a peninsula that juts into Coral Bay. Danes built the fort in 1717 after Governor Erick Bridel seized the island from the British and fortified it with nine-pound cannons mounted on the ramparts. Slaves reduced the fort to rubble during the revolt of 1733. The English built another battery here during their occupation in 1807–15, and a few iron cannons remain. The fort is on private land; you can ask at Skinny Legs restaurant in Coral Bay about directions to the ruins and whether it is currently OK to intrude on private property.

## 🏝 Beaches

In addition to the beaches listed below, several others in the vicinity offer good snorkeling and privacy. If you love to swim with the fishes, consider getting your flippers on at Hansen Bay, Long Bay or Privateer Bay, as well.

**TOP CHOICE** **Salt Pond Bay**          ACTIVITIES BEACH
Strap on your hiking shoes and snorkel mask for this essential South Shore beach, located a few miles from town down Rte 107. You will see a parking lot at the top of the hill and a broad trail leading down to the beach (a 10-minute walk). The bay itself provides excellent snorkeling in calm waters; keep an eye out for turtles and squid. At the beach's south end, the **Ram Head Trail** takes off and rises to a windswept cliff jabbing out into the sea. The trek is a 2-mile round trip through rocky exposed terrain, so bring ample water and sun protection. The **Drunk Bay Trail**, a beachcomber's delight, also takes off from the beach. See p103 for details. The beach has no facilities except portable toilets. It's on the Vitran bus route if you don't have a car. Watch your valuables here.

**Great Lameshur Bay**
**& Little Lameshur Bay**          SECLUDED BEACH
You reach these secluded beaches by following the bumpy dirt Lameshur Rd (Jeeps only) along the South Shore from Salt Pond Bay. The first cove you hit is Great Lameshur Bay, a stony beach that will likely be deserted. Continue down the road less than 450 yards and you'll reach Little Lameshur Bay, with a wide, sandy apron, picnic facilities and toilets. Beginners can snorkel around the rocks off the beach's west side and see snappers and other fish. Experienced snor-

kelers can head along **Yawzi Point**, the peninsula that separates the two bays. The long swim to the tip pays off with views of an active reef and big, coral-crusted rocks. Or walk the Yawzi Point Trail (p103) to the beach that pops up en route via the spur path (about 450 yards), and you won't have to swim as far.

### Haulover Bay
SNORKELING BEACH

You have to hike into this beach via a trail off hilly East End Rd, about 3 miles east of Coral Bay. The beach is gravelly and exposed, and the swells can make for a rough entry and cloudy visibility. But if you come on a calm day, you will find fish-rich snorkeling on the reef and coral heads – with no one else in sight and a superb view of the BVI to the east.

## 🏃 Activities

### Carolina Corral
HORSEBACK RIDING

(📞340-693-5778; www.carolinacorral.vi; Rte 107; rides adult/child $75/65; ⏰10am & 3pm Mon-Sat) Horseback-riding enthusiasts can saddle up a trusty steed or donkey with Carolina Corral for a 1½-hour guided jaunt on mountain roads and trails. The morning excursion is an easier one-hour ride. Call to make reservations, and be prepared for trips to depart on 'island time' (it can be a bit disorganized here).

### Crabby's Watersports
KAYAKING

(📞340-714 2415; www.crabbyswatersports.com; Rte 107; kayak per half/full day $30/45) Crabby's provides all kinds of gear on Coral Bay's waterfront next to Coccoloba Plaza. For kayaking, ask if they'll drop you off at Hurricane Hole so you'll have an easier paddle downwind back to the bay.

## 🛏 Sleeping

### Concordia Eco-Tents
ECO-TENTS $$

(📞340-693-5855, 800-392-9004; www.maho.org; tents $155-185, apt $160-250; ☒) On a cliff above Drunk Bay, Concordia's 'tents' are probably the most imaginative and environmentally sensitive accommodations on the island. Maho Bay Camps' developer, Stanley Selengut, has taken his eco-tent concept and pumped it up. Concordia has more than 25 'tent-cottages' on stilts, strung together by boardwalks up the steep hillside like at Maho. Only here, each 16ft by 16ft unit has a 2nd-floor loft and a private bathroom, with composting toilet and solar-

heated shower (still a bit chilly). The tents' fans and lights run on a 12-volt solar-generated electrical system, and the shower water comes from a rain-collection cistern under the tent. A kitchen (small refrigerator and two-burner propane stove) and sea view (more dramatic than at Maho) complete the package.

The resort has its own cafe, activities center for yoga and water sports, and swimming pool. It's a half-mile walk to the beach at Salt Pond Bay. Located about 2.5 miles south of Coral Bay, Concordia is even more quiet and isolated than Maho. You'll likely want a rental car, though patient souls can access it by public bus.

The Concordia camp also offers several studio apartments with upgraded amenities. These are, in essence, condos with lots of space, a full kitchen and stellar views. As with the eco-tents, you'll be walking up and down oodles of stairs to access the cafe, pool and other facilities.

### Estate Zootenvaal
APARTMENTS $$$

(📞340-776-6321; www.estatezootenvaal.com; Rte 10; apt $275-550) Robin Clair manages these four units overlooking a large crescent cove near the shores of Hurricane Hole. You can get one- or two-bedroom units perched on the hillside overlooking the water. Each unit has a full kitchen, deck and a decor splashed with soft tropical colors. Fans cool the rooms. There is no air con, telephone or TV. Cash only. The estate is located a short drive east of town via Rte 10 (East End Rd).

### Vie's Campground
CAMPGROUND $

(📞340-693-5033; Rte 10; campsites $35) Across the road from Vie's Snack Shack, a place of legendary West Indian cooking, Vie and her family have a handful of camping spots on a short but wide strand of beach. Some of the sites feature shade trees; others are out in the sun. An outhouse and solar shower on the premises are the only facilities. Make your reservations early for high season. The campground is located east of town; take Rte 10 (East End Rd) to Hansen Bay. You'll need a car to get here. Cash only.

## ✕ Eating

### TOP CHOICE ⌐ Donkey Diner
BREAKFAST $$

(📞340-693-5240; www.donkeydiner.com; Rte 10; breakfast $7-12, pizzas $13-23; ⏰8am-noon daily, to 8pm Wed, Fri & Sun) It has – that's right – kick-ass food and baked goods. It's the breakfast place of a traveler's dreams – cheery, welcoming and reasonably priced for good-sized plates of pancakes, stuffed French toast, omelets and biscuits and gravy. Bloody Mary's, mimosas and bottomless cups of coffee accompany the fare. A few nights a week the chefs toss house-made dough and bake thin-crust, 16-inch pizzas; call ahead to ensure you procure one. The diner is across from Coral Bay's elementary school, a hop and a skip past the Moravian Church on Rte 10. Cash only.

### Skinny Legs · BURGERS $

(☎340-779-4982; www.skinnylegs.com; Rte 10; mains $8-13; ☺lunch & dinner) Salty sailors, bikini-clad transients and East End snowbirds mix it up at this open-air grill. Overlooking a small boatyard, it's not about the view, but the jovial clientele and lively bar scene. Burgers win the most raves, so open wide for a cheeseburger, or tuck into a grilled mahimahi sandwich. Skinny Legs lets the good times roll just past the fire station on Rte 10 (East End Rd) in Coral Bay.

### Vie's Snack Shack · WEST INDIAN $

(☎340-693-5033; Rte 10; mains $7-13; ☺10am-5pm Tue-Sat) Vie Mahabir opened this plywood-sided restaurant next to her house in 1979, just after the government paved the road. She wanted to make a living while raising her 10 children. In the process, she perfected the art of conch fritters, garlic chicken with johnny-cakes and coconut tarts. Many islanders confess an addiction to her island-style beef pate. Vie and her daughter, who now helps run the business, also will let you lounge ($2.50 per day) or camp on her low-key beach. She's located east of town; take Rte 10 (East End Rd) to Hansen Bay. Cash only.

### Miss Lucy's · WEST INDIAN $$

(☎340-693-5244; Rte 107; mains $16-25; ☺lunch & dinner Tue-Sat, brunch Sun; 🍴) Miss Lucy, the island's first female cab driver and one heck of a cook, passed away in 2007 at age 91. Her restaurant lives on, as famous for its Sunday jazz brunch and piña colada pancakes as for its weekday conch chowder, jumbo crab cakes and toasted goat-cheese salad – all served at the water's edge under the sea-grape trees. Vegetarians can ask for the 'local trimmings' platter of pigeon peas, rice, sweet potato, fungi, plantain and sauteed veggies. Take Rte 107 to Friis Bay; it's en route to Concordia.

### Sweet Plantains · FUSION $$

(☎340-777-4653; www.sweetplantains-stjohn.com; Rte 107; mains $16-28; ☺dinner) This sophisti-cated bistro fuses West Indian, East Indian and Latin flavors. Nights are devoted to certain themes. Sunday and Monday are French–Caribbean, so you might find short ribs with red wine pan gravy. Wednesday and Thursday are Latin, so maybe you'll see ceviche. Friday and Saturday are for curries, so you'll fork into a coconut or spicy red concoction (these are good nights for vegetarians). The chefs can add wine pairings or a rum-tasting flight. The appetizers are all West Indian street foods.

### Island Blues · BURGERS $$

(☎340-776-6800; www.island-blues.com; Rte 107; mains $8-14; ☺lunch & dinner; 🛜) Let's see: we have bay views, coconut-lime drinks, juicy burgers and grilled cheese sandwiches, live music and lots of locals hanging out. Oh, and free wi-fi (ask the staff for the password). It adds up to a sweet deal on Coral Bay's waterfront, by Coccoloba Plaza.

### Shipwreck Landing · BURGERS, SEAFOOD $$

(www.shipwrecklandingstjohn.com/index.htm; Rte 107; mains $8-18; ☺lunch & dinner) This is a laid-back, dimly lit place to drink, play darts and nosh on the small menu of burgers and seafood dishes. The blackened Cajun shrimp and daily fish special draw a crowd of locals who sit on the deck overlooking the bay. There's live music most weekends and Wednesdays. It's in Coral Bay a short distance beyond Coccoloba Plaza.

### Larry's Tourist Trap · CAFE $

(☎340-774-0912; www.wedontneednostinking website.com; Rte 107; mains $5-12; ☺11am-6pm Tue-Sat) Larry is quite the character, and his quirky yellow snack shack reflects it. It's a teeny place with a smattering of plastic tables and chairs where you can eat Larry's hot dogs and fish tacos. If nothing else, stop for a drink (to no one's surprise, he has home-brewed beer available). It's a great place to fortify before tackling Salt Pond Bay, or refresh after. Take Rte 107 south out of Coral Bay; the Tourist Trap is right before you get to Salt Pond Bay.

### Cafe Concordia · INTERNATIONAL $$

(☎340-693-5855; www.maho.org; mains $17-25; ☺breakfast & dinner Tue-Sat) This eco-resort's restaurant offers sublime views of the waves rolling in. The menu changes daily, but expect main dishes such as grilled fish or squash tart with goat cheese (there's always one vegetarian item). Lighter bites include flat breads with manchego cheese or smoked gouda. There's no wait staff, so give your order to the bartender.

##  Entertainment

**Skinny Legs**                    LIVE MUSIC
(www.skinnylegs.com; Rte 10) This place draws caravans of islanders and travelers to the East End for some hearty parties. The attraction is a steady diet of live entertainment from throughout the archipelago. Bluegrass, calypso, reggae, country and rock fuel the fire. The crowd is largely continental and ranges from six to 60 years old – and *everybody* dances. Thursdays, Fridays and Saturdays are the hot nights.

**Sputnik**                        LIVE MUSIC
(Rte 10) Next to the Donkey Diner, this West Indian bar sets a lazy mood. It hosts occasional bands and events such as screenings by the St John Film Society.

## ⓘ Information

**Connections** (www.connectionsstjohn.com; per 30min $5) Internet access by Skinny Legs restaurant.

**Coral Bay** (www.coralbaystjohn.com) Community website.

## ⓘ Getting There & Away

The distance between Cruz Bay and Coral Bay on Centerline Rd is just over 8 miles, but it takes a good 30 minutes or so to drive it on the winding mountain roads. Watch out for feral donkeys. The public Vitran bus also makes the journey. There are no ferries from Coral Bay to elsewhere (you must return to Cruz Bay).

# St Croix

POP 53,200

## Best Places to Eat

» Harvey's (p119)
» Savant (p120)
» South Shore Café (p126)
» Cheeseburgers in Paradise (p126)
» Rowdy Joe's North Shore Eatery (p129)

## Best Places to Stay

» Hotel on the Cay (p117)
» Palms at Pelican Cove (p128)
» Arawak Bay Inn at Salt River (p128)
» Waves at Cane Bay (p128)
» Mt Victory Campground (p134)

## Why Go?

St Croix (pronounced *Saint Croy*) is the Virgins' big boy, and it sports an exceptional topography spanning mountains, a spooky rainforest and a fertile coastal plain that, once upon a time, earned it the nickname 'Garden of the Antilles' for its sugarcane-growing prowess.

Today divers and drinkers appreciate St Croix's charms. The former submerge to view the wall along the island's north shore. It drops at a 60-degree slope to a 12,000ft depth, offering a true look into 'the deep.' There's nothing quite like it anywhere in the world. Underwater enthusiasts also don mask and flippers to explore Buck Island Marine Sanctuary, an 18,800-acre coral reef system with an abundance of marine life. Landlubbers take solace sipping through the heady Cruzan Rum Factory and taking their pick of 18th-century windmills, plantations and forts to poke around.

## When to Go

Mid-December through April is the dry and sunny high season, when prices and crowds hit their peak. The island has a busy social calendar year-round. There's Agri-Fest in mid-February, which is like a big state fair and draws families from around the islands; the Half-Ironman Triathlon in May; the sticky-sweet Mango Melee in June; and the Christmas Fiesta, gifting concerts and pageants from December through early January. The quarterly Jump Ups (street carnivals) are a prime time to be on the island for some spontaneous cultural fun.

## History

When Christopher Columbus arrived at Salt River Bay in November 1493 and named the island 'Santa Cruz,' the indigenous community he encountered was a mix of warrior Caribs and Taíno. The Spanish, English, French and Dutch took turns battling over the island in the ensuing years. The Danes took control in 1734 and remained so for the next two centuries.

By 1792 the island had 197 plantations and 22,000 slaves; 18,000 worked in the fields. The white population still numbered fewer that 3000. Describing this epoch in island history, the poet Philip Freneau wrote, 'If you have tears prepare to shed them now… no class of mankind in the known world undergo so complete servitude…'. Meanwhile, sugarcane production soared to more than 40 million pounds of sugar per year. Windmills and oxen mills dotted the landscape.

When England's Parliament abolished slavery in 1834, the freeing of slaves in the British Caribbean colonies provoked cries for freedom in the Danish islands. The 1848 slave rebellion followed, leading to freedom for all slaves on St Croix and the other Danish Virgin Islands.

After the US bought the islands in 1917, it tried to revive St Croix's sugarcane plantations by importing laborers and merchants from Puerto Rico. A Puerto Rican community took root around Frederiksted, but the tired one-crop economy withered. Enter tax incentives and the Hovensa oil refinery, which is now one of the world's largest processors.

In 1989 Hurricane Hugo damaged or destroyed about 90% of island structures and left more than one-third of the population homeless. Since then, St Croix has weathered attacks from equally vicious Hurricanes Marilyn (1995) and Lenny (1999).

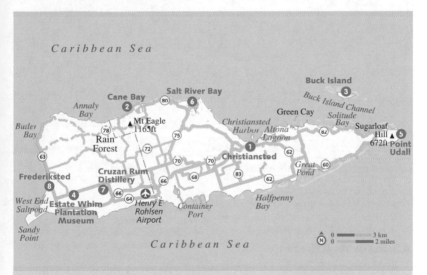

## St Croix Highlights

❶ Sip microbrews and explore the cannon-covered fort in the historic district of **Christiansted** (p112)

❷ Dive the wall and peer into the deep at **Cane Bay** (p118)

❸ Sail to **Buck Island** for a day of snorkeling, hiking and barbecuing (p123)

❹ Relive the sugarcane days at the **Estate Whim Plantation Museum** (p132)

❺ Hike to the wild East End beaches from **Point Udall**, the easternmost point in the USA (p123)

❻ See where Columbus landed, then kayak the bioluminescent water at **Salt River Bay** (p126)

❼ Drink the Virgin Islands' favorite attitude adjuster at its source at the **Cruzan Rum Distillery** (p133)

❽ Cycle or horseback ride on the lush rainforest trails around **Frederiksted** (p129)

**ST CROIX**

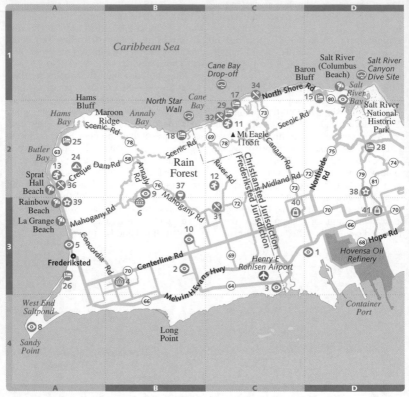

More than half of the island's residents are the descendants of former slaves; about 30% are second- or third-generation immigrants from Puerto Rico; and quite a few are young white Americans who come to run restaurants, inns and sports operations.

## 🎉 Festivals & Events

St Croix is the Virgins' most festive island. In addition to the events below, Jump Ups (music-filled street carnivals) take place four times per year.

**USVI Agri-Fest**          CULTURAL FAIR
(www.viagrifest.org; mid-Feb) The three-day event features island crafters, food stalls with superb examples of West Indian and Puerto Rican cooking, flora exhibitions and livestock contests. Of course, there is plenty of entertainment from bands that come from around the Virgin Islands.

**St Patrick's Day**          PARADE
(Mar 17) Cruzans go all out with a parade in Christiansted. Islanders dress in green and

find this day a perfect excuse to forget work and kick back at the beaches and pubs.

**St Croix Food
& Wine Experience**          FOOD FESTIVAL
(www.stcroixfoodandwine.com; mid-Apr) Celebrity chefs arrive for a week of gourmet feasting and drinking around the island.

**St Croix Half-Ironman Triathlon** TRIATHLON
(www.stcroixtriathlon.com; early May) Participants strive for Ironman qualification.

**Mango Melee**          FOOD FESTIVAL
(www.sgvbg.org; late Jun) The St George Village Botanical Garden celebrates the island's fruity bounty with sticky eating contests.

**Danish West Indies
Emancipation Day**          FIREWORKS
(Jul 3) Cruzans celebrate with a holiday from work, beach parties, family gatherings and plenty of fireworks over Christiansted's harbor.

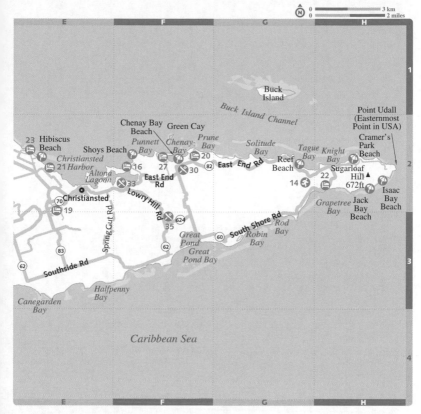

### Cruzan Christmas Fiesta    CULTURAL FAIR

(www.stxfestival.com; early Dec–early Jan)
Christmas is celebrated with a month
of pageants, parades and calypso
competitions, putting a West Indies
spin on the holiday season.

### ❶ Getting There & Around

#### AIR

**Henry E Rohlsen Airport** (STX; www.viport.
com) is on St Croix's southwest side and handles
flights from the US, many connecting via San
Juan, Puerto Rico or St Thomas. Major operators
from the US mainland include the following:

**American Airlines** (www.aa.com)

**Delta** (www.delta.com)

**United** (www.united.com)

**US Airways** (www.usairways.com)

Between St Thomas and St Croix, **Seaborne
Airlines** (www.seaborneairlines.com) flies cool
floatplanes from wharves at Christiansted and
Charlotte Amalie. The cost is around $80 each way.

#### BOAT

**VI Seatrans** (☑340-776-5494; www.govisea
trans.com) operates a passenger ferry between
Christiansted and Charlotte Amalie, St Thomas
(one way $50, 90 minutes). It sails twice on
Friday and Saturday, and once on Sunday and
Monday. Departures are from Gallows Bay,
about a 0.75-mile walk east of downtown Christiansted. Look for humpback whales during
winter crossings.

The cruise ship dock is in Frederiksted on the
island's west end.

#### BUS

**Vitran** (☑340-778-0898; fare $1) buses travel
along Centerline Rd between Christiansted and
Frederiksted. The schedule is erratic; buses
depart roughly every hour or two.

#### CAR

St Croix has several car-rental agencies, but
none of them seem to have many cars. Book
ahead for a vehicle if you can. Rentals cost about
$55 per day. Many companies, including those
listed, will pick you up at the airport or seaplane

# St Croix

dock. As in all the Virgins, you drive on the left. Roads on the island's west side, in the rainforest, are particularly rough.

**Budget** (☎340-778-9636; www.budgetstcroix. com)

**Centerline Car Rentals** (☎340-778-0450, 888-288-8755; www.ccrvi.com)

**Hertz** (☎340-778-1402; www.rentacarstcroix. com)

**Olympic** (☎340-773-8000, 888-878-4227; www.olympicstcroix.com)

### TAXI

Taxis are unmetered, but rates are set by territorial law. Prices are listed in the readily available free tourist guide *St Croix This Week*. The fare for one person from the airport to Christiansted is $16, to Frederiksted it is $12. The following taxi services get good marks from islanders:

**St Croix Taxi Association** (☎340-778-1088)
**Frederiksted Taxi Service** (☎340-772-4775)
**Cruzan Taxi Association** (☎340-773-6388)

## Christiansted

Christiansted is not only the island's major town but also a traveler's delight. For decades, its greatest appeal lay in its six-block historic district, which includes well over 100 residential, commercial and government buildings from the 18th and 19th centuries of Danish colonial rule. Here, the well-preserved fortress, flanked by gold, pink and brown West Indies neoclassical buildings, evokes the days when Christiansted was the capital of the Danish Virgin Islands and St Croix plantocracy society was awash with gold. The district abuts Kings Wharf, the commercial landing where, for more than 250 years, ships landed with slaves and set off with sugar or molasses.

Today the wharf is fronted by a boardwalk of restaurants, dive shops and a brewpub, with art galleries, wine bars and courtyard bistros tucked into the narrow lanes leading inland. It all comes together as a well-provisioned base from which to explore the island. The main arteries are King St (eastbound) and Company St (westbound).

## History

When the Danes purchased St Croix from the French in 1733–34, the Danish governor Frederick Moth designed Christiansted using Norway's picturesque town of Christiania (now Oslo) as a model. The new town would take its name from the reigning Danish monarch, Christian VI.

Moth drew up a town with a fort on its waterfront to protect the nearby commercial buildings of the Danish West India and Guinea Company and a rectangular grid of streets where the town was subdivided into building sites.

Thrilled with the development of the modern town and the burgeoning prosperity of their garden isle, the Danes moved the capital of the Danish West Indies here

from St Thomas in 1755, where it remained until 1871.

Many of the town's 18th-century buildings might have been lost to modernization if the sugar industry had not gone into serious decline in the 1820s. As the island fell into economic hard times, Christiansted settled into dormancy, and little changed here for almost 200 years.

## ◉ Sights

Fort Christiansvaern, the old Danish commercial and government buildings, and 27 acres at the heart of the town are now part of the **Christiansted National Historic Site** (☑340-773-1460; www.nps.gov/chri; ⊙9am-5pm), under the direct administration of the National Park Service.

**Kings Wharf**         COMMERCIAL DISTRICT
The heart of Christiansted's historic district, Kings Wharf is where merchants traded slaves for sugar in the 18th and early 19th centuries. The wharf is now home to a harborside boardwalk, small hotels, restaurants, shops, pubs, water-tour operators and the ferry to Protestant Cay. The wharf is the natural place for any walking tour of the town to begin.

**Fort Christiansvaern**       HISTORICAL SITE
(Hospital St; admission $3) Built of masonry and yellow Danish brick that came to the islands as ballast in sailing ships, this fort took shape between 1738 and 1749 over the ruins of a French bastion. Fort Christiansvaern (Christian's Defenses) is a four-point citadel and the best preserved of the five

---

### ST CROIX IN...

#### One Day

Ramble over cannon-dotted ramparts at **Fort Christiansvaern** and explore Christiansted's historic downtown district. If you have a car, drive out to **Point Udall**, the easternmost spot in the US, and hike down to secluded **Isaac and Jack Bays** to snorkel or lounge. If you're without wheels head to the beach at **Protestant Cay**, a stone's throw from downtown. Have drinks at the **Comanche Mill Yacht-less Club**, an old windmill turned gin mill on the boardwalk. At dusk, paddle through the glowing water at **Salt River Bay** in a see-through kayak.

#### Two Days

Motor west to sip at the **Cruzan Rum Distillery**, sniff local herbs at the **St George Village Botanical Garden**, and time warp to the sugar cane days at **Estate Whim Plantation Museum**. Follow it all up with snorkel around the pier in **Frederiksted**. Or stay on the island's east side and sail out on day trip to beautiful **Buck Island** marine sanctuary.

Danish forts in the West Indies. Its ramparts surround a central courtyard.

Though Danish soldiers quartered here until 1878, and the walls have protected citizens from the onslaught of pirates, hurricanes and slave revolts, the fort's guns have never been fired in an armed conflict. After 1878, the fort served as a prison and courthouse for the island. Cannons on the ramparts, an echoey claustrophobic dungeon and latrines with top-notch sea views await visitors who tour the site. The ticket you buy at the entrance here is also good for the Steeple Building. There's parking available in the lot next door to the fort ($2 per two hours).

**FREE** **Scale House**     HISTORICAL BUILDING
(King St) The Scale House, with its two-story, yellow-masonry construction and hipped roof, dates from 1856. This is the site where the Danish weighed hogsheads of sugar for export; imports were also weighed here,

to levy duty. You can see the scales as you enter the building. The 2nd floor was the weighmaster's office, while the rear of the building once garrisoned Danish soldiers. Now, this building is an information center for the National Park Service, where you can pick up brochures describing the national park buildings and historic Christiansted. The center also sells a good selection of local books.

**Customs House**     HISTORICAL BUILDING
(King St) This yellow-brick and masonry building with its sweeping 16-step entrance stairway stands between the fort and the Scale House at Kings Wharf. The building served as the Danes' customs house for more than a century. Begun in 1750, the building evolved over decades; the 2nd floor was added around 1830. While it has functioned in recent years as a post office, library and exhibition space, the interior is not currently open to the public.

# Christiansted

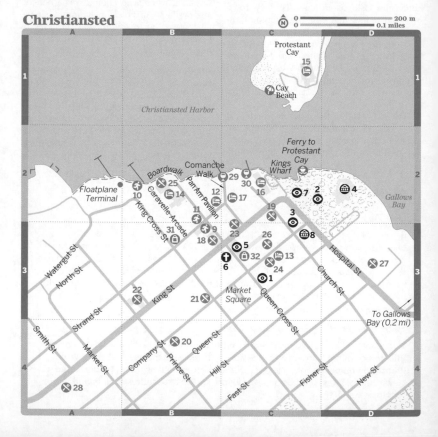

**FREE** **Danish West India & Guinea
Company Warehouse** HISTORICAL BUILDING
(Church St) Just across the intersection of
Hospital and King Sts stands a three-story
neoclassical building with dormers set into
the steep, hipped roof and a courtyard surrounded by a wall. Today, this building functions as a park administration building, but
it began life in 1749 as the headquarters
and warehouse for the Danish West India &
Guinea Company.

The courtyard here was the site of one of
the West Indies' most active slave markets
until the abolition of the slave trade in the
early 19th century. The building has also
served as military quarters and as the office
for the Panama Telegraph Company early in
the 20th century.

**Steeple Building** MUSEUM
(Church St; admission $3, free with fort ticket) The
white building with the Georgian steeple,
across Company St from the Danish West
India & Guinea Company Warehouse, was St
Croix's first house of worship, the Church of
Lord God of the Sabaoth. Lutherans erected
this edifice between 1750 and 1753, adding
the steeple four decades later. In 1831 the
government converted the building into a
military bakery. It has been modified several
times since then and put to use as a hospital
and school.

Today, the Steeple Building houses the
National Park Service Museum, with exhibits depicting life in old St Croix. There
are Taíno relics, agricultural exhibits and a
model of a working sugar plantation.

**Government House** HISTORICAL BUILDING
(King St) This three-story, U-shaped building,
mixing neoclassical and baroque elements,
fills a quarter of a block between King and
Company Sts, just west of the other historic
buildings at Kings Wharf. Begun as a private
home in 1747, Government House evolved
into one of the most elaborate governor's
residences in all of the Lesser Antilles. Various Danish governors bought up surrounding townhouses and joined them together to
form the current structure, which has galleries of colonnades surrounding a grassy
courtyard and ornamental garden. Visitors

**ST CROIX** CHRISTIANSTED

# Christiansted

**LOCAL KNOWLEDGE**

## OLASEE DAVIS: ST CROIX HIKING ASSOCIATION

Olasee Davis is an ecologist at the University of the Virgin Islands and a tour leader with **St Croix Hiking Association** (www.stcroixhiking.org). He's a lifelong Virgin Islander, and a resident of St Croix for more than 40 years.

### Favorite place to hike

The north bay, at Annaly Bay and Will Bay (next to Hams Bluff) near Maroon Ridge. 'Maroons' were slaves who ran away from the plantations. They came here because the topography – the mountains and forest – made it difficult to for anyone to find them. It's a no-man's-land. Some jumped off and killed themselves so as not to be recaptured. The virgin forest remains. It's an extremely historical and spiritual place.

can enter via the sweeping staircase on King St and explore the huge 2nd-floor reception hall, which is still used for some formal government functions. The period furnishings are gifts from the Danish government.

**Lutheran Church** CHURCH
(King St) Just beyond Government House as you move west on King St stands Christiansted's oldest church. Begun in about 1740 as the Dutch Reformed Church, this one-story, cruciform-plan house of worship became the property of the Lutherans in the early 1830s, when they moved here from the Steeple Building. The building is remarkable not only for its age, but also for the unusual three-tier Gothic tower added over the entranceway years after the original construction. This is still an active parish.

FREE **Apothecary Hall** EXHIBIT
(Queen Cross St; ◷10am-5pm Mon-Sat) On Queen Cross St, in between Company and Queen Sts, this little exhibit behind plexiglas shows what a local 19th-century pharmacy stocked with potions and pills looked like.

**Market Square** MARKET
(Company St) Frederik Moth laid out Market Square in 1735 as the site for the town's produce market. The square still attracts a few fruit and vegetable vendors (especially on Saturday morning) around the intersection of Company and Queen Cross Sts.

**Protestant Cay** BEACH
The small triangular cay, less than 200 yards from Kings Wharf, is a sweet little oasis. It's the site of a mellow resort whose wide, sandy beach and bar-restaurant are open to the public.

The **St Croix Water Sports Center** (www. stcroixwatersports.com) is here, offering jet skis,

snorkel gear, kayaks, sailboats and windsurfers. The beach offers protected swimming and snorkeling off the north side, as well as a vista that looks out over the sailboat anchorage, Fort Christiansvaern and Kings Wharf. For snorkeling, some swimmers rave you can see just as much underwater life here as at Buck Island.

The ferry ($4 round trip, five minutes) departs from the wharf in front of the Customs House; look for a step labeled Hotel on the Cay. As soon as the boat captain sees you, they'll drive over and pick you up.

## 🏃 Activities

Christiansted is chock-full of operators that book diving trips (see the boxed text, p118) and Buck Island snorkeling trips (see p123). More outdoor activities are listed in the Activities sections throughout this chapter.

### Boat Trips

Many travelers combine their sailing adventures with a trip to Buck Island (see p123). Another great option is the highly recommended **World Ocean School** (☎340-626-7877; www.worldoceanschool.org; 2½hr tours adult/child $45/30; ◷4:30pm Dec-May), which offers daily trips aboard the sharp-looking, historic schooner *Roseway*. Added bonus: sailing with these folks supports their nonprofit group that teaches local students sailing and leadership skills. Departures are from Gallows Bay.

### Fishing

Sportfishing enthusiasts head for the waters north of the island for a decent season of good fishing that runs from September to June. Kingfish, wahoo and bonito are usually the biggest catches, but sometimes the boats hook into marlin, yellowfin tuna and swordfish. Four-hour charters run about $500 on most of the boats, $900 for eight hours.

**Gone Ketchin'** (☑340-713-1175; www.gone ketchin.com; Salt River Marina) Cast a line with Captain Grizz on his boat that runs on recycled vegetable oil.

**Captain Carl** (☑340-277-4042; www.fish withcarl.com; Christiansted Harbor) Captain Carl hits the high seas in two boats: the 36ft *Mocko Jumbie* and 29ft *Keep It Reel*. Departures are from the dock in front of Rum Runners restaurant in downtown Christiansted.

**Jade Hook Fishing Charters** (☑340-244-9062; www.jadehookcharters.com; Christiansted Harbor) Captain Ryan motors 27ft *Jade Hook* to fish-rich zones close to the shore and offshore. Departures are from the dock in front of Angry Nate's restaurant in downtown Christiansted.

### Hiking

Hikers will love the guided eco-walks available. They depart from sites around the island. Fees vary.

**St Croix Environmental Association** (☑340-773-1989; www.stxenvironmental.org) In addition to hiking, this organization also offers bird-watching and snorkeling trips, as well as programs where you help count sea turtles; click the 'events' calendar' for listings.

**Ay-Ay Eco-Hikes** (☑340-277-0410, 340-772-4079; eco@viaccess.net) Island guide and herbalist Ras Lumumba offers tours to Maroon Ridge, Annaly Bay, Salt River Bay and more. Most treks take three to four hours and cost $50 to $60 per person; some trips are strenuous. Contact him for the schedule.

**St Croix Hiking Association** (www.stcroix hiking.org) This group sponsors a couple of hikes per month; click 'calendar' for the schedule.

### Windsurfing & Kitesurfing

Those seeking windsurfing instruction or board rental can head to **St Croix Water Sports Center** (☑340-773-7060; www.stcroix watersports.com) on Protestant Cay. Kitesurfers should contact **Kite St Croix** (www. kitestcroix.com), located in the island's East End. Make reservations at least two weeks in advance for lessons.

### Snorkeling

Protestant Cay has good snorkeling off its beach, as well as gear rental. The Christiansted-based dive company **St Croix Ultimate Bluewater Adventures** (☑340-773-5994, 887-567-1367; www.stcroixscuba.com; 1104 Strand St; 2hr tours $40-50) offers a west end snorkel tour around Frederiksted Pier and Sandy Point National Wildlife Refuge. It runs Tuesday, Thursday and Saturday at 10am and 2pm. You'll need to provide your own transportation to Frederiksted.

### ☞ Tours

Several operators offer four-hour island tours (about $45 per person) by van that go to the botanic garden, rum factory, Whim Plantation, Frederiksted and Salt River. They depart from King St near Government House, and must be reserved in advance.

**Tan Tan Jeep Tours** 4WD TOUR (☑340-773-7041; www.stxtantantours.com) Goes four-wheeling to the Annaly Bay tide pools, deep into the rainforest and to other hard-to-reach destinations. Tours range from 2½ hours ($70 per person) to eight hours ($140 per person).

**Eagle Safari Tours** (☑340-778-3313; ◷Mon-Sat)

**Rudy's Taxi Tours** (☑340-773-6803; ◷Mon-Sat)

**Sweeney's Safari Tour** (☑340-773-6700, 800-524-2026; ◷Mon-Fri)

To arrange a private tour, contact **Matthew Telesford** (☑340-773-9022, 340-277-8521), a reliable driver who knows the island well.

### 🛌 Sleeping

All of the hotels listed below are conveniently located and walkable to Christiansted's bars, shops and restaurants. Tax is an additional 18%, and some places tack on an energy surcharge (about $4).

**Hotel on the Cay** HOTEL $$ (☑340-773-2035, 800-524-2035; www.hotelon thecay.com; r $150-190; ❋@☎☲) A truly cool place to stay, this hotel sits just offshore on the sandy islet of Protestant Cay, accessible by a five-minute ferry ride (free for guests). It's good value for the spacious rooms with full kitchenettes, cooking utensils and bright tropical decor. The pièce de résistance: private balconies for taking in cool breezes, hearing waves lap the shore and watching pelicans dive-bomb for fish. True, the rooms

If you are a scuba enthusiast worth your sea salt, you'll be spending lots of time underwater in St Croix. It's a diver's mecca thanks to two unique features: one, it's surrounded by a massive barrier reef, so turtles, rays and other sea creatures are prevalent; and, two, a spectacular wall runs along the island's north shore, dropping at a 60-degree slope to a depth of more than 12,000ft. It gives a true look into 'the deep,' and there's nothing quite like it anywhere in the world.

The best dives on the north shore are at Cane Bay Drop-Off, North Star Wall and Salt River Canyon. The top west island dives are at the Butler Bay shipwrecks (including the *Suffolk Maid* and *Rosaomaira*) and at Frederiksted Pier. While almost all dive operators offer boat dives, many of the most exciting dives, such as Cane Bay, involve beach entries with short swims to the reef.

The operators listed here go to the various sites around the island and charge about $75 for one-tank dives and about $100 for two tanks (including equipment).

**Anchor Dive Center** (☎340-778-1522, 800-532-3483; www.anchordivestcroix.com; Salt River Marina) Specializes in dives in Salt River Bay's underwater 'canyon'.

**Cane Bay Dive Shop** (☎340-773-9913, 800-338-3843; www.canebayscuba.com; Cane Bay) A friendly five-star PADI facility, across the highway from the beach and the Cane Bay Drop-Off, and with shops in both Christiansted and Frederiksted.

**Dive Experience** (☎340-773-3307, 800-235-9047; www.divexp.com; Christiansted) This female-owned shop has a strong environmental commitment and offers 'green' diving courses.

**N2 The Blue** (☎340-772-3483; www.n2theblue.com; Frederiksted) Specializes in west-end wreck dives and Frederiksted Pier snorkel trips.

**Scuba West** (☎340-772-3701, 800-352-0107; www.divescubawest.com; Frederiksted) Specializes in west island dives, including awesome night dives on Frederiksted Pier (located across from the shop).

**St Croix Ultimate Bluewater Adventures** (☎340-773-5994, 887-567-1367; www.stcroix-scuba.com; 81 Queen Cross St, Christiansted) Another ultra-professional company that dives all over the island; it also offers west-end snorkel trips.

---

are a bit dated, but they're slated to undergo renovation. The property's broad, protected beach with all its water-sports vendors attracts a crowd for good reason. Wi-fi is in the public areas only.

**Company House Hotel**  HOTEL **$$**
(☎340-773-1377; www.companyhousehotel.com; 2 Company St; d incl breakfast $115; ❄@🛜🏊) Company House is the value pick of the downtown hotels. It is the sister property of King Christian Hotel, and as such guests have access to that entity's fitness center and continental breakfast. Rooms at Company House don't have views, a private deck or waterfront locale, but they're newly renovated, well maintained and offer free in-room wi-fi. To feel classy, take a seat at the piano bar in the lobby.

**Club Comanche Hotel**  HOTEL **$$**
(☎340-773-0210; www.clubcomanche.com; 1 Strand St; r $135-165; ❄🛜🏊) This downtown

property is set in a 250-year-old Danish mansion – once home to Alexander Hamilton (see boxed text, p119) – and has been lodging guests since 1948. The 23 rooms have been renovated recently with West Indian antique decor, new beds, flat-screen satellite TVs and in-room internet access, and the place now has a boutique-hotel vibe. There is a pool on the premises with a small deck. The good news: it's in the heart of Christiansted's entertainment district, right by the boardwalk; the bad news: the area can be noisy.

**King Christian Hotel**  HOTEL **$$**
(☎340-773-6330, 800-524-2012; www.kingchristian.com; 59 Kings Wharf; r incl breakfast $120-155; ❄@🛜🏊) You can't miss this three-story, peach-colored building that looks like a Danish warehouse (which it was 200 years ago) right next to the National Park Service sites. The 39 rooms are typical midrange, flowery-bedspread types; opt for a 'superior' room

with harbor view, which will brighten up the scene considerably. Most rooms have wi-fi, but ask for it specifically if you need it. Many of the island's dive operations and tour boats have offices on the hotel's 1st floor.

### Hotel Caravelle
HOTEL $$
(✆340-773-0687, 800-524-0410; www.hotelcaravelle.com; 44A Queen Cross St; d $170-190; ❊❋) Located on the waterfront, this 43-room property is similar in spirit to, though a bit fancier than, the King Christian Hotel. The more expensive rooms have harbor views. You can also get a harbor view by heading out to the pool and sundeck. You'll usually find deals on the website to whittle down the price.

### King's Alley Hotel
HOTEL $$
(✆340-773-0103; 57 King St; d $179; ❊❋) King's Alley has 35 rooms above a gallery of shops and restaurants right on the harbor. The set-up imitates a 19th-century Danish great house with colonial-style mahogany furniture and vaulted ceilings to match. Handsome rooms have French doors that open onto tiny but pretty balconies with a view toward the water.

### Carrington's Inn
B&B $$
(✆340-713-0508, 877-658-0508; www.carringtonsinn.com; r incl breakfast $125-165; ❊@❂❋) You won't get a beach here, but you will get lots of personalized attention from long-time owners Roger and Claudia Carrington. A cooked breakfast each morning, bathrobes, full concierge services and cookies at bedtime are all part of the package. The five rooms are each named and colored after a particular flower; all have a private bathroom, refrigerator, coffee maker and either a pool view or harbor view. There is a shared TV in the common room. The B&B sits on Herman Hill, overlooking Christiansted. It's about a 10-minute drive southwest of town

via Rte 70, so you'll need a car if you're staying here.

### Rental Accommodations
St Croix has no shortage of resort condominiums and villa compounds. Most cluster along the North Shore and East End, and most require a weeklong stay in high season. In addition to **VRBO** (www.vrbo.com), browse offerings from the following companies that focus on St Croix:

**Vacation St Croix** (✆340-718-0361; www.vacationstcroix.com)

**CMPI Vacation Rentals** (✆800-496-7379; www.enjoystcroix.com)

**Teague Bay Properties** (✆800-237-1959; www.teaguebaypropertiesrentals.com)

## ✖ Eating

Christiansted knows how to fill a stomach. On one hand, you'll find imaginative, upscale dining at chic little bistros. On the other, you'll find local holes-in-the-wall that specialize in budget-priced West Indian fare (King St offers a good row of these between King Cross and Smith Sts). Casual bar-restaurants that fall somewhere in the middle line the waterfront. Many eateries close on Sunday and/or Monday.

### TOP CHOICE Harvey's
WEST INDIAN $$
(✆340-773-3433, 11B Company St, mains $11-22; ⏱11am-4pm Mon-Sat) At breezy, 10-table Harvey's, a classic tropical cafe, you half expect Humphrey Bogart from *Casablanca* to wander in and order a drink at the bar. Conch in butter sauce, delicate grouper, sweet-potato-based Cruzan stuffing, rice and peas and many more West Indian dishes arrive heaped on plates. Look for the big mural outside of NBA star Tim Duncan; he used to wait table here before achieving his hoop dreams.

---

### ALEXANDER HAMILTON & THE 10 SPOT

You know that guy on your $10 bill? It's Alexander Hamilton, Christiansted's famed historic son. Hamilton was born on the neighboring island of Nevis in 1755, but spent his formative years in Christiansted. His was a hard-knock life – born illegitimately, orphaned by age 11, impoverished – but he worked hard and impressed the local merchants, who sent him to school in New York.

He flourished in the US and became a major voice during the Revolutionary War. George Washington appointed him to be the architect of the new country's economic policies. In 1789 Hamilton became the first secretary of the treasury – which is what earned him the honor of being on the 10 spot.

Hamilton died infamously in a duel with Aaron Burr in 1804.

**Sale e Miele** ITALIAN $$
(☎340-719-0510; 57C Company St; mains $14-23; ⊙lunch Tue-Sat, dinner Thu-Sat) This amiable trattoria serves authentic Tuscan cuisine at tables scattered in a shady courtyard. Calamari, lasagna, and ricotta-and-spinach quiche are some of the dishes written on the blackboard menu. The Italian owner and her husband source much of their produce from the local farmers market and use those ingredients as a starting point for the menu each week. There's a nice wine list to go with the flavors.

**Savant** INTERNATIONAL $$
(☎340-713-8666; 4C Hospital St; mains $17-28; ⊙dinner Mon-Sat; ⓙ) Cozy, low-lit Savant serves upscale fusion cookery in a colonial townhouse. You know you're in for something wild when you see the leopard-print curtains. The ever-changing menu combines spicy Caribbean, Mexican and Thai recipes; sweat over them in the air-conditioning indoors or outside in the courtyard. Reservations recommended, though you can walk in and try for one the handful of stools at the bar.

**Singh's Fast Food** WEST INDIAN $
(☎340-773-7357; King St; mains $6-12; ⊙lunch & dinner; ⓙ) When the roti craving strikes – and it will – Singh's will satiate with its multiple meat and tofu varieties. The steamy, four-table joint also serves shrimp, conch, goat, turkey and tofu stews – all while island music ricochets off the pastel walls. The best deal is to ask for a 'plate' and point to the items in the display case that you want, and staff will heap it on. Singh's caters to a constant flow of locals for takeaway.

**Avocado Pit** CAFE $
(☎340-773-9843; 59 Kings Wharf; mains $6-12; ⊙breakfast & lunch) Young staff pour strong coffee and fruity smoothies at this wee cafe overlooking the fort and harbor. The granola-and-yogurt wins raves for breakfast, while the wraps (spicy tuna, tofu or avocado) make a delicious lunch or Buck Island picnic fare. It's in the King Christian Hotel arcade.

**Kendrick's** INTERNATIONAL $$$
(☎340-773-9199; King Cross St at Company St; mains $27-36; ⊙dinner Mon-Sat) Chef David Kendrick's award-winning restaurant has long set the standard for Cruzan gourmands. You can sit inside the colonial cottage or eat in the courtyard. Fork into grilled rack of lamb or fettuccine with lobster medallions, or go for something lighter off the bar menu, like lobster nachos or barbecue tuna tacos.

**Tutto Bene** ITALIAN $$
(☎340-773-5229; www.tuttobenerestaurant.com; Hospital St, Gallows Bay; mains $20-33; ⊙dinner) There's no West Indian ambience and no ocean view, but that's not the point at Tutto Bene. It stands apart by cooking traditional Italian food that will rock your world. Generous portions of fish, chicken and meat mains and creative pasta dishes are served in a sophisticated yet casual room. It's located 0.5 miles east of town in the Boardwalk Building by Gallows Bay.

**Kim's Restaurant** WEST INDIAN $$
(☎340-773-3377; 45 King St; mains $9-14; ⊙lunch & dinner) Come here for dynamite West Indian cooking and friendly conversation with cook and manager 'Big Kim.' The ambience is simple with peach-and-white tablecloths and a courtyard; the menu is written on a dry-erase board. Try the curried chicken or Creole-style conch, both served with rice and salad.

**Bacchus** INTERNATIONAL $$$
(☎340-692-9922; www.restaurantbacchus.com; Queen Cross St; mains $26-40) Bacchus offers a sassy, eclectic menu of meat and seafood dishes. The setting is the 2nd floor of a historic townhouse, and the bait is the most complete wine list on the island. Get a fine pour to go with your hoisin-barbecue-sauced ribs or root-beer-braised rabbit over pasta. For dessert, scoop up the boozy sourdough-bread pudding.

**Lalita** VEGETARIAN $$
(☎340-719-4417; www.kalimacenter.org; 54 King St; mains $8-16; ⊙9:30am-9pm; ⓦⓙ) Raw-food nuts and vegans: Lalita is your place, serving everything from organic muesli to seaweed salad and hummus plates. The restaurant's bulletin board is a good resource for yoga and other healing-art classes; there's also free wi-fi if you want to check your email.

**Galangal** THAI $$
(☎340-773-0076; www.galangalstx.com; 17 Church St; mains $22-32; ⊙dinner Tue-Sat) Galangal offers swanky Thai food, with a couple of Vietnamese and Indonesian dishes thrown in for good measure. The sleek, Buddha-dotted space attracts a well-dressed crowd swirling wine glasses and gabbing over duck in red curry, green papaya salad and stir-fried beef and basil.

### Luncheria

MEXICAN **$**

(📞340-773-4247; 6 Company St; mains $8-12; ⏰lunch & dinner Mon-Sat) This fun Mexican cantina will quench your desire for margaritas and burritos, whether you order them to go or stay to eat in the laid-back, shaded courtyard.

### Rum Runners

BURGERS, SEAFOOD **$$**

(📞340-773-6585; www.rumrunnersstcroix.com; boardwalk at Hotel Caravelle; mains $12-24; ⏰breakfast, lunch & dinner; 🐾) Rum Runners consistently hosts throngs of visitors who come for the big menu of burgers, toasted sandwiches, seafood and drinks. Eat on the waterside deck and watch the tarpon swim up and hunt for food. A steel pan band plays for the popular Sunday brunch. Rum Runners is also always a friendly place to soak up brews.

###  Jaccar Organic Sorbets

SORBET SHOP **$**

(📞340-719-6999; Arawak Bldg, Gallows Bay; cups $3-4; ⏰10am-5pm Tue-Sat) Jaccar mixes local fruits like mango, soursop and carambola (aka starfruit) with organic blue agave nectar to make its healthful treats. The tiny takeaway shop also offers cookies and sweets (gummi worms, lollipops etc) made with agave nectar. All the spoons and cups are biodegradable. Jaccar is a bit tricky to find; it's tucked into the strip of shops in the Arawak Building, across the road from the post office in Gallows Bay, about a half-mile east of downtown.

## 🍷 Drinking

The best way to find out what's up is to check the entertainment section of **St Croix This Week** (www.stcroixthisweek.com) and the daily *St Croix Avis*. A healthy collection of gin mills lines the boardwalk along Kings Wharf; there is always live music on at one or the other of them throughout the week.

### TOP CHOICE Fort Christian Brew Pub

MICROBREWERY

(📞340-713-9820; www.fortchristianbrewpub. com; boardwalk at King's Alley Hotel; mains $17-23; ⏰lunch & dinner) Right on the boardwalk overlooking yachts bobbing in the sea, this open-air pub is primo for sampling VI Brewing Company's small-batch suds. Try the flagship Blackbeard Ale or Foxy's Lager (the brewmaster here doubles as the suds-maker at Foxy's on Jost Van Dyke). Happy hour between 4pm and 7pm attracts young continentals working on the island and rafts of travelers drawn to the waterfront. The scene can be a good spot to gain some local knowledge or get invited to a party. The New Orleans–style menu features jambalaya and spicy shrimp *étouffée* (a tomato-based stew), but we advise sticking to the beer and breeze.

### Comanche Mill Yacht-less Club

BAR

(📞340-773-0210; www.comanchemillyacht-less club.com; boardwalk at Comanche Walk) Set around an old windmill at the water's edge, the Yacht-less Club is hard to miss. It hosts a crowd of grizzled regulars in the afternoon, which morphs into a younger, clubbier group at night. The windmill used to pump sea water to the old pool at the Comanche Hotel. These days, the bar mostly pumps rum and beer. The afternoon crew is a bunch of characters.

### Hotel on the Cay

BAR

Steel pan aficionados head for Hotel on the Cay's bar on Tuesday night for the beach barbecue, which also has fire-eaters, broken-bottle dancing (yes, dancing on glass) and mocko jumbie stilt dancers.

##  Shopping

Christiansted will please visitors who like to buy pretty things. The ambience could hardly be more fetching, with historic colonial buildings, shady arcades, galleried sidewalks, cooling trade winds, sea views and the lilt of calypso pouring from a host of boutiques and shops. There are more than 30 Cruzan shopkeepers specializing in gold, gems and handcrafted jewelry. Several painters and photographers have galleries in town, too, with most on Company St near Queen Cross St. The **Art Thursday** (www.artthursday.com;

---

### JUMP UPS

Jump Ups are family-friendly street carnivals that happen four times per year in Christiansted, usually in mid-February, early May, early July and late November. Steel pan bands play. Mocko jumbies dance on stilts to ward off evil spirits. Stalls sell local food, drinks and crafts. And restaurants, shops and galleries stay open late. Families come from all over the island to party under the moonlight. Check the events calendar at **Go To St Croix** (www.gotostcroix.com) for upcoming dates.

⊙5-8pm 3rd Thu of month) free gallery hop takes place November through June.

There's worthy browsing in the old warehouses that open into courtyards and shopping pavilions between Strand St and the waterfront. These include the complexes at the Pan Am Pavilion, Caravelle Arcade and King's Alley. The Gallows Bay development on the east side of the harbor attracts a lot of snowbirds to the hardware store, bookstore and boutiques there. For big-box retailers you'll have to head out of town to the malls on Centerline Rd.

**Crucian Gold**                    JEWELRY
(www.cruciangold.com; 1112 Strand St) The studio where the Bishop family crafts their signature 'knot' designs in gold and silver.

**National Park Service Shop**    BOOKSTORE
(King St) The park service visitors center in the Scale House sells lots of locally authored books and educational kids' gifts.

**Riddims**                       MUSIC STORE
(www.riddimsmusic.com; 3A Queen Cross St) Good source for reggae and *quelbe* music from the Virgin Islands, plus clothing, hats, incense and other Caribbean cultural items.

## ❶ Information

### Dangers & Annoyances
The area west of King Cross St is littered with strip clubs, rowdy bars, prostitution, drugs and vagrants. Avoid this area after dark.

### Internet Access
**Strand Street Station** (☑340-719-6245; Pan Am Pavilion; per half hr $5; ⊙10am-5pm Mon-Sat, to 3pm Sun) Internet cafe with eight terminals; you can print, burn CDs and make photocopies here, too.

### Media
**St Croix This Week** (www.stcroixthisweek. com) Widely available free monthly magazine that has events listings and the cruise ship schedule.
**St Croix Avis** The island's daily newspaper.
**St Croix Source** (www.stcroixsource.com) Online news.

### Medical Services
**Governor Juan F Luis Hospital** (☑340-776-6311; ⊙24hr) Next to the Sunny Isle Shopping Center on Centerline Rd, 2 miles west of Christiansted.

### Money
There are couple of banks with ATMs on King St, near Prince St.

### Post
**Post office** (☑340-773-3586; cnr Company St & Market Sq)

### Tourist Information
**Visitors center** (☑340-773-1460; King St; ⊙10am-5pm) It's located in the historic Scale House and operated by the National Park Service. The knowledgeable staff can provide information on islandwide attractions, plus town and island maps.

### Websites
**St Croix Landmarks Society** (http://heritage trails.stcroixlandmarks.org) Maps to ruins and cultural sites islandwide.
**USVI Department of Tourism** (www.visitusvi. com) Official tourism site.
**VI Now** (www.vinow.com/stthomas) The low-down on beaches, cruise ship schedules, taxi rates, the weather and more.
**Go to St Croix** (www.gotostcroix.com) Comprehensive website with information on events, historic sites and nightlife, plus webcams to view the main towns.

## ❶ Getting There & Away

### Air
**Seaborne Airlines** (www.seaborneairlines.com) has floatplane services for the 20-minute jaunt to Charlotte Amalie, St Thomas. The terminal is at the boardwalk's western end. Planes depart multiple times daily; the cost is around $80 each way.

### Boat
**VI Seatrans** (☑340-776-5494; www.govisea trans.com) sails to Charlotte Amalie twice on Friday and Saturday, and once on Sunday and Monday (round trip $90, 90 minutes). Departures are from Gallows Bay, about a 0.75-mile walk east of downtown.

### Taxi
The taxi stand is at Kings St, near Government House. Rates are set by territorial law. Prices are listed in the free tourist guide *St Croix This Week*.

The following table shows rates per person to popular destinations from Christiansted. The price drops when more than one passenger goes to the destination. There's also an added $2-per-bag luggage fee.

| DESTINATION | COST |
| --- | --- |
| Gallows Bay | $6 |
| Airport | $16 |
| Frederiksted | $24 |
| Cane Bay | $24 |

# Buck Island

Buck Island floats 5 miles east of Christiansted. For such a small landmass – 1 mile long by 0.5 miles wide – this island draws big crowds. It's not so much what's on top but what's underneath that fascinates: an 18,800-acre frenzy of fish amid the coral reef system surrounding the island, known as **Buck Island Reef National Monument** (www.nps.gov/buis). President John F Kennedy designated it the first US underwater national monument in 1961. Unfortunately, coral bleaching has damaged much of the original protected area.

The sea gardens and a marked underwater trail create captivating **snorkeling** on the island's east side, and there's shallow **diving** around the point to the northeast. Snorkelers will see elkhorn coral grottoes and tropical fish (from blue tang to barracuda) along the marked trail. Be aware that during the fall and winter, the trade winds often blow hard at Buck Island, creating cloudy visibility and a significant chop on the reef, which can make it rough for newbies to the mask and fins.

On land, endangered hawksbill and green sea turtles come ashore on Buck Island's protected beaches. **Turtle Beach** is named for the critters and offers sheltered swimming, toilets and picnic sites with tables and cooking grills you can fuel with driftwood. The **hiking trail** that circles around the west end of the island is a moderate walk through tropical dry forest, bromeliads, guinea grass and giant tamarind trees. The walk takes about 45 minutes and leads to an observation point on the island's 340ft ridge.

Do not come to Buck Island expecting *Blue Lagoon* serenity. All sorts of tour boats from Christiansted congregate here. The vessels may be large powerboats, sleek catamarans or smaller sailboats. Pick the one that fits with your sense of adventure. Half-day trips ($65 to $70 per person) are usually aboard a fast powerboat and include time at the snorkeling trail and a quick visit to Turtle Beach. Full-day trips (from $85 to $90) are often aboard a sailboat and add a beach barbecue to the mix. Reserve in advance, as the trips book up quickly. All operators include snorkeling gear.

**Big Beard's Adventures** (☑340-773-4482; www.bigbeards.com; Queen Cross St by Kings Wharf, Christiansted) Trips are aboard catamaran sailboats.

**Caribbean Sea Adventures** (☑340-773-2628; www.caribbeanseaadventures.com; 59 Kings Wharf, Christiansted) Half-day trip is aboard a glass-bottom powerboat; full-day trip is on a catamaran.

**Teroro II** (☑340-718-3161; teroro@msn.com) A trimaran sailboat whose captain will entertain you completely; trips leave from Green Cay Marina, east of Christiansted via East End Rd (Rte 82).

# East End

The scalloped coastline and steep hills of the East End beg for a drive. East End Rd (Rte 82) unfurls along the beach-strewn northern shore, rolling all the way to Point Udall for sublime views and hikes to a turtle-inhabited eco-reserve. Circle back along South Shore Rd (Rte 60) for yet more dramatic seascapes. Lively restaurants and bars dot the way, and golfers and gamblers will find their groove in the area.

## ◉ Sights

Hospital Rd in Christiansted morphs into East End Rd a short distance beyond downtown.

**Point Udall** SCENIC OVERLOOK
(East End Rd) Point Udall is the easternmost geographic point in US territory, and it's well worth the drive out. As you face into a 25-knot trade wind, the vista from the promontory more than 225ft above the surf-strewn beaches is enough to make you hear symphonies. The triangular Millennium Monument marks the spot where St Croix ushered in the year 2000. Hikers will like the challenge of taking the steep trails down the hillside to isolated Jack and Isaac Bays on the point's south side, good for sunbathing, swimming and snorkeling in peace; look for the trailhead near the monument. The road is paved all the way out.

**Great Pond Bay** SALT POND
The large salt pond on the southeastern side of the island, bracketed by Rtes 62, 624 and 60, is home to dozens of varieties of migratory and wading waterfowl, such as egrets. The Boy Scout Camp Arawak is over on the western end of the wilderness, and you can find hiking trails from the camp leading to both Great Pond and the bay. The stunning, undeveloped area has a new visitor: the Wyndham Group, which has plans to build

**THE CASTLE & THE TELESCOPE**

As you near Point Udall, a couple of odd sights will catch your eye. First is the **Contessa's Castle**, a walled, Taj Mahal–like palace rising on a steep inland hill; you'll see it a few miles before you reach the island's tip. Rumors abound about the elderly inhabitant, a Bulgarian starlet who married a New York City real estate mogul. Supposedly when the flags are flying, she is on the island, but most of the time she lives in the US.

About a mile beyond the castle, by Cramer's Park, look for an 82ft-diameter dish antenna. It's the **Very Long Baseline Array Telescope**, one of 10 worldwide, and it records astronomical images.

a resort here. The project has long been delayed by environmental concerns, among other issues, so stay tuned to see if it ever gets off the ground.

### 🏖 Beaches

Beaches are listed in the order you'll encounter them when driving east from Christiansted.

**Buccaneer Beach**  ACTIVITIES BEACH
A crescent beach sheltered from the trade winds and popular with tourists, Buccaneer Beach is in front of the Buccaneer hotel, about 2 miles east of Christiansted off the East End Rd. If you are not a guest of the hotel, you must pay $4 to enter at the hotel gatehouse. You can take advantage of the changing facilities and beach restaurant, but the beach chairs and towels are reserved for hotel guests.

**Shoys Beach**  SNORKELING BEACH
This long crescent of sand just east of Buccaneer Beach is just as protected as the hotel beach but less touristy, and it's free. Lots of upscale Cruzans come here on weekends. Head off the point at the west end of the beach for good snorkeling. To get to Shoys, go to the gatehouse at the Buccaneer, but instead of following the road into the hotel, take the road that veers off to the right; check in with the guard to the gated community and follow the road to the beach. There are no facilities here.

**Chenay Bay**  ACTIVITIES BEACH
This beach lies a mile east of Shoys. The Chenay Bay Beach Resort is here with its bar-restaurant and water-sports concession renting out kayaks. Swimming at Chenay Bay is protected, and the water is shallow, which makes the area popular with families and children. There's good snorkeling if you stay to the right and follow the cove around the point.

**Reef Beach**  ACTIVITIES BEACH
Travelers will find Reef Beach at Tague (sometimes called Teague) Bay in front of Duggan's Reef restaurant, about 7 miles east of Christiansted on Rte 82. The water is a little rough, as the trade winds sometimes blow onto the beach. A lot of the sunbathers here are snowbirds and short-time guests staying in the condo developments in the surrounding area. For strong swimmers, there is good snorkeling on the offshore reef. The spot is also a favorite for windsurfing.

**Cramer's Park**  FAMILY BEACH
This is an attractive public beach on Rte 82. There are grills, picnic tables, bathrooms and a few shelters here. The park can get crowded with Cruzans on holidays and weekends. Most of the time, though, Cramer's Park is quiet. The water deepens gradually and is usually calm, making it good for children.

[TOP CHOICE] **Isaac Bay & Jack Bay**  SECLUDED BEACH
These two secluded beaches are near the southeast tip of the island. They offer no shade or facilities, and you'll have to work hard to reach them, but you'll be hard-pressed to find a more beautiful stretch of sand. The Nature Conservancy manages the area as part of a 301-acre eco-reserve, home to the largest nesting populations of green and hawksbill turtles on St Croix. The creatures are active from July to December.

Jack and Isaac Bays' coral reefs host more than 400 species of fish, including parrot-fish, blue tangs and four-eyed butterfly fish and sergeant majors. The snorkeling here is excellent, though swimmers should be careful of the riptides.

The beaches are popular with Cruzans and the young continentals working on the island. Nudism and topless bathing are common at Isaac Bay.

The most popular route to get to the beaches is to take the steep trail south from Point Udall. It is a good 20-minute hike down to Isaac Bay; the trail starts just before the Millennium Monument. You can also follow the unnamed road east from Rte 60 through the ruins of the vacation homes destroyed by Hurricane Hugo. A path leads along the shore from the end of the road.

### Grapetree Bay                    RESORT BEACH
Broad, long Grapetree Beach connects to the shore in front of the Divi Carina Bay Beach Resort, and the stretch makes for an ideal ramble. You can park at the resort and head down to the 1000ft strand. There is fair snorkeling off the East End. While there are no facilities at Grapetree, you'll find the full array at Divi.

## 🏃 Activities
### Golf
Hitting the links is the big thing to do on the East End.

**Reef Golf Course** (☑340-773-8844) Golfers on a budget will love this 9-hole public course on Rte 82 at Tague Bay. The greens fee is $20, plus $15 for a cart. You can rent clubs for $8. The grounds also have a driving range, as well as two tennis courts.

**Buccaneer Golf Course** (☑340-712-2144; www.thebuccaneer.com) The rolling, oceanside, 18-hole course at the Buccaneer is slightly less challenging than Carambola (see p128). The greens fee is $100 (including cart).

**Divi Carina Mini-Golf Course** (☑340-773-9700www.divicarina.com; adult/child $8/6; ⊙2-9pm Thu-Sun) Bring the kids and let them putt around.

### Windsurfing & Kitesurfing
If you're serious about windsurfing, bring your own board to the island and head for Chenay Bay, Shoys Beach or Reef Beach. You can also kitesurf at most beaches on the East End. **Kite St Croix** (www.kitestcroix.com) rents gear (half/full day $50/70) and offers instruction.

## 🛏 Sleeping
Several resorts rise on the East End's shores. You'll need a car if you plan on leaving the grounds.

**Buccaneer**                    HOTEL $$$
(☑340-712-2100, 800-255-3881; www.thebuccaneer.com; r incl breakfast from $310; ✻@🛜⛱🐾) The Buccaneer set the standard for Virgin Islands beach resorts back in the 1950s and still supplies plenty of luxury. There are 134 rooms in a complex of buildings and cottages surrounding the main three-story hotel that overlooks a cove and beach. The Buccaneer is geared for the active resort guest, with golf, tennis, water sports and a health spa, plus a children's program. Rates include free breakfast, in-room wi-fi, snorkel gear and kayaks. Four restaurants on the grounds provide a wide range of fare. Celebrities have long favored this resort. It's on East End Rd (Rte 82), about 2 miles from Christiansted.

**Divi Carina Bay Beach Resort**    HOTEL $$$
(☑340-773-9700, 877-773-9700; www.divicarina.com; r incl meals from $400; ✻@🛜⛱🐾) There are 180 oceanfront rooms, suites and one-bedroom villas at this resort. Teal-toned fabrics, wicker furniture, kitchenettes and satellite TVs outfit the pleasing units. Divi offers a lot of entertainment options: guests can choose from four restaurants and bars, two pools, a 1000ft beach, tennis courts, water sports, a mini-golf course and the island's only casino. Wi-fi is free in the public areas; it's available in some rooms, too, but you'll need to ask for it. There is a minimum three-night stay in high season. The resort is

---

## BEST BEACHES

» Isaac and Jack Bays (p124) The Nature Conservancy manages these gorgeous beaches as part of an eco-reserve for green and hawksbill turtles. The snorkeling on the reef is outstanding. You can only reach the area by hiking in.

» Protestant Cay (p116) This calm, water-sport-laden beach is a stone's throw from Christiansted.

» Cramer's Park (p124) It's a Cruzan family favorite for picnicking and swimming.

» Cane Bay (p127) The beach at Cane Bay is a divers' mecca, while landlubbers will find lots of friendly beach bars.

on Rte 60 at Grapetree Bay, on the southeast coast.

### Chenay Bay Beach Resort  APARTMENTS $$

(☑340-773-2918, 866-226-8677; www.chenaybay.com; apt from $250; ❄️🛜🏊🐾) Rising above the swells at Chenay Bay, this complex of 50 efficiency cottages (part of a timeshare complex) may well be the favorite destination of vacationing families on St Croix. The West Indian–style rooms have a satellite TV, refrigerator, stovetop and microwave. Sports equipment for snorkeling and kayaking are free, as is tennis. A restaurant on-site serves reasonably priced meals.

### Tamarind Reef Hotel  HOTEL $$

(☑340-773-4455, 800-619-0014; www.tamarindreefhotel.com; r $275-325; ❄️🛜🏊) Tamarind Reef's 38 motel-like rooms are nothing fancy, but the location overlooking Green Cay impresses. All units come with free wi-fi, a kitchenette and a private patio or balcony with a sea view. There are two beaches, protected by offshore reefs, and a large pool. The popular Galleon restaurant is at the marina next door. The hotel is about 3 miles east of Christiansted, on the northeast shore.

## ✗ Eating

### Cheeseburgers in Paradise  BURGERS $$

(☑340-773-1119; Rte 82; mains $8-14; ☉lunch & dinner; 🐾) You may indeed think it's paradise at this ever-popular stop for snowbirds and families. The setting is a roadside field with a small bar and kitchen building surrounded by a collection of open-air tables, some shaded with large umbrellas. The cuisine is light and informal Tex-Mex. The ambience says 'picnic.' Open wide for the nachos and the 'world famous cheeseburger,' or just come for a lick of soft-serve ice cream. This popular restaurant also puts on live music several nights a week, including reggae on Saturday and steel pan on Sunday, starting at about 6pm.

### 📋TOP CHOICE South Shore Café  CAFE $$

(☑340-773-9311; Rte 62 & Rte 624; mains $20-30; ☉dinner Wed-Sun) This gourmet bistro with an open-air setting sits by its lonesome near Great Pond. Most of Diane Scheuber's cuisine is Italian in style, such as sweet-potato ravioli with onions or tomato-based Sicilian clam chowder. Daily specials include a vegetarian option, plus Scheuber makes her own bread and ice cream. The rustic structure is an old dairy building. Reservations recommended.

### Pickled Greek  GREEK $$

(☑340-713-1868; www.thepickledgreek.com; Rte 82; mains $19-24; ☉dinner Mon-Sat) The trim blue-and-white building looks like it came straight from Santorini. Owner Papi does not dispel that notion with his grandmother's old country recipes for stuffed grape leaves, moussaka and gyros. He makes a vegan stew with squash, potatoes and corn. Don't forget to try the chickpea fries!

### Galleon  FRENCH, ITALIAN $$$

(☑340-773-9949; www.galleonrestaurant.com; Rte 82; mains $28-36; ☉dinner) The Galleon, located dockside at Green Cay Marina, is the choice of East Enders who are in the mood for fine French and Northern Italian dinners. *Fra diavola* (shrimp, mussels and fish in a spicy tomato sauce over linguini), coq au vin and duck confit are popular main dishes. To get here from Christiansted, take East End Rd (Rte 82) for about 3 miles and turn left at the marina sign.

## ☆ Entertainment

### Divi Carina Bay Beach Resort  CASINO

(Rte 60) Slots and the usual games are here in a plush but virtually windowless 10,000-sq-foot setting. Players will feel out of place if they do not dress the part of a high roller. There's live music nightly in the 'showbar.'

# North Shore

Luminescent bays, Chris Columbus' landing pad and hot dive sites await along the North Shore. Divers and beach lovers can choose from several cool little hotels to be near the action.

## ◉ Sights

### FREE Salt River National Historic Park  PARK

(www.nps.gov/sari) The Salt River Bay estuary, about 4 miles west of Christiansted on North Shore Rd (Rte 80), is the only documented site where Christopher Columbus landed on US soil. More importantly, Salt River is the site where, on November 14, 1493, Native Americans first tried to repel European intruders. Not only is Salt River the site where the Caribs first drew Spanish blood (at the so-called Cape of Arrows on the bay's eastern tip), but the shores are also the site of some of the earliest French, English and Danish colonial efforts.

St Croix offers a laundry list of singular activities:

» **Kayaking** (p127) Dip a paddle in a bioluminescent bay.

» **Four-wheel drive tours** (p117) Get off the beaten path – literally – to reach tide pools, the rainforest and secluded shores.

» **Diving** (p118) Go deep at the North Shore's wall.

» **Hiking** (p117) Step into the wilderness with local environmental groups or herbalists.

» **Snorkeling** (p123) Swim the underwater trail at Buck Island marine sanctuary.

» **Cycling** (p131) Go mountain biking in the rainforest or along the West End's back roads.

Don't expect bells and whistles; the park remains undeveloped beach. It is most easily viewed from a parking lot at the western entrance to the bay – built on top of the ceremonial ball court and Carib village that the Spaniards invaded more than 500 years ago. With modern yachts moored in the bay and the parking lot beneath your feet, it is difficult to picture either the Caribs or Columbus here. A **visitors center** (☺9am-4pm Tue-Thu Nov-Jun) sits uphill on the shore.

The 700 acres surrounding the Salt River estuary are part of an ecological reserve. Take one of the highly recommended kayak tours to experience it – especially at night, when the water glows with bioluminescent life. Daytime paddles will give you a sense of the diversity of birds, ranging from peregrine falcons to roseate terns, as you glide through red mangrove canals.

## 🏃 Beaches

**Hibiscus Beach**                 SNORKELING BEACH
Plenty of travelers head for palm-fringed Hibiscus Beach, less than 2 miles west of Christiansted off Northside Rd (Rte 75). There are two hotels with a beachside restaurant and bars here, and good snorkeling on the reef joining the coast at the west end of the beach. When the wind swings northeast, there may be an undertow.

**Salt River (Columbus Beach)**     FAMILY BEACH
Lying about 4 miles west of Christiansted off Rte 80 on the west side of Salt River Bay, this is the place where Columbus (actually his men) landed in 1493. While it has historical importance, there are definitely prettier beaches around the island.

**Cane Bay**                        DIVING BEACH
A long, thin strand along Rte 80 about 9 miles west of Christiansted, Cane Bay marks the border between some of the best reef dives on the island and the steep hills of the rainforest. This beach is a favorite with adventure travelers and sports-minded locals. There are several small hotels, restaurants, bars, dive shops and even some shade trees. Every month the island's young and restless (both Cruzans and continentals) head here on the night of the full moon to party till they drop. It's a great time, if you have the stamina.

## 🏃 Activities

### Diving
For the lowdown on diving the famous Wall on the North Shore, see the boxed text, p118. Most dive operators are based in Christiansted or Frederiksted. **Cane Bay Dive Shop** (☎340-773-9913, 800-338-3843; www.canebayscuba.com) is an exception, with a shop across the highway from Cane Bay Beach.

### Kayaking
Paddling Salt River Bay is a St Croix highlight. Day tours provide history on the Columbus site and its early inhabitants, as well as nature lessons on the area's rich bird life. Evening tours glide through the river's bioluminescent water while knowledgeable guides share local legends, folktales and ghost stories. Note the bioluminescence is best viewed during certain phases of the moon; call for the schedule. The companies listed here provide similar tours ($45 to $50 per person, two to three hours). The first two groups also rent kayaks (single/double per day $30/40).

**Virgin Kayak Tours** (☎340-778-0071; www.virginkayakco.com; Cane Bay) As well as tours, Virgin Kayak rents fast, foot-pedaled kayaks and has a small museum of indigenous art on-site. Tours weave in lots of history on the Taíno settlement of Salt River Bay. Cash only.

**Caribbean Adventure Tours** (☑340-778-1522; www.stcroixkayak.com; Salt River Marina) Tours with this organization are broken down into three types: a historical tour, an ecotour and a moonlight tour.

**Sea-Thru Kayak Adventures** (☑340-244-8696; www.seathrukayaksvi.com) This company does its tours in ubercool clear kayaks so you can see what's gliding in the water beneath you. It also offers daytime paddles at Cane Bay and various East End and West End locations. Sea-Thru has no bricks and mortar shop; make location arrangements by phone.

### Golf

Of St Croix's three golf courses, **Carambola Golf Club** (☑340-778-5638; www.golfcarambola.com) is the big enchilada. The Robert Trent Jones course has been ranked among the top 12 resort courses in the world. The 18-hole, 6834-yard, par-72 course spreads out through a valley on the edge of the rainforest on River Rd (Rte 69) about a mile south of the Carambola Beach Resort. The greens fee is $135, including a cart. Golf clubs rent for $35.

### 🛏 Sleeping

For all of these properties you'll need wheels to get out and about.

**Palms at Pelican Cove** HOTEL $$
(☑340-718-8920, 800-548-4460; www.palmsatpelicancove.com; 4126 La Grand Princesse; r $239-289; @�winfi🏊) This 40-room resort hotel overlooks a handsome beach about 2 miles west of Christiansted. The brightly painted rooms are comfy and a decent size, but they're not luxurious. The Palms' selling point is its homey vibe and waterside locale. Guests can use the free snorkel gear and tennis racquets (for the lone court); a morning yoga class (fee required) takes place on the beach. There's a pool, restaurant and beach bar. The free wi-fi is available in the public areas only.

**Hibiscus Beach Hotel** HOTEL $$
(☑340-718-4042, 800-442-0121; www.hibiscusbeachresort.com; 4131 La Grande Princesse; r incl breakfast $200-290; 🌀�winfi🏊) The Hibiscus stands just up the mile-long beach from the Palms at Pelican Cove. The 38 rooms spread through a collection of beachfront, colonial-style villas amid a coconut grove. Room decor is a bit dated, but each unit comes with a wind-cooled private patio or balcony. Snorkeling equipment is available for free, as is in-room wi-fi. There is a popular beachfront bar and restaurant here, with entertainment most nights of the week (noise alert) and views across the water to Christiansted.

**Arawak Bay Inn at Salt River** B&B $$
(☑340-772-1684; www.arawakbaysaltriver.co.vi; 62 Salt River Rd; r incl breakfast $140-160; 🌀@winfi🏊) The pick of the local litter for value, this peachy B&B opened in 2007 and has 14 bright rooms, each with different color schemes and decor. For those without a vehicle, it's isolated from the beaches and eateries, but the owners make amends by providing daily transportation to Christiansted and Cane Bay. The honor bar and telescope for guests to use to stargaze (or ship-gaze) are nice touches.

**Waves at Cane Bay** HOTEL $$
(☑340-778-1805, 800-545-0603; www.canebaystcroix.com; North Shore Rd; r $150-200; 🌀winfi🏊) This small, tidy hotel has pretty dang big rooms painted in tropical pastels. All 12 units have a balcony, kitchenette, cable TV and free wi-fi. But it's really all about location: you can snorkel or dive right off the rocks out front or lounge in the saltwater pool.

**Cane Bay Reef Club** HOTEL $$
(☑340-778-2966, 800-253-8534; www.canebay.com; 114 North Shore Rd; r $150-250; 🌀winfi🏊) The Reef Club is good value because each of the nine rooms is like its own little villa overlooking the beach. The decor is dated but all suites include small kitchens and private patios virtually hanging over the sea. There is a pool for bathing and a seaside sundeck. Cane Bay Beach and its diving, snorkeling and beach bars are 300 yards down the busy road.

**Carambola Beach Resort** HOTEL $$$
(☑340-778-3800; www.carambolabeach.com; North Shore Rd; r from $360; 🌀winfi🏊) The Carambola is the former Rockefeller resort, and it's posh. If you stay here, accommodations are in one of the red-roofed villas on the mountainside overlooking Davis Bay. There are about 150 suite-sized rooms with all the trimmings. Three restaurants, a world-class golf course, an on-site dive operator and tennis courts cater to the guests. The property belongs to Marriott's Renaissance brand.

Also recommended:

**Villa Greenleaf**  B&B **$$**
(☎340-719-1958, 888-282-1001; www.villagreen
leaf.com; r incl breakfast $275-300; ✳🈂🈂) Five
elegant suites fill the garden-surrounded
house.

**Club St Croix**  APARTMENTS **$$**
(☎340-773-4800, 800-524-2025; www.antilles
resorts.com; apt $200-265; ✳🈂) These condos
are part of the Antilles group, which manages several properties on St Thomas, as
well. It's a good beach location, though the
surrounding neighborhood is a bit sketchy.

**Colony Cove**  APARTMENTS **$$**
(☎340-773-9150, 800-524-2025; www.antilles
resorts.com; apt $235; ✳🈂🈝) Located beside
Club St Croix and under the same man-
agement; units have a washer and dryer.

## ✕ Eating

TOP
CHOICE / **Rowdy Joe's North
Shore Eatery**  INTERNATIONAL **$$**
(☎340-718-0055; North Shore Rd; mains $9-15;
☺lunch & dinner; 🈝) Walk up to the converted house, sit on the porch, and order off
the blackboard menu. The chef strives for
'good mood food' using ingredients from St
Croix's farms and fishers. Dishes might include the Cubano pork sandwich, Thai beef
salad with fermented black bean vinaigrette,
fish tacos or house-made pasta. Rowdy Joe's
has gained a loyal fan base for its ice cream
made on-site, with flavors such as French
vanilla praline, or order a margarita made
with local fruits.

**Eat @ Cane Bay**  INTERNATIONAL **$$**
(☎340-718-0360; www.eatatcanebay.com; mains
$9-14; ☺lunch & dinner, brunch Sun, closed Tue)
Eat @ Cane Bay lets the good times roll with
'food shots' – bite-sized gourmet servings of
fare such as smoked duck potpie. Located
across from Cane Bay Beach, the restaurant
also cooks burgers that are a cut above the
norm. Other delicious items on the menu in-
clude slow-roasted pulled pork and brisket,
along with wine and Belgian beers. The Sun-
day reggae brunch features eggs benedict,
crepes and bananas Foster pancakes among
the lineup.

**Off the Wall**  BURGERS **$$**
(☎340-778-4771; North Shore Rd; mains $8-15;
☺lunch & dinner) After a day of diving at Cane
Bay, climb out of the ocean and head to the

beach's east end, where this open-air pub
serves burgers, nachos and quesadillas to a
happy crowd of drinkers.

**Breezez**  INTERNATIONAL **$$**
(☎340-773-7077; mains $9-20; ☺lunch & dinner,
brunch Sun) Located at Club St Croix, a mile
west of Christiansted, Breezez is a popular
lunching place for folks spending the day at
Hibiscus Beach. The poolside operation serves
up burgers and a popular Sunday brunch.

# Frederiksted

Except for about every third day when
a cruise ship arrives, Frederiksted looks
the part of a classic Caribbean outpost – a
motionless village of colonial buildings
snoozing beside a painted teal-blue sea.
Though it's quiet much of the time, St Croix's
second-banana town is worth a visit to see
its first-rate collection of Victorian colonial
architecture, and to join its tour operators
for cool cycling, snorkeling and diving trips.
The jazzy little spot also hosts a vibrant
gay community.

## History

From the beginning of St Croix's sugarcane
industry, merchant ships from England's
North American colonies found this western
end of the island a convenient point for trans-
shipping cargo of slaves, cane and finished
goods without paying duty to the Danish gov-
ernment in Christiansted. To stop illegal traf-
fic at the spot, nicknamed 'Freedom City,' the
Danes decided to create an official port with a
fort as a deterrent to the smuggling.

Dramatic events highlight Frederiksted's
history during much of the 19th century.
First came the recession in the sugar in-
dustry. Next came the slave revolt of 1848,
when the black leader General Budhoe and
a legion of slaves gathered outside the fort
and threatened destruction of the island un-
til Governor Peter von Scholten issued his
Proclamation of Emancipation, which freed
all the slaves in the Danish West Indies.

Finally, on October 1 and 2, 1878, former
slaves, angered by the planters' refusal to pay
wages of more than 5¢ to 7¢ a day, went on
an island-wide rampage called the Fireburn,
which reduced Frederiksted to ashes. The
burned neoclassical colonial buildings were
rebuilt or replaced during the end of the 19th
century, giving Frederiksted's historic build-
ings the Victorian look you see today.

## ⊙ Sights

When cruise ships arrive, the town bustles. Shopkeepers fling open their doors, vendors set up stalls, and bands play in the park. Otherwise, it's pretty quiet around here. Check **VI Now** (www.vinow.com) for the ship schedule.

### Frederiksted Pier & Waterfront Park   PARK

The long pier that heads out to sea from the north end of Strand St has had its ups and downs in recent years. A decade or so ago, cruise ships docked here regularly. Then high crime rates drove them away. The community worked hard to address the issue, and it eventually got funding to revitalize the abutting area with a park, fountains and cobbled pedestrian paths stretching along the waterfront. In 2008 ships began to drift back in.

The palm-lined seafront has benches where you can sit and watch the scene. The pier is worth a stroll – except when ships are in, in which case only passengers are permitted past the gate. During quiet times, snorkelers and divers gravitate to the pier's pilings, which attract an extensive collection of marine life, such as schools of sea horses.

### Fort Frederik   MUSEUM

(admission $3; ⊙open when cruise ships in port) The deep red color of this fort at the foot of the town pier is what most visitors remember about the little citadel. The threatening paint job was meant to dissuade smugglers of a bygone era. The rubble-and-masonry structure came to life between 1752 and 1760 and owes its trapezoidal design to classic Danish military architecture of the period.

Governor Peter von Scholten issued his 1848 Proclamation of Emancipation here, which freed all the slaves in the Danish West Indies. Exhibits in the museum now housed inside explain the event, and also provide lessons on colonial architecture, the sugar industry and more.

The fort has served as a jail, courthouse, police station, fire station and telephone exchange. In 1976 island conservationists restored the structure. The local government now manages the property (unlike Christiansted's fort, which the federal government oversees).

### Caribbean Museum Center for the Arts   MUSEUM

(☑340-772-2622; www.cmcarts.org; 62 King St; suggested donation $3; ⊙11am-6pm Tue-Sat) Housed in an 18th-century Danish town-house on the waterfront, the Caribbean Museum hangs vibrant local and international artworks. The exhibits rotate regularly, and though the museum is not expansive, it's definitely worth a browse.

### Buddhoe Park   PARK

This small, tree-shaded park lies outside the eastern ramparts of Fort Frederik. Today, it's a good place to escape the sun on a hot day, but on July 3, 1848, the spot was a wild place when Moses 'General Budhoe' (also spelled 'Buddhoe') Gottlieb led 'all the Negroes in this part of the country in revolt.' Bells sounded from every church and plantation on the island, and 6000 to 8000 slaves, all armed with machetes and bludgeons, congregated here in front of the gate to Fort Frederik to demand and receive their freedom.

### Victoria House   HISTORICAL BUILDING

(7-8 Strand St) This large residence, near Market St, sits back from the sidewalk and rises three stories as one of the most elaborately detailed buildings in the Virgin Islands. Largely destroyed in the 1878 fire, the house has been rebuilt in a Victorian 'gingerbread' style, including a great deal of ornamental latticework. The house remains a private residence and is not open to the public.

### Market Square   MARKET

(near Market St & Queen St) If you head east on Market St from Strand St into the heart of the small town, you will find Market Square, where the corners of the blocks have been cut away at the intersection of Market and Queen Sts to make room for vendors. This has been Frederiksted's marketplace for 250 years, but don't expect a lot of vendors now that most islanders shop at the supermarkets on Centerline Rd. On most days, you will find fresh produce in the market shed on the southeast corner, and this can be a good place to pick up a mango to quench your thirst.

### St Patrick's Roman Catholic Church   CHURCH

(near Market St & Hospital St) This Catholic church lies a block east of Market Square. It's interesting because of its unusual synthesis of architectural styles. Built in 1848, with a three-story brick bell tower, it is basically Gothic Revival, but the gabled ends of the nave and transept are reminiscent of the Spanish Mission style. A high masonry wall encloses the church and its cemetery. Masses are in English and Spanish.

### St Paul's Episcopal Anglican Church
CHURCH
(near Hospital St & King Cross St) The church dates from 1812 and is the oldest house of worship in town. Although much of the church has its roots in Danish colonial neo-classicism, the most outstanding part of the structure is its crenellated English Gothic bell tower.

### Athalie MacFarlane Petersen Public Library
CULTURAL CENTER
(Strand St near Queen Cross St; ☺9am-5pm Mon-Fri) Also called the Bell House for its second owner, this building at the south end of Strand St dates from 1803. There is not only a small library inside but also a cultural center that supports local arts and crafts events. It is a good stop if you want a peek inside Frederiksted's Victorian buildings.

## 🐾 Beaches

**Fort Frederik Beach** is the public strand just north of the fort and pier. When the prevailing trade winds blow, this beach remains as sheltered as a millpond; you can swim off the beach for some excellent snorkeling around the pier (as long as no ships are in).

**Sand Castle Beach** is the nickname for the strand in front of the Sand Castle on the Beach and Cottages by the Sea lodgings, about a mile south of Frederiksted along the waterfront road. It provides calm water, good snorkeling and great sunsets.

**La Grange, Rainbow** and **Sprat Hall Beaches** are north of Fort Frederik Beach on Rte 63. They're all actually the same beach, but you can get a beer at the south end, where there are several pubs and restaurants. Young Cruzans and continentals make this a party scene on weekends.

## 🏃 Activities

### Freedom City Cycles
CYCLING
(☎340-277-2433; www.freedomcitycycles.com; 2 Strand St) The shop will rent you a mountain bike (half/full day $20/35) to cruise the back roads. Better yet, book a tour ($40 per person) and pedal past sugar-plantation ruins and onward to Hams Bluff; more difficult rides bounce over rainforest trails. The shop is located a half block inland from the pier.

### St Croix Ultimate Bluewater Adventures
SNORKELING, DIVING
(☎340-773-5994, 887-567-1367; www.stcroixscuba. com; tours $50) The shop is in Christiansted, but it offers a snorkel trip from Frederiksted

on Tuesday, Thursday and Saturday at 10am and 2pm to check out the pier and a reef near Sandy Point National Wildlife Refuge.

### N2 The Blue
SNORKELING, DIVING
(☎340-772-3483; www.n2theblue.com) Specializes in West End wreck dives and Frederiksted Pier snorkel trips; the shop is located across from the pier on the first side street next to the police station.

### Scubawest
DIVING
(☎340-772-3701, 800-352-0107; www.dives cubawest.com; 330 Strand St) Specializes in wreck dives near shore and trips to explore the outer reaches of Frederiksted Pier.

## 🛏 Sleeping

With its out-of-the-mainstream, laissez-faire ambience, Frederiksted is the center for gay life on St Croix. All of the hotels listed here are gay-friendly.

### Cottages by the Sea
APARTMENTS $$
(☎340-772-0495, 800-323-7252; www.caribbean cottages.com; apt $160-220; 127A Estate Smithfield; ✳🛜♿) This 20-cottage compound sits on a quiet beach about a mile south of Frederiksted. The friendly, hands-on staff make the place feel like a beach camp. All cottages have whimsical decor and a kitchen, TV and private patio. You'll need a car to get around with ease. Four-night minimum stay required.

### Frederiksted Hotel
HOTEL $$
(☎340-772-0500, 800-595-9519; www.frederik stedhotel.dk; 442 Strand St; r $110-150; ✳@▨) This Danish-owned, bright-blue hotel sits right in the middle of downtown. Four floors are built around a courtyard and small pool, and many rooms have patios overlooking the pier. The 36 units each have tiled floors and standard hotel-style furnishings, plus a refrigerator.

### Sand Castle on the Beach
HOTEL $$
(☎340-772-1205, 800-524-2018; www.sandcastle onthebeach.com; 127 Estate Smithfield; r/ste incl breakfast from $149/259; ✳🛜▨) On the beach about a mile south of Frederiksted, this multi-story, four-building establishment with 21 rooms is one of the few gay- and lesbian-oriented hotels in the USVI. The motel-like rooms come with kitchenettes; most have sea views. There is also a video library and gas grills for cookouts, or you can have lunch or dinner at the oceanside restaurant aptly named the Beach Side Cafe.

## ✕ Eating

**Polly's at the Pier**  CAFE **$**
(☑340-719-9434; 3 Strand St; mains $5-9; ☺breakfast & lunch) Beloved by cruise-ship passengers, Polly's serves coffee, tea, sandwiches and omelets three doors down from the pier. It has internet terminals and free wi-fi for customers. Polly's also scoops several flavors of locally made Armstrong's Ice Cream.

**Mahogany by the Sea**  INTERNATIONAL **$$**
(☑340-772-0732;  www.mahoganybythesea.com; 37 Strand St; mains $24-28; ☺dinner) Mahogany calls itself a sports bar and grill, but it's classier than that (though a few flat-screen TVs do appear around the bar). The menu ranges from baked oysters with Brie to shrimp creole to vegetarian lasagna, with more locals than tourists stopping by to dig in. The open-air, second-story venue offers good views of the harbor. Bands play on Thursday, and DJs spin on Friday. The restaurant sits at the southern end of the town's waterfront.

**Coconuts on the Beach**  TEX MEX **$$**
(☑340-719-6060;  www.coconutsonthebeach-stx. com; 72 LaGrange; mains $8-15; ☺lunch & dinner) The casual beach bar serves nachos, jalapeño-spiced burgers and wraps. If nothing else, go for a drink and watch the sunset. It's about a five-minute walk north of town.

**Blue Moon**  CARIBBEAN, CAJUN **$$**
(☑340-772-2222;  www.bluemoonstcroix.com; 7 Strand St; mains $25-29; ☺lunch Tue-Fri, dinner Tue-Sat, brunch Sun) Considered one of the best restaurants on the island, Blue Moon dishes up Caribbean and Cajun cuisine in an atmospheric colonial warehouse. There's live jazz Wednesday and Friday nights and during Sunday brunch.

**Turtles**  SANDWICHES **$**
(☑340-772-3676; www.turtlesdeli.com; 37 Strand St; mains $7-10; ☺8:30am-5:30pm Mon-Sat) Chow down on hulking sandwiches with homemade bread, or sip a fine cup of coffee, at beachfront tables under sea-grape trees.

**Sunset Grille**  BURGERS, SEAFOOD **$$**
(☑340-772-5855; sandwiches $7-13, dinner mains $17-33; ☺lunch & dinner) Ahh, swing in beachfront hammocks while awaiting your fish and island dishes. Located 2 miles north of Frederiksted on Rte 63.

## ☆ Entertainment

The **Sunset Jazz Festival** (admission free; ☺6pm 3rd Fri of month) brings throngs of locals and visitors to the waterfront park. Check **St Croix This Week** (www.stcroixthisweek.com) and the daily *St Croix Avis* to see what's on in Frederiksted.

**Blue Moon**  LIVE MUSIC
(☑340-772-2222; 7 Strand St) Friday is the big night, when both locals and continentals jam the place for live jazz and the chance to find romance.

**Rhythms at Rainbow Beach**  LIVE MUSIC
(☑340-772-0002) On Sunday afternoon, less than a mile north of Frederiksted on Rte 63, Rhythms has live reggae and R&B in a beachside setting. The scene draws a lot of the island's hard bodies to party on, dude.

## ℹ Information

### Dangers & Annoyances

Be mindful: lonely beaches are no place to go without a group of friends. In particular, stay away from the Sandy Point National Wildlife Refuge at the southwest corner of the island. A red-light district exists in Frederiksted on King St for three blocks or so south of the intersection with Market St.

## ℹ Getting There & Away

### Taxi

Frederiksted's taxi stand is at Market Square. It can take up to an hour to drive between here and Christiansted (fare from $24, depending on number of passengers).

# West End

The area around Frederiksted has two very distinct sides to its topography and character. First, there are the wild mountains and beaches of the so-called rainforest area in the island's northwest pocket. South of the mountains is the broad coastal plain that once hosted the majority of sugar plantations. Today, the area is largely a modern commercial and residential zone where most of St Croix's population lives, but sprinkled among the few patches of undeveloped land bordering Centerline Rd are some remarkable heirlooms from the colonial era, including the Whim Plantation.

## ◉ Sights

**Estate Whim Plantation Museum**  MUSEUM
(☑340-772-0598;  www.stcroixlandmarks.com; Centerline Rd; adult/child $10/5; ☺10am-4pm Mon-Sat) Just a few miles outside Frederiksted on Centerline Rd lies one of St Croix's most

striking evocations of its colonial sugarcane history. Only a few of the original 150 acres of Whim Plantation survive as the museum, but the grounds thoroughly evoke the days when 'King Cane' ruled the island.

The fully restored and furnished neoclassical great house stands at the heart of the grounds. For the purposes of cooling, it has only three rooms, which are ventilated by huge windows. Walls built of coral, limestone and rubble, bonded with a mortar of molasses, insulate the house and have given it the strength to stand up against hurricanes since the 1790s.

As you tour the grounds, you'll see animal-mills and windmills as well as steam engines used for grinding cane. Buildings like the cookhouse (where they serve johnnycakes), bathhouse, watch house, caretaker's cottage and slave quarters are also on the grounds. Some are restored to their vintage state; others function as exhibition galleries and the museum store. The tombstone of Anna Heegaard, the black companion of Governor von Scholten, is also on the grounds.

Guided tours of the great house leave every 30 minutes. Don't forget to ask for the Landmarks Society's map to other ruins around the island.

### Cruzan Rum Distillery     DISTILLERY
(☎340-692-2280; www.cruzanrum.com; 3 Estate Diamond, Rte 64; adult/child $5/1; ☺9:30-11:30am & 1-4pm Mon-Fri) To find out how the islands' popular elixir gets made, stop here for a distillery tour. The journey through gingerbread-smelling (from molasses and yeast), oak-barrel-stacked warehouses takes 20 minutes or so, after which you get to sample the good stuff. The company store offers low prices on specialty rums like 'tropical banana.'

The Nelthropp family, Cruzan Rum's owners, have had a corner on the market since 1760 – right up until Captain Morgan opened its distillery nearby in 2010. The Cruzan factory is about 2 miles east of Whim Plantation off of Centerline Rd on Rte 64.

### St George Village Botanical Garden     GARDEN
(☎340-692-2874; www.sgvbg.org; Centerline Rd; adult/child $8/1; ☺9am-5pm) If you continue east on Centerline Rd after leaving the Cruzan Rum factory, you soon see St George Village Botanical Garden on the highway's north side. This 16-acre park built over the ruins of an indigenous settlement and a colonial sugar plantation does for the flora and fauna what Whim Plantation does for the grandeur of plantation days. A self-guided tour takes you on trails among the ruins of the rum factory, great house, shops, dam and aqueduct. There are more than 1500 species of tropical plants, including a profusion of orchids and hibiscus, as well as the much-admired cactus garden.

### FREE St Croix Leap     ART STUDIO
(☎340-772-0421; Mahogany Rd (Rte 76) Brooks Hill; ☺8:30am-5pm Mon-Fri, 10am-4pm Sat) Tucked into a steep hillside at the heart of the rainforest on the Mahogany Rd is the unusual outdoor woodworking and sculpture studio called St Croix Leap. Here, master sculptor 'Cheech' leads a band of apprentice woodworkers in transforming chunks of fallen mahogany trees into all manner of art and housewares. Bring your bug repellent.

### Lawaetz Family Museum     MUSEUM
(☎340-772-1539; www.stcroixlandmarks.com; Mahogany Rd (Rte 76); adult/child $104; ☺10am-4pm Tue, Thu & Sat) Less than a quarter-mile beyond

---

**DON'T MISS**

## CALEDONIA RAIN FOREST

Most of St Croix's rain falls over the mountains on the northwest corner of the island, producing a thick, damp forest of tall mahogany, silk cotton and white cedar. Although this area is commonly called 'rainforest,' only about 40 inches of rainfall here per year. That's actually less than half the amount a true rainforest receives, but no matter. This place looks the part, with clouds, dripping trees, earthy smells, slick roads and muddy trails.

The best hiking, mountain biking and off-road exploring is here along the unpaved tracks of the Creque Dam Rd (Rte 58) and the Scenic Rd (Rte 78). If you don't have the time, inclination or vehicle to do off-road exploring, you can still see the rainforest by following Mahogany Rd (Rte 76) as it cuts through the spooky woods; it's twisty and pot-holed, so be careful.

the entrance to St Croix Leap lies this plantation museum. Look for the light-blue sign for 'Little La Grange' and follow the dirt track up the hill between ruins of the old sugar mill and factory to the great house.

Set amid virtual jungle and steep hills, this plantation belies the myth that sugarcane could only be raised on St Croix's coastal plain. For the most part, the place and its furnishings retain the ambience of the plantation when it became the Lawaetz family homestead slightly more than 100 years ago. Now, family heir Irene Lawaetz acts as your hostess, giving you a guided tour of the house. New trails have been opened to make the grounds an exceptional place for hiking, losing yourself in birdsong and kicking back for a picnic lunch. It's a rustic place that stands in contrast to the grandeur of Whim Plantation.

### Sandy Point National Wildlife Refuge
NATURE RESERVE

(☑340-773-4554; ⊙10am-4pm Sat & Sun) In the 1980s, the US Fish & Wildlife Service purchased almost 400 acres that included the peninsula and shores of Sandy Point at the extreme southwest end of St Croix. The area is now a nature reserve with more than 3 miles of vacant beaches that are important nesting grounds for the mammoth leatherback sea turtle. Hawksbill and green turtles nest here as well. The Fish & Wildlife rangers constantly monitor the beaches during the nesting season from February to July, and the beach may well be closed when the 1000lb leatherbacks are coming ashore at night to lay their eggs.

By day, bird-watchers enjoy the area, as it is a nesting ground for endangered brown pelicans, terns and oyster catchers. To see the turtles, you may be able to join one of the night tours sponsored by the Fish & Wildlife Service or perhaps even volunteer for beach patrol. Check with the Fish & Wildlife Service or the St Croix Environmental Association (☑340-773-1989; www.stxenvironmental.org) about guided tours and turtle-watching programs, especially during the April through August nesting season. While Sandy Point is a wild and beautiful area, locals know it as a place that attracts a bad element. Car break-ins do happen, so take precautions.

### Doc James Race Track
RACE TRACK

(☑340-778-1395; Rte 64) This old, small-scale thoroughbred-racing operation is open spo-

radically. Call for a racing schedule and post time. It stands just south of the airport.

### Captain Morgan Rum Distillery
DISTILLERY

(www.diageo.com; Rte 66) The makers of Captain Morgan Rum are slated to open a LEED-certified visitors center in 2012. Diageo, the company that owns the brand, also owns Guinness, among other well-known booze brands, so expect an entertaining tour for the masses at the new facility.

## 🏃 Activities

### Bird-watching

The West End Salt Pond at Sandy Point on the southwest tip of the island is a good spot for seabirds like egrets and brown pelicans. (You can also see these birds in abundance around Great Pond off the Southside Rd.) You may also see several species of grebes and herons. The rainforest trails along Scenic Rd lead you into the territory of parakeets, canaries and hawks like the 'killy killy' sparrow hawk. Hummingbirds and bananaquits are common around the flowering ruins of many of the island's old estates, including the St George Village Botanical Garden.

### Horseback Riding

Paul & Jill's Equestrian Stables (☑340-772-2880, 340-332-0417; www.paulandjills.com; Rte 63; 1½hr tours $90) offers trail rides that lead through hidden plantation ruins and the rainforest to hilltop vistas. Cash or traveler's checks only. The stables are located 1½ miles north of Frederiksted on Rte 63.

### Hiking

Hiking to Hams Bluff on the island's tip-top northwest corner unfurls views of sea-pounded cliffs. Visiting with a guide is a good idea; see p117 for some recommendations.

## 👉 Tours

The St Croix Landmarks Society (www.stcroixlandmarks.org) sponsors house tours at regular intervals during the year, where you get to go inside homes not normally open to the public, as well as on 'ruins rambles.' Check the website's calendar for schedules.

## 🛏 Sleeping & Eating

🏕 Mt Victory Campground CAMPGROUND $

(☑340-772-1651, 866-772-1651; www.mtvictorycamp.com; Rte 58; campsites/equipped tents/cottages $30/85/95; ☒) This is a terrific facility set on a small working farm, where you'll fall asleep to a lullaby of croaking frogs and wake to birdsong. The three perma-tents and two cottages are similar screened-in dwellings, each with a kitchen with cold-water sink, a propane stove and cooking utensils. There's no electricity, and guests share the solar-heated bathhouse. It feels remote, but the beach is only a few miles down the hill. Cash or traveler's checks only.

**Northside Valley**                    APARTMENTS **$$**
(☑340-772-0558;          www.northsidevalley.com; 2 Estate Northside; villas per week $1000-1500; ❄) A step up in amenities from Mt Victory Campground, Northside Valley offers eight concrete-and-tile villas with private bathrooms and bamboo sheets, all washed using environmentally friendly cleaning supplies. There is a one-week minimum stay. It's on the beach near Butler Bay.

**Country Snack Stand**               JUICE BAR **$**
(☑340-772-0604; Rte 76; ☺10am-6pm) In the heart of the rainforest, a few miles east of Montpellier Domino Club, Trinidad native Hazel Smith blends eight fruits – mango, starfruit, passionfruit, tamarind, papaya, guava, gooseberry and pineapple – into a heckuva smoothie. She also pours ginger beer, coconut water and other local drinks and sells avocados, bananas, mangos and more from her garden. It's a good place to pick up sauces and other local treats, too.

## ☆ Entertainment

**Montpellier Domino Club**                    BAR
(☑340-772-9914; ☺10am-5pm) This open-air West Indian bar-restaurant lies deep in the rainforest. Some folks come to drink the *mamajuana* (spiced rum), but the big attractions are the famous beer-guzzling pigs Hurricane Roger and Grunt. Tourists line up to pay $1 to watch the pigs gnaw open cans of nonalcoholic brewskis and swill the contents. It costs you $2 a can to feed the pigs yourself (mind the spray!) and $3 to shoot a video. It's certainly not kosher (the animals live in confined pens), but you've never seen anything like it. The porkers used to drink the real thing until

offspring were born suffering the symptoms of alcohol withdrawal.

**Candlelight Concert Series**          LIVE MUSIC
(☑340-772-0598; www.stcroixlandmarks.org; Centerline Rd; ☺Oct-Apr) The Landmarks Society, which oversees the Whim Plantation, hosts an intimate classical musical series on the atmospheric grounds. Concerts take place on Friday and Saturday night one weekend per month. Tickets cost $45.

**Island Center for the Performing Arts**                    LIVE MUSIC
(☑340-778-5272; Rte 79) This is St Croix's venue for theater, cabaret and performances by local and internationally recognized classical ensembles and pop music stars. The center is just north of the Sunny Isle Shopping Center.

**Caribbean Community Theater**     THEATER
(☑340-778-3596; www.cct.vi; Rte 79) The CCT is a very active local theater troupe, performing more than four shows annually in the Sidney Lee Theater, within the Island Center.

**Caribbean Dance Company**          DANCE
(☑340-778-8824) This dance company takes pride in its capacity to preserve and perform Afro-Caribbean traditions of storytelling, music and dance. It usually performs its big February show at the Island Center.

**Sunny Isle Theaters**                 CINEMA
(☑340-778-5620) Shows first-run Hollywood films; the theaters are in the Sunny Isle Shopping Center.

## 🔒 Shopping

**La Reine Farmers Market**               FOOD
(Centerline Rd; ☺11am-3pm Sat) The Department of Agriculture runs this market, which is chock-full of colorful herbs, yams, collard greens, beets, mangos, guava, pumpkin and more. Sweet-tooths can browse the homemade jams, chutneys, pies and tarts.

**Sunny Isle Shopping Centre**           MALL
(Centerline Rd; ☑340-778-5830) It's the main mall on the island, featuring several big-box retailers.

# Tortola

POP 19,600

## Best Places to Eat

» Sugar Mill Restaurant (p156)

» Mrs Scatliffe's Restaurant (p153)

» Road Town Bakery (p146)

» The Dove (p146)

» De Loose Mongoose (p160)

## Best Places to Stay

» Sugar Mill Hotel (p156)

» Hummingbird House (p144)

» Village Cay Hotel & Marina (p144)

» Serendipity House (p159)

» Heritage Inn (p152)

## Why Go?

Among Tortola's sharp peaks and bougainvillea-clad hillsides, you'll find a mash-up of play places. Guesthouses and mountain villas mingle with beachside resorts. *Bon Appétit* cooks make island dishes next to elderly Mrs Scatliffe, who prepares them from her garden. You even get your choice of full moon parties – artsy with Aragorn or mushroom-tea-fueled with Bomba.

About 80% of the BVI's 25,000 citizens live and work on Tortola, so it's not surprising there's a lot of choice here. It's also the territory's governmental and commercial center, plus its air and ferry hub. And for all the sailors out there: Tortola is the Caribbean's charter boat capital.

Beyond busy Road Town, Cane Garden Bay's turquoise water and music-fueled nightlife beckons. Surfers will find plenty of groovy beaches and to top it all off, Tortola's funky West Indian settlements add local character to the scene.

## When to Go

Mid-December through April is the prime weather high season, when visitors from northern climes descend and set sail in charter boats. Big bashes take place in spring and summer, including the BVI Spring Regatta (early April), BVI Music Festival (late May), HiHo windsurfing races (late June) and the year's biggest bash: the Emancipation Festival (late July to early August). Tortola also gets busy each month during the full moon when the parties at Bomba's and Aragorn's fire up the night.

## History

Although no definitive record exists, many historians speculate that Tortola was the island that Columbus called Santa Ursula when he sailed past in 1493. The island got its present name around 1515, when outriders from Puerto Rico passed this way in search of gold. They called the island Tortola, which means 'turtle dove' in Spanish, after encountering flocks of the cooing birds. Most have since flown the coop (except on neighboring Guana Island).

The island was formally claimed by Holland in 1648, when the Dutch West India Company established a settlement and built a fort on the site that is now the Fort Burt Hotel. In 1666, a band of British drove the Dutch out and claimed the island for England.

In the 18th century an enterprising group of English religious dissidents known as Quakers arrived. Famed for their work ethic, business acumen and devotion to pacifism, they established plantations throughout Tortola. Their surnames – Callwood, Lettsome etc – are still the most common among islanders.

In the 1960s modern sailors discovered the BVI's fair winds and pristine anchorages, and bareboat yacht-charter companies – led by the Moorings – set up shop to serve them, using Tortola as their base. Soon sailors came by the tens of thousands from the US and Europe to charter cruising sailboats. And so began the modern development boom. Some 90% of the commercial buildings and homes on the island date from the last 35 years or so.

### ★★ Festivals & Events

**BVI Spring Regatta**  SAILING
(www.bvispringregatta.org; late Mar-early Apr) The granddaddy of Tortola's myriad yacht races has become one of the Caribbean's biggest parties. It features seven days of small- and large-craft races and provides a time-honored excuse to swill beer, sip rum, listen

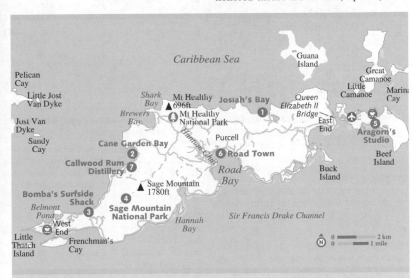

## Tortola Highlights

① Kick back on the dramatic strand of sand at **Josiah's Bay** (p158)

② Dance to reggae at the beach bars along **Cane Garden Bay** (p151)

③ Knock back a beer with the board-toting crowd at **Bomba's Surfside Shack** (p157)

④ Hike the trails at lush **Sage Mountain National Park** (p150)

⑤ Ring in the new moon with fungi music, stilt walkers and fire jugglers at **Aragorn's Studio** (p160)

⑥ Set sail on a charter boat from **Road Town** (p143)

⑦ Check out the atmospheric copper vats and wooden casks at the **Callwood Rum Distillery** (p150)

**TORTOLA**

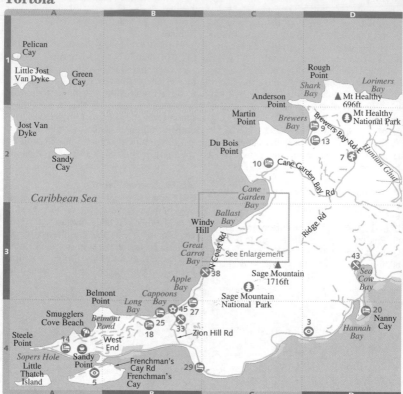

to live music and party with sailors and crew from around the world.

**BVI Music Festival**                    MUSIC
(www.bvimusicfestival.com; late May) This festival brings big-name acts such as Percy Sledge and Wyclef Jean to wail at Cane Garden Bay in late May.

**Highland Spring HIHO**         WINDSURFING
(www.go-hiho.com/hshiho; late Jun) Windsurfers and stand-up paddleboarders converge for the weeklong Hook-In-Hold-On races, which zip around Virgin Gorda, Anegada and the Out Islands, too.

**BVI Emancipation Festival**       CULTURAL
(www.bvitourism.com; late Jul–early Aug) The BVI's premier cultural event, when Tortola rocks from East End to West End, celebrating its African-Caribbean heritage. Activities feature everything from a beauty pageant and car show to 'rise & shine tramps' (noisy

parades led by reggae bands in the back of a truck that start at 3am) to horse racing. The celebration marks the 1834 Emancipation Act that abolished slavery in the BVI; it coincides with a string of public holidays.

**Virgin Islands Fungi Fest**           MUSIC
(www.vifungifest.com; mid-Nov) The weekend-long Fungi Fest brings musicians from around the islands to a Road Town park for nonstop concerts.

### ❶ Getting There & Around

**AIR**

**Terrence B Lettsome Airport** (EIS; ☎284-494-3701) is on Beef Island, connected to Tortola by a bridge on the island's East End. It is a 25-minute drive between the airport and Road Town. All flights from the USA, Canada and Europe connect through a hub (usually Puerto Rico or St Thomas, but also Antigua). Main airlines include:

**Air Sunshine** (www.airsunshine.com) Via St Thomas.

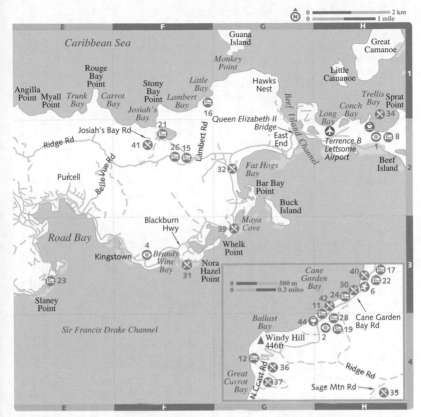

**American Eagle** (www.aa.com) Via San Juan.

**Cape Air** (www.flycapeair.com) Via San Juan.

**LIAT** (www.liatairline.com) Via Antigua.

Smaller airlines with regularly schedule service to/from Caribbean destinations include:

**BVI Airways** (www.gobvi.com) Antigua, St-Martin/Sint Maarten and Dominica

**WinAir** (www.fly-winair.com) Antigua and St-Martin/Sint Maarten

### BOAT

Tortola is a ferry hub to the rest of the Virgins. The two main ports of entry are at Road Town and West End; a smaller dock at Trellis Bay on Beef Island has boats to Virgin Gorda's north-end resorts. See the **BVI Welcome Guide** (www.bviwelcome.com) for cost and schedule details. Most ferries do not operate after 5pm. See the Transportation chapter (p241) for more information on the main ferry routes.

### CAR

Public transportation is nonexistent and taxi fares add up in a hurry, so rent a car if you want to do much exploring of the island and its beaches. However, driving can be a bit tricky: the roads are narrow and twisty, and they go up and down Tortola's mountains via brake-smoking switchbacks. Watch for cows and goats on the road, as well as the ubiquitous speed bumps. Islanders drive on the left.

There are several car-rental agencies on Tortola. High-season rates begin at about $55 per day. While they can run as high as $90, you'll get a better price for a weekly rental.

**Avis** (284-494-3322; Road Town)

**Dollar** (284-494-6093; www.dollarcar.com; East End)

**Hertz** Airport (284-495-2763); Road Town (284-494-6228); West End (284-495-4405)

**Itgo Car Rentals** (284-494-5150; www.itgobvi.com; Road Town) Good prices; located at Wickhams Cay 1.

### TAXI

Taxis are widely available in the main tourist areas. Rates are set. You can download the rate sheet from the **BVI Tourist Board**

(www.bvitourism.com); click 'Getting Around.' The fare from Road Town to the West End or airport is the same ($27). Reliable taxi companies:
**Beef Island Taxi Association** (☏284-495-1982)
**BVI Taxi Association** (☏284-494-3942)

**Scato's Bus and Taxi Service** (☏284-541-7541; www.scatosbusntaxi.com)
**Waterfront Taxi Stand** (☏284-494-4959)
**West End Taxi Association** (☏284-495-4934; www.westendtaxi.com)

# Road Town

Let's be honest: the BVI's capital is nothing special – no mega sights to see or scenery to drop your jaw. But there's nothing wrong with Road Town, either (unless it's all the traffic and exhaust fumes). It's a perfectly decent place to spend a day or night, and most visitors do exactly that when they charter their own boat or take the ferries to the outlying islands.

The town takes its name from the island's principal harbor, Road Bay, which has served as a 'roadstead' (staging area) for fleets of ships for centuries. It remains a convenient place to stock up on food, drinks and money before journeying onward.

Most of the town's pubs and restaurants are along Waterfront Dr. Main St, Road Town's primary shopping venue, is a nice retreat for anyone seeking shade and quiet. The narrow street winds along the western edge of town and has a collection of wooden and stone buildings dating back about 200 years.

Be aware that while Road Town has little street crime, the main areas can become suddenly desolate after dark.

## ◉ Sights

### JR O'Neal Botanic Gardens                          GARDEN
(cnr Botanic Rd & Main St; admission $3; ☺8am-4pm) The Botanic Gardens are a four-acre national park and a pleasant refuge from Road Town's traffic, noise and heat. Benches are set amid indigenous and exotic tropical plants and there is also an orchid house, lily pond, small rainforest and cactus grove.

The herb garden is rife with traditional bush medicine plants. It's about two blocks north of the town's main roundabout.

### FREE Lower Estate Sugar
### Works Museum                                        MUSEUM
(Station Rd; ☺9am-3pm Mon-Fri) There are no bells and whistles here, but if you're keen to take your time and read about the area's history, this museum is an old sugar mill is a worthy stop. A group of friendly volunteers runs it, and they'll be happy to talk you through the intriguing displays. You'll learn how the McClevery slaves built the dwelling in 1780, and how molasses, sugar and rum were produced until the 1940s. Later, the government had a cotton gin on-site. Other rooms hold a hodgepodge of exhibits on local shipwrecks, fauna and flora (don't forget to check out the sugarcane growing by the front door). Yet another room serves as a gallery showcasing local artists' works.

Reach it by taking Waterfront Dr past the roundabout for 0.25 miles, to where Waterfront intersects with Station Ave. Head up Station and you'll see the museum a short distance up the road.

### Government House                                    MUSEUM
(Main St; admission $3; ☺9am-3pm Mon-Fri, to 1pm Sat) Standing at the extreme south end of Main St like one of those imperial symbols you may have seen in Penang and Rangoon, this whitewashed manor is a classic example of British colonial architecture. Once the home of England's appointed governor to the BVI, it is now a small museum with period furniture and artifacts.

---

## TORTOLA IN...

### One Day

Browse **Main St** or sniff your way around the **Botanic Gardens** in **Road Town**. Taxi over to **Cane Garden Bay** for fun in the sun. Stay for dinner and listen to live music at one of the famous beach bars – **Quito's Gazebo**, **Myett's** or **Elm's** will have someone rocking the stage.

### Two Days

Pick a direction: east to **Trellis Bay** lets you check out **Aragorn's Studio**, learn to **windsurf** and chow down at **De Loose Mongoose**. Or you could veer off at **Josiah's Bay** to surf and have dinner at **Secret Garden**. Or you can go west and ramble around **Sopers Hole**, then steer up the coast to **Bomba's Surfside Shack**, the **North Shore Shell Museum**, ending with dinner at the **Sugar Mill Restaurant**.

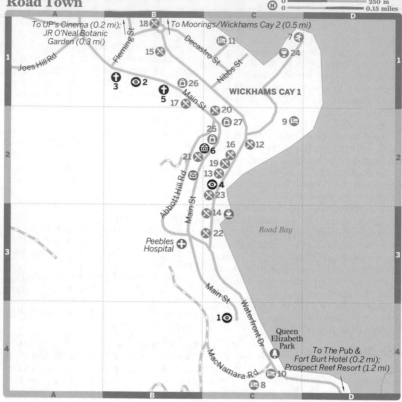

To UP's Cinema (0.2 mi);
JR O'Neal Botanic
Garden (0.3 mi)

To Moorings/Wickhams Cay 2 (0.5 mi)

Joes Hill Rd

Fleming St

Decastro St

Nibbs St

WICKHAMS CAY 1

Main St

Abbott Hill Rd

Main St

Peebles Hospital

Road Bay

Main St

Waterfront Dr

Queen Elizabeth Park

To The Pub &
Fort Burt Hotel (0.2 mi);
Prospect Reef Resort (1.2 mi)

MacNamara Rd

---

### Main Street
HISTORICAL BUILDINGS

If you start at Government House and meander down Main St, here are some of the
historic buildings you'll see (in order):

#### VI Folk Museum
(admission free; ⊗8:30am-4:30pm Mon-Fri)
This tiny museum north of the post office
on Main St is in a traditional West Indian
house and contains pre-Columbian, planta-
tion-period and marine artifacts as well as
a gift shop.

#### St George's Episcopal Church
This neat Anglican chapel is another sur-
vivor of the 18th century but was rebuilt in
the early 19th century following a hurricane.
Inside is a copy of the 1834 Emancipation
Proclamation that freed Britain's slaves in
the West Indies. It's rarely open other than
Sunday and during morning services.

#### HMS Prison
Located at the heart of Main St, these stark,
white rubble walls date back to the 18th century and mark the oldest building in Road
Town. The prison sits empty these days.

#### Methodist Church
(☎284-495-9619) Flanking the north side of
the prison, this working Methodist house
of worship dates from 1924. It's a fine example of classic West Indian timber-framed
construction.

### Sir Olva George's Plaza
PLAZA

Once Road Town's primary street market,
this shady square, stretching between the
waterfront ferry terminal and the post office, is now a courtyard with ficus trees surrounded by the customs house and other
government buildings. It's a good place to
relax and watch the local citizens go about

their business while you're waiting for a ferry.

**Queen Elizabeth Park**                              PARK
This small community park bordering the western side of the harbor south of Government House is a good place to cool off in the trade winds while letting the kids loose on the little playground.

**Fort Burt**                         HISTORICAL BUILDING
Only the foundations and the magazine remain of this small fort that once guarded the mouth of Road Harbour. It was constructed by the Dutch and later rebuilt by the English, who claimed the islands in 1672. The Fort Burt Hotel and its restaurant now crown the site.

## 🏃 Activities

### Boat Trips
Boat charters are big, big business in the BVI, and Road Town is where it all happens (primarily from the Moorings at Wickhams Cay 2). For more information on bareboat or crewed boat charters, including a list of reputable companies, see our 'Chartering a Boat' chapter (p37).

The day-sail operators below run trips to the Baths, Cooper Island, Salt Island

and Norman Island, among others. A full-day trip costs around $110, and typically includes soda, beer and snorkel gear.

**Lionheart** (www.aristocatcharters.com; Village Cay Marina) This one is a 48ft catamaran.

**White Squall II** (www.whitesquall2.com; Village Cay Marina) Feel the wind in a traditional, 80ft schooner.

### Diving
Boats go to all the major local dive sites. Expect to pay around $85 for a one-tank dive and $120 for a two-tank dive.

**BVI Scuba Co** (www.bviscubaco.com; Inner Harbor Marina) Located near the cruise ship dock, by the Hertz rental car outlet.

**We Be Divin'** (www.webedivinbvi.com; Village Cay Marina) Look for the Aquaventure Scuba office, which works in conjunction with We Be Divin'.

### Cycling
Cycling on Tortola can be particularly hair-raising along the heavily trafficked roads of the south shore, but the back roads along the north shore can be delightful as long as you enjoy hill climbs. Last Stop Sports is the best place to rent well-maintained trail bikes. The **BVI Mountain Bike Club** (search

# TORTOLA TRIP TIPS

» The two main resources for lodging, transportation and activities information are the **BVI Tourist Board** (www.bvitourism.com) and **BVI Welcome Guide** (www.bviwelcome.com).

» The **Tourist Board's Facebook page calendar** (www.facebook.com/britishvirginis) has the lowdown on upcoming festivals and full moon parties.

» The airport and main ferry terminal have information desks where you can pick up a useful road map and the BVI Welcome Guide. Many restaurants and resorts also carry the map and guide.

» Although everything looks close on the map, the ruggedness of Tortola's topography makes for slow travel. It takes at least 45 minutes to travel the 14 miles from Sopers Hole at the West End to the airport on Beef Island at the East End.

for them on Facebook) organizes races and social events.

## Multi-Sport

**Last Stop Sports** (www.laststopsports.com; Wickhams Cay 2) carries a huge array of equipment. Rent kayaks ($30/40 per single/double) and windsurfing equipment (from $55 per day), as well as surfboards, bicycles, fishing rods and dive gear. Located on the Moorings dock.

The apparel company and sponsor of Tortola's big June windsurfing competition, **HiHo** (www.go-hiho.com; Wickhams Cay 2) also has surfboard and paddleboard rentals from $45 per day. Located near the entrance of the Moorings/Wickhams Cay 2 complex.

## ☞ Tours

Almost all taxi drivers will do island tours. Expect to pay around $65 or $70 for a two-hour drive. If you're arriving by ferry, there's a taxi stand to the right of the dock.

## 🛏 Sleeping

Road Town does have a couple of lower-priced options, but remember: you get what you pay for here. A 7% hotel tax is added to bills. Higher-end places also tack on a 10% service charge.

### TOP CHOICE Hummingbird House    B&B $$

(☑284-494-0039; www.hummingbirdbvi.com; Pasea; r incl breakfast $140-155; ✳@🛜≋) This is a real B&B (the BVIs' only one), run by long-time UK transplant Yvonne. Tile floors, batik decor and thick towels fill the four breezy rooms; you'll feel like you're staying in a friend's big ol' guest room. Breakfast is a full cooked affair served poolside. There are surcharges to use the air-conditioner (per night $20) and internet (per 30 minutes $5), though wi-fi access is free. Hummingbird is located in the leafy Pasea neighborhood (near Wickhams Cay 2), a 25-minute walk from town, or $5 cab ride.

### Village Cay Hotel & Marina    HOTEL $$

(☑284-494-2771; www.villagecayhotelandmarina.com; Wickhams Cay 1; r $150-225; ✳@🛜≋) Located smack in the middle of Road Town overlooking the bay's yacht slips, Village Cay is a sweet place to rest your head, especially if you want to schmooze with fellow boaters. The 23 rooms, suites and condos have first-class amenities for less than you'll find elsewhere in town. The free wi-fi is available in the common areas only (no in-room access). A lot of yacht charterers like to 'chill' here before or after going to sea, so it books up fast. If nothing else, come for a drink at the pier-side bar-restaurant.

### Moorings-Mariner Inn    HOTEL $$

(☑284-494-2333; www.bvimarinerinnhotel.com; Wickhams Cay 2; r $220-395; ✳🛜≋) Located on the water at Wickhams Cay 2, the Mariner Inn stands adjacent to the docks supporting the Moorings' mammoth fleet of charter sailboats. The place consistently bustles with guests leaving on or returning from yacht charters. The 40 rooms in the two-story building have balconies and upper-end amenities. There's a lovely swimming pool; a long, festive outdoor bar (where you can use the free wi-fi); and an ATM, restaurant and convenience store onsite. It's a 20-minute walk (or $5 cab ride) from downtown.

### Maria's by the Sea    HOTEL $$

(☑284-494-2595; www.mariasbythesea.com; Wickhams Cay 1; r $160-280; ✳🛜≋) Maria's is on the harbor (no beach) at Wickhams Cay 1. If you like watching the coming and going of charter yachts from a seaside pool and sundeck, this expansive three-story operation with 40 units may be for you. All rooms have balconies, kitchenettes and tropical but plain-Jane decor. At press time, the property was adding new rooms. There's free wi-fi in the common areas and in some rooms on the lower level (ask for it if you need it, though be aware it's spotty).

**Fort Burt Hotel** HOTEL $$
(☎284-494-2587; www.fortburt.com; Waterfront Dr; r/ste from $115/240; ✳@🛇🖂) The hotel rises out of the ruins of a 300-year-old Dutch fort that once guarded the harbor from a steep hillside. The 10 rooms and eight suites have business amenities, free wi-fi and access to the main pool; most have sweeping sea views and some of the suites even have private pools. Be ready to climb lots of steps to get to your room. It's a trek to Road Town's center, though there's a good restaurant-bar onsite.

**Treasure Isle Hotel** HOTEL $$
(☎284-494-2501; www.pennhotels.com; Waterfront Dr; r $190-275; ✳@🖂) A popular stop for yacht charterers, this 65-room hillside hotel is laid out around a sundeck and pool on grounds bursting with shade trees and flowers. It has a definite business hotel vibe – rooms have solid, beige-and-white decor, along with work desks and speedy wired internet access – but at the same time, staff isn't very helpful in catering to business travelers' needs (ie processing reservations, arranging taxis etc). The hotel is located across Waterfront Dr from the Moorings/Wickhams Cay 2 complex, and is a 20-minute walk (or $5 cab ride) from downtown.

**Sea View Hotel** HOTEL $
(☎284-494-2483; seaviewhotel@surfbvi.com; cnr Waterfront Dr & MacNamara Rd; r/apt incl tax $85/125; ✳🖂) If you're looking for a budget option, this is it. Located at the southern end of town, the property has about 20 small rooms and 'efficiency' apartments (includes a kitchenette); the latter have a porch and kitchen. It's nothing fancy (and despite the name, there's no view), but the motel-like rooms are clean and well kept.

**NAVIGATING ROAD TOWN** 145

For such a small community, it can be daunting finding your way around Road Town. The difficulty comes from the mule-paths-turned-paved-streets that twist, turn and change names capriciously. Here are some basic rules to stay oriented:

» Finding specific buildings is a bit of a challenge because few places have precise street addresses. Both Tortolians and this guide describe locations as being on a certain street near some prominent landmark like the post office or traffic roundabout.

» The traffic roundabout at the heart of town is the best landmark. It's the easiest place to see and hear (screeching brakes and revving engines). Most of Road Town's principal arteries lead to and from this heart.

» Main St, despite its name, has become a seldom-traveled byway. Most traffic follows Waterfront Dr around the harbor, skirting the old town.

Unfortunately, the hotel fronts a busy road so noise can be a problem.

**Hotel Castle Maria** HOTEL $$
(☎284-494-2553; MacNamara Rd; r $110-160; ✳@🛇🖂) Located up the hill behind the Sea View Hotel, this 30-room property offers decent value with its harbor-view rooms, which have thick wood furnishings and private balconies. The non-view interior rooms tend to be dark, and all rooms are somewhat faded and spooky.

##  Eating

Tortolians love to eat out, and Road Town has restaurants to match every wallet.

---

**THE OFFSHORE BANKING BIZ**

Besides sailing, the BVI's other renowned business is sheltering companies from taxes. It has rivals in the trade – the Cayman Islands, Bermuda, Switzerland – but it also has a specialty: offshore incorporation. According to a recent survey done by KPMG, around 41% of all the offshore companies in the world can be found in the BVI. To look at it another way: this population of 25,000 people hosts 450,000 active registered companies. Road Town is the hub for the trade, and the many 'trust companies' you see around are the agents that form and administer offshore entities. For around $1500, they'll fill out the paperwork and put you in business, too.

Internationally schooled chefs have begun to bring imagination and sophistication to island menus, so many now go beyond the usual grilled chicken, conch and fish dishes. There are even a few vegetarian options hiding around town.

### TOP CHOICE Road Town Bakery
BAKERY $

(☎284-494-0222; Main St; sandwiches $5-8; ☺7am-6:30pm Mon-Sat, to 2pm Sun) New England Culinary Institute students bake the goods here. The small counter mostly serves take-away, though you can eat at the four outdoor tables along with the chickens pecking for scraps. The soups and sandwiches are dandy, but it's the pumpkin spice muffins, brownies and fat slices of cake that will set you free.

### Roti Palace
WEST INDIAN $$

(☎284-494-4196; Abbott Hill Rd; rotis $10-14; ☺10am-5pm Mon-Fri) On a side street that leads up the hill off Main St (look for Samarkand Jewelers and go up the stairs beside it), this cramped little restaurant serves some of the island's best roti at its open-air plastic tables. Fiery chutney sets off the chicken, beef, conch or vegetable fillings, which you can try to tame with a cold beer. The older woman who runs the Palace keeps erratic hours, so you might want to call first to make sure she's there.

### Dove
FRENCH $$$

(☎284-494-0313; Main St; mains $20-45; ☺dinner Tue-Sat) The cozy, French-flaired Dove, set in a historic house, is pretty much the top address in town. The menu changes but you might see pan-seared foie gras, dry aged steaks, charcuterie platters, even some sushi. For something lighter, head upstairs to the wine bar for tapas. Oh, did we mention the wine? The list at the Dove is supposedly the BVI's longest.

### Capriccio di Mare
ITALIAN $$

(☎284-494-5369; Waterfront Dr; mains $10-17; ☺breakfast, lunch & dinner Mon-Sat) Set on the porch of a classic West Indian house across from the ferry dock, this Italian cafe draws both locals and travelers. Breakfast includes pastries and cappuccino. Lunch and dinner feature salads, pasta dishes and pizza, with plenty of wines to wash it all down.

### Le Grand Cafe
FRENCH $$

(☎284-494-8660; Waterfront Dr; mains $24-32; ☺lunch & dinner; ☎) The open air Le Grand Cafe concocts its escargot, foie gras and seafood dishes using provisions flown in from

French St-Martin. Croque monsieur and tomato and goat cheese panini with frites satisfy for lunch. The open-air terrace, carved from a classic West Indian house, becomes a happenin' scene at night with DJs and live music.

### Midtown Restaurant
WEST INDIAN $$

(☎284-494-2764; Main St; mains $8-15; ☺breakfast, lunch & dinner) Friendly Midtown attracts a local following for breakfast, lunch and dinner. The place is a storefront operation right out of the 1950s, with a dining counter and menu board hung over the grill. Johnnycakes, pancakes, eggs, bacon, toast and coffee make a bountiful breakfast. Lunch and dinner feature curried conch and beef, baked chicken, oxtail stew, whelk and salt fish.

### The Pub
BURGERS, SEAFOOD $$

(☎284-494-2608; Waterfront Dr; mains $15-30; ☺lunch Mon-Sat, dinner daily; ☎) On the waterfront near Fort Burt, The Pub has been a Road Town institution for years. You can dine on the deck at the harbor's edge on steaks, ribs, lobster and fresh fish. The jerk chicken wrap is a lunchtime favorite, and any time you go you can choose from the 20-plus beers behind the bar.

### French Deli
BAKERY $

(☎284-494-2195; Wickhams Cay 2; sandwiches $6-8; ☺8am-6pm Mon-Fri, to 3pm Sat) This deli/bakery abounds in gourmet cheeses and meats from Europe. Vegetarians get decent options, too, including tofu, hummus or veggie sandwiches. At breakfast, grab an espresso and a ham and cheese croissant and you're good to go for about $5. Eclairs, mini pies, chocolatey brownies and other sweet treats tempt from the bakery case. If you're going on a picnic, the French Deli is a dandy place to stock up. Take Waterfront Dr to the Moorings/Wickhams Cay 2; it's located near the entrance to the complex.

### Pusser's Pub
PIZZA, BURGERS $$

(☎284-494-3897; www.pussers.com; Waterfront Dr; mains $12-24; ☺lunch & dinner) Pusser's English-style, nautical-themed pub gets lively with pizza, burger and sandwich eaters whooping it up at brass-ringed tables. High marks go to the smoked turkey and gouda sandwich and the macaroni and cheese plate.

### Nature's Way
VEGETARIAN $

(☎284-494-6393; Waterfront Dr; mains $5-10; ☺lunch) It's a bit tricky to find, located at the rear of a health food store. But vegetar-

## TOP VIEWS WHILE EATING & DRINKING

These venues rise to the occasion.
» Drake's Point at Fort Burt (p147)
» Bananakeet Cafe (p153)
» Mountain View (p154)

ians will be pleased they persevered for the red beans and rice, veggie burgers, lasagna and tofu dishes sold at the takeout counter. They start ladling it out between 10:30am and 11am, and by 1pm it's gone. Look for the Quastiskey Building by the roundabout; Nature's Way is on the first floor.

**C&F Bar & Restaurant**  WEST INDIAN **$$**
(☏284-494-4941; mains $15-28; ⊘dinner Mon-Sat) For totally authentic West Indian cuisine, come to this neighborhood joint in Purcell Estate, east of Road Town. It's worth the trouble it takes to find (take a cab your first trip – about $8 from the ferry dock). Tortolians show up in droves to consume barbecue seafood and curry dishes from chef Clarence Emmanuel.

**Sabroso Churrasco Grill**  BARBECUE **$$**
(☏284-541-0202; Waterfront Dr; mains $9-14; ⊘lunch & dinner Mon-Sat) Look for the yellow and lime-green house set back from the road – or just follow your nose toward the smell of slow-cooked meats. Beef brisket, roast pork and rotisserie chicken are heaped on to plates with a side of cornbread. Marinated pork and chicken pesto sandwiches are also available, as are chicken wings with thyme and garlic gravy. If you have food allergies, staff make an effort to work around it.

**La Dolce Vita**  ICE CREAM **$**
(☏284-494-8770; Waterfront Dr; ice cream $3-5; ⊘10am-8pm Mon-Thu, to 9pm Fri-Sun) La Dolce Vita scoops real-deal gelato – awesome rich creamy goodness in flavors like chocolate chip, biscotti, cookies and cream and 20 or so more. The owner lived in Italy and honed her craft there. She even makes soy flavors for vegans.

**Three Sheets Sports Bar**  BURGERS, SEAFOOD **$$**
(☏284-494-8295; Waterfront Dr; mains $13-22; ⊘lunch & dinner; 🛜) This breezy, casual pub sits across from the ferry dock, and its free wi-fi and satellite TV make it a swell place to hang out if you're waiting for a boat. It's got a standard menu of burgers, wraps and fish

dishes. You can sit in the air-conditioned bar or outdoors on the roof terrace.

**Bazz Natural Juices**  SMOOTHIES **$**
(Waterfront Dr; smoothies $3-5; ⊘varies) Listen for the roar of blenders near where the road curves in toward Wickhams Cay 1. The good folks at this outdoor stand mix up all manner of healthy, fruity, frosty beverages – and they'll add alcohol if you like.

## 🍸 Drinking & Entertainment

Many of the bars and pubs listed below also host live music, but on most nights they're simply dedicated to helping you raise a glass. Have a skim through the Eating section, too, for spots to grab a drink as well as a meal.

Check the free weekly tabloid **Limin' Times** (www.limin-times.com) or the website **BVI Music** (www.bvimusic.com) for the local scoop when you're on Tortola.

**The Pub**  PUB
(Waterfront Dr; 🛜) Though it has been around for years, this is still one of the most happening gin mills in Road Town. It's a good place to meet charter boat crews and network with the regulars, who are mostly middle-age expats. There's a happy hour from 5pm to 7pm and live music on Thursday and Friday.

**Drake's Point at Fort Burt**  BAR
(Waterfront Dr) This hip restaurant-bar sits up high by the fort. Come for happy hour from 5pm to 7pm and drink in the views along with your beer. It hosts occasional live music, and shows rugby matches on the telly.

**Bar Fly**  BAR
(Main St; ⊘Tue-Sat) This urbane wine bar, where staff pour $2 reds and whites during happy hour from 5pm to 6:30pm, is above the Dove restaurant.

**Pusser's Pub**  PUB
(Waterfront Dr) Pusser's attracts an early-evening crowd of sailors and expats. The two-for-one drink specials are a big draw during the lengthy 4pm to 7pm happy hour.

**Bat Cave**  BAR
(Wickhams Cay 1) The Bat Cave is a backroom bar off the Spaghetti Junction restaurant, across from cruise ship dock. There is a pool table here and a small harborside deck to catch the trade winds. You'll find lively conversation and a pulsing sound system that pumps out classic rock. The crowd is a mix of travelers and expats between 25 and 40.

## Village Cay
BAR

(Wickhams Cay 1) The Village Cay always has a lively crowd tossing back adult beverages.

## Le Grand Cafe
CAFE

(Waterfront Dr) It's a place to sip wine or martinis, not slug down beer in your shorts and T-shirt. The scene is very chic, with low lights and the scent of French cooking and Brazilian or French jazz filtering through the open-air terrace. The music gets friskier as the night unfolds. The crowd is mostly under-25 expats, including many Europeans.

## UP's Cinema
CINEMA

(☑284-494-2098; Pickering Rd) Located across from the Recreation Ground (reach it by veering west, or left, from the roundabout), UP's is the only theater on the island, featuring an almost endless list of action films. It also hosts occasional DJs and dance nights.

## 🛍 Shopping

When cruise ships sail into port, craft hawkers come out in droves around Wickhams Cay 1 and set up canopied stalls filled with tchotchkes. Head over to Main St for more sophisticated wares. Note that there isn't really much in the way of shopping compared to what you'll find in Charlotte Amalie, St Thomas (the Virgins' other big cruise ship port).

## Sunny Caribbee Spice Shop
SOUVENIRS

(www.sunnycaribbee.com; Main St) It's a favorite for its colorful array of island-made seasonings like 'rum peppers' and 'mango magic.' Spices are also packaged as hangover cures and bad-spirit repellents. Yummy smelling natural soaps and shampoos use ingredients such as lime, chamomile and coconut. The adjoining gallery sells paintings, pottery, jewelry and dolls by local craftspeople. The building, a born-again West Indian cottage, is a visual delight.

## Pusser's Company Store
SOUVENIRS

(www.pussers.com; Waterfront Dr) A footpath runs south from Main St near Sunny Caribbee to Tortola's other famous shopping venue. Attached to Pusser's Pub, the fun store sells logoed clothing and accessories, as well as bottles of Pusser's Rum – the blend served on Her Majesty's Royal Navy ships for 300 years.

## Serendipity Books
BOOKSTORE

(Main St) It stocks an excellent selection of adult and children's books, including works by West Indian and BVI authors.

## Latitude 18
CLOTHING

(Main St) For those in need of flip-flops, sunglasses, Kipling bags or good-quality souvenir T-shirts, Latitude 18 stocks them all.

## Riteway Food Market
FOOD

(Pasea; ⊙7:30am-10pm Mon-Sat, to 9pm Sun) This is the main supermarket, located just beyond Wickhams Cay 2 at the roundabout there. Self-caterers can load up.

## ❶ Information

Branches of Scotiabank, FirstBank and First Caribbean are all found on Wickhams Cay 1 near Decastro and Nibbs Sts. All have ATMs.

**Bits 'n' Pieces** (Wickhams Cay 1; per 30min $3; ⊙closed Sun) Internet access: has four computer terminals and a printer.

**Peebles Hospital** (☑284-494-3497; Main St; ⊙24hr) Offers complete emergency services.

**Tourist office** (www.bvitourism.com; ⊙8:30am-4:30pm Mon-Fri) Drop by the tiny office at the ferry terminal for a free, useful road map or BVI Welcome Guide book.

## ❶ Getting There & Away

### Boat

Road Town is a hub for boat travel. It holds:

» The BVI cruise ship dock (at Wickhams Cay 1).

» The main charter boat dock (the Moorings at Wickhams Cay 2).

» The main ferry dock for boats to Virgin Gorda, Anegada and St Thomas.

**TO VIRGIN GORDA (SPANISH TOWN)** Ferries sail almost every hour during the daytime (round trip $30, 30 minutes):

**Smith's Ferry** (☑284-494-4454; www.smiths ferry.com)

**Speedy's** (☑284-495-5240; www.speedysbvi. com)

**TO ST THOMAS (CHARLOTTE AMALIE)** Ferries depart around 6am, 10am and 2:30pm (one way $30, 45 minutes direct). There's a $5 departure tax paid at the window by the departure lounge:

**Native Son** (☑284-495-4617; www.nativeson ferry.com) Goes via West End.

**Road Town Fast Ferry** (☑284-494-2323; www. roadtownfastferry.com) Goes direct.

**Smith's Ferry** (☑284-494-4454; www.smiths ferry.com) Goes via West End.

**Speedy's** (☑284-495-5240; www.speedysbvi. com) Goes direct.

**TO ANEGADA ROAD TOWN Fast Ferry** (☑284-494-2323; www.roadtownfastferry.

No idea how to hoist a jib? Don't know your shortboard from your longboard? Don't worry. Several local companies can teach you:

» **Island Surf & Sail** (p149) Provides surfing, windsurfing and stand up paddleboarding lessons.

» **Rob Swain Sailing School** (p149) Get the mooring balls ready: you can be on the water and ready to go in two days.

» **Sistership Sailing School** (p149) Specializes in teaching women, couples and families.

» **Boardsailing BVI** (p159) Glide over Trellis Bay during a two-hour windsurfing lesson.

com) departs Monday, Wednesday and Friday at 6:45am and 3:30pm (round trip $45, 1½ hours).

**TO PETER ISLAND** The **Peter Island Ferry** (☎284-495-2000) departs from the CSY dock at Baughers Bay. It makes the 30-minute trip six times daily (round trip $20, free for restaurant customers); call for the times. To get to the dock, follow Waterfront Dr past Wickhams Cay 2 to Blackburn Rd.

**NIGHT FERRY FROM ST THOMAS** Most ferries stop running after 5pm, but **Road Town Fast Ferry** (☎284-494-2323; www.roadtownfastferry.com) has a night service that departs Red Hook, St Thomas at 9pm Thursday through Sunday and goes to Road Town (one way $35).

### Taxi

Following are costs to popular destinations from Road Town (these are per one passenger; fares go down for multiple passengers):

| DESTINATION | COST |
| --- | --- |
| Cane Garden Bay | $24 |
| Cappoon's Bay | $27 |
| West End | $27 |
| Airport | $27 |

# Around Road Town

Southwest of Road Town the road hugs the shoreline around Sea Cow Bay. A couple of big resorts are here, offering a slew of wet and wild activities.

## 🏃 Activities

**Dolphin Discovery**                     DOLPHIN SWIM
(www.dolphindiscovery.com/tortola; Prospect Reef Resort) A 'swim with the dolphins' program operates at Prospect Reef offering a variety of options for close encounters, ie being towed by the animal's dorsal fin, getting a ride on the dolphin's belly or just paddling

around with the creatures. Keep in mind though that these are wild animals brought here forcibly, a practice that is widely condemned by environmental groups. Kids must swim with a paying adult companion. Rates start at $70 per person.

**Island Surf & Sail**                           SURFING
(☎284-494-0123; www.bviwatertoys.com; Nanny Cay) It rents all kinds of boards and sail equipment, and provides surfing, windsurfing and stand up paddleboarding lessons here, as well as kayak tours. There's another branch at Sopers Hole.

**Blue Water Divers**                           DIVING
(☎284-494-2847; www.bluewaterdiversbvi.com; Nanny Cay) PADI-certified with four boats to get you to the good spots. It, too, has another branch at Sopers Hole.

**King Charters**                           BOAT TRIP
(☎284-494-5820; www.kingcharters.com; Nanny Cay) Head out for a day-sail on King's 46-foot motor yacht.

**Rob Swain Sailing School**       SAILING LESSONS
(www.swainsailing.com; Nanny Cay) Learn to sail with lessons from Swain's well-rated school.

**Sistership Sailing School**       SAILING LESSONS
(www.sistership.com; Nanny Cay) Focuses on instruction for women, couples and families.

##  Sleeping & Eating

**Nanny Cay Resort & Marina**           HOTEL **$$**
(☎284-494-2512; www.nannycay.com; d $180-260; ❄@⏛) Located 3 miles west of Road Town, Nanny Cay describes itself as 'an island unto itself' – the description fits. The 42-room resort has two pools, two restaurants, a marina, a windsurfing school, dive shop, mountain bike center, boutiques and a mini market – in short, it's a self-contained pleasure dome on a 25-acre islet. Rooms have

kitchenettes, private balconies and wooden cathedral ceilings. Nanny Cay competes with Village Cay Hotel & Marina in Road Town for the boater set; Village Cay has the slight edge.

**Prospect Reef Resort**   HOTEL $$
(☎284-494-3311, 800-356-8937; www.prospect reefbvi.com; r $155-480; ❋❄) Tortola's largest resort lies just beyond Fort Burt on the western border of Road Town. The 137 rooms come in several configurations, from garden studios to two-bedroom villas. The place has certainly seen better days, but as long as you're not expecting luxury, there's decent value to be had here. While there's no beach, the Olympic lap pool can satisfy the swimming urge. Tennis, fishing and yacht charters are at your doorstep.

**Crandall's**   BAKERY $
(☎284-494-5240; Prospect Reef; ❂breakfast & lunch Mon-Sat) Long lines (well, long for Tortola, with seven people or so) form at the counter of this little bakery. The draw? Pates, whose warm spiced meat plumps a flaky crust. They come in chicken, beef, turkey or salt fish varieties, and you can get two of them plus a johnnycake for less than $8. A cuppa bush tea goes nicely with the fare. Crandall's is located across the street from the Riteway supermarket at Prospect Reef.

**Struggling Man's Place**   WEST INDIAN $$
(☎284-494-4163; mains $10-20; ❂lunch & dinner) Past Prospect Reef en route to Nanny Cay (about 1½ miles west of Road Town) you'll come across Struggling Man's Place. Not much more than a converted fisherman's shack, this small, sea-view restaurant has a funky ambience, with friendly service and a nice mix of West Indians and travelers. Try the pumpkin soup or curried mutton and don't miss the free guavaberry brandy at the bar.

## Cane Garden Bay Area

A turquoise cove ringed by steep green hills, Cane Garden Bay is exactly the kind of place Jimmy Buffet would immortalize in song – which he did in 1978's 'Mañana.' The area's perfecto 1-mile beach and throngs of rum-serving bars and restaurants make it Tortola's most popular party zone. Rid yourself of visions of a sprawling resort area, however. The sheer mountains dominate the landscape, so everything hugs the water along a small strip of road.

Cane Garden Bay lies only a few miles as the crow flies from Road Town, but the winding, precipitous roads travel over the mountains, making it about a 25-minute drive.

## ◉ Sights

**Sage Mountain National Park**   PARK
(Ridge Rd; admission $3; ❂sunrise-sunset) At 1716 feet, Sage Mountain rises higher than any other peak in the Virgin Islands. Seven trails crisscross the 92-acre park, including the main trail that leaves from the car park and moseys up through a pseudo rainforest. A sign showing all the routes is at the trailhead.

The park is not a rainforest in the true sense because it receives less than 100 inches of rain a year. However, the lush area possesses many of the characteristics of one and offers cooling breezes and spectacular vistas of both the US and British Virgin Islands. Travelers should keep an eye out for the 20-foot-tall fern trees that have not changed since the days of the dinosaurs. Hummingbirds, kestrels and martins are a few of the birds you may see. Allow two hours for your rambles. The Mountain View restaurant at the trailhead is good for post-trek refreshment.

To get here, start in Carrot Bay and follow the Windy Hill Rd to a four-way stop. Turn right and you're on Ridge Rd, which will take you to the turnoff for Sage Mountain Rd.

**Callwood Rum Distillery**   DISTILLERY
(Cane Garden Bay; admission $2; ❂7:30am-5pm) Just off the North Coast Rd at the west end of Cane Garden Bay stands a stone plantation building dating back more than 300 years. The Callwood family has been producing rum here for generations, using copper vats and wooden aging casks in much the same fashion as they have for centuries. A small store sells the delicious local liquor and offers tours through the atmospheric structure (highly recommended). The distillery is the oldest continuously operated one in the Eastern Caribbean.

**North Shore Shell Museum**   MUSEUM
(Carrot Bay; admission free but donation requested; ❂varies) It's more of a folk art gallery/junk shop than museum, but it's funky by whatever name you call it. It has so many shells

## WHERE THE WAVES ARE: SURFING HIGHLIGHTS

Surf season in Tortola is between November and March. Good waves can break as late as May, though after March they're much less frequent. Hurricanes also produce quality surf in September and October.

**» Apple Bay (aka Cappoons Bay)** This is the water in front of Bomba's Surf Shack on the West End. When the wind blows right, you can sit in the lineup and listen to reggae music waft over from the bar. Then you can ride up to the shore and grab a cold beer. It's an easy break and attracts loads of surfers.

**» Cane Garden Bay** The break at the bay's northern point is mythic. Only one problem: you need a 6ft to 7ft swell, which happens less than a dozen times a season. But when it does come, it's an excellent long ride. Hardcore surfers get weak at the knees thinking about it.

**» Josiah's Bay** Josiah's, on the East End, wins the best all-round award for Tortola surfing. It's a beach break, with a constantly changing wave that's rideable in an array of conditions (except when it's bigger than 5 feet; then it becomes tough to paddle out and deal with rip tides). Families come to Josiah's to watch the scene on weekends, and many even join the action.

it looks like it was built from a mound of beached conch. The hours vary depending on when the proprietor, Egbert Donovan, is around to show you through. He'll also encourage you to buy something or to eat in the upstairs restaurant.

**FREE** **Mt Healthy National Park**    PARK
(☉sunrise-sunset) This small preserve of less than an acre stands above Brewers Bay and features Tortola's only intact remains of a stone windmill, once part of an 18th-century sugar plantation. You'll be on your own to poke around the place.

### 🏖 Beaches

**Cane Garden Bay**    ACTIVITIES BEACH
Cane Garden Bay is probably the beach on the postcard that drew you to the BVI in the first place. It's Tortola's most famous and popular beach. The gently sloping crescent of sand hosts plenty of beachside bars and water-sports vendors. It's a popular yacht anchorage, and becomes a full-on madhouse when cruise ships arrive in Road Town and shuttle passengers over for the day. The party continues most nights and weekends, too, with a congenial mix of West Indians, sailors and travelers grooving to all manner of live music. If you're looking for the BVI equivalent of spring break, this is it.

**Brewers Bay**    ACTIVITIES BEACH
Travelers like Brewers Bay, a palm-fringed bay on the north shore, east of Cane Garden Bay. There are two beach bars, a campground, guesthouse and excellent snorkeling on the coral heads that pepper the bay. The beach is always tranquil because getting here involves an expensive cab ride as well as a brake-smoking ride down steep switchbacks.

### 🏃 Activities

**Cane Garden Bay Pleasure Boats & Water Sports**    BOAT TRIPS
(☎284-495-9660) It rents 18- to 28 foot outboards with bimini tops and VHF radios. Rates start at about $150 a day. You can rent snorkel gear and bodyboards ($35 to $40 per day), too.

**Shadow's Ranch**    HORSEBACK RIDING
(☎284-494-2262; Ridge Rd) Shadow, a friendly West Indian man you might well meet at the Elm Beach Bar at Cane Garden Bay, offers horseback riding through Sage Mountain National Park or down to the beach at Todman's Estate. He works with several of the resorts; call for customized trips and rates.

### 🛏 Sleeping

Most of the Cane Garden Bay beach options are fun but not fancy. You'll have to move away from the party zone to find more elegant digs. And while you could feasibly stay at Cane Garden Bay itself without a car, you'll need wheels to stay at any of the other lodgings not sitting right on the bay.

### Heritage Inn
APARTMENTS **$$**
(☎284-494-5842; www.heritageinnbvi.com; Windy Hill; 1-/2-bedroom apt $200/315; ❄❄) High on Windy Hill between Cane Garden Bay and Carrot Bay, this place has nine spacious apartments that seem to hang out in thin air. If you like the feel of a self-contained oasis with a pool, sundeck, restaurant and bar, Heritage Inn could be for you. The villas are spacious with full kitchens, balconies and great views of the sunset over Jost Van Dyke and St Thomas. There's a minimum stay of three nights. You will need a car to get around from here.

### Mongoose Apartments
APARTMENTS **$$**
(☎284-495-4421; www.mongooseapartments. com; Cane Garden Bay; apt $200; ❄) Elroy and Sandra Henley designed and built this three-story apartment building on the hillside farm that Elroy's mother once worked. Each of the six large units has a living room, full kitchen (including a blender for frosty drinks), bath and bedroom as well as a private balcony. The common area has books and board games, and the beach – where lounge chairs and kayaks await guests – is a two-minute walk through a coconut palm grove. There's a $10 surcharge to use the air-conditioning, and a three-night minimum stay requirement.

### Cane Garden Bay Cottages
APARTMENTS **$$**
(☎284-495-9649; www.canegardenbaycottages. com; Cane Garden Bay; apt $195; ❄) These four peach cottages sit in a coconut grove across the road from the beach. Each one-bedroom unit is decked out with blond wood and wicker furnishings, a kitchenette, a dining area and patio. A three-night minimum stay is required. The office is at Myett's.

### Lighthouse Villas
APARTMENTS **$$**
(☎284-494-5482, 284-495-0230; www.light housevillas.com; Cane Garden Bay; apt per week from $1225; ❄❄) Located next to Quito's Ole Works Inn, Lighthouse's airy, white-washed villas are a real step up. Each unit has French doors leading out onto a big balcony, as well as a kitchen, cable TV and wired internet hookup. Even though it is by Quito's bar, noise isn't as noticeable here as it is at the inn. Rentals are per week.

### Elm Beach Suites
GUESTHOUSE **$$**
(☎284-494-2888; www.elmbeachsuites.com; Cane Garden Bay; r $140-150; ❄) Just a few yards west along the beach from Rhymer's Beach Hotel, Elm Beach Suites offers one of the warmest welcomes on the island. Elvet Meyers and Lianna Jarecki have five one-bedroom suites in this two-story, beige-and-violet guesthouse. You get bright fabrics, nice wicker furniture, cable TV and kitchenettes in the suites and air-con in the bedrooms. The patios have expansive sea views. Be prepared for noise, as you're on the beach surrounded by party bars (including Elm's own bar).

### Rhymer's Beach Hotel
HOTEL **$**
(☎284-495-4639; www.canegardenbaybeachhotel. com; Cane Garden Bay; r $100; ❄) Smack on the beach and right in the center of the action, Rhymer's was one of the area's first inns. The big pink concrete building, with its restaurant and laundry, shows serious signs of hard use, but the price and energy of the place make up for it. Rooms are mostly studios with TVs, kitchenettes, ceiling fans and patios. There's free wi-fi in the restaurant.

### Ole Works Inn
HOTEL **$$**
(☎284-495-4837; www.quitorymer.com; Cane Garden Bay; d with hill/beach view from $110/145; ❄❄) Reggae master Quito Rymer built this bright yellow, 18-room inn within the walls of a centuries-old rum factory. Rooms are fairly small and dated, though that may change as Quito has recently turned the property over to new managers. Noise from Quito's bar across the street can be a problem if you are a light sleeper. On the other hand, if you like action, you're right in the thick of it, just steps from the beach.

### Sunset Vacation Apartments
APARTMENTS **$**
(☎284-495-4751; www.sunsetvacationapartments. com; Cane Garden Bay; apt $100; ❄) Near the Callwood Rum Distillery at the west end of Cane Garden Bay, Sunset has no-frills, one and two-bedroom apartments in a two-story ranch-style building. There is no sea view here, as the road is set back 100 yards from the beach, but each apartment has a kitchen and private balcony to catch the breeze. The convenience store/small bar on the property has some of the cheapest beer in Cane Garden Bay. The property is a good choice for budget travelers.

### Carrie's Comfort Inn
APARTMENTS **$**
(☎284-495-9544; www.stanleycomfort.com; Cane Garden Bay; apt $100; ❄) Carrie's is another worthy budget option. It rests on the hill above the east end of the bay. There are 16 one-bedroom apartments with kitchenettes in the two-story motel-style building. The units are spacious and airy, freshly decorated

## ℹ RENTAL ACCOMMODATIONS

Tortola has loads of private villas for rent around Cane Garden Bay and elsewhere. They're typically top-end, though you might find a few one-bedroom places for $250 per night or two-bedroom places for $400 per night. Rentals are usually by the week.

» **Areana Villas** (☎284-494-5864; www.areanavillas.com) Local company that manages 30 or so properties around the north shore.

» **Purple Pineapple** (☎305-396-1586; www.purplepineapple.com) Big company with properties around the Caribbean, including Tortola, at a wide range of price points.

» **McLaughlin Anderson Luxury Villas** (☎340-776-0635, 800-537-6246; www.mclaughlinanderson.com) A St Thomas-based company that represents swanky properties around Tortola.

» **Vacation Rental by Owner** (www.vrbo.com) Say to heck with the management companies, and work out all the details with the property owners themselves; VRBO's website acts as a clearinghouse. Many visitors swear by this method.

with colorful fabrics and well maintained. Individual balconies give you a bird's-eye view on the bay and beach that lie one-eighth of a mile down the steep hill. If you're staying for a week or more, ask about the budget villas (from $900 per week) on offer.

**Icis Vacation Villas**     APARTMENTS $$
(☎284-494-6979; www.icisvillas.com; Brewers Bay; apt incl breakfast $150-290; ❄) Though the villas are relatively modern, the grounds surrounding them give you the feel of being on an old plantation. The one- and three-bedroom villas and studios lie inland about a one-minute walk from the beach. All units have a private patio, air-con, full kitchenette and cable TV. There is an open-air restaurant and bar on the property; a continental breakfast is included in the rates.

**Brewers Bay Campground**     CAMPGROUND $
(☎284-494-3463; Brewers Bay; campsites/equipped tents $20/40) Tortola's only commercial campground is around the bend from Cane Garden Bay, although it's a hell of a ride over zigzagging mountain roads. The sites sit under sea-grape trees and tall palms right on the beach. You can bring a tent or use the prepared sites (which include two cots, linens and a cook stove; the latter are worn and gloomy, so you're better off with your own gear. Everyone shares the cold-water bathhouse and flush toilets. There's a beach bar for beer and other sustenance. The extensive reef system offshore in the bay makes for excellent snorkeling, and exploring the reef is the major daily activity for campers. The pros here are the great beach and low price; the cons are the campground's dilapidated nature and deep isolation. Cash only.

## ✕ Eating

Many of the beach restaurants turn into bars at night, offering live music, dancing or just solid boozing time.

**TOP CHOICE** **Mrs Scatliffe's Restaurant**     WEST INDIAN $$$
(☎284-495-4556; Carrot Bay; mains $29-36; ☺dinner) Senior citizen Mrs Scatliffe serves West Indian dishes on her deck, using fruits and veggies she yanks straight from her garden. You must call for reservations before 5pm, since she'll be making the chicken-in-coconut or conch soup just for you. Dinner will be at 7pm, and Mrs S will be singing gospel songs to accompany the meal. Suffice to say it's a one-of-a-kind experience. She's in the yellow building across from the primary school, about a hundred yards up a bushy street off the North Coast Rd. Cash only.

**Palm's Delight**     WEST INDIAN $$
(☎284-495-4863; Carrot Bay; mains $9-18; ☺dinner) Located right on the water's edge, this family-style West Indian restaurant serves up great cheap eats and local ambience. The menu includes pates, rotis, fish Creole and 'honey stung' chicken. Friday nights provide a lively scene, with families eating on the patio and a bar crowd watching cricket or baseball on the TV.

**Bananakeet Cafe**     INTERNATIONAL $$
(☎284-494-5842; Windy Hill; mains $22-36; ☺dinner daily, brunch Sun) Bananakeet is the poolside restaurant-bar at the Heritage Inn (see p152), whose claim to fame is the sweet sunset view from atop the hill. Return diners praise the coconut shrimp, jerk pork

tenderloins with banana chutney and lamb chops. If nothing else, pop in for a happy hour drink from 4pm to 6pm. It offers a free shot at sunset.

### North Shore Shell Museum Bar & Restaurant                    WEST INDIAN $$

(☑284-495-4714; Carrot Bay; mains $9-19; ☺breakfast, lunch & dinner) This zany mix of folk art gallery and eatery, owned by Egbert Donovan, specializes in delicious big breakfasts (pancakes are a specialty) and grilled fish dinners. The staff often lead the patrons in making fungi music by blowing and banging on conch shells. You might want to call before coming, as hours can be erratic.

### Rhymer's                         BURGERS, SEAFOOD $$

(☑284-495-4639; Cane Garden Bay; mains $15-33; ☺breakfast, lunch & dinner) Beachside Rhymer's (attached to the eponymous hotel) caters to the crews off yachts who are sick of cooking aboard. The dinner menu includes fish, ribs and conch, but breakfast is the big attraction, when folks stuff their face with eggs, French toast and bacon. The bar draws beachgoers seeking refreshment.

### Elm Beach Bar                   BURGERS, SEAFOOD $$

(☑284-494-2888; Cane Garden Bay; mains $16-34; ☺lunch & dinner) The Elm is the smallest and perhaps the most welcoming of all the beachfront eateries on Cane Garden Bay. Try the fruit platters or get the BBQ ribs with Jamaican festival sauce and coconut curried rice.

### Stanley's Welcome Bar     BURGERS, SEAFOOD $$

(☑284-495-9424; Cane Garden Bay; mains $15-35; ☺lunch & dinner) On the beach as well, Stanley's has been popular with yacht crews and surfers for years. It is a cheeseburger-in-paradise kind of place that also serves pasta, salads, fresh fish, steak and lobster.

### Big Banana                       BURGERS, SEAFOOD $$

(☑284-495-4606; Cane Garden Bay; mains $18-34; ☺breakfast, lunch & dinner) The Big Banana is one of the largest, busiest and loudest restaurant-bars on the beach, serving up dishes like coconut shrimp, BBQ chicken and ribs. There's pizza, too.

### Quito's Gazebo                           SEAFOOD $$

(☑284-495-4837; Cane Garden Bay; mains $16-33; ☺lunch & dinner, closed Mon) Set on the beach, Quito's is a legendary pub due to its namesake, calypso-crooning owner. The food is fine: rotis, conch fritters and fresh salads make for popular light lunches. At night, grilled items such as snapper fill the menu.

### Mountain View                       INTERNATIONAL $$

(☑284-495-9536; Ridge Rd; mains $11-28; ☺lunch & dinner) High on the mountain at the entrance to the trails at Sage Mountain National Park, this restaurant serves dishes like chicken roti and curried conch. It works best as a lunchtime destination after a hike; dinner is by request only. The name doesn't lie: the view of Tortola and the surrounding islands impresses.

## ☆ Entertainment

Cane Garden Bay is Tortola's hot spot for live music. Check the free weekly tabloid **Limin' Times** (www.limin-times.com) or the website **BVI Music** (www.bvimusic.com) to find out what's on. Or just stroll down the beach and listen for the sounds that groove you. The volume really ratchets up when Cane Garden Bay hosts the **BVI Music Festival** (www.bvimusic-festival.com) and big name players descend on the village in late May.

### Quito's Gazebo                         LIVE MUSIC

(☑284-495-4837; Cane Garden Bay) This bar-restaurant takes its name from its pre-eminent act, Quito Rymer, whose band has toured with Ziggy Marley. You can dance up a storm to Quito's reggae rhythms, and hundreds pack the restaurant on weekends to do just that. The crowd ranges from 16 to 60 and is a rich blend of travelers, expats, yacht crews and West Indians. Quito plays solo on Tuesday and Thursday at 7pm, and with his group on Friday at 9:30pm.

### Elm Beach Bar                          LIVE MUSIC

(☑284-494-2888; Cane Garden Bay) Elm's is worth checking out if you are looking for an intimate and welcoming beachside bar to kick back with a few friends and friendly Tortolians. The Elmtones, a rock/blues cover band, play frequently. On Memorial Day, the bar rocks when it becomes the official Tortola headquarters for crews racing in Foxy's Woodenboat Regatta.

### Myett's                                LIVE MUSIC

(www.myettent.com; Cane Garden Bay) Myett's is the competition down the beach. It draws a lot of people off the charter boats and features local bands nightly during high season. Very different kinds of bands play here: rock, country, pop, Deadhead and even country and western.

## Getting There & Away

Getting to Jost Van Dyke from Cane Garden Bay is a requirement for many visitors, so local outfitters heed the call with water taxi services. **Cane Garden Bay Pleasure Boats & Water Sports** (☑284-495-9660) boats depart around 10am most days; prices vary. Look around the beach near Rhymer's and the Big Banana for other water taxis, as well.

# West Island

The western end of Tortola draws a large number of travelers, as it is home to many resort hotels and villa rentals, a couple of spectacular beaches, vistas of the offshore islands, distinctive restaurants and legendary bars.

## ⊙ Sights

**Sopers Hole**     MARINA
(www.sopershole.com) A major anchorage on the West End, Sopers Hole is the site of a 16th-century pirate's den. The marina and shopping wharf bustle with great restaurants, bars and water sports operators, and provide amenities such as a grocery store and ATM. The ferry terminal for vessels going to and from Jost Van Dyke, St John and St Thomas (Red Hook) is here, too.

**Fort Recovery**     HISTORICAL BUILDING
This fortification near the West End is the BVI's oldest intact structure. It has a turreted gun emplacement with 3-foot-thick walls that date from Dutch construction in 1660. The Villas of Fort Recovery Estate now surround the building.

**Dungeon**     HISTORICAL BUILDING
Built in 1794 by the Royal Engineers, this is a ruined fort located halfway between Road Town and West End. It was nicknamed 'the Dungeon' because its underground cell holds remnants of what might be prisoners' graffiti.

## 🏄 Beaches

**Apple Bay**     SURFING BEACH
The beach at Apple Bay (which also includes Cappoons Bay) has long been 'the surfing beach.' In actuality, there's not much beach to be had, other than the bit down by Sebastian's hotel. The action is out on the water – and at the infamous Bomba's bar (see p157).

**Long Bay**     RESORT BEACH
Long Bay is an attractive mile-long stretch of white-sand beach that extends west of Apple Bay. A top-end resort and clutch of rental villas line its eastern portion. The western end offers slightly less development and good swimming. Beach joggers come here for workouts during the early morning and evening. Visitors can use the resort's beach restaurant for food and drink. And just to confuse you: there is another Long Bay on Tortola's eastern end at Beef Island.

**Smuggler's Cove**     SECLUDED BEACH
An undeveloped beach at Tortola's western tip, Smuggler's Cove used to be a secluded patch of island where you could risk topless or nude sunbathing. Now the dirt track to the beach gets clogged with rental Jeeps and folks trying to escape the predictable scenes at their beach resorts. You can't blame them: the cove is a gorgeous piece of real estate (pretty enough that Hollywood staged a remake of *The Old Man and the Sea* here in the late 1990s). There's a bar and snack stand, and good snorkeling off the beach.

To reach it, drive past the Long Bay resort and keep bearing right (ie near the water) for about 1 mile. Hold on to your teeth: the road is unpaved and very bumpy. The vegetation hides parked cars (and potential thieves) from the beach's view, so take care of your valuables.

## 🏃 Activities

**Island Surf & Sail**     SURFING
(☑284-494-0123; www.bviwatertoys.com; Sopers Hole) It rents all kinds of boards and sail equipment, and provides surfing, windsurfing and stand up paddleboarding lessons, as well as kayak tours.

**Blue Water Divers**     DIVING
(☑284-494-2847; www.bluewaterdiversbvi.com; Sopers Hole) It's PADI-certified and will get you to the good spots.

**Kuralu**     BOAT TRIP
(☑284-495-4381; www.kuralu.com; Sopers Hole) Offers day sails aboard a 50ft catamaran; trips vary, but they can go to Jost Van Dyke, Norman Island and/or Peter Island for snorkeling and swimming.

**Aristocat Charters**     BOAT TRIP
(☑284-499-1249; www.aristocatcharters.com; Sopers Hole) Offers day sails on a 48ft catamaran to Norman Island or Jost Van Dyke for snorkeling and general frivolity.

## 🛏 Sleeping

**Sugar Mill Hotel**  HOTEL $$$
(📞284-495-4355, 800-462-8834; www.sugarmill
hotel.com; Apple Bay; studio/ste from $325/365;
❋🛜🏊) In a league of its own for ambience,
intimacy and customer service, this bou-
tique hotel rises from the ruins of the Apple-
by Plantation that gave Apple Bay its name.
Guests stay in the studios and suites hidden
on the steep hillside among mahogany trees,
bougainvillea and palms. The large, gracious
rooms have a kitchenette, balcony and free
wi-fi. A small beach lies at the foot of the
hotel. The centerpiece of the property is its
gourmet restaurant.

**Villas of Fort Recovery Estate**  HOTEL $$$
(📞284-541-0955, 800-367-8455; www.fort
recoverytortola.com; Waterfront Dr; r from $310;
❋@🛜🏊) Standing alone on the southwest
coast, these suites have the privacy and iso-
lation that some travelers crave. The one-,
two- and three-bedroom units are spread
out along a private beach in the shadow of
the old fort's martello tower. The pool sits
in a garden of hibiscus, oleander and palms.
Everything is top drawer, and the views of St
John and Norman Island to the south and
west are expansive. Bonus: staff offer free
yoga and pilates classes on the dock each
morning.

**Sebastian's on the Beach**  HOTEL $$
(📞284-495-4212, 800-336-4870; www.sebastians
bvi.com; Little Apple Bay; r $135-245; ❋🛜) Sebas-
tian's is well known for its friendly staff and
its pretty stretch of beachfront. The rooms
come in a wide range of styles and sizes. The
higher-end ones open out to the beach and
have a balcony, while the lesser-priced ones
are across the road, away from the beach,
in a courtyard sans views. Take a good
look around before deciding; room decor
and brightness vary even within the same
price bracket. All rooms are straightforward
motel-style, with flowery bedspreads and a
mini-refrigerator. There's a good onsite res-
taurant (with free wi-fi) if you're feeling too
lazy to travel elsewhere.

**Jolly Roger Inn**  INN $
(📞284-495-4559; www.jollyrogerbvi.com; Sop-
ers Hole; d $85-106; ⊘closed Aug & Sep) On the
north side of Sopers Hole, next to the ferry
dock, this is the place to drop your bags if
you're taking an early or late boat. Five very
basic rooms sit above the busy Jolly Roger's
restaurant. Configurations range from a unit

with private bathroom and air-conditioning,
to others that share a bathroom and have no
air-con.

**Long Bay Beach Resort & Villas**  HOTEL $$$
(📞284-495-4252, 866-237-3491; www.longbay.
com; Long Bay Rd; r from $300; @🛜) Long Bay
is Tortola's only large, full-scale resort, home
to several pools, tennis courts, jogging trails,
restaurants, bars and a pitch-and-putt golf
course. The property spreads out along the
bay of the same name at the west end of the
island. It offers more than 70 rooms plus additional private homes and rental villas hidden among the vegetation of a north-facing
hill. Amenities and views vary, but you can
count on a balcony or deck, tile floors and
tropical decor.

For longer-term rentals, try the following:

**Bananas on the Beach**  APARTMENTS
(📞284-495-4318; www.beachrentalsbvi.com; Little
Apple Bay; apt per week $1115; ❋🛜) Ocean-
front studio apartments.

**Casa Caribe**  APARTMENTS
(📞860-693-9482; www.casacaribe.net; Little
Apple Bay; apt $185-225; 🛜) Waterfront villas
with full kitchens and telephones; five-
night stay required.

## 🍴 Eating

**TOP CHOICE Sugar Mill
Restaurant**  INTERNATIONAL $$$
(📞284-495-4355; www.sugarmillhotel.com; Apple
Bay; mains $28-38; ⊘dinner) The Sugar Mill
restaurant wins our award as Tortola's best.
Owners Jeff and Jinx Morgan, contributing
writers for *Bon Appétit* magazine, over-
see the menu, cooking and presentation of
meals in the restored boiling house of the
plantation's rum distillery. Here you dine
by candlelight on haute cuisine, with dishes
like wild mushrooms in puffed pastry or
leg of lamb with roasted peppers, spinach
and feta filling, brought out by ace servers.
Wines, cocktails and decadent desserts com-
plete the sensory experience. Reservations
are a must.

**Jolly Roger**  PIZZA, SEAFOOD $$
(📞284-495-4559; www.jollyrogerbvi.com; Sopers
Hole; mains $12-30; ⊘breakfast, lunch & dinner,
closed Aug & Sep) Located near the West End
ferry landing, the JR (as they call it) has a
hearty waterfront pub scene in the evening
and serves food long after most of the competition's kitchens have closed. Pizza is the

## BOMBA'S FULL MOON FESTIVITIES

**Bomba's Surfside Shack** (☑284-495-4148; Cappoon's Bay), near Apple Bay, has achieved mythic status in the Caribbean –think bras, booze, full moons and trippy mushroom tea.

The place truly is a shack, built from a mishmash of license plates, surfboards and graffiti-covered signposts espousing carnal wisdom such as 'Wood is Good!'. Bras and panties are woven throughout, along with snapshots of topless women. Very often, sitting smack in the middle of these photos and wearing a wide grin along with his trademark sunglasses, is Bomba.

Bomba started his bar-restaurant more than 30 years ago to feed the surfers who still ride the waves curling out front. Today the shack is famous for its monthly full moon parties, which feature an outdoor barbecue, live reggae and plenty of dancing and drinking. Bomba also serves free psychoactive mushroom tea (mushrooms grow wild on Tortola and are legal), and up to 500 people, both tourists and locals, show up for his bacchanals. Note to those who don't wish to end up topless in photos: mind your intake of tea and rum punch.

Even if you're not on-island during the full moon, the Bomba Shack is a sight to behold. Stop by for a beer with the surfers. The shack also hosts live bands on Wednesday and Sunday evenings.

popular beer chaser here, though the chefs serve up delicious grilled fish with Asian-tinged sauces, too. Locals and travelers flock to the Caribbean barbecue and live music on Friday and Saturday nights.

**Sebastian's on the Beach**   INTERNATIONAL $$
(☑284-495-4212; www.sebastiansbvi.com; Little Apple Bay; mains $17-33; ⊙breakfast, lunch & dinner; 🛜🍴) Sebastian's has been a favorite of travelers for years, offering beachfront dining for all three meals. Banana pancakes and rum-soaked French toast hit the plates for breakfast, rotis and burgers for lunch, and spicy chicken wings, stewed conch and vegetarian casserole for dinner.

**Pusser's Landing**   BURGERS, SEAFOOD $$
(☑284-495-4603; www.pussers.com; Sopers Hole; mains $14-27; ⊙lunch & dinner; 🛜) This fun pub offers outdoor harborside seating and a Margaritaville ambience. The seafood-based dinners are a bit pricey for their quality; it's best to stick to snacks and booze (happy hour is from 5pm to 6:30pm). There's also free wi-fi.

**Fish Fry**   SEAFOOD $
(Zion Hill Rd; Apple Bay; mains from $8) On Zion Hill Rd, in the clearing opposite the Coco Plums restaurant (which had closed at press time, so it may have a new name by now), is the 'fish fry tree.' On various nights the surrounding West Indian settlement gathers

for a cookout of grilled snapper or flying fish with sweet potato, peas and rice. Ask around as to what night it might be happening.

**D' Best Cup**   CAFE $
(Sopers Hole; sandwiches $6-10; ⊙breakfast & lunch; 🛜) Tucked in among the shops at the marina, D' Best Cup is a local chain serving sweet cappuccino, espresso and coffee drinks, as well as smoothies, omelets and sandwiches.

## ☆ Entertainment

The most famous bar on Tortola would have to be Bomba's Surfside Shack.

**Pusser's Landing**   LIVE MUSIC
(www.pussers.com; Sopers Hole; 🛜) Pusser's cranks up live entertainment almost every night of the week. There is usually a lively after-work crowd for the happy hour specials like cheap chicken wings and $1 discounts on all drinks. Depending on the night, you get live steel pan, calypso, reggae or fungi music. The crowd is a mix of local expats, travelers and sailors off charter boats.

**Jolly Roger**   LIVE MUSIC
(www.jollyrogerbvi.com; Sopers Hole; ⊙closed Aug & Sep) Jolly Roger has bands Friday and Saturday nights. The music is typically West Indian or country and western and draws 30-somethings from the surrounding West End villas.

## 🔒 Shopping

The Sopers Hole wharf has outlets of Road Town's top shops. Try Pusser's for the rum of Her Majesty's Royal Navy, then Sunny Caribbee Spice Company for herbal hangover cures for when you drink too much of it. Other boutiques include:

**BVI Apparel Company**                    CLOTHING
T-shirts, pottery, jewelry and other island souvenirs; Cuban cigars, too.

**Zenaida's**                    ACCESSORIES
Sarongs and straw bags, as well as funky jewelry, fill the shelves.

## ❶ Getting There & Away

The West End has a busy little passenger ferry terminal. You'll need to pay a $5 departure tax if you're going to St John or St Thomas.

**TO JOST VAN DYKE/TORTOLA New Horizon Ferry** (☑284-495-9278; round trip $25) sails the 25 minute trip five times daily (twice in the morning, three times in the afternoon); cash only.

**TO ST JOHN Inter-Island** (☑340-776-6597; www.interislandboatservices.vi; round trip $45) sails three times daily at 9:15am, 12:15pm and 4:15pm (later on Friday and Sunday). It takes about 30 minutes.

**TO ST THOMAS** A couple of companies alternate departures to Red Hook four or five times per day. The trip takes 35 minutes:

» **Native Son** (☑284-495-4617; www.nativesonferry.com; one way $25)

» **Smith's Ferry** (☑284-494-4454; www.smithsferry.com; one way $28)

# East Island

Tortola's eastern end is a mix of steep mountains, remote bays and thickly settled West Indian communities. Surfers and windsurfers find their hot spots out this way. Many visitors also land at **Beef Island** – literally – which is the site of the BVI's main airport, as well as a fiery arts collective that ramps up during the full moon. Beef Island floats off Tortola's tip, connected to the mainland by a two-lane bridge.

## ◉ Sights

**Ruins of St Philips Church**                    HISTORICAL BUILDING
(Blackburn Hwy) The walls of this church on the north side of Blackburn Hwy in Kingstown, east of Road Town, are all that remain of a community of freed slaves established in 1833 as the 'Kingstown Experiment.' Most of the worshippers here were survivors from the wreck of a slave ship in about 1815. They were given this reservation and place of worship after working for some years as plantation laborers. The building is quite dilapidated and as it's not an official historical site, there are no amenities here.

**Aragorn's Studio**                    ARTS CENTER
(www.aragornsstudio.com; Trellis Bay, Beef Island) Local metal sculptor Aragorn Dick-Read started his studio under the sea-grape trees fronting Trellis Bay, the broad beach just east of the airport. It grew to include space for potters, coconut carvers and batik makers, many of whom you can see at work in the now-sprawling arts center. Aragorn also helped build the traditional Carib dugout canoe you'll see on the beach. The vessel has made journeys following old Carib routes in South America and the Leeward Islands. For information on Aragorn's family-friendly full moon parties, see p160.

## 🏖 Beaches

**Josiah's Bay**                    SURFING BEACH
An undeveloped gem on the north shore near East End, Josiah's Bay is a dramatic strand at the foot of a valley that has excellent surf with a point break in winter. Many say it offers Tortola's best surfing. Lifeguards patrol the water, and a couple of beach bars serve cold Red Stripes and snacks. They also rent boards, so you paddle out to catch your own wave. While there are usually surfers here, it's never jam-packed, and retains the feel of a lazy outpost. The privacy and wildness of Josiah's appeals to travelers who want to veer off the beaten path and have a rental 4WD to get there. Several charming and inexpensive guesthouses lie inland on the valley slopes.

**Lambert Bay**                    RESORT BEACH
East of Josiah's Bay, Lambert Bay used to be called Elizabeth Beach before the Lambert Beach Resort developed it in the late 1990s. If you make the trek down the steep hill to the resort and park in its lot, you will find a wide, palm-fringed beach. (If you miss the resort turnoff, you'll end up at Tortola's prison.) You can get drinks and food at the resort. In winter, when there is an Atlantic Ocean swell coming out of the north, the undertow here and at Josiah's Bay can be dangerous.

## Long Bay

FAMILY BEACH

Not to be confused with the resort-clad Long Bay on Tortola's West End, *this* Long Bay stretches along Beef Island's northwest side. It's shallow, calm and sandy-bottomed, and so a winner for families and children (though it does drop off quickly; flotation devices are a good idea for little ones). The beach's charms are no secret, and you'll likely have the company of picnicking Tortolians (especially on weekends), but it never feels crowded. The beach borders a nesting area for terns and a salt pond that attracts egrets. There are no amenities, and some noise from the airport does impinge on the idyll. To get here, drive over the bridge to Beef Island and hang a left shortly thereafter, just past the salt flats.

## Trellis Bay

WINDSURFING BEACH

Trellis Bay, a broad semicircular beach east of the airport on Beef Island, is a crowded yachting anchorage and the landing for Virgin Gorda's North Sound Express ferry, as well as water taxis to Bellamy Cay (see p160), Marina Cay and Scrub Island. It's also home to a renowned windsurfing operator (see p159), Aragorn's Studio, restaurants, a general store and a funky guesthouse. All in all, it's an entertaining place to wait for a flight or laze around for an afternoon.

## 🏃 Activities

### Boardsailing BVI

WINDSURFING

(www.windsurfing.vi; Trellis Bay) The biggest windsurfing operator on the islands, with loads of gear for beginners to advanced surfers. Two-hour lessons take place out front in the bay; money-back guarantee if you aren't sailing by the end. If you don't see the equipment guys on the beach, head into the Trellis Kitchen and Cybercafe, and they'll help you out.

## 🛏 Sleeping

### Serendipity House

APARTMENTS $$

(☏284-499-1999; www.serhouse.com; Josiah's Hill; apt $90-205; ❄❄🐾) For tropical seclusion about half a mile from Josiah's Bay, this is one of the best values on Tortola, with special deals for longer stays. Canadians Carol and Bill Campbell welcome travelers with their invitation to 'spend a vacation, not a fortune.' There are four units, ranging from a studio apartment to a two-bedroom villa. Each have a TV and kitchen (fully equipped in the larger units, kitchenettes in

the smaller ones). The pool area is a nice hangout, with a gas grill and hammock.

### Tamarind Club

HOTEL $$

(☏284-495-2477; www.tamarindclub.com; Josiah's Hill; r incl breakfast $139-199; ⊘closed Aug & Sep; ❄❄) Just 100yd down the hill from Serendipity House, near Josiah's Bay, the eight rooms at this red-roofed West Indian–style building surround a central garden and pool. The rooms have batik-print decor, but are a bit dark; each has a private veranda. The onsite restaurant serves good local dishes, and the swim-up bar is a fine touch.

### Beef Island Guest House

GUESTHOUSE $$

(☏284-495-2303; www.beefislandguesthouse. com; Trellis Bay; r incl breakfast & tax $150) Located on Trellis Bay next to De Loose Mongoose restaurant, this place is a five-minute walk to the airport and therefore an excellent choice for anyone with a late arrival or early departure. Set on a thin beach among a grove of low coconut palms, the one-story guesthouse looks more like a contemporary West Indian home than an inn, but the four rooms have unexpected character, with beam ceilings and all rooms featuring a private bathroom and fan.

### Near-D-Beach Limin' Bar & Hostel

HOSTEL $

(☏284-443-7833; www.josiahsbaybvi.com; Josiah's Bay; r without/with bathroom $60/80) This no-frills hostel in Josiah's Bay caters mostly to surfers, since it's only a five-minute walk from the popular surfing beach. The three rooms each have a queen-size bed and simple furnishings; they all share gender-segregated, cold-water bathrooms and a game-filled common room. There's also a studio apartment with a private, hot-water bathroom and kitchenette. A funky bar (with snacks) and free wi-fi in the common areas round out the deal. Cash only.

### Josiah's Bay Inn

APARTMENTS $$

(☏284-495-2818; josiasbayinn@hotmail.com; Josiah's Bay; apt from $100) These are the folks who own the Grapetree bar on Josiah's Bay beach, so you'll get first dibs on their surfboards to rent. The one- to four-bedroom apartments aren't fancy, but they're pleasantly furnished with tile floors, whitewashed walls, a kitchen and deck. It's a 10-minute walk to the beach. No credit cards.

**TORTOLA**

## FIREBALL FULL MOON PARTY

Aragorn's Studio and the Trellis Bay Kitchen combine to put on the **Trellis Bay Full Moon Party** (www.windsurfing.vi/fullmoon.htm), which is the artsy, family-friendly alternative to Bomba's raucous event (see p157). The party kicks off around 7pm with fungi music, stilt walkers and fire jugglers. At 9pm Aragorn sets his steel 'fireball sculptures' ablaze on the ocean – a must-see.

**Lambert Beach Resort**    HOTEL **$$**
(☎284-495-2877; www.lambertresort.com; r $169-270; ❄@🤶🏊) This resort is on a long, white strand of beach near the northeast corner of the island. Most of the 38 units are large, one-bedroom suites contained in a four-unit villa. Bodyboards, kayaks and fishing rods are available to guests for free (though note that the water can have a strong undertow during winter months), and there's a large pool with a swim-up bar. Alas, the resort has experienced some hard times and ownership changes of late, so how it evolves remains to be seen. The restaurant recently closed, which means you'll have to travel a fair distance for meals.

## ✖️ Eating

Any of the Trellis Bay eateries are good places to hang out if you're waiting for a flight or a boat.

**TOP CHOICE** **De Loose Mongoose**    CAFE **$$**
(☎284-495-2303; www.beefislandguesthouse.com; Trellis Bay; mains $15-25; ◷breakfast, lunch & dinner Tue-Sun) Next to the Beef Island Guest House, this windsurfer hangout is a great place to have breakfast, eat lunch or watch the sunset over dinner. Try the conch fritters, arguably the BVI's best. Guests sit at brightly hued picnic tables on a screened-in porch. Sunday night is a big barbecue, when there's live blues and soca music.

**Secret Garden**    CARIBBEAN **$$**
(☎284-495-1834; Josiah's Bay Plantation; mains $19-33; ◷dinner Wed-Mon) One of the most delightful places to eat on Tortola, Secret Garden sets its outdoor tables amid the distilling buildings of an old plantation. Suzanne Allen's imaginative fare ranges from grilled swordfish Creole to coconut chicken or Bajan flying-fish pie. She also shakes up specialty cocktails such as watermelon sangria and passionfruit martinis. Reservations required.

**Last Resort**    SEAFOOD **$$**
(☎284-495-2520; Bellamy Cay; mains $25-38; ◷dinner) Located on an islet in Trellis Bay, the Last Resort is a little place with a big personality, renowned for its baked mahimahi and other surf and turf options. When the chef steps out and joins the band, the real fun begins. The open-air venue is popular with cruising sailors, but landlubbers can call for ferry service from the resort's hotline telephone at the Trellis Bay ferry dock, and staff will pick you up. If you like a good-humored night on the town, the Last Resort delivers.

**Brandywine Bay**    ITALIAN **$$$**
(☎284-495-2301; Sir Francis Drake Hwy; mains $28-45; ◷dinner Mon-Sat) This is chef David Pugliese's signature restaurant, lying a mile east of Road Town, overlooking Sir Francis Drake Channel. Here you can eat haute Mediterranean dishes served on a candlelit, breeze-cooled terrace. Menu items include dishes like roasted duck in mango sauce, veal chop with ricotta, lamb ravioli and the house-made mozzarella. Reservations are essential. Brandywine's sister restaurant is Capriccio di Mare in Road Town.

**Pusser's East**    PIZZA, SEAFOOD **$$**
(☎284-495-1010; www.pussers.com; Fat Hogs Bay; mains $12-24; ◷lunch & dinner) Yep, it's another goodtime Pusser's, joining the outlets in Road Town and Sopers Hole. This one is on the waterfront at Hodge's Creek, with a seaside 100-foot porch and views out toward Peter, Salt and Cooper islands. The menu ranges wide, with pizza and fried chicken the house specialties. Happy hour rings in from 4pm to 7pm, when drinks are two for the price of one – a prime time to visit.

**Trellis Bay Kitchen & Cybercafe**    CAFE **$$**
(www.windsurfing.vi; Trellis Bay; mains $8-18; ◷7am-7pm; @) Stop in for all-day breakfasts, such as bagel sandwiches or porridge, or for West Indian plates, including curried goat, crab cakes, steamed mahi mahi and rotis. It costs

$5 per 15 minutes to surf the web. The cafe shows **free movies** on Wednesday nights at 7pm.

**Calamaya's**　　　　　BURGERS, SEAFOOD **$$**
(284-495-2403; Hodge's Creek Marina; mains $10-20; ☺breakfast & lunch) Located at Hodge's Creek Marina, a few miles east of Road Town on the Blackburn Hwy, waterfront Calamaya's serves a menu of Caribbean-tinged bites such as rotis, wraps, burgers and salads.

**D' Best Cup**　　　　　CAFE **$**
(Trellis Bay; sandwiches $6-10; ☺breakfast & lunch) Trellis Bay has another outlet of this local chain serving cappuccino, espresso and coffee drinks, as well as omelets and sandwiches.

##  Drinking

These restaurants and lodgings double as nifty places to grab a drink.

**De Loose Mongoose**　　　　　CAFE
(www.beefislandguesthouse.com; Trellis Bay; ☺Tue-Sun) Sip your beverage of choice while watching key sporting events on satellite TV at the outdoor gazebo.

**Near-D-Beach Limin' Bar & Hostel**　　BAR
(www.josiahsbaybvi.com; Josiah's Bay) The hostel's bar has a funky, tiki-esque ambience with a thatched, open-air pavilion fronting a bird-filled pond.

**Pusser's East**　　　　　PUB
(www.pussers.com; Fat Hogs Bay) It pours beer, the namesake rum and more on the waterfront.

##  Shopping

**Aragorn's Studio** (www.aragornsstudio.com) The place to go for one-of-a-kind, locally made wares. You'll find high-quality copper and steel iconographic sculptures, woodcut print T-shirts and traditional Caribbean arts and crafts, such as coconut carvings. You can also buy something from the small selection of organice products that Aragorn brings in from his farm.

## ✪ Getting There & Away

The dock at Trellis Bay bustles with small ferries heading to Virgin Gorda and the Out Islands; see those chapters for further information.

**TO VIRGIN GORDA North Sound Express**
(284-495-2138) ferries depart to both Spanish Town (round trip $40) and North Sound (round trip $65) several times daily (except no service Sunday). Reservations required.

**TO MARINA CAY** The **Marina Cay Ferry** (284-494-2174; free) departs at 10:30am, 11:30am, 12:30pm, 3pm, 4pm, 5pm and 6pm. It operates by request thereafter. The trip takes 10 minutes.

**TO SCRUB ISLAND** The **Scrub Island Ferry** (284-440-3440; free) sails from 7am to 11pm (hourly, on the hour).

# Virgin Gorda

POP 3500

## Best Places to Eat

» Mermaid's Dockside Bar & Grill (p168)

» Mad Dog (p169)

» Thelma's Hideout (p169)

» Bath & Turtle (p169)

» Clubhouse Steak & Seafood Grille (p173)

## Best Places to Stay

» Guavaberry Spring Bay Homes (p168)

» Leverick Bay Resort (p172)

» Bitter End Yacht Club & Resort (p172)

» Virgin Gorda Village Hotel (p168)

## Why Go?

Virgin Gorda is the BVI's rich, plump beauty, beloved by movie stars and feisty billionaires. You'll understand their ardor once you've seen her national parks. The otherworldly, granite megaliths at the Baths put on the main show. Boulders hulk over the shore and form sea-filled grottoes, making for a wet and wild climb up, over and around them to Devil's Bay. Trekkers can summit Virgin Gorda Peak and then head south to meander around wind-pounded Copper Mine National Park. Sea dogs can take ferries over to Bitter End Yacht Club to sail, kitesurf and drink with the yachtsfolk.

It's the way these extraordinary sights blend with easy access, good restaurants, and no rampant commercialism that catapults Virgin Gorda to most-favored-island status. A prosperous, well-tended atmosphere permeates. Sure, you'll probably come across roaming chickens sooner or later, but they will be snowy white and an islander will have named them all.

## When to Go

Mid-December through April is the high season, when prices go up but all the businesses are in full swing. Virgin Gorda's main events throughout the year also get a lot of attention. The late February/early March BVI Kite Jam attracts a hip group for activities around North Sound. The Virgin Gorda Easter Festival brings revelers for parades and bands in Spanish Town, usually in late March or April. The two weeks leading up to Christmas are also a local party time in Spanish Town.

## History

After leaving St Croix in 1493, Christopher Columbus sailed north and anchored to the southeast of Virgin Gorda. He named the island the 'Fat Virgin' because to him, its silhouette resembled a full-bodied woman sleeping on her back.

Virgin Gorda thrived in the centuries that followed. Large plantations on the island produced sugarcane, ginger, indigo and cattle. By 1812, the island's population reached an all-time peak of 8000. Alas, the plantation economy soon collapsed, and Virgin Gorda sat all but abandoned until the 1960s. That's when Laurence Rockefeller constructed the Little Dix Bay resort, which brought jobs, roads and utilities and put the island back on the map.

## ✨ Festivals & Events

Spanish Town around the yacht harbor fills with mocko jumbies (costumed stilt walkers representing spirits of the dead), fungi bands, a food fair and parades for the **Virgin Gorda Easter Festival** (www.bvitourism.com), held Friday through Sunday during the Christian holiday (usually late March or April).

The **BVI Kite Jam** (www.bvikitejam.com; late Feb–early Mar) is a weeklong event packed full of 'freestyle, sliders, big air and wave riding' around North Sound, Necker Island and Anegada. Sir Richard Branson is the co-founder and an active participant.

## ❶ Getting There & Around

### AIR

**Virgin Gorda Airport** (VIJ; ☏284-495-5621) is on the Valley's east side, about a mile from Spanish Town. At press time, only private charters were permitted to fly in. **Air Sunshine** (www.airsunshine.com), a commercial carrier with flights from St Thomas, is trying to change that. In the interim, it flies into Tortola's airport and provides a free ferry to Spanish Town.

### BOAT

Check the **BVI Welcome Guide** (www.bviwelcome.com) for schedules. Between Spanish Town and Road Town, Tortola, ferries sail almost every hour during the daytime (round trip $30, 30 minutes):

VIRGIN GORDA

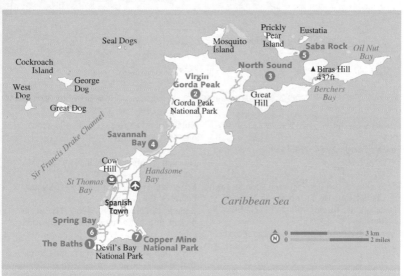

## Virgin Gorda Highlights

❶ Wade around boulders and through grottoes at sunrise at **the Baths** (p165)

❷ Hike to island-spanning views atop **Virgin Gorda Peak** (p170)

❸ Sail or kitesurf in the bay at **North Sound** (p172)

❹ Walk the long beach at **Savannah Bay** (p171)

❺ Join the yachties for happy hour at **Saba Rock** (p173)

❻ Snorkel in the protected pools at **Spring Bay** (p167)

❼ Explore the forlorn, windswept ruins of **Copper Mine National Park** (p166)

VIRGIN GORDA

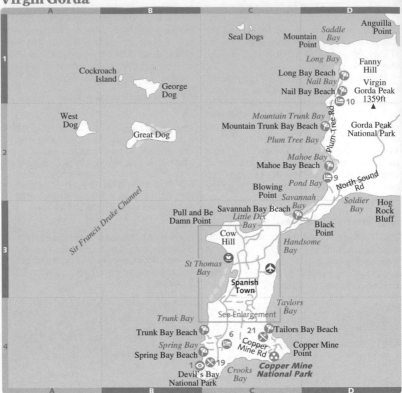

**Speedy's** (☏284-495-5240; www.speedysbvi.com)

**Smith's Ferry** (☏284-494-4454; www.smithsferry.com)

There are direct services between Spanish Town and Charlotte Amalie, St Thomas on Tuesday, Thursday and Saturday (round trip $70, 90 minutes):

**Speedy's** (☏284-495-5240; www.speedysbvi.com)

There is also a service between Spanish Town and Red Hook, St Thomas (via Cruz Bay, St John) on Thursday and Sunday (round trip $80, 75 minutes):

**Inter-Island** (☏340-776-6597; www.interislandboatservices.vi)

Ferries run from Trellis Bay/Beef Island, Tortola (ie the airport) to both Spanish Town (round trip $40) and North Sound (round trip $65) several times daily (Monday to Saturday, no service Sunday):

**North Sound Express** (☏284-495-2138) Reservations required.

Free public water taxis zip to resort areas from North Sound's Gun Creek:

**Bitter End Ferry** (☏284-494-2746) Departs hourly on the half hour.

**Saba Rock Ferry** (☏284-495-7711) Call for pickup; free, but driver usually expects a tip.

### CAR

Virgin Gorda has several Jeep rental companies that will pick you up from the ferry and drop you off almost anywhere on the island. You'll pay $55 to $85 per day.

**Mahogany Car Rentals** (☏284-495-5469; www.mahoganycarrentalsbvi.com)

**Speedy's Car Rental** (☏284-495-5240; www.speedysbvi.com)

### TAXI

Taxi fares are set. The rate from the North Sound resorts or Gun Creek to Spanish Town is $30 one

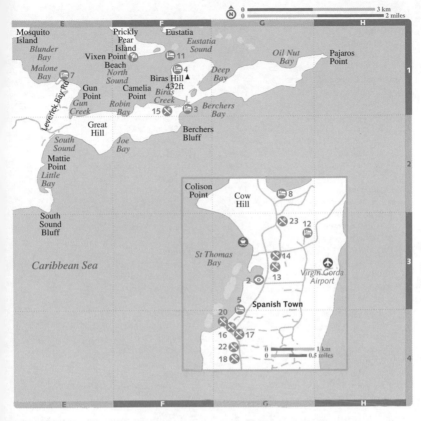

way; from the ferry dock to the Baths is $8 round trip. Reliable companies include the following:

**Andy's Taxis** (☑284-495-5252, 284-495-5160)

**Mahogany Taxi Service** (☑284-495-5469)

## Spanish Town & the Valley

Spanish Town isn't a town so much as a long road with businesses strung along it. It's the commercial center of Virgin Gorda, and probably gets its name from a (severe) corruption of the English word 'penniston,' a blue woolen fabric used long ago for making slave clothing on the island, rather than from any Spanish connections. Islanders referred to their settlement as Penniston well into the 1850s.

The harbor dredged here in the 1960s is home to today's Yacht Harbour, the heart of Spanish Town. Overall the settlement is a sleepy place, but it has shopping, dining and nightlife with a fresher mix of West Indians, expats and travelers than you get at the island's resorts.

## ⊙ Sights

**The Baths**                                    PARK
(admission $3; ☉sunrise-sunset) This collection of sky-high boulders, near the island's southwest corner, marks a national park and the BVI's most popular tourist attraction. The rocks – volcanic lava leftovers from up to 70 million years ago, according to some estimates – form a series of grottoes that flood with sea water. Wander around them and you'll see shafts of sunlight sparking the rocks' kaleidoscope of colors. The area also makes for unique swimming and snorkeling; the latter is distinctive as many boulders lurk under water, too.

The Baths would easily live up to its reputation for greatness if it wasn't overshadowed

# Virgin Gorda

by the adjacent **Devil's Bay National Park** to the south, and the cool trail one must take to get there. Actually, there are two trails. The less exciting one takes off behind the taxis at the Baths' parking lot. The trail you want though leaves from the Baths' beach and goes through the 'Caves.' During the 20-minute trek, you'll clamber over boulders, slosh through tidal pools, squeeze into impossibly narrow passages and bash your feet against rocks. Then you'll drop out onto a sugar-sand beach.

While the Baths and Devil's Bay stir the imagination, the places are often overrun with tourists. By 9am each morning fleets of yachts have moored off the coast, and visitors have been shuttled in from resorts and cruise ships. All you have to do though is come at sunrise or late in the afternoon, and you'll get a lot more elbow room. Make sure to lather up with insect repellent.

The Baths' beach has bathrooms with showers, a snack shack and snorkel gear

rental ($10). Taxis run constantly between the park and ferry dock (round trip $8).

**Yacht Harbour** MALL
(www.virgingordayachtharbour.com) The dredged harbor at Spanish Town came as a result of Laurence Rockefeller's construction of Little Dix Bay. Today, the development is known as Yacht Harbour and contains many of the island's essentials services (ie banks) as well as popular places to eat, shop and drink. While the style of this mall seems more like what you would find in Southern California than in the West Indies, Yacht Harbour is well kept without being sterile or banal.

**FREE** **Copper Mine National Park** PARK
(☼sunrise-sunset) You've got to drive along one heck of a winding road to reach this forlorn bluff at Virgin Gorda's southwest tip, but it's worth it to see the impressive stone ruins (including a chimney, cistern and mine-shaft house) that make up Cop-

per Mine National Park. Cornish miners worked the area between 1838 and 1867 and extracted as much as 10,000 tons of copper, before abandoning the mine to the elements. A couple of trails meander through the ruins, and the hillside makes an excellent place for a picnic as the blue sea pounds below.

## 🏊 Beaches

Beachcombers can wander for hours along Virgin Gorda's 14 beaches. Note that all of Virgin Gorda's shores are public beaches by law. However, there's not always public access, meaning you might have to tramp through a resort to reach your perfect strand of sand.

### Spring Bay                     SNORKELING BEACH
An excellent beach with national park designation, Spring Bay abuts the Baths to the north. The beauty here is the Baths'-like setting without the crowds. Hulking boulders dot the fine white sand and there's clear water and good snorkeling off the area called 'the Crawl' (a large pool enclosed by boulders and protected from the sea). Sea grape trees shade a scattering of picnic tables, but that's the extent of the facilities.

To get here, watch for the Spring Bay sign just before Guavaberry Homes on the road to the Baths. There's a parking area, and you'll pass a little swing set on the path down to the beach.

### Trunk Bay                      SECLUDED BEACH
This long, unpopulated beach lies north of Spring Bay. It's primo for sun, sand and swimming, though not snorkeling. It's not particularly easy to reach; look for a rough, unmarked trail leading through the boulders at Spring Bay's north end.

### Taylors Bay                    SECLUDED BEACH
Taylors Bay, a beach off Copper Mine Rd on the southeast side of the island, sees few visitors. It is probably the best place to come for sunbathing in the buff because the chance of offending anyone is quite slim. The surf can be rough since the bay faces east.

## 🏃 Activities

### Diving
**Dive BVI** (www.divebvi.com; 1-/2-tank dive $85/110) at Yacht Harbour and Leverick Bay, has several fast boats that can take you diving at any of the BVI sites.

### Boat Trips
Several day-sail operators depart from Yacht Harbour and offer a variety of trips to Anegada and the Out Islands; a minimum of four to six people is required. The boats usually stop for snorkeling breaks and lunch somewhere (food is not included in the price, though beer and soda are).

**Dive BVI** (www.divebvi.com; (full-day trips from $85) This dive operator offers well-run snorkel trips aboard a catamaran.

**Spirit of Anegada** (www.spiritofanegada.com; half-/full-day trips $65/95) A red-sailed 44ft schooner.

**Double 'D'** (www.doubledbvi.com; full-day trips from $89) A 50ft sloop.

## 🗺 Tours
**Andy's Virgin Gorda Tours** (☎284-495-5252; www.virgingordatours.com) offers several options to see the island by bus, including a half-day 'Highlights' tour (per person $16) that takes in the Baths, Savannah Bay, and Gorda Peak and Copper Mine national parks. This is the same Andy's that operates one of the local taxi fleets.

---

## VIRGIN GORDA IN...

### One Day

Spend the morning splashing around **The Baths**. For fewer people and better snorkeling, kick over to **Spring Bay**. Sit on the porch at **Mad Dog** and revive with a piña colada. Hopefully you remembered to call ahead and make reservations at **Thelma's Hideout** for a West Indian dinner.

### Two Days

Hike up **Virgin Gorda Peak** for sweet views from the top. Reward the effort with a trip to one of the North Sound resorts. **Bitter End Yacht Club** fulfills with kitesurfing lessons, snorkeling tours and monumental buffets. Or ferry over to **Saba Rock** for happy hour.

## 🛏 Sleeping

Lodging is pricey on Virgin Gorda, with no real budget options during high season. The island has loads of private villas for rent. They're typically top-end, though you might find a few one-bedroom places for $250 per night or two-bedroom places for $400 per night. Rentals are usually by the week.

### TOP CHOICE Guavaberry Spring Bay Homes
COTTAGES $$

(☎284-495-5227; www.guavaberrspringbay.com; cottages $235-300; @🛜) A stone's throw from the Baths, plopped amid similar hulking boulders, Guavaberry's circular cottages come with one or two bedrooms, a kitchen, dining area and sun porch. The setting amazes. Only some units have air-conditioning, so ask for it when booking if you need it. There's a common area with wi-fi (for a small fee), games, books and cable TV, and a commissary stocked with alcohol, snacks and meals to cook in your cottage. The office has internet terminals, and staff are a fountain of knowledge who can arrange all manner of tours. It's a short walk to both the Baths and Spring Bay beach (where Guavaberry provides chairs for lounging). Payment by cash or check only.

### Virgin Gorda Village Hotel
HOTEL $$

(☎284-495-5544; www.virgingordavillage.com; r from $250; ❄🛜🏊♿) You can rent out one of these one to three bedroom condos. Although it's not on the beach, the large pool and garden setting give it the feel of an oasis. Tennis courts, a gym, spa, children's playground and restaurant-bar on site round out the package. The property is on North Sound Rd at the north end of the Valley, about 1 mile from Savannah Beach. The bar has free wi-fi.

### Bayview Vacation Apartments
APARTMENTS $$

(☎284-495-5329; www.bayviewbvi.com; apt $140-165; ❄🛜) Each of these apartments, behind the restaurant Chez Bamboo, has two bedrooms, a full kitchen, dining facilities and an airy living room. It's plain-Jane ambience, with faded rattan furnishings, but it can be a good deal, especially if you have three or four people. There is a roof deck for sunbathing and there's free shuttle pickup from the ferry docks.

### Fischer's Cove Beach Hotel
HOTEL $$

(☎284-495-5252; www.fischerscove.com; d/cottages $165/190) Surrounded by gardens and located just a few steps from the beach, Fischer's Cove is made up of eight triangular-shaped cottages and a main hotel building with 20 no-frills studios. The cottages have full kitchens, but no phones, TVs or air-con (they're also located by a drainage ditch). The hotel units do have phones and TVs, and a few also have air-con. The popular open-air restaurant overlooks the property's beach. It's a 15-minute walk from the main ferry dock, and the best lodging option if you're carless, being near the Yacht Harbour amenities as well.

### Little Dix Bay
HOTEL $$$

(☎284-495-5555, 888-767-3966; www.littledixbay.com; r from $750; ❄🛜🏊) This is the resort that rocketed Virgin Gorda to glory, and it remains the island's swankiest, celebrity-filled digs. An army of staff keep the grounds and 98 rooms perfectly coiffed, while it wafts an overall South Seas vibe. Free use of water sports gear (Hobie Cats, kayaks, snorkel gear) is included; wi-fi costs $20 per day.

Also recommended:

### Tropical Care Services
RENTAL ACCOMMODATIONS

(☎284-495-6493; www.tropicalcareservices.com) Virgin Gorda-based company that manages a handful of properties, including some near the Baths. Rates are fairly reasonable for the island.

### Purple Pineapple
RENTAL ACCOMMODATIONS

(☎305-396-1586; www.purplepineapple.com) Big company with properties around the Caribbean, including Virgin Gorda, at a wide range of price points.

### McLaughlin Anderson Luxury Villas
RENTAL ACCOMMODATIONS

(☎340-776-0635, 800-537-6246; www.mclaughlinanderson.com) A St Thomas-based company that represents swanky properties around the island.

## 🍴 Eating & Drinking

Dinner reservations are a good idea. Some places charge an extra 5% to pay by credit card.

### TOP CHOICE Mermaid's Dockside Bar & Grill
SEAFOOD $$

(☎284-495-6663; mains $16-27; ☺lunch & dinner) Mermaid's is indeed dockside, on a breezy pier over the true-blue water. It specializes in seafood with Spanish flair. Staff grills your mahi mahi, snapper or other fish right on the dock and plates it up alongside rice and pigeon peas and lots of veggies. Sunset vistas compliment the casual, open-air vibe. It's located on the road leading west from the roundabout.

### Mad Dog                            SANDWICH SHOP $
(☑284-495-5830; mains $8-12; ☺10am-6pm; ☎) Expats and tourists often gather at this airy little pavilion set among the rocks where the road ends at the Baths. They can't resist the fat sandwiches – turkey and bacon wins particular plaudits – to help take the edge off the killer, secret-recipe piña coladas.

### Thelma's Hideout                    WEST INDIAN $$
(☑284-495-5646; mains $17-25; ☺breakfast, lunch & dinner) Find this West Indian hangout on the side road leading to Little Dix Bay resort. Seating is in an open-air courtyard, and there is a stage where a band plays during high season. Thelma will serve you breakfast, but most travelers come here for her conch stew. You must make dinner reservations by 3pm for a table that night.

### Bath & Turtle                     PIZZA, BURGERS $$
(☑284-495-5239; mains $14-21; ☺breakfast, lunch & dinner; ☎) In a courtyard surrounded by the Yacht Harbour mall, this casual pub cooks up pizza, quesadillas and seared ahi tuna salad. At night it's a fun scene, with live music on Wednesday. A lending library and free wi-fi add to the general goodwill B&T generates.

### Mine Shaft Café                        SEAFOOD $$
(☑284-495-5260; www.mineshaftbvi.com; sandwiches $15-18; mains $20-30; ☺lunch & dinner) You can't beat the location, perched high on a hill overlooking the Atlantic Ocean on Copper Mine Rd. The food is pretty good, too, including burgers (even the veggie variety), wraps and mains like lobster in rum-lemon-cream sauce. Owner Elton Sprauve throws a monthly full-moon party, complete with live music, warm breezes, cheap rum punch and grilled meats. If you can't make that shindig, at least come here for a view-tastic sunset cocktail. Kids will enjoy puttering around the mini-golf course.

### Rock Cafe                              ITALIAN $$
(☑284-495-5482; www.bvidining.com; mains $20-38; ☺dinner) Nestled among the boulders at the traffic circle south of Spanish Town, this place has indoor and outdoor dining, plus a popular terrace bar that rocks with live music several nights per week. The cuisine is mostly Italian, with pizzas, pastas, mahi mahi, snapper and other fresh fish. Many locals think it bakes the best lobster on the island.

### Giorgio's                              ITALIAN $$$
(☑284-495-5684; www.giorgiobvi.net; mains $38-46; ☺dinner) Peasant food meets Tuscan gastronomy in dishes like black squid tagliatelle, lobster risotto and braised beef ravioli – all served with homemade pasta, of course. Chef Giorgio Paradisi is a serious oenophile, with 250 Italian wines to compliment the fine dining experience in his classy, exposed-brick setting. Reservations required.

### Chez Bamboo                    FRENCH CARIBBEAN $$$
(☑284-495-5752; small plates $8-14, mains $25-45; ☺dinner) Just north of Yacht Harbour, this bistro (in a converted West Indian home and yard) couldn't be in a better setting, amid candlelight and tropical plants. The chefs specialize in French Creole Caribbean cuisine; there's also a small plates menu with saltfish croquettes and hummus – items that go nicely with the happy hour martinis from 5pm to 6pm. Some folks come away saying the food is overpriced... Still, the yacht owners pour in, so reservations are a good idea. Mad Dog and Bath & Turtle are Chez Bamboo's sister restaurants.

### LSL Bakery & Restaurant           WEST INDIAN $$
(☑284-495-5151; mains $20-25; ☺breakfast, lunch & dinner Mon-Sat, dinner Sun) Chef Margaret brings her home-cooking skills to the table for dishes like butter-wine-sauced conch, mango chutney-topped lamb chops and garlic shrimp. During the day, lots of kids pop over from the school across the street for chocolate cake slices, guava tarts and raisin-filled baked treats. Sunday's dinner revolves around an outdoor barbecue. LSL is located on the road to the Baths.

### Dixie's Bar & Restaurant               BURGERS $
(☑284-495-5640; mains $6-10; ☺breakfast, lunch & dinner Mon-Sat) Dixie's is a great cheap-eats diner across from the ferry dock. Come for eggs and toast for breakfast, a fish burger for

lunch, fried chicken and beer for dinner, and ice cream and milkshakes anytime.

### Top of the Baths
FUSION $$

(☑284-495-5497; www.topofthebaths.com; mains $20-34; ☺breakfast, lunch & dinner Tue-Sun; ) On a hillside above the Baths, this restaurant offers indoor and outdoor dining to a clientele who often come from visiting yachts. The lunch menu includes wraps, veggie burgers and conch fritters. Dinner dishes are Caribbean fusions such as seafood risotto, sweet potato snapper and Thai shrimp. A kids menu is available. Bonus: there's a swimming pool to dip into.

### Island Pot
WEST INDIAN $$

(☑284-495-6554; mains $8-15; ☺lunch & dinner Wed-Sat) Island Pot specializes in barbecue. You can eat in or take away (a popular option for locals). It's near the roundabout, across from the gas station.

### Buck's Food Market
DELI $

(☑284-495-5423; www.bucksmarketplace.com; ☺7am-7pm) The island's main grocery store has a deli counter for sandwiches and snacks that many locals pair with a bottle of beer; located in the Yacht Harbour mall.

## ☆ Entertainment

Most restaurants have live music at least one night a week. Ask around as to which place is the hot spot during your visit or check the sporadic listings in the **Limin' Times** (www.limin-times.com).

### Bath & Turtle
LIVE MUSIC

(Yacht Harbour mall) Also known as the Rendezvous Bar, this courtyard restaurant in the mall pushes back the tables and becomes a hot nighttime venue for expats working on the island and travelers. The crowd ranges from the college set to older yacht captains ready to kick up their heels. Local bands play Wednesday night and cover classic reggae and dance tunes.

### Mine Shaft Café
LIVE MUSIC

(www.mineshaftbvi.com) It always has a fired-up crowd for happy hour, but once a month the place really rocks for the full-moon party. On Tuesday nights, a DJ spins island tunes, and Friday nights it's all about calypso.

### Chez Bamboo
LIVE MUSIC

(☑284-495-5752) Chez Bamboo is a hip after-dinner destination for drinks. On Friday night, jazz, blues or calypso fills the air.

The crowd is largely couples and groups of friends, mostly expats and travelers.

### Sam's Piano Bar
LIVE MUSIC

(www.bvidining.com; Rock Cafe restaurant) Musicians tickle the ivories every night starting at 8pm.

##  Shopping

Virgin Gorda won't do much for shopaholics. About the only place to fill your bag is in Spanish Town's Yacht Harbour mall, which holds several little boutiques including the following:

**Flamboyance** Exotic perfumes.

**Margo's Jewelry Boutique** Handcrafted coral, pearl and gold jewelry.

**Virgin Gorda Craft Shop** Locally produced straw hats, dolls, books and other mementos.

**Thee Artistic Gallery** Crystal, coins and nautical-themed trinkets.

## ❶ Information

The Yacht Harbour mall holds most of the island's services, including banks and laundry.

**Chandlery Ship Store** (Yacht Harbour mall; per 10min $5; ☺7am-5pm Mon-Fri, 8am-noon Sat) Has a couple of internet terminals.

**Nurse Iris O'Neal Clinic** (☑284-495-5337; ☺9am-4:30pm Mon-Fri) On the ridge road in the Valley near the airport. There's a physician on staff, but for hospital services you must go to Tortola.

**Virgin Gorda Baths** (www.virgingordabaths.com) The website for a tour operator, but it has good general information about the island, attractions and beaches.

# Mid-Island

Steep mountain slopes rise along Virgin Gorda's mid-section, culminating at hike-worthy Gorda Peak National Park. Pretty beaches fringe the western coast.

## ◉ Sights

### Gorda Peak National Park
PARK

At 1359 feet, Gorda Peak is the island's highest point. The park protects all of the island above 1000 feet and creates a nature preserve of 265 acres. Both of the trails leading to the summit branch off North Sound Rd and are well marked.

If you are coming from the Valley, the first trailhead you see marks the start of

## BEST BEACHES

» **Spring Bay** (p167) It's the Baths' next-door neighbor, sporting the same big-bouldered beauty but without the crowds. Snorkelers have fun here. It's probably the best beach to go to if you're short on time.

» **Savannah Bay** (p171) It's a gorgeous strand for walking unfettered on white sand and gaping at sunsets. Many return visitors to Virgin Gorda say this is their favorite beach.

» **Vixen Point** (p172) You'll need a boat to reach this shore on Prickly Pear Island where there's sheltered swimming and a fun beach bar.

the longer trail (about 1½ miles). This trail makes a moderate climb to the summit, where you will find a few picnic tables, an observation tower and a portable toilet. The second trailhead is farther north along North Sound Rd. From here, you have a relatively easy half-mile climb to the summit. En route on both trails you'll see Christmas orchids, bromeliads (pineapple family members) and hummingbirds. The lookout tower at the top provides vistas of the entire archipelago.

### 🏖 Beaches

A short distance north of the Valley, **Savannah Bay** features more than a mile of white sand, largely protected from the worst of the northerly swells that come during the winter by a barrier reef. Except for the beaches of Anegada, no other beach provides the same opportunities for long, solitary walks. Sunsets here can be fabulous. There are no facilities and not much shade, so come prepared. A small sign off North Sound Rd points the way; the road leads to a little parking area.

Heading north, the strand of gently curving beach and vivid blue water at Mango Bay Resort is called **Mahoe Bay**. You'll have to park at and walk through Mango's facilities to reach it, but staff is nonchalant.

**Mountain Trunk Bay**, **Nail Bay** and **Long Bay** lie north of Mahoe Bay and run nearly undisturbed for about 1 mile all the way to rugged Mountain Point. Resort and villa development along these strands has taken away some of the privacy. Waters are generally calm.

### 🛏 Sleeping

**Mango Bay Resort**  APARTMENTS **$$**
(☏284-495-5672; www.mangobayresort.com; apt from $195; ❋) Located on the beach at Mahoe Bay, the resort is a compound of Italian-style duplex villas. They range in size from studios to three-bedroom properties. Each villa is equipped with a small porch, kitchen, TV/DVD player and barbecue grill, along with free access to the resort's kayaks and snorkeling gear. The latter is useful as there's great snorkeling along the reef just offshore. Some units have wi-fi; the most expensive villas also have a pool. Mango Bay is isolated, with no dining options on site, so you'll need a car.

**Nail Bay Resort**  APARTMENTS **$$**
(☏284-495-5875, 800-871-3551; www.nailbay.com; apt from $250; ❋≋) The resort is on the grounds of a 147-acre sugar plantation in the shadow of Virgin Gorda Peak. There is a wide range of accommodations at this resort, from standard hotel rooms and suites to apartments and seaside villas with as many as five bedrooms. Most of these units are privately owned and managed by the resort. All rooms come with a kitchen, TV/DVD player, barbecue grill and balcony. There are three secluded beaches here, which are great for strolling, but the centerpiece of the resort is the Sugarcane Restaurant, with its swim-up bar overlooking Drake Channel. You will want a rental Jeep if you stay here, as Nail Bay is secluded and at the end of a long, rough road. Some units have wi-fi.

## North Sound

Beyond the mid-island mountains is North Sound, Virgin Gorda's only other settlement besides Spanish Town. It's main job is to serve the big resorts and myriad yachts anchored in the surrounding bays. A mini-armada of ferries tootle back and forth from the Sound's Gun Creek to Bitter End Yacht Club and Saba Rock Resort, both excellent for a happy hour drink and sea views at their bars, even if you're not staying there.

## Beaches

**Berchers Bay**, a reef-protected beach, stretches along the ocean side of the Biras Creek Resort. It's your best beach option if you're staying at or visiting Biras Creek or the Bitter End Yacht Club.

You need a boat to access **Prickly Pear Island** in North Sound (it's possible to rent one; see the listed boat trip outfitters). On the island's south side, you'll find **Vixen Point**, with a long, broad stretch of white sand, sheltered swimming and a beach bar. There is also a secluded beach on the north side of Prickly Pear. And the island's name? It comes from all the cacti dotting the salt-ponded landscape.

## Activities

North Sound's protected waters make it top-notch for all manner of splashy activities. Bitter End and Leverick Bay are ground zero for the action.

### Boat Trips

**Bitter End Yacht Club**
(www.beyc.com) It has the biggest collection of watercraft for rent, including kayaks, Hobie Waves, windsurfers and 11ft Boston Whalers, to name just a few, for $40 to $50 per hour. It is most renowned though for its sailing school. Beginners can learn to steer, trim sails, pick up moorings and more in two three-hour sessions for $200. The school also teaches windsurfing and advanced sailing classes, as well as offering special classes for kids.

**Leverick Bay Watersports**
(www.watersportsbvi.com; ⊙Mon-Sat) This joint rents powerboats (from $400 per day), dinghies with outboards (from $90 per day) and kayaks (from $12 per hour).

### Diving

Common dive sites that companies go to include the Dogs, Ginger Island and the wrecks of the *Rhone* and *Chikuzen;* see the Out Islands (p191) for more on these locations. Prices are around $85 for a one-tank dive and $110 for a two-tank dive. Snorkelers are usually welcome to join diving companies' excursions.

**Dive BVI** (www.divebvi.com; Leverick Bay) is well-regarded operator is one of the BVI's most active, offering trips to all the hot

spots; there's another outpost at Spanish Town's Yacht Harbour.

**Kilbride's Sunchaser Scuba** (www.sunchaserscuba.com; Bitter End Yacht Club) was started by BVI diving pioneer Burt Kilbride; it offers trips to Anegada's wreck-strewn Horseshoe Reef as well as popular night dives.

### Kitesurfing

**Carib Kiteboarding** (www.caribkiteboarding.com; classes from $75) allows you to take advantage of the trade winds and get airborne. It provides gear and lessons for all levels of experience and is located at Bitter End Yacht Club.

### Snorkeling

**Bitter End Yacht Club** (www.beyc.com; 90 min tour $15) offers daily snorkeling tours at 10:30am and 2pm. It costs an extra $6 for gear rental. Sign up at the Watersports Center near the ferry dock.

## Sleeping

Many places have minimum stay requirements (ranging from three to seven days) during high season. For luxury villas, try **Virgin Gorda Villa Rentals** (☑284-495-7421, 800-848-7081; www.virgingordabvi.com), which manages properties at Leverick Bay and Mahoe Bay.

**Leverick Bay Resort**          HOTEL **$$**
(☑284-495-7421, 800-848-7081; www.leverickbay.com; r from $149; ❋⟨⟩❄) When you see the purple, green and turquoise buildings splashed up the hillside, you'll know you've arrived at Leverick Bay, located on North Sound near Gun Creek. The resort mixes hotel, condo and villa accommodations; the 14 hotel rooms are the best deal. Each has two double beds, rattan furnishings, free wi-fi and a private balcony. Then there's the access you have to the beach, marina, tennis court, dive shop, spa, market, internet cafe – oh, and the popular restaurant, too.

**Bitter End Yacht Club & Resort**   HOTEL **$$$**
(☑284-494-2746, 800-872-2392; www.beyc.com; d incl meals $760-1100; @⟨⟩❄⛵) This all-inclusive resort at the east end of North Sound has 85 hillside villas adorned with batik bedspreads and teak floors. Some villas have hammocks, wrap-around verandahs and are open to the trade winds, others have air-con and decks and none have TVs. Rates include three meals a day and unlimited use of the

resort's bountiful equipment for sailing, windsurfing, kayaking and much more. It's a great place for active couples or families who like to spend their days on the water. Children are well catered to with sailing, snorkeling and crafts classes. Wi-fi is available in the public areas only.

### Saba Rock Resort
HOTEL **$$**

(☎284-495-9966, 284-495-7711; www.sabarock.com; r incl breakfast from $150; ✻🛜) On a fleck of island just offshore from Bitter End Yacht Club, Saba Rock Resort is a charismatic boutique hotel with eight rooms, a restaurant and a bar. It's the most laid-back place to get your North Sound resort experience, catering largely to boaters who want a reasonably priced night off their vessel. It's nothing fancy, but nice touches include the free breakfast, free wi-fi and private balconies. A free water shuttle ferries guests here from Gun Creek or Bitter End (call Saba to arrange a pickup).

### Biras Creek Resort
HOTEL **$$$**

(☎284-494-3555, 877-883-0756; www.biras.com; r from $675; @🛜🏊) A neighbor to Bitter End on the eastern shore of North Sound, Biras Creek is an exclusive oasis for up to 70 guests. The 140-acre property fills a narrow isthmus between North Sound and the open Atlantic. The rooms are individual cottages, the best of which front the Atlantic so you hear the roar of the waves as a nighttime lullaby. They're well appointed, though not outrageously luxurious, as you might expect at this price. Each guest gets his or her own mountain bike, and there are excellent trails among the sea grape tree forest for cycling and hiking. Horseback riding is another option. Meal plans are available at the resort's chic restaurant for an additional fee. Wi-fi is available in the public areas only. Biras' owners are developing the land at Oil Nut Bay for villas, so expect more company around this part of North Sound in the years to come.

## ✖ Eating

### Fat Virgin's Café
CAFE **$$**

(☎284-495-7052; www.fatvirgin.com; mains $10-20; ◷lunch & dinner; 🛜) This cafe is the budget diner's delight of North Sound. Travelers must come to the little bistro (and little boutique) that rises from the Biras Creek Resort's dock by boat, located on the west side of the property. The roti stuffed with curried chicken rocks the palate, or you can opt for a good ol' hot dog, burger or BLT sandwich to go with the sensibly priced beer. Ask about the daily West Indian specials (Mondays are devoted to rotis) and Friday night Chinese specials.

### Clubhouse Steak & Seafood Grille
STEAK, SEAFOOD **$$$**

(☎284-494-2745; brunch/dinner buffet $30/45; ◷breakfast, lunch & dinner) Of Bitter End Yacht Club's three restaurants overlooking North Sound, the Clubhouse rules the roost. There is an a la carte menu here, but most people order the buffet. It's monumental in both variety and substance, with roasted meats, grilled fish and shellfish leading the way. The Sunday brunch is popular. Make reservations early, as the Clubhouse is a favorite of the boating crowd. If you don't have your own vessel, catch the free Bitter End Ferry that departs Gun Creek hourly on the half hour.

### Biras Creek Restaurant
INTERNATIONAL **$$$**

(☎284-494-3555; www.biras.com; 4-course prix fixe dinner $85; ◷breakfast, lunch & dinner) Overlooking North Sound from an elegant, tiki-style pavilion, the resort's hilltop restaurant is about as highfalutin as it gets. The four-course set menu changes daily, but honey-coated shrimp brochette or lentil-cream-sauced, ham-wrapped salmon are examples of what to expect. A swig of house port wraps up the affair. Reservations are mandatory, and there's a dress code (trousers and collared shirt for men). The resort's free ferry picks up restaurant guests at Gun Creek at three-quarters past the hour.

### Leverick Bay Restaurant
ITALIAN, SEAFOOD **$$$**

(☎284-495-7154; www.therestaurantatleverickbay.com; mains $30-45; ◷breakfast, lunch & dinner) Oven-fired pizzas and burgers are the domain of lunchtime, while New Zealand lamb, lobster ravioli and mahi mahi on coconut risotto are some of the items filling plates for dinner, accompanied by something from the hearty wine list. The Friday night pig roast, with stilt dancers and live music, attracts throngs of locals and visitors. The restaurant sits beachside and provides nice views of the water.

## 🍷 Drinking

### TOP CHOICE Saba Rock Bar
PUB

(www.sabarock.com) Saba Rock is a very cool place for a drink, especially during happy hour from 4:30pm to 5:30pm. Check out all the shipwreck booty on site, such as the cannon from the RMS *Rhone*. Also, keep an eye out for big fish and turtles lurking in the water by your table. Food is served here, but the bar is what you're after. Come over on the free ferry from Gun Creek or Bitter End (call 284-495-7711 to arrange a pickup).

**Crawl Pub** PUB
(www.beyc.com) This breezy pub at Bitter End Yacht Club is a local hot spot, especially for workers from the area's resorts.

**Jumbies Beach Bar** BAR
(www.therestaurantatleverickbay.com) The beachside bar at Leverick Bay has happy hour from 5pm to 6pm, when oysters and mussels accompany drinks at discounted prices.

 **Shopping**

**Pusser's Company Store** CLOTHING
(Leverick Bay) Shopping in this part of Virgin Gorda is limited to the resorts' gift shops, of which Pusser's at Leverick Bay is the most interesting. It sells tropical apparel and the namesake rum.

# Jost Van Dyke

POP 200

## Best Places to Eat

» Foxy's Tamarind Bar
(p178)

» Ali Baba's (p178)

» Corsairs (p179)

» Sandcastle Restaurant
(p182)

» Sidney's Peace & Love
(p183)

## Best Places to
Stay

» Perfect Pineapple (p180)

» White Bay Campground
(p180)

» Sandcastle Hotel (p181)

» White Bay Villas & Seaside
Cottages (p181)

## Why Go?

Jost (pronounced 'yoast') is a little island with a big personality. It may only take up 4 sq miles of teal-blue sea, but its reputation has spread thousands of miles beyond. A lot of that is due to calypsonian and philosopher Foxy Callwood, the island's main man.

In the late 1960s, free-spirited boaters found Jost's shores, and Foxy built a bar to greet them. Its good-time reputation spread far and wide, and soon folks such as Jimmy Buffett and Keith Richards were dropping by for a drink.

Today Jost is no secret to yachters and glitterati but, despite its fame, it remains an unspoiled oasis of green hills fringed by blinding white sand. There's a small clutch of restaurants, beach bars and guesthouses, but blissfully little else. As one local put it, 'When Main St is still a beach, you know life is good.'

## When to Go

Mid-December through April is the dry and sunny high season on the 'barefoot island'. Jost also packs a crowd over Memorial Day weekend in late May, for Foxy's Woodenboat Regatta; around Halloween in late October for Foxy's Cat Fight Regatta; and on New Year's Eve, for Foxy's blowout to end all blowouts. Fridays and Saturdays are the best days to be on the island for live music, barbecues and other festivities. Many places close entirely in September and early October.

## History

For over 400 years Jost has been an oasis for seafarers and adventurers. A Dutch pirate (the island's namesake) used the island as a base in the 17th century. In the 18th century it became a homestead for Quakers escaping religious tyranny in England. Quaker surnames, such as Lettsome and Callwood, survive among the islanders, mostly descendents of freed Quaker slaves.

Once Foxy Callwood built his bar in the late 1960s, the tide ebbed and flowed for a quarter century and not much changed. Electricity arrived in 1991 and roads were cut a few years later.

### ★★ Festivals & Events

**Foxy's** (www.foxysbar.com) sponsors the main events, which rage island-wide.

**Foxy's Woodenboat Regatta** (late May) It draws classic wooden yachts from all over the Caribbean for four days of light racing and heavy partying.

**Foxy's Cat Fight Regatta** (late Oct) Ditto the above, only substitute catamarans for wooden boats and add a costumed Halloween party at the end.

**New Year's Eve** (Dec 31) Hundreds of boats show up in Jost's harbors on New Year's Eve. Party Central is Foxy's, where there is constant live reggae and calypso. The other island beach bars are full of action as well.

### ⓘ Getting There & Around

**BOAT**

Most visitors arrive by yacht. Landlubbers can get here by ferry from Tortola or St John. Ferries land at the pier on the west side of Great Harbour. It's about a 10-minute walk from the pier to the town center.

**New Horizon Ferry** (☑284-495-9278; round trip $25) Sails five times daily to/from Tortola's West End (twice in the morning, three times in the afternoon); it's a 25-minute trip; cash only.

**Inter-Island** (☑340-776-6597; www.inter islandboatservices.vi; round trip $70) Sails twice daily to/from Red Hook, St Thomas, and Cruz Bay, St John. It leaves Jost at 9:15am and 3pm. No service Wednesday or Thursday.

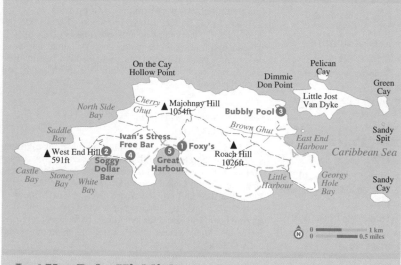

## Jost Van Dyke Highlights

**①** Hoist a namesake lager and hear improvised calypso at **Foxy's** (p178)

**②** Sharpen your ring-toss skills with a Painkiller at the **Soggy Dollar Bar** (p182)

**③** Splash in the waves and sea fizz at **Bubbly Pool** (p182)

**④** Pour yourself a drink using the honor system at **Ivan's Stress Free Bar** (p182)

**⑤** Pick a night, pick a bar for live music and a beach barbecue at **Great Harbour** (p178)

### One Day

Start at **White Bay**, rich with groovy beach bars to kick back, suck down tropical drinks and watch folks stumble in off their yachts. Conduct your own research along the strip: Who makes the best rum drinks? Best conch fritters? As the afternoon wears on, head to **Great Harbour**'s waterfront to meet Foxy and friends.

### Two Days

Hopefully you already stopped into **JVD Scuba** and made arrangements to go diving or take a snorkeling/hiking ecotour. Or head over to **Bubbly Pool** and follow up with a meal at **Little Harbour**.

**Dohm's Water Taxi** (☑340-775-6501; www.watertaxi-vi.com) A customized, much pricier way to get between Jost and St John/ St Thomas.

**CAR**

A car is more of a luxury than necessity on Jost. Expect to pay $60 to $80 per day for a 4WD.

**Abe & Eunicey** (☑284-495-9329)
**Paradise Jeep Rental** (☑284-495-9477)

**TAXI**

Taxis wait by the ferry dock. Fares are set. Following are costs to popular destinations from Great Harbour (these are per one passenger; fares go down for multiple passengers):

| DESTINATION | COST |
| --- | --- |
| White Bay | $10 |
| Little Harbour | $12 |
| Bubbly Pool | $20 |

## Great Harbour

In Jost's foremost settlement, Main St is a sandy path lined with hammocks and open-air bar-restaurants. Kick off your shoes, grab a frosty beverage, and join the vibe. To reach the actual 'town' (school, shops etc) where island life takes place, follow one of the lanes that lead behind the bars.

### ◎ Sights & Activities

Stretching the length of its little namesake town, Great Harbour Beach is perfectly adequate for sunbathing but it isn't good for swimming (shallow water, turtle grass and isolated patches of dead coral).

The one-stop shop for activities is **JVD Scuba** (www.jostvandykescuba.com), on Main St. It can set you up for just about anything. There's good **diving** (one/two tank $85/115)

at 30 unmarked dive sites around the island, where it's common to see turtles, dolphins and spotted eagle rays. The shop can arrange full-day **ecotours** that combine snorkeling, bird-watching and hiking; times and prices vary according to demand. It also offers **kayaking** and **fishing** equipment and trips. In addition, island innkeepers can make arrangements with water-sports vendors on Tortola to meet your diving, sailing and boating needs.

Jost has quite a collection of **hiking trails** that lead over the mountains to the rugged north shore and isolated east and west ends. It is easy to get lost on these trails. Get

### KNOW BEFORE YOU GO

» There are no banks on Jost. Most places accept credit cards, but a few do not, so make sure you bring cash. The closest bank is in Sopers Hole at Tortola's West End, where there are ATMs.

» Book ahead for accommodations, as there are relatively few options and demand is high.

» The island has a couple of small shops that stock limited food and supplies, but you're better off bringing provisions from Tortola or St John if you're self-catering during your stay.

» Updated websites about Jost are hard to come by. Your best bets are **White Bay Villas** (www.jostvandyke. com) and the **BVI Tourist Board** (www.bvitourism.com) for a smattering of restaurant, activity and transport info.

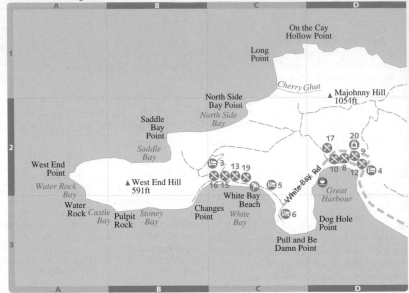

information from island hikers and/or hire a local to take you on a guided hike.

## 🛏 Sleeping

**Ali Baba's**                                    GUESTHOUSE **$$**
(📞284-495-9280; www.alibabasheavenlyrooms
bvi.com; r from $160) This long-standing restaurant recently began offering rooms on its 2nd floor. The compact, white-washed, wicker furnished units face the beach and have a wind-cooled balcony from which to view the action. Given the location, noise can sometimes be an issue.

**Sea Crest Inn**                                    APARTMENTS **$$**
(📞284-495-9024, 340-775-6389; seacrestinn@hot mail.com; apt from $145; ❄) The gracious owner, Ivy Chinnery Moses, has four large studio apartments, each with a kitchenette, TV, queen-size bed, private bathroom and balcony. It's on the waterfront just east of Foxy's.

**Paradise Guest House**                    GUESTHOUSE **$**
(📞284-495-9281; r from $85; ❄) On the 2nd floor above her bakery, Christine rents a couple of basic rooms with a shared porch and private bathroom.

## 🍴 Eating & Drinking

Since most of Jost's businesses cater to the crews off visiting yachts, almost all of the restaurants and bars stand by on VHF radio channel 16 to take reservations and announce nightly events. A list of favorite spots follows, but there are plenty more to choose from – wander down Main St to have a look.

**TOP**
**CHOICE** Foxy's Tamarind
**Bar**                                    BURGERS, SEAFOOD **$$**
(📞284-495-9258; www.foxysbar.com; mains $22-42; ⊙lunch & dinner) Foxy's is the place of legends. The yachting crowd has been partying here for almost five decades and raising hell on the beach. Local bands play several nights a week (usually Thursday through Saturday) in season and draw a mix of islanders and party animals off the boats. The light fare is a mix of rotis and darn good burgers, while the dinner mains are mostly meat and seafood. On Friday and Saturday night staff fire up the barbecue. What's more, Foxy has his own microbrewery on site, so fresh tap beers accompany the food. The best time to catch Foxy hanging out and singing his improvisational calypso is around 10am; prepare for him to embarrass you (in a fun way). Make dinner reservations by 5pm.

**Ali Baba's**                                    BURGERS, SEAFOOD **$$**
(📞284-495-9280; www.alibabarestaurantandbar bvi.com; mains $22-38; ⊙breakfast, lunch & dinner) Ali Baba's has a lazy, down-island atmosphere

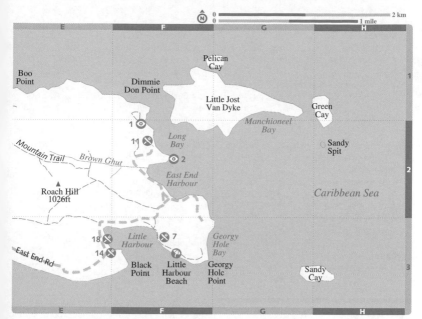

on its open-air patio. Patrons come for fresh fish and the Monday-night pig roast. The West Indian conch, lime-garlic shrimp and pumpkin soup rank as favorites. Breakfast draws a group of coffee-drinking locals. Make dinner reservations by 6pm.

**Corsairs**  PIZZA, SEAFOOD **$$**
(⌨284-495-9294; www.corsairsbvi.com; mains $25-40; ⊙breakfast, lunch & dinner) Corsairs provides a variation on the usual seafood theme with a menu of pizzas and pastas, along with eclectic Tex-Mex, Thai and other fusion dishes. Most incorporate seafood in some fashion, including fish tacos, shrimp fettuccine and lobster in coconut-pumpkin sauce. The bar hosts limbo contests and the BVI's only Jagermeister machine (you've been warned...). Beach barbecues take place on Sunday and Tuesday.

**Christine's Bakery**  BAKERY **$**
(⌨284-495-9281; mains $3-10; ⊙breakfast & lunch) Christine doesn't start baking when the roosters wake up, but she's got the settlement filled with the scents of banana bread, coconut and coffee by 8am, which is about as early as anyone starts to move around here. Grab an egg sandwich for breakfast; burgers and sandwiches are available for lunch. Go early for the best selection. The

bakery is just inland from the customs office (look for the sign with arrow).

**Rudy's Mariner's Rendezvous**  BURGERS, SEAFOOD **$$**
(⌨284-495-9282; mains $17-35; ⊙lunch & dinner) Congenial Rudy George runs this bar, restaurant and convenience store rolled into one. The breezy eatery serves delicious seafood; lobster and local fish are the specialties, along with burgers and ribs.

## 🔒 Shopping

**Fox Hole**  SOUVENIRS
Foxy has a large shop attached to his restaurant that sells all manner of Foxy souvenirs – T-shirts, hats, shorts etc – as well as high-quality jewelry, sportswear and Cuban cigars.

**Ice House**  FOOD
Across Back St from Christine's Bakery, Daisy and Joyce Chinnery run this little store where you can pick up fresh mangos and homemade mango chutney (ask for it).

## ℹ️ Information

Travelers will find brochures and postings of island events at the customs office and police station (next door) on Great Harbour's waterfront.

# White Bay

With Jost's most striking beach – and the jovial birthplace of the rum-soaked Painkiller cocktail – you'll find yourself at White Bay at some point during your visit. It's a primo place to stay, thanks to its multi-budget lodging options and highly entertaining beach bars. It's a hilly, 1-mile, bun-burning walk from Great Harbour.

## ⊙ Sights & Activities

**White Bay Beach** is by far Jost's most attractive shore. The long white crescent near the southwest end of the island lies pressed to the sea by steep hills. A barrier reef shelters the water from swells and waves, which makes for good swimming and a protected anchorage.

A water-sports vendor at the beach's west end rents **pedal boats** and floats a **water trampoline**. It caters mostly to cruise ship passengers who come over for day trips. Besides that, White Bay's activities are wriggling your feet in the crazy-white sand, drinking and people-watching.

## ⊨ Sleeping

**TOP CHOICE** **Perfect Pineapple**   GUESTHOUSE **$$**
(☑284-495-9401; www.perfectpineapple.com; ste from $160; ⊛) Foxy's son Greg owns this great-value property set on a steep hill back from the beach. The three one-bedroom suites each have a full kitchen and private porch with ocean views. He also rents a couple of larger cottages on site (one with one bedroom, the other with two bedrooms). The family owns Gertrude's restaurant down on the beach if you don't want to cook your own meals, and there's a little convenience store with internet access available here, too.

**White Bay Campground**   CAMPGROUND **$**
(☑284-495-9358, 340-513-1095; www.ivanscampground.com; campsites/equipped tents $20/40, cabins $65-75) This is one of Virgin Islands' most popular stops for backpackers. Ivan Chinnery, the owner, mixes it up by offering bare sites (the best of the bunch are right on the beach, where you can string your hammock between sea-grape trees), equipped platform tents (with beds, linens) and cabins (add electricity to the beds and linens). Everyone shares the communal kitchen and cold-water bathhouse. The tents, cabins and facilities are very bare bones, which may explain why Ivan added a couple of apartments with private bathrooms (see below). The property is a bit of a hike east from the main strip of White Bay watering holes, though with the Stress Free Bar on site, you might not find the need to leave. If you do, look for the path over the rocks on the beach.

### Ivan's Stress Free Guesthouse
APARTMENTS **$$**

(☎284-495-9358, 340-513-1095; www.ivansstress
freeguesthouse.com; r $150-375; ❄@) This is
Ivan's more upscale lodging on the premises.
The upstairs holds a one-bedroom suite that
can accommodate up to five people; there's a
sleeper sofa and full kitchen. The downstairs
is a studio suite for two people, with a micro-
wave and refrigerator. There's a minimum
stay of three nights.

### Sandcastle Hotel
HOTEL **$$**

(☎284-495-9888; www.soggydollar.com; d $285-
310) Situated smack on the beach, the Sandcastle offers four cottages and two hotel
rooms, all sans phone and TV (and only
the hotel rooms have air-conditioning). The
grounds host the infamous Soggy Dollar
Bar, which is the most popular of the strip's
venues, so there's always an active scene
here. Kids under 16 are not permitted as
overnight guests.

### White Bay Villas & Seaside Cottages
APARTMENTS **$$$**

(☎410-571-6692, 800-778-8066; www.jostvan
dyke.com; cottages per week from $2000; ❄@♿)
Located far up a hill at White Bay's east
end, the property consists of seven pretty
cottages and three villas in configurations
of one to three bedrooms. All have kitch-
ens, coolers and decks with killer views.
Staff are first-rate pros at arranging what-
ever you need (including child care). Rent-
als typically are for weekly stays, but you
might snag a three- or five-night opening.
It's quite secluded, located more or less
between Great Harbour and the White
Bay strip, so prepare to walk if you're sans
wheels.

## 🍴 Eating & Drinking

Ask around about live music – musicians
such as Reuben Chinnery strum at different
bars throughout the week.

---

## ONE FOXY FELLA

Mention you have recently returned from the BVI in a casual conversation at some first-
world watering hole and there's a good chance someone will ask, 'Did you go to Foxy's?
How's Foxy?' The question will have the tone of a traveler ruminating on a long-lost
friend. And Foxy has legions of them.

Foxy (born 'Philiciano') Callwood started life as one of seven children on Jost Van
Dyke in 1938. Since then, this barefoot man with the dreadlocks and guitar has be-
come probably the most famous person in the BVI. The keys to Foxy's celebrity are
his irreverent, deep and infectious laughter, the persistent twinkle in his eye and the
ability to offer up a melody or piece of philosophy to make each person he meets feel
worthy. Best of all, the man exudes a disarming euphoria owing more to his guitar
than to the bottle of beer he has forgotten on your table. 'I always happy,' you can hear
him telling himself and anyone who will listen, as the troubadour wanders around
Foxy's Tamarind Bar in a T-shirt and ragged jeans. 'I am so happy my cup is full and
running over.'

The public first met Foxy in 1968, when his mother set up a booth on the beach for
a festival at Jost and proclaimed it 'Mama's Booth & Foxy's Bar'. 'Somebody told us to
put a little kitchen on da booth, so we did,' says Foxy. 'Den Mama left, and I was stuck
with it.' Soon word spread among sailors about this jolly fellow on Jost Van Dyke who
could make up a calypso melody in the time it took you to crack a cold beer from his
cooler.

Over the last few decades, Foxy has prospered. And, as he's done so, he has passed
the hat around and made large donations to build a high school on the island and to
build an island sloop to teach local kids about their heritage. He will tell anyone who will
listen, 'Don't put all these hillsides in condos; educate our young people to grow mangos
up dere or build and sail boats.' In 2008 he was honored as a Member of the Order of
the British Empire for his commitment to conservation and philanthropy on Jost. That's
right: he's 'Sir Foxy' now!

And how did he get his crafty nickname? He isn't saying. But one island woman has
this to say: 'What would you call a fella dat done gone out with two sisters at da same
time, and dem not even carin'?'

**Soggy Dollar Bar & Sandcastle Restaurant**   BURGERS, SEAFOOD $$
(☎284-495-9888; www.soggydollar.com; 4-course meals $40; ☺breakfast, lunch & dinner; 🛜) The infamous Soggy Dollar takes its name from the sailors swimming ashore to spend wet bills. It's also the bar that invented the Pain-killer, the BVI's delicious-yet-lethal cocktail of rum, coconut, pineapple, orange juice and nutmeg. The attached restaurant is something special, offering cinnamon-rum French toast for breakfast and a fixed-price, four-course candlelit meal for dinner (call by 4pm to reserve). And when you're not drinking or eating? Play the ring-toss game, and find out how freakin' addictive swinging a ring onto a hook can be. This place is always hopping.

**Ivan's Stress Free Bar & Restaurant**   SANDWICHES $$
(☎284-495-9358; www.ivanscampground.com; mains $9-15; ☺breakfast & lunch daily, dinner Thu) Ivan's is a Jost institution and an excellent place for younger travelers to network. It's open all day, but if no one is around you simply grab your own drinks and sandwiches at the shell-strewn bar using the honor system. The Thursday-night cookouts (fish, chicken and ribs) draw a crowd. Ivan's is located at White Bay Campground.

**One Love Bar & Grill**   BURGERS, SEAFOOD $$
(☎284-495-9829; www.onelovebar.com; mains $14-22; ☺lunch & dinner) Foxy's son Seddy owns this reggae-blasting beach bar. He'll wow you with his magic tricks, and certainly magic is how he gets the place to hold together – old buoys, life preservers and other beach junk form its 'walls.' Lobster quesadillas, burgers and pasta dishes fill plates. Seddy usually closes when the sun sets.

**Jewel's Snack Shack**   BURGERS $
(☎284-495-9286; mains $5-9; ☺11am-4pm) Saucy Jewel cooks fine burgers, hot dogs and fries, and scoops ice cream.

**Gertrude's**   BURGERS, SEAFOOD $$
(☎284-495-9104; mains $12-22; ☺lunch & dinner) Next door to Jewel's, Gertrude's is another low-key beach bar with tasty sandwiches, rotis and fish dishes to go with her cocktails.

# Little Harbour & Around

This is Jost's quieter side, with just a few businesses. It's a popular stop for yachts that descend on the harbor, especially on weekends.

## ◉ Sights & Activities

**Bubbly Pool**   SWIMMING HOLE
This natural whirlpool formed by odd rocky outcrops is reached via a goat trail from Foxy's Taboo restaurant. When waves crash in, swimmers experience bubbling water like that of a Jacuzzi. Don't worry: it's enclosed and safe. Bring a picnic and stay a while. The folks at Taboo can provide directions; it's a 20-minute walk.

**Little Harbour Beach**   BEACH
Little Harbour's east edge has a thin, steep strand of white sand perfect for sunbathing and swimming in water protected from wind and waves.

**Diamond Cay National Park**   PARK
Travelers who follow the road all the way to the east end of Jost will see a tiny offshore island at the southern end of Long Bay. This is the 1¼-acre Diamond Cay National Park. Pelicans, boobies and terns nest here. There

---

**DON'T MISS**

### SHIP AHOY

No, it's not the booze playing tricks with your eyes. If you walk round back of Foxy's complex, you really do see a 32ft wooden sloop rising from the yard. It's the handiwork of the **JVD Preservation Society** (www.jvdps.org) or, more accurately, the local teenagers employed by the society to construct the *Endeavor II*.

It's part of a nonprofit project to provide Jost's kids with traditional boat-building skills and to keep them from straying into off-island temptations. The society pays the boys and girls for their efforts, they stay on the island and learn a time-honored trade, and in the process Jost preserves its culture.

The group has been hammering away since 2004; the *Endeavor II* is scheduled for completion, er, sometime soon. The kids will then learn to sail the sloop, as well as study local marine science and conservation.

## SANDY CAY & GREEN CAY

If you have a boat or kayak, you might want to check out the small **Sandy Cay** off the southeast coast of Jost. It is the quintessential desert island, with a broad apron of sand on the west side and good snorkeling on the fringe reef both north and south of the island. There are also some short hiking trails. The island is a favorite picnic stop for yachts, so you probably won't have the place to yourself.

Even smaller than Sandy Cay is **Green Cay**, an islet off the east end of Little Jost, featuring adjacent Sandy Spit with its lone coconut palm rising above the beach. This is a terrific place to stop for lunch or a swim if you are kayaking in the vicinity of Little Jost Van Dyke.

is good snorkeling nearby on the coral heads in shallow Long Bay as well as along the south side of Little Jost Van Dyke. Be very careful of the boats and dinghies moving through the anchorages here.

 **Eating & Drinking**

At time of research, a new bakery was slated to open behind Foxy's Taboo in the yellow, white and orange building, which should be handy for picnic provisions en route to Bubbly Pool.

**Foxy's Taboo**          BURGERS, SEAFOOD **$$**
(☎284-495-0218; mains $13-25; ☺lunch & dinner) Foxy teams up with daughter Justine at Foxy's Taboo to serve easy, breezy dishes such as pizza and pepper-jack cheeseburgers for lunch, and more sophisticated fare (say lobster-stuffed tilapia) for dinner, all accompanied by Foxy's microbrews. Taboo sits in a scenic dockside building by Diamond Cay.

**Sidney's Peace & Love**    BURGERS, SEAFOOD **$$**
(☎284-495-9271; mains $20-45; ☺lunch & dinner) The specialty here is lobster, but Sidney's serves up plenty of West Indian fish dishes, along with burgers and barbecue.

Pour your own drinks to go with the goods at the honor bar. T-shirts left behind by visiting revelers decorate the rafters. 'Time flies when you're doing very little,' as the T-shirts proclaim (though in slightly different wording). Saturday night rocks particularly hard with charter yacht crews.

**Harris' Place**          BURGERS, SEAFOOD **$$**
(☎284-495-9302; mains $19-40; ☺breakfast, lunch & dinner; ☎) Amiable Cynthia Jones runs this harborside pavilion known for homey comfort food. Burgers, pork, ribs, chicken and fruit smoothies make appearances. On Monday night, feast on all-you-can-eat lobster in garlic-butter sauce.

**Abe's by the Sea**              SEAFOOD **$$**
(☎284-495-9329; mains $20-40; ☺lunch & dinner; ☎) Abe's open-air restaurant is indeed by the sea, and boats dock right up beside it. Lobster, conch, fish, chicken and spare ribs rule the menu. The pig roast on Wednesday night during the winter is the big event and often features live fungi music. Abe also runs a convenience store and car rental shop from here.

# Anegada

POP 200

## Best Places to Eat

» Potter's by the Sea (p188)

» Cow Wreck Beach Bar & Grill (p188)

» Pam's Kitchen & Bakery (p189)

» Big Bamboo Bar & Grill (p190)

» Dotsy's Bakery & Sandwich Shop (p190)

## Best Places to Stay

» Neptune's Treasure (p188)

» Cow Wreck Villas (p188)

» Anegada Beach Cottages (p188)

» Keel Point Cottages (p188)

## Why Go?

The easternmost Virgin is located just 12 miles away from its brethren, but you'll think you've landed on another planet. Anegada's pancake-flat, desert landscape looks that different, and its wee clutch of restaurants and guesthouses are that baked-in-the-sun mellow. Flamingos ripple the salt ponds. Giant rock iguanas hide under blooming cacti. And ridiculously blue water laps at beaches with whimsical names like Loblolly Bay and Flash of Beauty.

You've probably seen 'Anegada lobster' on menus throughout the islands. Indeed, this is where it's sourced. Dinners consist of huge crustaceans plucked from the water in front of your eyes and grilled on the beach in converted oil drums.

Some travelers find Anegada to be too sleepy, but if listening to waves and walking solitary beaches rank high on your list, this is your island. It's a mysterious, magical and lonesome place to hang your hammock for a stretch.

## When to Go

Mid-December through April is the dry and sunny high season, when prices ramp up but all the businesses are in full swing. The late February/early March BVI Kite Jam and the late June Lobsta Regatta bring more visitors than usual to the island. May and early December are good shoulder season times when bargains and fair (if a bit wet) weather intersect. November through July is lobster season, so they're widely available and at their juiciest during these months.

## History

Anegada is a killer island. Literally. It takes its name from the Spanish word for 'drowned' or 'flooded,' and that's what it did to more than 300 ships in the early years – it sunk them. The island is so low (28ft above sea level at its highest) that mariners couldn't see it to get their bearings until they were trapped in the surrounding coral maze known as Horseshoe Reef. Some of these wrecks are legendary, such as that of the HMS *Astrea,* a 32-gun British frigate, and the *Paramatta,* an English steamship.

In the 17th century, the island became the chronicled haunt of pirates, including Billy Bones and Normand. The reclusive settlers who followed in their wake subsisted on fishing, vegetable plots and salvaging the wrecks on the reef.

## ⭐ Festivals & Events

**BVI Kite Jam** (www.bvikitejam.com; late February–early Mar) A weeklong event packed full of 'freestyle, sliders, big air and wave riding' around Virgin Gorda, Necker Island and Anegada. Sir Richard Branson is the cofounder and an active participant.

**Anegada Lobsta Regatta** (late Jun) Boat race followed by a beach party at Potter's by the Sea.

**Anegada Desert Duel Bicycle Race** (mid-Sep or Oct) The BVI Mountain Bike Club sponsors the heated event; check the Facebook page for info as the time frame varies.

## ℹ Getting There & Around

### AIR

Tiny Captain Auguste George Airport lies a mile northwest of the Settlement in the island's center. There is no commercial service, only charter planes from Tortola and Virgin Gorda. The following companies offer day-trip packages for around $155:

**Fly BVI** (www.bviaircharters.com)

**Island Birds** (www.islandbirds.com)

### BICYCLE & SCOOTER

If you feel like you have the stamina to ride on rough, dusty roads in the hot sun (not an easy

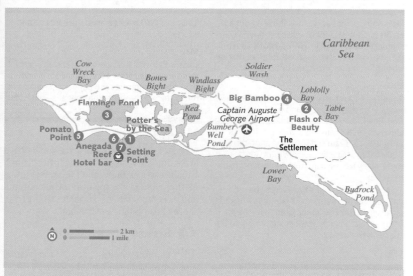

## Anegada Highlights

**1** Crack into a grilled, spiced lobster at **Potter's by the Sea** (p188)

**2** Snorkel over colorful fish and coral at **Flash of Beauty** (p190)

**3** Catch a glimpse of the pink flock at **Flamingo Pond** (p186)

**4** Swing in a hammock at the **Big Bamboo** (p190)

**5** Walk the deserted beach at **Pomato Point** (p187)

**6** Join the party at the **Anegada Reef Hotel bar** (p189)

**7** Cast a line for some world-class fishing on the flats around **Setting Point** (p187)

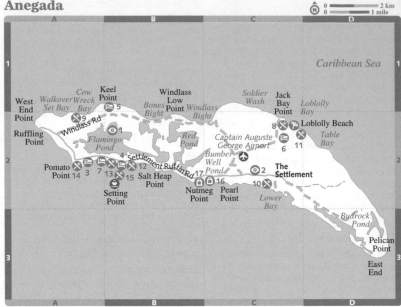

ANEGADA

feat), you can rent a bike near the ferry dock at **Lil Bit** (☑284-495-9932; bikes per day $20, scooters per day $40 to $50). **Scooth Tooth** (☑284-544-5433; www.scoothtooth.com) rents wheels for similar prices and offers tours.

**BOAT**

**Road Town Fast Ferry** (☑284-494-2323; www. roadtownfastferry.com; round trip $45) sails from Road Town, Tortola, on Monday, Wednesday and Friday at 6:45am and 3:30pm; it departs Anegada at 8:30am and 5pm. The boat makes a quick stop at Spanish Town, Virgin Gorda, en route. Many travelers use this public ferry to do a day trip.

Several Tortola- and Virgin Gorda–based day-sail operators also make jaunts to Anegada, including **Bitter End Yacht Club** (www.beyc. com), which runs a 'blue water excursion' to the island on Wednesdays.

**CAR**

Jeep rentals cost about $75 per day at the **Anegada Reef Hotel** (☑284-495-8002; www. anegadareef.com) by the ferry dock. **DW Jeep Rentals** (☑284-495-9677; dwjeep@hotmail. com) at Nutmeg Point can cost a bit less.

Anegada has one main road, Settlement Ruffin Rd, which starts at the airport and swings by The Settlement. From there it heads west to the ferry dock at Setting Point. It's paved for this portion, but as you move onward around the island the pavement gives way to packed sand. Unpaved

trails and 4WD tracks lead to the East End and interior.

**TAXI**

Taxis wait by the ferry dock. You can arrange a three-hour island tour for around $55. In addition, open-air shuttles ($8 per person round trip) run to the beaches from the Anegada Reef Hotel.

## West End

If you take the ferry to Anegada, you'll arrive at Setting Point, by the Anegada Reef Hotel, which serves as the island's unofficial information center. The majority of restaurants and accommodations sprinkle around the shore of Anegada's western half.

### ◉ Sights

FREE **Flamingo Pond**                    NATURE RESERVE
The large salt pond at the island's West End hosts a flock of flamingos. These birds were once plentiful on Anegada and other cays in the BVI, until hunters seeking their tender meat and feathers decimated the population. In 1992, biologists reintroduced flamingos to Anegada by bringing in birds from Bermuda. In 1995 the Anegada colony had its first hatchlings, and by 2001 the flock had grown to more than 50. Now, biologists

are hoping the flock will attract migrating flamingos to increase the gene pool.

You can see the birds wading on the far north side of what is now called Flamingo Pond. Please keep your distance: flamingos require hundreds of feet of buffer between them and apparent threats such as humans. The BVI National Parks Trust has designated Flamingo Pond and its surrounding wetlands as a bird sanctuary, and you can see egrets, terns and ospreys nesting and feeding in the area, too.

**FREE** Wilfred Creque's Pomato Point
Museum                                    MUSEUM
(☏284-495-9466) This tiny 'museum' – it's actually a side room of the Pomato Point Restaurant – exhibits a bizarre mix of archaeological relics and shipwreck items that owner Wilfred Creque (pronounced *CREEK*-ee) collected from local waters. You can see doubloons, gin bottles, musket balls, ship timbers, crockery from steamship lines and Taíno artifacts. It's usually open in the evening, when dinner guests can view the collection. At time of research, it was closed for repairs but due to reopen soon.

## 🏝 Beaches

Gorgeous, secluded **Cow Wreck Bay** stretches along the island's northwest end and offers good snorkeling in its shallow waters. Rent **kayaks** ($50 per day) at the beach bar, or just kick back in a lounge chair under one of the thatched-umbrella shelters. The beach at **Pomato Point** is prime for solitary walks on endless acres of untouched sand.

## 🏃 Activities

### Fishing

There is world-class **fishing** year-round on the flats around Setting Point and Salt Heap Point on the south shore. The Vanterpools are the first family of fishing guides: Clinton Vanterpool was a guide for President Jimmy Carter, who was so impressed he wrote about it in his memoir *An Outdoor Journal*. His son, Danny Vanterpool, now runs **Danny's Bonefishing** (☏284-441-6334; www.dannys bonefishing.com; per half/full day $300/500) to much acclaim.

The Anegada Reef Hotel can arrange **deep-sea fishing charters** (per half/full day $700/1100). Anglers cast for wahoo and tuna year-round, mahimahi from October to June and marlin from September to June.

### Diving & Snorkeling

**North Shore Divers** (www.diveanegada. com) has a shop at the Big Bamboo restaurant for snorkel-gear rental ($5 per hour); there's good snorkeling from shore there (Loblolly Bay, East End). The company also has dive packages (one-/two-tank dives $85/125). Experienced divers can inquire about checking out the *Paramatta* and *Astrea* shipwrecks.

### Kayaking

Rentals are available at **Cow Wreck Beach Bar & Grill** (per day $50). Put in there, or at the dock south of the Settlement, from

**ANEGADA**

### One Day

Rent a car or scooter and check out the beaches at **Cow Wreck Bay** or **Loblolly Bay**. If you're without wheels, taxi shuttles run frequently to these places, especially Loblolly. Snorkel, sip a frosty drink at the beach bar, swing in a hammock. Take a peek at the island's unique wildlife at the **Flamingo Pond** and **Rock Iguana Hatchery**. For dinner, it's trite but true: have the lobster. **Potter's by the Sea** fires up a fine one.

### Two Days

Well, you've already seen all the sights. Sooo, back to the beach? Or arrange an activity – **diving**, **fishing**, **kayaking** or **cycling** (only for the brave).

which you can paddle through the southern shore's flats and mangroves to Setting Point.

## 🛏 Sleeping

**TOP CHOICE** **Cow Wreck Villas**     APARTMENTS **$$**
(☎284-495-8047; www.cowwreckbeach.com; 1-/2-bedroom apt $250/375; ▣) Most of the day it'll just be you and the wandering bovines who share the grounds at Cow Wreck. Three sunny yellow-and-green cottages front the perfect, hammock-strewn beach. The owner, Bell, is lovely and so are dishes she cooks at the restaurant, Cow Wreck Beach Bar & Grill.

**Neptune's Treasure**     HOTEL **$$**
(☎284-495-9439; www.neptunestreasure.com; s/d from $108/148; ▣🖥) Neptune's nine simple, color-washed rooms sit right on the sand and garner lots of loyal patrons. It's the best-value lodging on the island, and well managed to boot. For slightly more space, ask for one of the end units, which are a tad larger. A good restaurant and bakery are on site; store leftovers in your room's mini refrigerator. Neptune's is a 15-minute walk west from the ferry dock.

**Anegada Beach Cottages**     COTTAGES **$$**
(☎284-495-9234; www.anegadabeachcottages.com; cottages from $250) Pomato Point is the site of these three concrete bungalows on stilts, a short walk from Pomato Point Restaurant. They're the island standard – unfussy, clean, on the beach, with a kitchen. The difference here is a little extra peace and privacy (plus your own palapa hut by the waves).

**Keel Point Cottages**     APARTMENTS **$$$**
(☎284-441-0296, 284-495-8019; www.keelpoint cottages.com; 1-/2-bedroom apt $250/300) These four peach-colored cottages are situated at – yes – Keel Point, a short distance from Cow

Wreck. They're on the beach, but up a dune in a protected setting. They're equipped with wicker furniture, a full kitchen, a TV and sun deck. The crowning glory: jeep rental is included as part of the package.

**Anegada Reef Hotel**     HOTEL **$$**
(☎284-495-8002; www.anegadareef.com; d garden/ ocean view $175/200; ▣@) The island's first and largest hotel, this seaside lodge by the ferry dock has the feel of a classic out-island fishing camp. The property's 16 rooms and two-bedroom villas are nothing fancy – with tropical motel-style wares – but the fishing dock, restaurant and beach bar here are Anegada's social epicenter. For those on budgets: if you ask nicely, the owners will let you pitch a tent ($20) in the garden.

## 🍴 Eating & Drinking

All of the main restaurants also have bars if you just want a beverage.

**TOP CHOICE** **Potter's by the Sea**     SEAFOOD **$$$**
(☎284-495-9182; www.pottersbythesea.com; mains $25-50; ⊙dinner; 🖥) Potter's is the first place you stumble into when departing the ferry dock. Potter lived in Queens, New York, and worked in the restaurant biz there for years, so he knows how to make customers feel at home while serving them ribs, fettuccine, curried shrimp and lobster. Graffiti and T-shirts cover the open-air walls; live bands occasionally play. The bar is open all day, and there's free wi-fi.

**Cow Wreck Beach Bar & Grill**     SEAFOOD **$$$**
(☎284-495-8047; www.cowwreckbeach.com; mains $24-53; ⊙lunch & dinner) The open-air restaurant at sublime Cow Wreck Beach features lobster, conch and shellfish cooked over local wood on the outdoor grill. Chef Bell's conch fritters win applause. The bar

pours the usual assortment of tropical drinks plus the 'cow killer'.

### Pam's Kitchen & Bakery
BAKERY $

(☎284-495-9237; mains $7-12; ⊙8am-5pm) Pam is back! After a lengthy stateside stint, she has returned to her bakery next to Neptune's Treasure and is once again cranking out loaves of herb bread, key lime pies, cinnamon rolls and brownies. It's a terrific breakfast stop for an egg sandwich, or for a lunchtime savory snack like a burger or fish pâté. Her homemade chutneys and hot sauce give a jolt to local conch and fish.

### Lobster Trap
SEAFOOD $$$

(☎284-495-9466; mains $22-50; ⊙lunch & dinner) The Lobster Trap's grilled version of the namesake crustacean approaches perfection on a menu that includes the usual seafood suspects. Adding to the pleasure: the twinkly garden setting on the main anchorage's waterfront. There is a dinghy dock for boaters.

### Neptune's Treasure
SEAFOOD $$$

(☎284-495-9439; www.neptunestreasure.com; mains $22-50; ⊙breakfast, lunch & dinner) The Soares family, originally Portuguese fisherfolk from the Azores, has run this restaurant and hotel of same name for more than 35

---

## KNOW BEFORE YOU GO

» The public ferry sails from Road Town, Tortola to Anegada on Monday, Wednesday and Friday morning and returns around 5pm, making day trips possible.

» There are no banks on Anegada. Most places accept credit cards, but a few do not, so make sure you bring cash.

» For dinner, you'll have to choose a restaurant ahead of time and call by 4pm for reservations. Without this advance warning, most venues won't have enough food on hand.

» Anegada has some fierce mosquitoes; be prepared with strong repellent. Stinging red ants can also be a problem.

» The island has a couple of tiny shops that stock limited food and supplies, but you're better off bringing provisions from Tortola if you're self-catering during your stay.

---

Cracking an Anegada lobster is a tourist rite of passage. Every restaurant serves the massive crustaceans, usually grilled on the beach in a converted oil drum and spiced with the chef's secret seasonings. Because the critters are plucked fresh from the surrounding waters, you must call ahead by 4pm to place your order so each restaurant knows how many to stock. Most places charge around $50 to indulge. Note that lobster fishing is prohibited from August 1 through November 1 so stocks can replenish, thus they're not on menus (nor is conch) during that time.

years. They remain the BVI's main commercial fishers, so the swordfish, yellowfin tuna and mahimahi are hot off the boat. The meat-and-seafood menu is similar to the island's other waterfront establishments, but it's served in an air-conditioned dining room rather than the great outdoors.

### Anegada Reef Hotel
SEAFOOD $$$

(☎284-495-8002; www.anegadareef.com; mains $22-50; ⊙breakfast, lunch & dinner) This is Anegada's traditional hot spot. A lot of folks cruising in yachts show up in the anchorage off the dock and make a beach party at the open-air bar while the fish and lobster sizzle on the grill. Breakfast consists of bacon and eggs, lunch brings on the burgers and sandwiches (try the tuna melt).

### Pomato Point Restaurant
SEAFOOD $$$

(☎284-495-9466; mains $26-50; ⊙lunch & dinner) It's another of the open-air options for fish and shellfish, typically served with West Indian rice, salad and desert. The sunsets here can't be beat, and you can browse the room of shipwreck relics while waiting for your food.

### Lil Bit
ICE CREAM $

(⊙7am-late) This is your one-stop shopping strip for ice cream, snacks at the mini-mart, laundry machines and bicycle rentals, all on the road to the ferry.

 Shopping

### Purple Turtle
SOUVENIRS

It sells all kinds of island goodies (pottery, T-shirts etc); conveniently located near the Anegada Reef Hotel.

# East End

The Settlement, Anegada's only town, anchors the East End. The wee West Indian village is a picture of dead cars (you can get them on the island, but you can't get them off), laundry drying in the breeze and folks feeding goats and chickens. There are a couple of teensy shops where you can buy food and supplies. The iguanas and beaches are the draws.

## ◎ Sights

**FREE** **Rock Iguana Hatchery**    HATCHERY
(☺8am-4pm) The BVI National Parks Trust started the facility because feral cats were eating the island's baby iguanas, endangering the rare species. So workers now bring the babes to the nursery's cages to grow safely. After two years, they're big enough to be released back into the wild, where they'll sprout to around 5ft from tip to tail. The hatchery sits behind the government administration building; just let yourself in.

## 🏝 Beaches

**Loblolly Bay** stretches along the northeast shore, about 2 miles from the Settlement. Facilities include thatched-umbrella shelters, bathrooms, a pay shower ($3 per use) and the Big Bamboo bar-restaurant. **North Shore Divers** (www.diveanegada.com) has a shop on site for snorkel gear rental ($5 per hour). If it's not open, head to Big Bamboo and ask for assistance. You can swim over a widespread area here and see spotted eagle rays and barracudas.

**Flash of Beauty** is just east of Loblolly. It, too, has a bar-restaurant, bathroom facilities and excellent snorkeling. You'll swim through a more compact area but with bigger coral and lots of funny-looking fish.

The water is roughest at both beaches from November to March. Open-air shuttles ($8 per person) make frequent runs to Loblolly Bay from the Anegada Reef Hotel.

## 🛏 Sleeping

**Loblolly Beach Cottages**    APARTMENTS $$
(☎284-495-8359; www.loblollycottages.com; per week 1-/2-bedroom $1190/1925; ❄) Four summery cottages sit down a potholed road a short drive from the beach. The Green and Pink abodes each have one bedroom, while the Orange and Purple ones have two bedrooms. All have a deck with plastic chairs, a full kitchen and TV/DVD/music system. They're set close together, so they're not terribly private.

## ✕ Eating & Drinking

If you want dinner here, don't forget to call ahead make reservations.

**Big Bamboo**    SEAFOOD $$
(☎284-495-2019; mains $14-40; ☺lunch & dinner) Located on the beach at Loblolly Bay's west end, Aubrey Levons' tiki-esque restaurant-bar specializes in island recipes for lobster, fish and chicken. Staff grab the lobsters from the trap out front in the sea; you're welcome to join them and choose your prey. Sandwiches are available for those with less-hearty appetites. Thirsty? Get a drink at the bar and take it to one of the hammocks swinging from the sea-grape trees. The Bamboo always packs a crowd.

**Flash of Beauty**    SEAFOOD $$
(☎284-495-8014, 284-441-5815; mains $10-40; ☺lunch & dinner) After you finish snorkeling the rich waters out front, climb up the shore to Flash of Beauty's restaurant-bar. It's slightly more of a drinks-and-sandwich place than Big Bamboo, but the menu and prices are similar. The bartenders make a mean 'bushwhacker' – a milkshake-esque drink using seven liquors. It's located on the beach at Loblolly Bay's east end.

**Dotsy's Bakery & Sandwich Shop** BAKERY $
(☎284-495-9667; sandwiches $6-12, pizzas $10-20; ☺8:30am-7pm) Locals come to Dotsy's small, tin-roofed building in the Settlement for fresh-baked breads, breakfasts, fish and chips, burgers and pizzas. It's one of the few 'down home' eateries geared more to locals than tourists.

## 🛍 Shopping

There are two small crafters' shops near each other at Nutmeg Point, west of the Settlement. They keep whimsical hours.

**Pat's Pottery**    SOUVENIRS
Pat has one-of-a-kind, hand-painted platters, pitchers, mugs and bowls for sale. She also carries island-made dolls and Christmas ornaments.

**VNJ's Gift Shop**    SOUVENIRS
Vera specializes in hand-painted ceramics.

# Out Islands

## Includes »

## Best Places to Eat

» William Thornton (p193)

» Cooper Island Beach Club (p195)

» Pusser's Marina Cay Restaurant & Bar (p196)

» Pirates Bight (p193)

» Deadman's Bay Bar & Grill (p194)

## Best Places to Stay

» Cooper Island Beach Club (p195)

» Pusser's Marina Cay Hotel (p196)

» Peter Island Resort (p193)

## Why Go?

The BVI's 'out islands' – a Creole expression for remote or undeveloped cays – are a wonderful mix of uninhabited wildlife sanctuaries, luxurious hideaways for the rich and famous, and provisioning stops for sailors. With more than 40 little landmasses to choose from, you're bound to find something to suit your taste. Cooper Island floats affordable cottages, while Peter, Scrub and Guana Islands kick it up a notch with luxury resorts. Norman Island holds buried treasure and a rowdy floating bar. Salt Island lures divers to the wreck of the RMS *Rhone*. Countless other isles – Ginger, the Dogs, Fallen Jerusalem – offer nothing but beaches and blue sea.

Most of the islands are reachable only by charter or private boat. If you don't have your own vessel, try making arrangements with a day-sail operator.

## When to Go

Happy hour is always a jolly good time to visit islands such as Norman and Cooper Islands and Marina Cay thanks to their rollicking bars. Divers and snorkelers heading to sites such as the Dogs, Fallen Jerusalem and the Indians at Pelican Island will fare better earlier in the day when the winds are lighter and the crowds are fewer. As elsewhere in the BVI, mid-December through April is the Out Islands' high season, when tour operators and business are going full force. Several places close in September, the low season's peak.

## ❶ Getting There & Around

While most of the Out Islands are reachable only by dive boat or charter boat, there are three islands you can get to by public ferry from Tortola: Peter Island (from Road Town), and Marina Cay and Scrub Island (both from the docks at Trellis Bay/Beef Island on the east end).

## Norman Island

It's all about buried treasure on **Norman Island** (www.normanisland.com). Or so they say. The hype surrounding the BVI's largest uninhabited landmass is almost too much to bear.

Some chroniclers say Norman Island is the prototype for Robert Louis Stevenson's *Treasure Island*, and Stevenson based it on accounts his seafaring uncle told him while in the region.

Documented history does indeed show a rich past on Norman. After the crew of the Spanish galleon *Nuestra Señora de Guadalupe* mutinied in 1750, they buried several chests of silver coins on the island. Locals from Tortola dug it up. But did they find it all?

Another story centers on the French pirate Normand, who left Anegada and settled here (giving the island his name) with booty he'd ransacked from various ships. Rivals killed Normand, but never found the loot. And so rumors of silver and gold persist.

You'll feel the pirate spirit all over the island. It lingers at **the Caves** off Treasure Point, where Mr Fleming and the fictional Long John Silver allegedly hid their cache. These days the Caves is a mega-popular snorkeling site, with a mob of sailboats, dinghies and swimmers clustered around the entrance. The water inside the caverns is shallow (about 5ft deep) and brimming with silversides, glassy sweepers and little lobsters.

**The Bight** is adjacent, an anchorage with more than 100 moorings and two fantas-

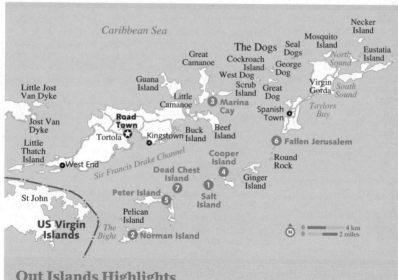

## Out Islands Highlights

❶ Snorkel or dive at the RMS *Rhone* shipwreck by **Salt Island** (p195)

❷ Party with scalawags at the pirate ship on **Norman Island** (p192)

❸ Knock back a 'painkiller' and watch the sun set on **Marina Cay** (p196)

❹ Kick off your shoes, snorkel the bay and fork into good food at **Cooper Island Beach Club** (p195)

❺ Hike the trails and beaches of wild **Peter Island** (p193)

❻ Explore the ancient toppled rocks at **Fallen Jerusalem** (p198)

❼ Dive where Blackbeard ditched his men with nothing but a saber and a bottle of rum at **Dead Chest Island** (p198)

**DON'T MISS**

## OUT ISLANDS' BEST SNORKEL SITES

» **Dry Rocks East** The shallow ridge by Cooper Island attracts sergeant majors, barracuda and other big fish, who flock to the surge created by the area's winds and currents.

» **The Caves** Three large caves dot Norman Island, where squid, coral and fish large and small like to hang out and feed.

» **Cistern Point** Coral-covered ledges and multihued fish surround this rocky point extending off Cooper Island.

» **The Indians** Several pinnacles rise near Pelican Island and offer good viewing of glassy sweepers and other fish.

» **RMS Rhone – Stern** While the renowned Salt Island shipwreck is best known as a dive site, its stern lies in water shallow enough for snorkelers to see the bronze propeller, rudder and aft mast from the surface.

tic bars, including one aboard a converted schooner. Except for the beaches at the Bight and at Benures Bay on the east side, the island is so overgrown it is virtually impenetrable. Depending on the season and traffic, you may find a trail open between the beach at the Bight and Spyglass Hill. The hike takes about half an hour each way; running into wild goats and cattle is not uncommon.

### ✖ Eating & Drinking

You have two choices: one on land, the other at sea. Both places bring in live West Indian bands or just crank Bob Marley and Jimmy Buffett over high-voltage sound systems. Weekends are always a huge party scene.

**TOP CHOICE** **William Thornton** BURGERS, SEAFOOD **$$**
(☎284-496-8603; www.williamthornton.com; mains $12-24; ☺lunch & dinner) Moored in the Bight and flying the Jolly Roger, the 'Willy T' is a 100ft schooner converted into a restaurant-bar. Jumbo prawns, barbecue ribs, fish and chips and burgers are really just side dishes for the all the booze that goes down the hatch. Belly shots and the infamous 'shotski' (you'll have to see it to believe it) fire up the crowd. Many a patron has been known to jump off the deck nude after a few too many.

**Pirates Bight** BURGERS, SEAFOOD **$$**
(☎284-496-7827; www.piratesbight.com; sandwiches $12-18, mains $20-35; ☺lunch & dinner) This open-air pavilion on the beach at the Bight serves vegetable rotis, roasted chicken, conch fritters and grilled mahimahi sandwiches among its burger and seafood arsenal. Kick back in the waterside ham-

mocks and beach chairs; there are rafts for kids to play on. The 4pm cannon shot signals the start of happy hour, when the crowd becomes a bit more frisky.

### ❶ Getting There & Away

Norman Island lies about 6 miles south of Tortola. You'll need your own boat to get here. Luckily, almost all day-sail operators have Norman on their itineraries.

## Peter Island

This lofty L-shaped island, about 4 miles south of Tortola, is the BVI's fifth-largest landmass and home to the luxurious Peter Island Resort. After a history of low-key cotton and tobacco growing, the island's fortunes changed in the 1960s when Norwegian millionaire Peter Smedwig bought it and built the resort. He ran it until his death in the late 1970s, when the founders of Amway Corporation took it over.

The island remains lush and wild, except along the shores of Deadman's Bay and Sprat Bay where the buildings huddle. There are five pristine beaches, excellent diving and snorkeling sites and paths for hiking and trail biking.

Anyone with reservations can come to the resort's restaurants via the Peter Island Ferry from Road Town.

### 🛏 Sleeping & Eating

Both restaurants are popular with visiting yachties, so be sure to make reservations.

**Peter Island Resort** HOTEL **$$$**
(☎284-495-2000, 800-346-4451; www.peterisland.com; r from $740; 🅿@🛜🏊) Named one

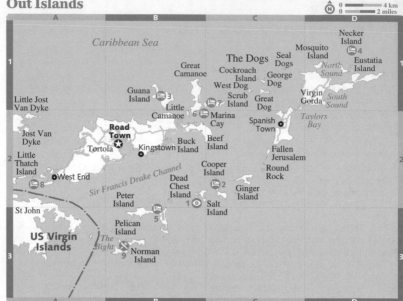

of the 'best places to stay in the world' by *Conde Nast Traveler* magazine, the property offers rooms in a variety of configurations, ranging from four-bedroom villas to the original A-frame cottages built in the 1960s. All have balconies. Amenities include water sports, tennis courts, bicycles, a fitness center and Ayurvedic spa. Staff is top-notch, as you'd expect, and can arrange private, candlelit dinners on the beach. There's free wi-fi in the lobby.

**Deadman's Bay Bar & Grill** INTERNATIONAL **$$** (☑284-495-2000; www.peterisland.com; mains $21-38; ☺lunch & dinner) This is the more casual venue of the island's two, set right on the beach. Wood-fired pizzas are the house specialty, along with a changing array of mains such as grouper and herb risotto, Caribbean gumbo and spicy salmon. A steel pan band plays Sunday afternoons and Wednesday evenings (when there's a West Indian buffet).

**Tradewinds** INTERNATIONAL **$$$** (☑284-495-2000; www.peterisland.com; mains $25-55; ☺dinner) Tradewinds is the resort's main restaurant, featuring gourmet West Indian and continental cuisine served on German china alongside fine wines in Italian crystal. There's a dress code for dinner:

no coats and ties, but trousers and collared shirts are required.

### ⓘ Getting There & Away

The **Peter Island Ferry** (☑284-495-2000; round-trip $20, free for restaurant customers) departs from the CSY dock at Baughers Bay in Road Town. It makes the 30-minute trip six times daily; call for the times. To get to the dock, follow Waterfront Dr past Wickhams Cay 2 to Blackburn Rd. Guests staying overnight can make arrangements for pick up at Tortola's Trellis Bay/Beef Island or from Charlotte Amalie on St Thomas.

## Cooper Island

Lying about 4 miles southeast of Tortola, Cooper Island is a moderately hilly cay and is virtually undeveloped except for the Cooper Island Beach Club on Manchioneel Bay. The inlet has a long, narrow beach that is sheltered from the easterly trade winds; this protection and the club's restaurant make it a popular anchorage for cruising yachts.

Cooper offers superb snorkeling off Cistern Point, a rocky peninsula surrounded by coral-covered ledges and multihued fish. **Sail Caribbean** (www.sailcaribbeandivers.com)

# Out Islands

has a full-service dive shop on the island that also rents kayaks, sailboards and sunfish sailboats.

Don't forget to say hello to the wild goats wandering the beachy paths.

## 🛏 Sleeping & Eating

**Cooper Island Beach Club** HOTEL **$$**
(☎284-495-9084, 800-542-4624; www.cooper-island.com; cottage $250; ◎closed Sep) It's not really a 'club' at all, but a casual property where it's just fine to be barefoot. The handful of bright cottages each have one king bed or two twin beds, a kitchenette, balcony and open-air shower. Solar panels provide 70% of the electricity and heat the water. Ceiling fans keep you cool at night.

**Cooper Island Hideaways** COTTAGES **$$**
(☎513-232-7173; www.cooperisland.com; cottage per week $1995) The owners rent out two simple villas: the Pink Beach House for two people, and the Hideaway for up to six people. Both have a kitchen, outdoor shower and solar power for ceiling fan and iPod docks. The cottages are located at Manchioneel Bay by the Beach Club. Rentals typically are for one week, but shorter time frames are sometimes available.

**TOP CHOICE** **Cooper Island Beach Club Restaurant** BURGERS, SEAFOOD **$$**
(☎284-495-9084; www.cooper-island.com; sandwiches $11-14, mains $26-32; ◎lunch & dinner, closed Sep; ☎) Cooper's bar-restaurant is a premiere gathering spot for boaters. Tuna nicoise, jerk chicken and other fat sandwiches come out of the kitchen for lunch. Happy hour sets the mood from 5pm to 6pm. Then it's time for dinner, when mussels in coconut-curry sauce, vegetable-and-herb pasta and baked red snapper fill plates. Nice eco-touches include the teak bar stools made from recycled fishing boats, and the kitchen's fryer oil being turned into bio-diesel for the generator. Reservations for dinner are a must. Free wi-fi.

## ❶ Getting There & Away

You'll need your own boat to get to Cooper Island, unless you're staying at either of the lodgings, in which case staff will make shuttle arrangements. Many day-sail operators come to Cooper.

# Salt Island

This uninhabited, T-shaped island, measuring a mile in both directions, lies just a dinghy ride west of Cooper Island. The salt making that gave the island its name still goes on here, and you can hike to various salt ponds to see it in action (though 'action' isn't quite the word for watching seawater evaporate and leave behind a crust of white crystals).

The real attraction is offshore at the wreck of the RMS *Rhone*. The *Rhone* was

---

## WILLIAM THORNTON

Odd but true: the *Willy T* party boat is named after a studious Quaker. William Thornton was born on Jost Van Dyke in 1759. He was educated in Scotland as a physician, but was also a self-taught architect, painter and inventor. He wasn't just fooling around: he went on to design the US Capitol building in Washington DC. George Washington and his administration had a contest, and Thornton's plan won for its 'grandeur, simplicity and convenience'. He received $500 and a city lot. He later went on to become the first US Secretary of Patents.

## WRECK OF THE *RHONE*

On the sun-washed morning October 29, 1867, the captain of the RMS *Rhone* thought the hurricane season was over. He was at Peter Island picking up fuel and cargo and preparing to depart for England with 147 passengers.

Built just two years earlier, the *Rhone* was one of a new, faster class of British steamships, 310ft long and 40ft abeam. She had been designed and built to run the Union blockade of the South during the American Civil War, but she launched too late for that service.

Around 11am, the sky grew leaden, and hurricane-force winds began to blow. The *Rhone* struggled to pass Salt Island, but the waves and wind drove her ashore. Seawater burst in and hit the hot boiler. Instantly, it exploded, and the ship broke in half and sunk. Only 23 people survived.

The stern with its propeller now lies in 20ft to 40ft of water. The forward half lies nearby and intact under about 80ft of water. Divers salvaged copper, cotton, liquor and $20,000 worth of money and gold. The BVI National Parks Trust moved in to preserve the wreck in the 1970s, long after divers had picked it clean.

a Royal Mail Steamer that crashed against the rocks off the island's southwest coast during a hurricane in 1867. Now part of a national park, the steamer's remains are extensive and have become an exotic habitat for marine life. It's one of the most famous dive sites in all of the Caribbean, and was a principal set in the film classic *The Deep*. Snorkelers can access it, too, since the ship's stern is in shallower water. Back on land, a stone wall to the west of the old island settlement surrounds the graves of nine of the 124 souls who perished on the *Rhone*.

A lot of people come to the wreck aboard charter boats that either anchor off the beach at Salt Island Bay or pick up one of the moorings placed by the park at Lee Bay near the wreck. Almost every dive shop in the Virgin Islands offers trips to the *Rhone*.

## Marina Cay

Lying just northeast of Tortola's airport, Marina Cay is the perfect little isle centered on a groovy beach bar-restaurant. Writer Robb White immortalized the 8-acre knob as the setting for his classic 1953 memoir *Our Virgin Island* (later a film with Sidney Poitier and John Cassavetes). The place remains ideal for sunset gazing.

The anchorage on the cay's north side offers exceptional shelter. It is almost always packed with about 50 yachts, whose crews come ashore for drinks, entertainment and dinner. There is a small beach off the west end and good snorkeling on the shallow reef.

**Pusser's Marina Cay Hotel**  HOTEL **$$**
(☑284-494-2174; www.pussers.com/t-marina-cay.
aspx; r incl breakfast from $250; 🛜) This wee hotel offers four simple rooms and two villas that surround the great house, which has an intimate and cool library for relaxing. There are no phones or TVs, letting you concentrate instead on the views from the private balconies. Staff can arrange all manner of water-sports rentals.

**Pusser's Marina Cay
Restaurant & Bar**  SEAFOOD **$$**
(☑284-494-2174; mains $22-35; ⊘breakfast, lunch & dinner; 🛜) The open-air restaurant on a deck at the beach jumps with yacht crews as well as travelers coming over for dinner from Tortola. Grilled yellowfin tuna, mahimahi and jumbo shrimp make appearances, cooked in a choice of sauces from Trinidad, Martinique, Cuba and the Bahamas. Happy hour is always a good time. Order up your 'painkiller' (made with Pusser's own rum, of course) at the beach bar or – better yet – the hilltop bar, hewn from Robb White's old porch. Live bands play on various nights.

### ❶ Getting There & Away

The **Marina Cay Ferry** (☑284-494-2174; free) departs from Trellis Bay/Beef Island on Tortola's east end at 10:30am, 11:30am, 12:30pm, 3pm, 4pm, 5pm and 6pm. It operates by request thereafter. The trip takes 10 minutes.

## Scrub Island

Scrub Island flew under the radar until 2010, when the **Scrub Island Resort** (📞877-890-7444; www.scrubisland.com; r from $750; ✳@🛜🏊) opened. The highly developed property has all the bells and whistles: two beaches, a 55-slip marina, a spa and a pool with waterfall and swim-up bar. The 26 standard rooms, 26 one-bedroom suites and smattering of hillside villas are decorated with local art, bright print fabrics and teak furniture. The resort's restaurants include a high-end Euro-Caribbean venue and a more casual Asian-style eatery. **Dive BVI** (www.divebvi.com) has an outpost here, but beyond that there's not a ton to do for nonguests on the island.

### ❶ Getting There & Away

The **Scrub Island Ferry** (📞284-440-3440; free) sails from Trellis Bay/Beef Island on Tortola's east end from 7am to 11pm (hourly, on the hour).

## Necker Island

About 1 mile north of Virgin Gorda, **Necker Island** (📞212-994-3070; www.neckerisland.virgin.com) is one of the world's most luxurious retreats. The private isle belongs to Richard Branson, famous adventurer and founder of Virgin Atlantic Airways and Virgin Records. A who's who of celebrities has stayed at his exclusive haven: Oprah brought her staff here, Posh and Becks spent their 10th anniversary here, Google founder Larry Page got married here, and the list goes on (Beyonce, Jimmy Fallon, Sarah Ferguson, Steven Spielberg...).

The 74-acre property has lodging for 28 people. A magnificent great house, crafted with Balinese architecture, stands atop the island's low hill and provides 10 double bedrooms that open onto private balconies. Spacious studios, each with one double bedroom and full facilities, stand about 500 yards from the great house. An unobtrusive staff prepares meals, serves drinks and offers water-skiing, sailing and – wait for it – your own private submarine (with driver). It's all included in the island's $53,000 per night fee.

Too much for your bank account? Come during one of the 'Celebration Weeks,' when you can book an individual room and share the island with others. Rates start at $26,500 per couple per week.

Don't even think of 'swinging by' Necker unless you have a verifiable invitation.

LOCAL KNOWLEDGE

### CASEY MCNUTT – DIVER

McNutt is president of the BVI Scuba Organization and general manager/owner of **Dive BVI** (www.divebvi.com).

**Best site for experienced divers**

The *Chikuzen* (a 250ft wreck north of Tortola) is great if you're looking for an out-of-the-ordinary dive. It's an attraction for big animals, like reef, bull and lemon sharks, and unique critters.

**Best site for newbie divers**

Ginger Island and Cooper Island have wonderfully protected sites with colorful reefs at moderate depths.

**Best sites if your time is limited**

The *Rhone* is always the 'must do' dive, but it can be a bit advanced in some conditions. To take in great color and marine life with more consistent conditions, try the Indians off Norman Island.

**Favorite 'secret' spots**

I love Thumb Rock and Devils Kitchen on Cooper Island. The boulders that create Thumb Rock are great places to look for nurse shark, eel, lobster and passing rays. Devils Kitchen has a fascinating ledge to swim under and the colors of the rock wall are a brilliant red color (hence the name).

# Guana Island

Lying a mile off Tortola's northeast tip, this undeveloped island of steep green peaks is the seventh-largest island in the BVI. Guana takes its name from a rock formation called the 'Iguana Head' that juts out from a cliff at the island's northwest corner.

Today the 850-acre island is a private nature reserve, home to flamingos, red-legged tortoises, seven sandy beaches and miles of hiking trails. Alas, the splendor is only available to the 32 guests staying at the all-inclusive **Guana Island Club** (📞212-482-6247, 800-544-8262; www.guana.com; r from $1250; ☺closed Sep;@☏). The resort's 'rooms' (they're individual stone cottages, to be precise) are models of simple elegance. They have no air-con, telephones or TV, but they do have windswept private porches, spacious bathrooms and – a concession to modern times – wi-fi. Rates include three meals a day, from a breakfast buffet to evening cocktails and snacks, as well as use of tennis courts, kayaks, snorkel gear and sailboards. Hiking the island's trails, watching the wildlife and swimming are the principal activities here. Children are welcome, but must be closely supervised by their parents.

A private ferry picks up guests from Trellis Bay/Beef Island on Tortola's east end. Visiting mariners can anchor off the beach at White Bay and enjoy the excellent snorkeling in the bay and along the cliffs that stretch to Monkey Point, but note Guana does not welcome nonguests to its grounds or trails.

# The Dogs

This clutch of six islands lies halfway between Tortola and Virgin Gorda. The Dogs take their name from a now-extinct monk seal known as *lobo marina* (sea wolf). These animals had colonies on the isles before hunters harvested them into oblivion. Today the BVI National Parks Trust protects the islands, and they are sanctuaries for both birds and marine animals. The bridled tern, sooty tern, roseate tern and red-billed tropicbird all nest here. Snorkeling around each of the islands is superior. Sometimes the schools of glassy sleepers can be so thick you are enveloped in a cloud of fish. Scuba divers will want to check out **Joe's Cave**, **Flintstones** and **Wall-to-Wall** just off the coast of West Dog.

A dive boat or charter boat are the only way to reach the Dogs. Pick up one of the park's moorings. It's best to come early in the day.

# Ginger Island

Ginger Island is a dramatic piece of uninhabited real estate east of Cooper Island. It has sheer cliffs on its north and south sides and a perfect cove to the east. Some of the BVI's best coral formations grow just offshore. Renowned dive sites include **Alice in Wonderland**, a deep-water reef with surreal, 15ft, mushroom-shaped staghorn coral; and **Ginger Steps**, another deep-water reef where sharks and eagle rays make appearances. You'll need to board a dive boat or charter boat to get here.

# Fallen Jerusalem

A 30-acre island lying 0.5 miles southwest of Virgin Gorda, Fallen Jerusalem is a gem of a national park that's often overlooked. It takes its name from its appearance: it is strewn with large boulders like those found at the Baths on Virgin Gorda, but here, the boulders appear to be the tumbled ruins of some ancient city with what look like clearly defined roads and foundations. The island's entire fringe makes for rewarding snorkeling (in calm weather). If you want to escape the almost relentless tourist traffic at the nearby Baths, Fallen Jerusalem is the place to come.

The area is accessible only by dive boat or charter boat. Pick up one of the moorings on the north side of the island. An ocean swell often stirs up the seas, so come early when the winds are lighter and the swells are at their lowest.

# Dead Chest Island

Half a mile north of Peter Island, this island looks like a giant vermilion mushroom covering 30 acres of land. Reputedly the place where the pirate Blackbeard left 15 men with a saber and a bottle of rum to fight out their differences, the uninhabited island and its legend are the prototype for TV's survival shows and the setting that spawned the doggerel ending in 'yo ho ho and a bottle of rum.'

Today, the island is a national park and bird sanctuary for noddies, boobies, gulls and terns. There is good diving at **Dead**

## OUT ISLANDS' BEST DIVE SITES

» **Wreck of the RMS *Rhone*** This famous 310ft shipwreck sits in just 20ft to 80ft of water off Salt Island, making it an accessible wreck-dive for all levels.

» **Blond Rock** A pinnacle between Dead Chest and Salt Islands, this coral ledge has many caves, crevices and deep holes.

» **Alice in Wonderland** This spot off Ginger Island has some of the best deep-water coral formations in the BVIs.

» **The Indians** Just off Pelican Island, three cone-shaped rock formations rise from 36ft underwater to 30ft above water.

» **Angel Reef** Off Norman Island, this site is a crossroads for species from different habitats, with shallow canyons rising to the surface.

**Chest West** and **Painted Walls**, where sponges and cup corals light up the sides of canyons with brilliant yellow, crimson, red, blue, white and orange.

As with many of the national park islands, you must come here on a dive boat or charter boat and pick up one of the moorings. An ocean swell generally makes mooring here a rough ride.

## The Indians/Pelican Island

Pelican is a small island about 0.5 miles north of Norman Island. Three pinnacles of rock nearby called the Indians are the main attraction, beloved by divers and snorkelers alike. Snorkeling is best in the shallows on the Indians' eastern side if the seas are calm. The diving on the western side features 50ft drops with elkhorn, stag and brain coral.

You'll need your own boat to get here. Come early, when the winds are lighter and the mooring area is less crowded.

## Little Thatch Island

Palm-fringed, blue-sea-kissed Little Thatch is so stereotypically pretty that MasterCard once featured it in a series of TV commercials as the ultimate island getaway.

You'll need a credit card to visit – the island's private owners, who live at one end of the 54-acre expanse and are only occasionally in residence, rent out a lone villa: **Seagrape Cottage** (☎284-495-9227; www.seagrapecottage.net; villa peak/off peak per week $7875/6065; ❄❀). The West Indian-style house has a wrap-around veranda, terracotta floors, bamboo decor and a draped four-poster bed in its one bedroom. The fully equipped kitchen comes stocked to your request. Outside a king-size hammock, hot tub and barbecue grill beckon – alongside your own beach, of course. Snorkeling gear and a private boat dock are included gratis.

Little Thatch floats a short distance off Tortola's West End. The resident caretakers can arrange transportation. Casual visitors on boats are not welcome.

## Mosquito Island

This 125-acre island looks like a green gumdrop and guards the entrance to Virgin Gorda's North Sound. Mosquito takes its name from the Miskito Indian tribe who left relics here. It is a private island that remains largely undeveloped...for now. Richard Branson bought it a few years ago, and plans reportedly are underway to turn Mosquito into an ecoresort with 20 villas and a beachfront restaurant powered by wind turbines and solar panels. Stay tuned.

# Understand the US & British Virgin Islands

## population per sq mile

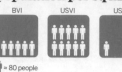

BVI  USVI  USA

🚹 ≈ 80 people

# US & British Virgin Islands Today

## Economic Perils

Both the US and British Virgin Islands use the US dollar as their currency, and both import most of their goods – cars, clothes, food – from America. They also get most of their tourists from America, so when the economy there melted down in 2008, the islands felt the fallout. In the USVI especially, where tourism accounts for 80% of GDP and employment, hoteliers, restaurant owners, taxi drivers and shopkeepers have struggled. And though the BVI depends on tourism for only about 45% of its income, the other pillar of its economy – offshore company registration – nosedived in the economic downturn, too. Accountants, lawyers and other tax-haven professionals have seen far fewer wealthy clients. Both territories strive to diversify with new, tax-incented business, such as the Captain Morgan distillery on St Croix, but such opportunities are few, so it's back to courting cruise ships and honeymooners.

» Population USVI: 109,700

» Population BVI: 25,400

» GDP per capita USVI: $14,500

» GDP per capita BVI: $38,500

» Life expectancy USVI: 79.3 years

» Life expectancy BVI: 77.6 years

## Green Tension

Everyone wants a piece of paradise, and in the 1980s, developers provided it. St Thomas and Tortola, in particular, saw resort and villa construction boom with reckless abandon. The pace had slowed by the time the new millennium rolled around, when islanders realized the environmental impact, but the tension between development and sustainability remains a major issue.

Take the situation on St John with Maho Bay Camps. The ecofriendly tent resort has drawn visitors to its forested, beachfront hillside for more than 30 years. Alas, it sits on leased land, and as the lease ends, the owners are wrestling with temptation to sell to developers. The Trust for Public Land has rallied to acquire the property. So far though, the green hills' fate remains undecided. Resort developments on St Thomas' West

## Dos and Don'ts

» Greet locals with a 'good day' or 'good evening' before asking questions or discussing business. Good manners are prized.

» Men without shirts and women in bathing suits or other skimpy attire are frowned upon anywhere besides the beach.

» The Virgins are on 'island time.'

» Don't expect things to run like clockwork. Whether catching a ferry or having a meal, allow more time than you would back home.

» Topless and nude sunbathing are illegal, though it is overlooked at a few discreet beaches.

## Top Books

» **Treasure Island** (Robert Louis Stevenson) Norman Island supposedly inspired the 1883 yarn about buried treasure and the pirate Long John Silver.

» **Musings of an Island Girl** (Henrita Barber) Essays by a *VI Daily News* columnist.

## BVI belief systems
(% of population)

| Other | Methodist |
|-------|-----------|
| 40 | 33 |

| Catholic | Anglican |
|----------|----------|
| 10 | 17 |

## USVI belief systems
(% of population)

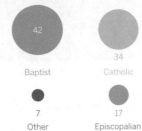

| Baptist | Catholic |
|---------|----------|
| 42 | 34 |

| Other | Episcopalian |
|-------|--------------|
| 7 | 17 |

End, St Croix's East End and Tortola's East End have also faced opposition from conservationists in recent years.

## Crime

The Virgin Islands have seen a marked increase in drug-related violent crimes over the past few years. This has occurred as Latin American producers shift transportation routes away from cartel-plagued Mexico and into the Caribbean. With the drugs has come a steady flow of illegal firearms that invariably end up in the wrong hands. The USVI saw a record 66 homicides committed in 2010, which is 10 more than in 2009. Most crimes happen away from tourist areas, but not always: in early 2010 a stray bullet killed a young tourist at Coki Beach.

## Politics

Elections in November 2010 returned Democrat John de Jongh to the governor's seat, the top post in the USVI leadership. It is his second consecutive term, and he'll hold the role until 2014. Democrats have dominated the post over the past two decades; they also control the USVI Senate, with 10 of the 15 seats. The Independents hold three seats, while the conservative Independent Citizen's Movement holds two seats. The Republicans hold none.

The BVI held elections in 2007, when Ralph T O'Neal took the helm as premier. He's a member of the VI Party, which is more inward focused and promises to help the 'little man.' Its main competition is the National Democratic Party, which looks toward outside interests and development. The next election will be in fall 2011. It is expected to be tight, as the VI Party has to address contentious issues about its handling of water and sewage contracts.

While English is the islands' official language, you'll hear unique phrases such as 'limin' (pronounced 'lime-in'; means 'relaxing') and 'wind at your back, mon' (a parting comment that means 'I hope you have an easy day').

» **Adrift on a Sea of Blue Light** (Peter Muilenburg) Graceful tales of life at sea by a long-time St John boat captain.

» **The Caribbean Writer** (www. thecaribbeanwriter.org) Journal of works by regional authors, published by University of the VI.

## Top Films

» **The Deep** (1977) Nick Nolte and barely clad Jacqueline Bisset treasure hunt on the *Rhone*.

» **Open Water** (2003) The Virgins provide the shark-infested waters for two stranded divers.

## Playlist

» **BVI Music** (www.bvimusic. com) The lowdown on BVI musicians: who they are, where they play, plus song downloads.

» **Iyaz** (www.iyazmusic.com) Tortola-born hip-hop singer.

» **Jamesie & the Allstars** St Croix quelbe band.

# History

Pirates, plantations and colonial power-brokering set the storyline for the Virgin Islands. From fierce indigenous tribes to scallywags named Blackbeard and Bluebeard to bloody plantation revolts, the islands have seen their share of drama.

The Virgins lie in the path of trade winds blowing from the Iberian Peninsula, so it's probably no surprise Christopher Columbus washed up on shore here and put the islands on the map in 1493. The ensuing centuries saw Spain, Denmark, Holland, France and England fight for territory in the Virgins as part of the land grab throughout the Caribbean. Denmark and England were the eventual victors. The Narrows strait between St John and Tortola served as the demarcation line: islands to the east were British controlled, islands to the west were Danish controlled. This boundary still exists to this day.

No matter who claimed them, all the islands were freewheeling pirates' dens, thanks to the bevy of secure and unattended harbors. The islands soon grew rich producing sugar and cotton using slave labor; the surviving tumbledown windmills are remnants of this turbulent period. The US entered the picture during WWI, when it bought Denmark's islands.

Several colonial forts, warehouses and plantation buildings have been preserved over the years, especially in the USVI, and these are the main historical sites visitors will see as they travel in the islands.

## Early Peoples

The first wave of Arawak Indians from South America arrived here AD 100. They traveled from the Orinoco Basin in Venezuela, island-hopping through the Lesser Antilles in swift, mammoth canoes that could carry 100 people. They settled on St Croix and brought with them well-developed skills in pottery making, fishing, canoe building and farming.

Around 1300, a second wave of Arawak, the Taíno, arrived and set up a community at Salt River Bay on St Croix as well as settlements on

Several black women gained their freedom and were part of mainstream St Thomas society in the early 19th century, according to the 1803 'Proceedings and Register of the Free Colored.'

FREEDOM

## TIMELINE

| C 1300 | 1493 | 1588 |
| --- | --- | --- |
| Taíno Indians, and later the Caribs, settle the islands. They leave behind petroglyphs and ceremonial temples on St John, and pottery shards and ball courts on St Croix. | Columbus arrives at St Croix's Salt River Bay, scuffles with locals, then sails away to Puerto Rico – but not before naming the islands after European maidens. | Spain loses claim to the islands when England defeats the Spanish Armada overseas. England, France and Holland issue 'letters of marque' allowing privateers the right to claim territory. |

the north shore of St John and St Thomas. These wayfarers were less skilled at pottery but better than their predecessors at grinding tools and procuring jewels from stones. The Taíno were also adept at agriculture.

Early Spanish chroniclers described the Taíno as short people with straight dark hair, high cheekbones and muscular, copper-colored bodies. Most of the Taíno wore no clothes. The copper coloring of their skin was actually a body paint made from plant and mineral dyes. They favored red, white and blue hues for their faces. While the body paints were considered fashionable to some degree, they primarily functioned as protection against insects, the tropical sun and evil spirits.

But no body paint could protect the Taíno against the invasion of the Caribs. Master mariners and ruthless warriors, this tribe of Indians left the northern shoulder of South America during the 15th century and launched a reign of terror, wiping out the Taíno as the invaders moved north through the Lesser Antilles. By 1493 the Caribs had overrun and mingled with the major Taíno settlements in the Virgin Islands. The boundary between Carib and Taíno sovereignty lay between the Virgin Islands and Puerto Rico.

## Christopher Columbus

Following his first voyage to the Caribbean in 1492, Christopher Columbus returned to the court of King Ferdinand and Queen Isabella of Spain. He had excellent news: by sailing 33 days west from the Azores, he had discovered the 'Indies,' a land where it was perpetually summer and the rivers flowed with gold. Upon hearing this report, the Spanish monarchs vested Columbus with the title 'Admiral of the Ocean Sea' and allowed him to assemble a fleet for a second voyage. So off he went with 17 ships and more than 1200 pilgrims, mariners and soldiers under the flagship nicknamed *Maríagalante*. The fleet departed the Spanish port of Cádiz

**Top Historic Sites**

» Annaberg Sugar Mill Ruins, St John

» Fort Christiansvaern, St Croix

» Fort Frederik, St Croix

» Estate Whim Plantation Museum, St Croix

» Salt River National Historic Park, St Croix

### FIRST BLOOD AT ST CROIX

On November 14, 1493, Columbus' ships anchored off Salt River Bay at the island Columbus named Santa Cruz (St Croix). When a landing party of 25 men headed for a Carib village on shore, the inhabitants scattered, but as the Spanish rowed back to their flagship, they surprised a Carib canoe coming around the point. The Caribs – four men and two women – let loose a flock of arrows on the Spaniards in their open boat.

Arrows wounded two sailors – one mortally – before the Spaniards rammed the canoe, forcing the Indians to swim. But the Caribs swam to a rock and fought on. At last, the Spaniards succeeded in taking the Caribs as prisoners, but they had gained respect for these fierce warriors. Columbus named the site of this conflict on St Croix 'Cabo de Flechas' (Cape of Arrows).

| 1665 | 1717 | 1733 | 1760 |
|---|---|---|---|
| The Danes claim St Thomas and follow up by building Fort Christian on the main harbor. They build lots of pubs and name the colony Taphus, Danish for 'brew pub.' | Danish planters drive the British off St John. The territory is now set – Danes west, English east – with the Narrows Strait between St John and Tortola the border. | St John's slaves revolt against oppressive conditions. They destroy plantations and drive off the white gentry, but within a few years the cane-growing system is back in place. | The Cruzan Rum Distillery begins working its magic on molasses. There is no banana rum or 'diamond' label liquid yet, but the marketing department is working on it. |

on September 25, 1493, and sighted land on November 3 – an island in the Lesser Antilles that Columbus named 'Dominica' because it came into sight on Sunday morning. In the following weeks, the Spanish fleet worked its way north through the Leeward Islands, where it encountered the Caribs.

Taíno captives guided Columbus north and then west along the southern coast of the archipelago. He named these islands 'Santa Ursula y Las Once Mil Vírgenes' (St Ursula and the 11,000 Virgins) in honor of a 4th-century princess raped and murdered along with an alleged 11,000 maidens in Cologne by marauding Huns. Historians believe that the great Admiral himself named the large islands in the group, but none can agree which he might have called Santa Ursula. The earliest Spanish charts of the islands identify San Tomes (St Thomas), San Juan (St John), Tortola (Turtledove) and Virgen Gorda (Fat Virgin).

After sailing past the Virgins, Columbus traveled to the west to Vieques, Puerto Rico and Jamaica for the first time, and revisited Cuba and Hispaniola, which he had encountered on his first voyage.

## The Age of Piracy

The Taíno and Caribs may have lived in peace on the Virgin Islands for another 15 years before the Spanish (who were establishing colonies to the west on Puerto Rico and Hispaniola) began raiding the Lesser Antilles for slaves. Rather than endure the wrath of Spain, the Indians who remained in the Virgin Islands fled south. Although the Virgins were abandoned by the Indians before the mid-16th century, few Spaniards tried to colonize the islands.

The islands of the Caribbean remained under Spanish control until the English defeated the Spanish Armada in 1588. In the aftermath of the destruction of the Spanish Navy, England, France and Holland were quick to issue letters of marque to mariners. These letters appointed the 'privateers' agents of the crown and gave them the rights to explore, claim territory and protect their claims in the name of the country that employed them. The letter of marque also gave the privateers rights to destroy or seize enemy shipping. One king's privateer was every other king's pirate.

By 1595 the famous English privateers Sir Francis Drake and Jack Hawkins were using the Virgin Islands as a staging ground for attacks on Puerto Rico and Spanish shipping. In the wake of Drake and Hawkins came French corsairs and Dutch freebooters as well. All knew that the Virgin Islands had some of the most secure and unattended harbors in the West Indies. Places such as Sopers Hole at the West End of Tortola and The Bight at Norman Island are legendary pirates' dens.

Blackbeard (Edward Teach) was operating in the Virgin Islands before 1720, as were a collection of other rascals including Henry Morgan and

**Off-the-Beaten-Path Historic Sites**

» Estate Catherineburg Sugar Mill, St John

» Copper Mine National Park, Virgin Gorda

» Lower Estate Sugar Works Museum, Tortola

» Cinnamon Bay Archaeological Dig, St John

» Mt Healthy National Park, Tortola

---

**1792**

Plantation life is well entrenched by now. St Croix has 197 plantations and 22,000 slaves; 18,000 work in the fields. Sugarcane production soars. Windmills dot the landscape.

DONALD C. & PRISCILLA ALEXANDER EASTMAN / LONELY PLANET IMAGES ©

» Estate Whim Plantation

**1805**

Tortola racks up exports of 2500 barrels of sugar, representing its peak in production. The island's population is 1300 whites and about 9000 slaves.

**1834**

The English Parliament emancipates all slaves in the British colonies. Afterward, many blacks leave Tortola for Trinidad, where a booming economy demands laborers.

'Calico' Jack Rackham with his female consorts and partners in plunder, Anne Bonny and Mary Read.

# The First Colonists

A big cast of colonial characters weaves in and out of the 17th century. In 1621 the British established a colony on St Croix to raise tobacco, watermelons and sweet potatoes but, after four months, Spaniards from Puerto Rico ousted them. In 1625 the English were back on St Croix – and so were the Dutch, who set up a colony of their own. Squabbles between these settlements came to a head in 1645 with the murder of the Dutch governor, and the Dutch abandoned their colony, but England's sovereignty over the Virgins was far from a sure thing.

Dutch buccaneers settled on Tortola in 1648, and in 1650 a force of 1200 Spaniards from Puerto Rico drove the English off St Croix. Within

## AVAST! LADIES OF PLUNDER

Boatloads of pirates sailed through the Virgin Islands in the early 1700s. Most were indistinguishable in their eye patches and wooden legs, except for two buccaneers: Anne Bonny and Mary Read.

Anne was the daughter of a respectable Charleston, South Carolina, family, who showed her wild ways early by marrying James Bonny against her father's wishes. Bonny was a small-time pirate working out of Nassau and, while he was out cavorting, he wanted Anne to stay home and cook for him. Instead, she began a series of affairs.

'Calico' Jack Rackham ultimately won her heart. 'Come sail away with me,' the sharp-dressed scallywag presumably said.

Anne disguised herself in men's clothing (women on ships were considered bad luck), and wielded her pistol and cutlass so fiercely no one questioned her gender. Well, one pirate did, and she stabbed him through the heart.

The thing that finally gave her away was pregnancy. Jack dropped her off in Cuba to have the baby, which died shortly after birth.

After Anne returned she discovered another woman on board. Mary Read also donned men's garb as a disguise. Anne walked in on her getting dressed and found out the truth. The two became pals.

The good times ended in 1720. The governor of Jamaica sent his troops to capture Jack's gang. They waited until the pirates were drunk and celebrating a recent ship-taking. The only crew left sober to defend the ship? Anne and Mary. They tried their best, but were outgunned.

The crew was condemned to hang, except for Anne and Mary, who were both pregnant. Mary died in jail. Anne was ransomed by her rich father and returned to Charleston. Some stories say she became a respectable society lady and lived to age 84. Others say she went back to life on the high seas.

| 1848 | 1867 | 1867 | 1878 |
|---|---|---|---|
| Moses 'General Budhoe' Gottlieb leads the slave revolt on St Croix. The group takes over Frederiksted. Danish Governor Peter von Scholten feels the heat and grants colony-wide emancipation. | By now the islands are known as refueling stations for steamers on trade routes. After one such stop, the RMS *Rhone* sinks in a hurricane off Salt Island. | US President Abe Lincoln's Secretary of State, WH Seward, tries to buy St Thomas, St John and St Croix from Denmark for $7.5 million. Congress vetoes the deal. | St Croix's plantation workers, pushed to the limit by a labor dispute, riot and torch Frederiksted and the surrounding plantations. Three women lead the uprising, known as the Fireburn. |

the same year, the French sailed from St Kitts and drove the Spanish off St Croix. During the next 83 years, the French governed St Croix and imported African slaves to work the tobacco and sugar plantations.

The Danes started their own initiative in 1665, when the Danish king granted a royal commission to establish a colony on St Thomas. The colony floundered from the start, and collapsed after English privateers plundered it. At about the same time, the English drove the Dutch off Tortola and brought that little settlement firmly under the British rule.

But the Danes returned to St Thomas, and by 1680 it was under the rule of the Danish West India and Guinea Company. It claimed 50 plantations with a population of more than 300, more than half of whom were slaves. In the same year, the British enticed planters from Anguilla to start tobacco and sugar farming on Virgin Gorda and Tortola.

Meanwhile, with English colonies in the Virgin Islands east of St John, and the Danes on St Thomas to the west, St John remained disputed territory. Finally, in 1717, the Danes sent a small but determined band of soldiers, planters and slaves to St John to drive the British out. The Narrows between St John and Tortola became the border that has divided the eastern Virgins from the western Virgins for close to 300 years.

**Top Towns for Historical Architecture**

» Charlotte Amalie, St Thomas

» Christiansted, St Croix

» Frederiksted, St Croix

## Slavery & Plantocracy

The West Indies grew rich producing sugar and cotton for Europe. In pursuit of profits, the Danish West India and Guinea Company declared St Thomas a free port in 1724, and purchased St Croix from the French in 1733. At this point, there were about 5000 African slaves in the Danish West Indies and fewer than 2000 in the British Virgin Islands. By the end of the century, the number of slaves exceeded 40,000. Something had to give – and it did.

In 1733 harsh living conditions and oppressive laws drove the slaves on St John to revolt. After eight months, during which the slaves destroyed most of the plantations on the island and killed or drove off the white gentry, Danes and loyal slave militias as well as English and French forces brought the rebellion under control. Once again it was business as usual. The Danish Virgin Islands, in particular, turned a pretty profit supplying smuggled goods to support the American Revolution, which had begun in 1776. One of the emerging US leaders, Alexander Hamilton, spent much of his youth on St Croix.

## Rebellion & Liberation

In the early 1800s, sugar production in Europe and American tariffs on foreign sugar cut into the islands' profits. The deteriorating economy put everyone in a foul mood. On Tortola, slaves plotted a rebellion in 1831;

### 1917
During WWI, the US fears German armies might invade Denmark and claim the Danish West Indies. The US pays the Danes $25 million in gold for the islands.

### 1927
The US Congress grants American citizenship to residents in the USVI.

### 1949
Following WWII British citizens in the BVI clamor for more independence and demonstrate for a representative government; they soon get a presidential legislature.

» Christiansted, St Croix

JOHN NEUBAUER / LONELY PLANET IMAGES ©

white citizens barely quelled the revolt before it got started. Fearful and economically discouraged, half the white population abandoned the British Virgins for good.

In the Danish Virgins, the government began to create more options for slaves to gain their freedom but waffled over universal emancipation even as the English Parliament decreed the end of slavery in all British colonies (including the BVI) in 1834. Finally, during the summer of 1848, blacks on St Croix claimed by force their freedom and right to be treated as equal. They marched on the town of Frederiksted, threatening to burn it to the ground, until Danish Governor Peter von Scholten felt the heat and granted colony-wide emancipation. For freeing the slaves, he was recalled to Denmark and tried for treason

But the black population remained in economic bondage. Life in the islands was dismal. Average wages for field workers were less than $0.15 a day. A series of labor revolts left the plantation infrastructure in ruins.

## Enter the USA

Meanwhile, the US was negotiating with Denmark to buy the Danish-controlled Virgins. President Abraham Lincoln's astute secretary of state, William Henry Seward, saw the islands' role as a waypoint and coaling station for steam ships and realized the strategic value of the Virgins relative to the Caribbean Basin. The deal was almost done in 1867, but the US Congress rejected the idea of paying $7.5 million (more than they paid for 'Seward's Folly', Alaska) for the islands. The US made another bid in 1902, but this time the Danish parliament rejected the offer, hoping that the Germans might offer them a sweeter deal.

As WWI began in Europe, the US grew concerned that German armies might invade Denmark and claim the Danish West Indies. Finally, the US paid the Danes $25 million in gold for the islands in 1917.

The US Navy then took control, which resulted in tensions with the local population. The US tried to enforce Prohibition here, an unusual concept for an economy tied to the production, sale and distribution of rum. In 1931 President Herbert Hoover traveled to the Virgins, stayed for less than six hours and made a speech in which he declared, 'It was unfortunate that we ever acquired these islands.'

## Self-Rule Begins

In 1934 President Franklin D Roosevelt visited the islands and saw the potential that Hoover had missed. Soon, the US instituted programs in the Virgins to eradicate disease, drain swamps, build roads, improve education, create hotels for tourists, attract cruise ships and even sell rum under a label that Roosevelt himself designed. In 1936 the US Congress passed the Organic Act, which gave the territory its first steps toward

QUEEN

During and after slavery, plantation workers had a tradition of choosing a 'queen' for each plantation. This tradition came from West Africa and was an extension of the matriarchal society existing in the workers' former homelands.

| 1967 | 1969 | 1978 | Mid-1980s |
|---|---|---|---|
| The BVI becomes an independent colony with its own political parties, Legislative Council and elected premier. The following year, the USVI wins the right to elect its own governor. | The Moorings charter-boat company opens for business in Tortola with three boats. Today it boasts 700 vessels, the largest fleet in the Caribbean. | Sir Richard Branson buys a forlorn atoll called Necker Island for around $325,000. At today's lodging rates, it would take him less than two weeks to make his money back. | The BVI starts providing offshore registration to companies that want to incorporate in the islands. The financial services industry takes off, pleasing those who seek tax relief. |

self-governance by letting islanders vote in local elections. WWII, the associated sugar boom, and the construction of naval and military bases in the islands brought full employment to the US islands for the first and only time since European colonization.

During this era, social conditions in the BVI lagged behind the improvements in the USVI, and citizens from the sparsely populated British colony migrated to work in the USVI, particularly St Thomas – a trend that continued through most of the 20th century.

Following WWII, both British and US citizens in the islands clamored for more independence. In 1949 BVI citizens demonstrated for a representative government and got a so-called presidential legislature the next year. In 1954 the US Congress passed the second Organic Act, which established an elected legislature in the USVI. During the 1960s Britain's administrative mechanisms for its Caribbean colonies kept changing shape, and by 1967, the BVI had become an independent colony with political parties, its own Legislative Council and an elected chief minister. The next year, the USVI won the right to elect its own governor, Cyril King (after whom the airport is named).

Florence Lewisohn has two short but well-researched volumes on the islands' history, *St Croix Under Seven Flags* and *Tales of Tortola and the British Virgin Islands*.

## The Bloom of Tourism

When Cuba's doors closed to American tourists in 1959, the Virgin Islands were ready for the rush of sunseekers. Cruise ships began making St Thomas their featured stop, and yachties discovered the superb cruising in the islands east of St Thomas, particularly around St John and the BVI.

The next four decades in the islands brought unprecedented growth in the tourism industry, with dozens of luxury hotels and hundreds of guesthouses, condominiums and vacation villas popping up on the shores and hillsides of both the US and British Virgins. Concurrently, the islands' population mushroomed.

The islands have endured more than their share of political corruption scandals – nepotism, cronyism and bribery have long been a way of life. Also, some unexpectedly violent crimes have rocked the Virgins, including the Fountain Valley Massacre on St Croix in 1972. The biggest stories in recent years have been hurricanes. Several major storms have nailed the islands since 1989. Hugo (in September 1989) and Marilyn (in September 1995) were the most devastating, with Luis (September 1995) and Lenny (November 1999) not far behind. Yet each storm brings improvements in the building codes, and more conscientious preparedness.

The focus of the new millennium has been on balance: where to draw the line between development and sustainability? And how to even out the economy beyond tourism, which has proved vulnerable to global financial downturns? Alas, even paradise has its predicaments.

| 1989 | 1995 | 1996 | 2007 |
|------|------|------|------|
| On September 17 and 18, Hurricane Hugo smashes into both territories, one of the worst storms on record. The eye passes over St Croix, leaving one-third of the population homeless. | Hurricane Marilyn hits the territories on September 15 and 16, not long after Hurricane Luis swept through. The USVI is declared a federal disaster area. | The US government hands over Water Island to the territorial government. Residents are now allowed to purchase the land they occupy, instead of leasing it | The USVI begins its fifth attempt to draft and ratify a constitution for greater self-determination. It's still in the works at time of research. |

# Island Life

While the US and British Virgin Islands both wear the veneer of their respective motherlands, it's West Indian culture that comes through strongest in local music, cuisine, spirituality and family life.

## Living in the Virgin Islands

One of the best places to get an insight into the local lifestyle is at the mom-and-pop restaurants that West Indian entrepreneurs are fond of erecting in the settlements and along country roads. These gathering places, such as Vie's Snack Shack on St John and LSL Bakery & Restaurant on Virgin Gorda, attract a clutch of neighbors to drink bush tea (from leaves, roots and herbs), soft drinks or Carib beer and linger at tables and benches outside to discuss the news of the day – especially the latest twist in a political or commercial corruption scandal.

Join the group and watch a basketball or cricket match on TV, hear the proprietor's newest calypso or reggae tunes, and sense the love of life that infuses Virgin Islanders. You'll pick up on a value system that places a high priority on family, friends and a love of the islands as well as relishing the time to enjoy them. Here you get a sense that work is often not an end in itself, it's a means of expanding one's social network – and laughter is worth more than gold.

## USVI Life

The US islands show their American affiliation with conveniences such as shopping malls and fast-food restaurants. On St Thomas and St John, most people work in the tourism industry. On St Croix, many work in manufacturing jobs at the petroleum refinery and rum distilleries.

The USVI ranks 79th in the world for per capita GDP, at $14,500. Twenty-nine percent of the population lives below the poverty line, and housing projects pop up throughout the islands.

Black people outnumber white by more than four to one and dominate the political and professional arenas. There is a large population of immigrants. About one-third of USVI residents were born elsewhere in the Caribbean. Large communities from the BVI and French-speaking St-Barthélemy live around St Thomas, and many Puerto Ricans have settled on St Croix.

About 13% of the population is white, many of them US mainlanders who've come to escape the politics and busyness of American life, or to retire in the sun.

## BVI Life

In the BVI, West Indian and American influences are more overt than anything British, though you will sense the UK's hand in the formal institutions of government, education, religion and the law. But go to the grocery store and you're more likely to find Oreo cookies than McVitie's

People who are island-born or children of island-born parents, often called 'belongers,' claim a special social status. In the USVI, belongers hold the bulk of government jobs. In the BVI, belongers get first priority when it comes to purchasing land or getting a job.

BELONGERS

biscuits, and Carib beer than Newcastle Ale. And you'll pay for them in US dollars, the local currency since 1959.

Compared to their US cousins, the British Virgin Islands are better off financially, ranking 24th in the world for per capita GDP at $38,500. In general, most people live quite comfortably. Unemployment and crime rates are both low here, as well.

The population is a mix of professional people working in financial services (ie lots of accountants, trust lawyers and investment brokers), folks working the tourist trade and adventurers whose biochemistry is intricately tied to the seas. Many are UK and US expats, especially in the financial services industry, where foreign workers fill around 80% of jobs.

While the local Rasta culture isn't large, it exists in scattered pockets on St Thomas, St John, St Croix and Tortola. Rasta restaurants are good bets for vegetarians, since many embrace 'ital' principles for healthy life energy and avoid meat, shellfish, eggs and dairy products.

## Food & Drink

In the Virgin Islands, West Indian cooking – more properly called Creole cuisine – is far from the peas-and-rice or goat-on-a-stick stereotypes often associated with Caribbean food. Creole cuisine is, perhaps, the most sophisticated fusion cuisine on the planet. West Indian dishes draw on breads and roots from the Carib and Taíno Indians, meats from the Europeans, spices and vegetables from Africa, India and China, and cooking styles from Asia and the Slave Coast of western Africa.

### Vegetables & Stews

Soups and stews are staples in West Indian cooking. Recipes incorporate unique island vegetables and fruits to add texture, taste and vitamins. Okra is a favorite ingredient; it's not native to the islands, but was smuggled in from Africa by slaves. Squash, plantain, eggplant, christophene (like a potato/cucumber cross), paw paw (green papaya), scallions, mamey apple, batata (tropical sweet potato), tannia (a root vegetable) and West Indian pumpkin are other commonly used items. Dasheen (taro root) is a tuber with the taste of a potato. The green leaves of this plant are a primary ingredient in the islands' famous callaloo soup, which also may contain okra, hot pepper, pork and fish.

Generally, cast-iron pots are used for 'boilin' down' soups or stews such as pepperpot, combining oxtail, chicken, beef, pork and calf's foot with hot pepper and cassareep (from cassava). Tannia soup is another traditional offering, as is calabeza (pumpkin soup).

Starch is also a main ingredient of islanders' diets. You get starch in the form of ground provisions (ie roots such as yam and cassava) that are boiled, mashed or steamed. You also get this in fungi (pronounced *foon*-ghee), which is made from cornmeal and has the look and texture of

## ISLANDS PROVERBS & WITTICISMS

| | |
|---|---|
| Buddy, me a walkin' behin' | Discretion is the better part of valor |
| Yo' mout' is a one-room house | Speak up, or, used ironically, You talk too much |
| If yo' put yo' ear a mango root, yo' will hear de crab cough | Patience is a virtue |
| Bettah fo' sure dan for sorry | Haste makes waste |
| Man got two wife; him sleep hungry | You can get too much of a good thing |
| Yo' a run from de jumbie a' meet de coffin | Out of the frying pan, into the fire |
| Not so cat walk dey does mouse | Don't judge a book by the cover; literally, 'The idle cat may pounce on the mouse' |
| De longes' prayer got amen | Nothing lasts forever |

polenta. Island cooks usually serve fungi with fish and gravy, and many West Indian families eat 'fish-and-fungi' weekly. Another popular dish is accra, a fried mixture of okra, black-eyed peas, pepper and a little salt.

## Meat & Fish

Meat dishes are primarily curried or barbecued with tangy spices. Islanders also serve the Jamaican-style 'jerked' barbecue, using meat marinated in lime, ginger, sugar and Scotch bonnet peppers and cooking over pimento wood. Daube meat is a pot roast seasoned with vinegar, native seasonings, onion, garlic, tomato, thyme, parsley and celery. Souse is another spicy one-pot dish made from boiled pig's feet and head with a sauce of limes and hot pepper.

Commercial fishing of conch and lobster is forbidden from August 1 to November 1 to let stocks replenish, so you're less likely to find the items on menus during that period.

All manner of fish and shellfish make it to the local table, including 'ole wife' (triggerfish), doctorfish, flying fish, grouper, grunt, red snapper, squid, West Indian topshell (whelk) and crab. Anegada lobster is a much-loved specialty. The cooks bake, grill, stew or boil the daily catch. Queen conch that is tenderized, marinated and diced into salads is a local favorite, as is grilled mahimahi (aka dorado). Fish lovers should also try a bowl of conch stew made with onion, tomato, sweet pepper and sherry. Salt cod is an ingredient and a taste left over from the days of the islands' trade with sailing ships from New England.

Every chef has his or her own secret-recipe 'native seasoning' to flavor the dishes, usually a mix of salt, ground hot pepper, cloves, garlic, mace, nutmeg, celery and parsley.

## Bread & Finger Foods

Johnnycakes (a corn flour griddle cake) accompany most meat and fish dishes. They also make a tasty breakfast meal when lathered with homemade fruit preserves.

The Virgin Islands have a tradition of quick-serve finger foods. Most of them are deep-fried in animal fat, contain coconut meat or oil and taste like your next addiction. Pate (pronounced paw tay) is the most popular of these dishes. It is a fried pastry of cassava (yucca) or plantain dough stuffed with spiced goat, pork, chicken, conch, lobster or fish – akin to an Latin American empanada.

Another popular dish is roti (pronounced root-ee), a relative of the Mexican burrito. Roti are flatbread envelopes stuffed with curried meat, fish or poultry, often served with a tangy mango chutney.

## Fruit & Desserts

Thanks to the nearly perfect tropical climate and enterprising traders during colonial times, the Virgin Islands are a fruit lovers' paradise today.

The plantain pops up frequently on island plates. Like most fruits in the islands, it was first introduced as an exotic import.

Mangos are probably the most popular fruit and fruit tree in the islands, and the practice of kicking back under the nearest mango tree to taste some of the bounty is alive and well throughout the Virgins.

Coconuts, limes, lemons, cocoplums, soursop, guava, gneps and carambola (star fruit) are big sellers in the local produce markets. Many of these fruits are combined with the juice of hot peppers, salt and sugar to produce a dozen different varieties of chutney and hot sauce that islanders consume with enthusiasm.

One of the Virgins' most popular after-dinner treats is homemade ice cream, which is actually frozen custard flavored with fresh mango, soursop, papaya or coconut. For special occasions, bakers serve up sweet-potato pie and sweet-potato pone (a mix of mashed sweet potatoes, sugar, eggs, lemon, dry wine, cinnamon, chopped almonds and raisins).

ISLAND LIFE FOOD & DRINK

» Anegada lobster – Hulking crustaceans plucked from the water in front of your eyes and grilled on the beach in converted oil drums.

» Fungi (*foon*-ghee) – A polenta-like cornmeal cooked with okra, typically topped by fish and gravy.

» Pate (*paw*-tay) – Flaky fried-dough pockets stuffed with spiced chicken, fish or other meat.

» Callaloo – Spicy soup with okra, various meats, greens and hot peppers.

» Roti – Fiery chutney sets off the curried chicken, beef, conch or vegetable fillings in these burrito-like flatbread wraps.

» Johnny cakes – Thick, spongy cornflour cakes cooked on the griddle.

» Conch fritters – The delicious local shellfish gets battered and fried in the chef's secret seasonings.

## Nonalcoholic Drinks

While the Virgin Islands have all the soft drinks and many of the juices found in mainland USA, they also shake up beverages that are unique to the islands.

Ginger beer is a nonalcoholic beverage that comes from a fermented mix of ginger root, water and sugar. Maubi (like Puerto Rico's *mauvi*) is the foamy juice made from the fermented bark of the carob tree, with spices and brown sugar. The islands' traditional practice of 'bush medicine,' descended from Africa, has created bush teas, made from more than 400 of the islands' leaves, roots and herbs. Many of these teas come with names like 'tamarind,' 'worry vine,' 'worm grass' and 'Spanish needle.' Each tea cures specific illnesses like gas, menstrual pain, colds or insomnia.

Many restaurants pour sorrel, a lightly tart, bright-red cold tea that's high in vitamin C and made from the flowers of the sorrel plant.

## Rum & Beer

Rum is the national drink, and it plays a major role in island social life. The historic Callwood Rum Distillery on Tortola and the Cruzan Rum and Captain Morgan factories on St Croix pump out much of the elixir. Rums from neighboring Puerto Rico, the world's largest producer, also flood the market.

More than 20 brands of rum are available at local bars. Beyond brand-name preferences, the choice of which rum to drink boils down to three options: white (like the local Cruzan offering), gold or añejo (aged, often from Puerto Rico). Dark rums are largely the products of Jamaica and other former British colonies, such as Barbados.

White rums are the lightest. They're distilled and aged for as little as a year and are often mixed with orange or tomato juice. Gold rums must be distilled and aged for three years, and this beverage is often an ingredient in the popular piña colada or the 'Painkiller.' The longest aged, most flavorful and expensive rums are añejo. These amber beverages are often sipped straight or on the rocks.

Adventuresome drinkers may want to take a risk and imbibe a bit of 'pinch.' These are homemade, illegal rums that can be either blinding firewater or the smooth, treasured drinks of connoisseurs.

Islanders drink plenty of beer, too. Carib is the most popular brand; it's brewed in Trinidad and marketed throughout the Eastern Caribbean. For microbrews, Virgin Islands Brewing Company taps Blackbeard's Ale

in the USVI and Foxy's Lager in the BVI, while St John Brewers pours
Mango Pale Ale and other citrusy suds throughout the USVI.

# Music

The Virgin Islands have a rich musical heritage rooted in West African
folk music and drumming, and tinged with colonial influences from England, Ireland, Spain, France, Denmark and Holland.

Reggae and calypso are the two types of music heard most often. Their
catchy tunes blast from vehicles and emanate from shops, restaurants
and beach bars. Quelbe and fungi (pronounced *foon*-ghee, like the island
food) are two types of Virgin Island folk music.

The best time to hear local bands is during major festivals like carnival on St Thomas and St John, the Virgin Gorda Easter Festival and St
Croix's quarterly 'jump up' street parties, to name just a few.

## Calypso

This music originated in Trinidad in the 18th century as satirical songs
sung in a French patois by slaves working the plantations. Many of the
songs mirrored slaves' discontent and mocked their colonial masters,
while other songs were competitions in which two singers tried to top
each other's insults. Lyrics were generally ad-libbed. Contemporary calypso is almost always sung in English and composed and rehearsed in
advance. The most popular songs contain biting social commentary, political satire or sexual innuendo, laden with double entendres and local
nuances. In most cases, the melodies and rhythms of the songs are well
established. Mainly the lyrics change from song to song.

Calypso and carnival have been linked for well over 100 years in Trinidad, and that link is equally strong in the Virgin Islands, where festivals always feature a contest for the 'King of Calypso.' Among the classic
calypsonians popular throughout the islands are the Mighty Sparrow,
Shadow and David Rudder, who are all from Trinidad. Foxy Callwood of
Jost Van Dyke is the BVI's legendary 'calypso mon.'

## Reggae

Born in Jamaica and derived from a mix of ska (a 1950s blend of R&B
with calypso), blues, calypso and rock, reggae is the famous back-beat
sound of social protest popularized by Bob Marley and Jimmy Cliff. Today, the reggae sound dominates the airways as well as the clubs of the

**Best Fests
for Island
Music**

» St Thomas
Carnival

» St John
Carnival

» BVI Emancipa-
tion Festival
(Tortola)

» VI Fungi Fest
(Tortola)

» Cruzan Christ-
mas Fiesta

ISLAND LIFE MUSIC

## TOP FIVE COCKTAILS

» Painkiller – Jost Van Dyke's Soggy Dollar Bar supposedly invented this sweet mix
of rum, coconut, pineapple, orange juice and nutmeg. It's now the Virgins' signature drink and poured throughout the islands.

» Bushwhacker – Local bars blend vodka, rum and five or so sweet, creamy liqueurs into a potent icy treat. It may taste like a plain ol' milkshake, but note what
happens when you try to stand up.

» Rum Punch – Remember the rhyme: 'One of sour, two of sweet, three of strong,
four of weak.' That's lime juice, grenadine, rum and soda, respectively, for those
mixing at home.

» Piña colada – OK, it was invented in Puerto Rico. But the revered, creamy glassful – a swirl of rum, coconut milk and pineapple juice – is oft sipped in the Virgin
Islands too.

» Shark Tank – With 64 ounces of blue-hued booze (five rums and three liqueurs)
served in a fish bowl with straws, it's wise to share this adult beverage. You'll only
find it at Duffy's Love Shack on St Thomas.

Virgin Islands. Local bands not only cover all of the Marley classics, but many play original works. St Croix has a particularly active scene. Keep an ear out for Dezarie, Inner Visions and Bambu Station.

## Soca

Blend soul and calypso and you get soca, a dance music with bold rhythms, heavy on the bass sound. Soca started in Trinidad in the 1970s, and you are sure to hear its rhythms in Virgin Island clubs. Listen for songs by Super Blue (from Trinidad).

## Quelbe

Quelbe is the official music of the US Virgin Islands. The indigenous style blends jigs, quadrilles, military fife and African drum music, with *bamboula* rhythms from the Ashanti in West Africa and cariso lyrics (often biting satire) from slave field songs. The music evolved when self-taught island musicians playing in the colonial fife and drum bands (basically colonial propaganda machines) blended their skills with the illegal cariso songs of the field.

As quelbe bands evolved in the 19th and early 20th centuries, they turned into an ensemble of banjo, flute, guitars, steel triangle, squash (dried gourd) and 'ass pipe' (bass). Since the 1960s, quelbe bands have added alto saxophone and electric guitar. The sound of the music remains percussive and distinctly rustic. CDs of popular quelbe groups, like Stanley and the Ten Sleepless Knights and Jamesie and the Allstars, are widely available in island stores.

## Fungi

Prominent in the BVI, fungi is similar to quelbe and is the local variation on scratch band music played throughout the West Indies. Bands use a host of homemade percussion instruments – whatever they can 'scratch up' – like washboards, ribbed gourds and cowbells to accompany a singer and melody played on a recorder or flute. Like calypso, fungi music favors satirical lyrics. The Lashing Dogs are a well-known BVI fungi band. A good place to hear the music live is at the Trellis Bay Full Moon party on Tortola each month.

## Steel Pan

Another import from Trinidad, steel pan music began in the 1940s when musicians started hammering out the bottoms of steel oil drums, tuning different sections to different pitches. In the Virgin Islands, pan drum players usually perform as soloists, as background music in restaurants and bars, but like Trinidad, the USVI also have huge steel pan bands like the Rising Stars Young Steel Orchestra, which plays at festivals and tours internationally.

# Arts

## Dance

A predecessor of square dancing in the USA, quadrille dancing in the islands descends from the formal dances of the European planters in the 18th century. Denied the public practice of African dances like the *bamboula*, slaves imitated the formal dances of their masters during holiday celebrations. But, of course, the slaves put an African spin on the music using the banjo, ukulele and flute to create pulsating rhythms. Dancers in full skirts transformed the jumpy steps of the European dance into smooth, hip-swaying movements. Today, the world-touring Caribbean Dance Company of St Croix preserves quadrille dancing (and revives the *bamboula*) for public entertainment at festivals and the performing arts centers on the islands.

## Architecture

The towns of Charlotte Amalie and Christiansted are the best place in the Caribbean to see examples of what is often thought of as traditional West Indian architecture. In fact, this architecture is a loose adaptation of the English Georgian (neoclassical) style from the late 18th century. At their best, the West Indies classics are two or three stories tall with arched galleries for pedestrians on the 1st and 2nd floor verandas, 'welcoming arms' exterior staircases and hipped roofs. Construction materials are a mix of ship-ballast brick, 'rubble' (a blend of coral, molasses and straw) and wood.

Exteriors feature soothing pastel shades of yellow, turquoise, lime and sometimes pink. Window shutters keep out inclement weather and hot sunlight. Large rooms with high ceilings help buildings 'breathe' the trade winds.

Frederiksted, rebuilt in the late Victorian era after it was destroyed by labor riots, is a repository of Victorian buildings.

## Painting & Sculpture

The most celebrated painter to come from the Virgin Islands is Camille Pissarro. Born in St Thomas in 1830 as Jacob Pizarro, the son of Spanish Jews, he grew up on Main St in Charlotte Amalie. Eventually, he became an accomplished painter, moved to Paris and changed his name to Camille Pissarro. The Virgin Islands, particularly St Thomas Harbor, inspired the painter. His tropical pastoral paintings feature a dreamy sense of line and sun-washed colors. Because of his subjects and his interpretations, Pissarro gained recognition as one of the founders of the French Impressionist movement.

Today quite a few artists work on the islands. Aragorn's Studio on Tortola hosts a collective of potters, sculptors and coconut carvers. Tillett Gardens on St Thomas houses the studios of superb printmakers, crafters and artists working in watercolors and oils. On St Croix, Christiansted is chock-a-block with the galleries of contemporary painters, while the woodworkers of the St Croix Leap project carve chunks of fallen mahogany trees deep in rainforest.

## Literature

While the Virgin Islands have been the setting for quite a few works of imaginative literature, no islanders have yet produced a blockbuster. But it might be just a matter of time. The University of the Virgin Islands sponsors *The Caribbean Writer,* a journal of poems and short fiction by major writers from throughout the Caribbean.

The oral tradition of storytelling reaches all the way back to Africa and is still alive and well in the Virgins. Cultural festivals on the islands often feature modern storytellers who call children and the young at heart to the lawn under a shade tree for 'tim-tim time.' At these gatherings, you are likely to hear stories about the adventures of Anansi de Trickster. Anansi is the hero of the Bruh Nancy Tales, a series of West African folkloric stories that also gave rise to the US slave stories of Uncle Remus and Br'er Rabbit, recorded by Joel Chandler Harris.

## Religion & Spirituality

The Virgin Islands have a strong tradition of spiritual worship – mostly in Protestant faiths – and Sunday mornings sees legions of islanders dressed in their finery headed to church in family cars, taxis and church-owned buses. Services are packed, and on Sunday mornings you cannot

*Caribbean Carnival: Songs of the West Indies,* by Irving Burgie, evokes the islands' celebrations and traditional songs, including music and lyrics.

CELEBRATIONS

help but hear the singing of the congregations pouring through communities large and small. Church ministers hold substantial respect and power in island communities.

In the USVI, Baptists have the most worshippers, followed by Roman Catholics (mostly Puerto Rican and Dominican immigrants), who make up about one-third of all churchgoers. Episcopalians make up the next-largest group.

In the BVI, the Methodist church is the dominant force, followed by the Anglicans. Most other worshippers belong to Pentecostal faiths, such as the Seventh-Day Adventist Church.

Quite a few islanders also practice obeah. This is not a religion per se but a set of beliefs that derives from West African ancestral worship, animism, spirit worship and sorcery. Like voodoo in Haiti, and Santería in the Spanish Caribbean, obeah uses fetishes, herbs, potions and rituals to invoke spirits of ancestors to work magic in favor of the practitioner. For believers, these jumbies or duppies (spirits) are often considered the source of both good and bad fortune and are capable of bringing everything from love and wealth to an outrageous electric bill or a bad hair day.

After centuries of keeping obeah away from the prying eyes of imperial moralists and the Christian church, Virgin Islanders are still shy when it comes to talking about their beliefs in spiritualism. Nevertheless, plenty of islanders consult the 'obeah man' or 'obeah woman' when they are about to make an important decision like buying a house or getting married. If you are living in a West Indian neighborhood, you will no doubt hear adults tell unruly children that 'de jumbies gonna getcha.'

**Top Spots for Local Art**

» Aragorn's Studio, Tortola

» Christiansted galleries, St Croix

» Camille Pissarro Gallery, St Thomas

» Tillett Gardens, St Thomas

» St Croix Leap, St Croix

# Island Landscapes

## The Archipelago

The Virgin Islands sit 1100 miles southeast of Miami and 40 miles east of Puerto Rico. Approximately 90 hilly islands comprise the archipelago. The USVI contributes three large land masses and close to 50 little islets and cays, while the BVI adds four main islands and 32 smaller ones.

St Croix is far and away the largest island, followed by (in order) St Thomas, Tortola, St John, Anegada, Virgin Gorda and Jost Van Dyke. In all, the Virgins have a total coastline of 166 miles and represent an area about twice the size of Washington, DC.

As throughout the Caribbean Basin, the Virgin Islands owe their existence to a series of volcanic events that took place along the dividing line between the North American and Caribbean Plates. These eruptions built up layers of lava and igneous rock, creating islands with three geographical zones: the coastal plain, coastal dry forests and the central mountains. For all of the Virgins except St Croix, the coastal plain is a narrow fringe, and for all of the islands except easternmost Anegada (a pancake-flat atoll), a ridge of mountains of 1000ft or more run west to east across the landscape and dominate their interiors.

Sage Mountain on Tortola is the highest point in the islands at 1780ft. Except where houses have encroached, the mountain slopes are dense subtropical forests. All of the timber is second- or third-growth: the islands were stripped for sugar, cotton and tobacco plantations in the colonial era. Today, less than 7% of island land supports agriculture. The Virgins have no rivers and very few freshwater streams. Coral reefs thrive in the shallow waters near the shores of all the islands. The shores also host a few pockets of mangrove swamps, including Salt River Bay on St Croix.

## Wildlife on Land

### Mammals

Very few of the land mammals that make their home in the Virgin Islands are natives. Most mammal species have been accidentally or intentionally introduced over the centuries. Virtually every island has a feral population of goats and burros, and some islands have wild pigs, white-tailed deer, cattle, horses, cats and dogs – all descendants of domestic animals abandoned to the jungle eons ago. St John and Anegada are the most likely places to see such critters.

Other prevalent land mammals a visitor might encounter are the mongoose and numerous bat species. The mongoose was introduced to control the rat population in the days of the sugarcane plantations and has since overrun the islands.

**Islands by Area**

» St Croix:
84 sq mi

» St Thomas:
32 sq mi

» Tortola:
21 sq mi

» St John:
19 sq mi

» Anegada:
15 sq mi

You may have heard 'Lesser Antilles' or 'Eastern Caribbean' used to reference the Virgin Islands. The terms are interchangeable and apply to the broader archipelago that extends east and southeast from the Virgins to Trinidad and Tobago, just off Venezuela's northern coast.

BIRDS

## Snakes, Lizards & Frogs

The Virgins are home to just a few species of snake – none of which are poisonous – including the Virgin Island tree boa. A host of small and not-so-small lizards scurry around, including the 5ft-long rock iguanas of Anegada and the common green iguana found throughout the islands. Anoles (aka chameleons) and gecko lizards are ubiquitous. That little guy crawling up your hotel wall is probably a house gecko; it hangs near outdoor lights because it likes to feast on the insects that congregate there. Numerous toad and frog species hop through the Virgins, such as the piping frog and the giant toad (aka cane toad), which can grow up to 10 inches and secretes a poisonous white venom.

## Birds & Insects

The bananaquit, or 'yellow bird,' is the Virgins' official flyer. The coastal dry forest features more than 100 bird species, largely songbirds. Some of these are migratory fowl, such as the prairie warbler and the northern parula. Many are native species, like the Caribbean elaenia and the doctorbird.

One of the joys of winter beach visits is watching the aerial acrobatics of brown pelicans as they dive-bomb for fish. Wading birds such as egrets and herons are common at salt ponds. On Anegada, pink flamingos hang out in the ponds.

The islands also have an ample supply of pesky insects, including daytime-active mosquitoes and sharp-biting no-see-ums (aka teeny sand flies). The *Cyrtopholis bartholomei* tarantula, which can grow up to five inches in diameter, is common on St John; look for it on the ground as you hike forested trails. Small scorpions are not uncommon; their sting is similar to that of a bee.

Don't know your brown booby from your pie-billed grebe? Check out *A Guide to the Birds of Puerto Rico & the Virgin Islands*, by Herbert Raffaelle.

## Plants & Trees

Thousands of tropical plant varieties grow in the Virgin Islands, and a short drive can transport a nature lover between entirely different

---

### A HIGH WIND GONNA BLOW

The word 'hurricane,' denoting fierce cyclonic storms with winds in excess of 75mph, comes from the language of Taíno Indians and their god of malevolence, Jurakán. Generally, the 'seeds' of these storms begin to grow off the west coast of Africa near the Cape Verde Islands. They migrate across the equatorial girdle of the Atlantic to the southern Caribbean as upper-atmospheric disturbances driven by the easterly trade winds. Here, they linger and pick up moisture and energy until the Coriolis effect of Earth's rotation propels the growing storms north through the Caribbean and/or the Gulf of Mexico. Eventually, many of the storms pose a threat to the southern and eastern US coasts.

The official hurricane season is from June 1 through November 30. August and September see the most action. The following records from the National Oceanic and Atmospheric Administration show how many tropical storms/hurricanes have struck the Virgins' region between 1819 and 2001:

» July: 9

» August: 34

» September: 38

» October: 9

» November: 4

Good, long-range storm predictions (broadcast widely on TV and radio and in newspapers), thorough preparation and the nearly universal practice of building new houses and public and commercial buildings with cement block or reinforced concrete have gone a long way toward reducing casualties and property damage.

## POISON APPLES

In 1587 Sir Walter Raleigh paused at St Croix with a party of settlers on their way to North America. After the long sea voyage, the colonists were tempted by an abundance of fruit that looked like small light-green apples hanging from trees near the shore. A number of Raleigh's men and women ate the poisonous fruit and 'were fearfully troubled with a sudden burning in their mouths and swelling of their tongues so big that some of them could not speak.'

The colonists' nemesis was the fruit of the manchineel or 'poison apple' tree. The sap of this tree is so toxic that the Caribs used it to poison their arrows. On French Caribbean islands, locals often mark the tree with a skull and crossbones. Although the manchineel has been eradicated from many public areas in the Virgins, it is still around, especially on St John and less developed islands.

Because touching any part of this tree can yield caustic burns (the sap takes paint off cars), humans must avoid the manchineel. Even rain dripping off the leaves and bark will burn if it touches your skin. Although manchineels can grow as tall as 40ft and spread broad branches in a radius of 15ft from the trunk, most trees are much smaller. You will always find these trees near beaches or salt ponds, and you will know a manchineel by its small, green apples and shiny green elliptical leaves.

ecosystems. Mangrove swamps, coconut groves and sea-grape trees dominate the coast, while mountain peaks support wet forest with mahogany, lignum vitae, palmetto and more than 30 varieties of wild orchid. Look for aloe, acacia, turpentine tree, gumbo limbo, century plant and dildo cactus in the coastal dry forests.

Exotic shade trees have long been valued in this sunny climate, and you will see yards and public parks with silk-cotton trees, poincianas (with flaming red blossoms) and African tulip trees. Islanders often adorn their dwellings with a profusion of flowers such as orchids, bougainvillea and poinsettias, and tend lovingly to fruit trees that bear mango, papaya, carambola (star fruit), breadfruit, tamarind, plantain and gneps (a fruit the size of a large marble that yields a sweet, orange flesh).

Islanders also grow and collect hundreds of different roots and herbs, including *japona*, ginger root, anise and cattle tongue, as ingredients for 'bush medicine' cures. Psychoactive mushrooms grow wild (and are consumed) in the islands, particularly on Tortola.

Traveling in the Virgin Islands without an arsenal of your favorite bug repellent is tantamount to offering up your body as a human sacrifice to the Lord of the Flies; come prepared.

# Marine Life

## Corals & Other Invertebrates

Corals are sea creatures in the same invertebrate category as lobsters and octopuses. More than 40 types rise up in the Virgin Islands, including sea fans and yellow tube sponges.

Each coral is a tiny animal with a great gaping mouth at one end, surrounded by tentacles for gathering food. A reef is usually composed of scores of coral species, each occupying its own niche. Each species has a characteristic shape – bulbous cups bunched like biscuits in a baking tray for the star coral and deep, wending valleys for the well-named brain coral. Deeper down, where light is scarcer, massive corals flatten out, becoming more muted in color. Deeper still, soft corals – those without an external skeleton – predominate. These lacy fans and waving cattails look like plants, but a close perusal shows them to be menacing animal predators that seize smaller creatures such as plankton.

The reefs attract fish and other sea creatures to the delight of divers and snorkelers, but the ecosystems are extremely fragile and take thousands of years to form. Warming water temperatures, human encroachment and hurricanes have harmed many reefs in the Virgin Islands and throughout the Caribbean.

## Fish

More than 500 species of fish swim in local waters. Mangrove estuaries and vast coral reefs are the nurseries and feeding grounds for these tropical creatures. And it's not just sergeant majors, angelfish and grouper: the Virgin Islands are some of the best places in the world to get up close and personal with large barracudas, manta rays, moray eels and plentiful nurse sharks – carefully, of course! Most of the scary-sounding swimmers have a live-and-let-live attitude, so as long as you leave them alone, they'll return the favor.

Fan favorites for exotic fish include the colorful, bird-beaked parrotfish, the electric-hued blue tang, the purple-and-yellow fairy basslet, and the pointy longspine squirrelfish.

Tiny algae called dinoflagellates provide the spark for bioluminescence at places such as Salt River Bay, St Croix. The single-celled organisms light up when agitated, such as when brushed with a kayak paddle.

## Sea Turtles

Endangered sea turtles nest on local beaches, particularly on St Croix. The cast of characters includes the 220lb hawksbill, which has been hunted to near extinction for its valuable shell; the 400lb green turtle, a hefty vegetarian identifiable by its short rounded head; and the leatherback, whose 6ft length and 1500lb make him the big boy of the group.

Every two to seven years, turtles return to the beach where they were born to lay their eggs. Since they can live to be 80 years old, they'll make the same journey over and over. The leatherbacks gravitate to Sandy

---

### TRYING TO HANG ON

The Virgin Islands are home to several endangered species. Some of the most fragile include:

» **Leatherback turtle** It's said that the 1500lb behemoths have been roaming the earth since the age of the dinosaurs. Yet their numbers have dwindled as humans collect their eggs and harvest their meat for food. In addition, many of the leatherback's nesting beaches have succumbed to development, and the coral reefs they feed on are being destroyed by rising water temperatures and pollutants.

» **Hawksbill turtle** They face the same environmental pressures as leatherbacks, with an additional twist: hawksbills' shells are prized to make jewelry and decorative items.

» **Screech owl** This rare owl's call led to it being identified as a cuckoo bird in the Virgin Islands. The last recorded sighting was in 1980, and most sources now list the screech owl as extinct. Deforestation played a big role in its demise.

» **Virgin Islands tree boa** The brown-and-cream snake is quite rare to see. Its numbers plummeted when the mongoose was introduced to the Virgin Islands, although habitat destruction also played a role. Captive breeding programs at zoos and introduction of the boas to new islands have been successful in increasing the population.

» **Brown pelican** This athletic fish-lover is another success story. It nearly went extinct in the 1960s. Eating fish contaminated with the pesticide DDT caused the birds to lay eggs with thin shells that broke easily. After the chemical was banned and protections were put in place against hunting the pelican, it rebounded. It was removed from the endangered species list in 2009, though it is still being monitored.

» **Anegada rock iguana** There are just a few hundred left on Anegada, the iguana's traditional habitat, and on the scattering of Out Islands where they've been introduced. Anegada has had a rehabilitation program in place since 1997, and you can visit the facility to check on the big iguana's progress (see p190).

Point National Wildlife Refuge on St Croix's West End, while hawksbills climb ashore at Buck Island and various East End beaches. Green turtles likewise swim to St Croix's East End shores.

Snorkelers can also see green turtles on St John, where they graze the seagrass beds at Maho, Francis and Leinster Bays.

## Dolphins & Whales

From time to time visitors might catch a glimpse of dolphins or porpoises from the shore; it's more common to see them when you're out sailing, especially in the BVI.

The biggest thrill is spotting humpback whales. These mighty leviathans – weighing in at 36 tons – swim into local waters between February and April to breed. They mostly cruise the area north of St John and east of Tortola – though they're sometimes spotted from the ferry going south to St Croix, as well. Even if divers don't see humpbacks, they often hear their songs, which can travel for miles underwater.

## Conch & Starfish

Conch is easy to recognize by its big pink spiral shell. The snail-like creature inside can grow up to 12in in length and weigh up to 5lb. Perhaps more impressively, it can live for up to 40 years. Conch meat is a prized ingredient in Caribbean cuisine. In recent years, the government drew up laws to help protect the conch from overfishing, including a moratorium between August and November to let stocks replenish.

Starfish make occasional appearances along the sandy bottoms of beaches or in tide pools along shorelines.

SEA TURTLE

Sand temperature plays a major role in determining a sea turtle's sex; higher temperatures result in less incubation time and creates more females.

## National Parks

The USVI and the BVI have good reason to be proud of their national parks, as both territories have set aside large portions of their landscape to remain forever wild.

On the US islands, the National Park Service oversees the vast Virgin Islands National Park, which includes more than 9500 acres of wilderness on St John, 5600 acres of surrounding bays and sea gardens, plus Hassel Island in St Thomas Harbor. The park service also protects the marine sanctuary at Buck Island National Reef Monument, encompassing 18,800 acres of coral reef a stone's throw from St Croix.

The BVI National Parks Trust oversees 20 parks covering more than 1800 acres on land and in the sea. The most popular ones are the 96-forested acres around lofty Sage Mountain and the Rhone National Marine Park surrounding the 1867 wreck of the RMS *Rhone*. Whole islands such as the Dogs and Fallen Jerusalem are preserved. And the entire southwest coast of Virgin Gorda is a collection of national parks that includes the giant boulder formations at the Baths and Spring Bay.

## Sustainability & Environmental Issues

The Virgin Islands have long faced environmental challenges, including deforestation, soil erosion, mangrove destruction and a lack of fresh water. While islanders have a way to go toward undoing generations of environmental damage and preserving their natural resources, the past few decades have seen an increase in the level of awareness, resources and action dedicated to conservation efforts.

**Friends of the Virgin Islands National Park** (www.friendsvinp.org) and the **USVI Department of Planning & Natural Resources** (www.vifishandwildlife.com) have led the way. The **Nature Conservancy** (www.nature.org) and **Trust for Public Land** (www.tpl.org) also have stepped in. For instance, the Conservancy made a protected reserve out of the sea-turtle nesting grounds at St Croix's Jack and Isaac Bays – land once slated

Virgin Islands' law prohibits the removal of corals, shells, sand and other natural resources from beaches, so leave that gorgeous conch shell right where it washed up.

for residential development. The Trust for Public Land is currently trying to save the land at Maho Bay's eco-camp from being sold and developed.

## Population Growth & Urbanization

Without a doubt, population growth and rapid urbanization have posed the greatest threats to the islands' environment. The Virgin Islands traditionally have had a very high birthrate and historically have been a sanctuary for immigrants. As a consequence, the population mushroomed from about 40,000 people in 1970 to 140,000 today between the territories. On St Thomas and Tortola, almost all of the flat land has been developed, and houses hang on mountain slopes like Christmas ornaments. The growth and density have left public utilities like sewage-treatment plants in a constant scramble to keep pace.

## Deforestation & Soil Erosion

During the 18th century logging operations denuded many of the islands to make room for plantations. Subsequently, untold acres of topsoil have eroded. The demise of the agricultural economy in the late 19th century allowed the islands to reforest, and in recent years the island governments have set aside forested land as national parks (particularly on St John, Tortola and Virgin Gorda) and begun work on a series of forest conservation projects to slow erosion.

## Mangrove Destruction

As with the islands' other environmental problems, mangrove destruction was at its worst decades ago when the rush to develop business and housing lots saw the devastation of mangrove swamps around urban areas. Some bays now lined with marinas, hotels and businesses, such as the harbor at Road Town, were mangrove estuaries just 50 years ago. Environmentalists began fighting to preserve the Virgin Islands' remaining mangrove estuaries in the 1980s, and the late 1990s brought some victories in this arena, helping preserve the mangroves at Paraquita Bay on Tortola, Salt Pond Bay on St Croix and Mangrove Lagoon on St Thomas.

## Freshwater Shortage

If not for the miracle of desalination plants, which make freshwater out of seawater, the Virgin Islands could not support even a quarter of its population – let alone the hotel guests. When a hurricane strikes, islands lose power and the desalination facilities shut down. Islanders with enough foresight and money keep rainwater cisterns for such emergencies, but folks without these reserves suffer.

**Top National Parks**

» Virgin Islands National Park

» Buck Island Reef National Monument

» Sage Mountain National Park

» The Baths

» Rhone National Marine Park

» Fallen Jerusalem

---

### CORAL BLEACHING

The record-high temperatures of water across the Caribbean are killing beneficial types of algae that corals depend on symbiotically to survive, which results in the process called 'bleaching'. Specifically, the algae is the source of the coral's color, so when it leaves, the coral becomes white. And while coral can survive the bleaching itself, it becomes vulnerable to disease and predators afterward.

The Virgin Islands experienced a particularly hot period in 2005 that wiped out about half of its coral colonies. The marine sanctuary at Buck Island National Reef Monument, offshore from St Croix, was particularly hard hit.

In 2010 local waters again started to warm to dangerous levels, until Hurricane Earl blew through and cooled down the temperature. While environmentalists are helpless to stop the bleaching process, they do have action plans in place to study it and learn from coral's adaptive abilities.

» **Reef Environmental Education Foundation** (www.reef.org) This one's for the scuba buffs in the crowd. REEF asks divers to fill out a survey sheet documenting marine life in the area they've just explored, which REEF then compiles and uses to monitor the region's health.

» **Friends of Virgin Islands National Park** (www.friendsvinp.org) Volunteer for beach clean-ups or trail clean-ups to remove invasive plant species on St John; takes place at 8am every Tuesday and Thursday from November through April.

» **St Croix Environmental Association** (www.stxenvironmental.org) This has programs (from $35) where you can help count sea turtles.

## Invasive Species

Lionfish first appeared in Virgin Islands' waters in late 2008. Striped with venomous spines and the homeliest thing you ever did see, it is native to the Pacific but started showing up in the Caribbean in the 1990s, probably released by aquarium hobbyists. The voracious creature multiplied quickly and began consuming native fish (it can eat as many as 20 per day) and competing with others for food. It has no known predators in the Caribbean, and now biologists fear a full-on invasion that will wreak havoc on local fisheries and reefs.

Biologists attribute its arrival in the Virgins to undersea currents and ballast water from boats traveling from elsewhere in the Caribbean. So far, they've been spotted only around St Croix and St John.

# Survival Guide

>

# Directory A–Z

## Accommodations

The Virgin Islands offer a wide range of lodging, including campgrounds, guesthouses, hotels, private villas and luxury resorts. The USVI and BVI tourist offices (see Tourist Information, p234) publish listings of accommodations that you can access online.

### Amenities

» While air-conditioning is widely available, it is not a standard amenity, even at top-end places. If you want it, be sure to ask about it when you book.

» Most properties offer free wi-fi in the lobby or common areas. In-room wi-fi is less common. Again, if you want it, ask for it when booking.

» If having a TV or telephone in your room is important,

check, although satellite/cable TV is pretty common.

### Discounts

» In the low-season (May through mid-December), prices can plummet by as much as 40%.

» Check the hotel websites listed throughout this book for special online rates. The usual online travel-booking websites also offer discounted room prices in the Virgin Islands, though selection is limited.

### Prices

» The price indicators in this book refer to the cost of a double room. Prices listed in this book are for peak-season travel and, unless stated otherwise, do not include taxes (which can be up to 17% in the BVI and 18% in the USVI). If breakfast is included and/or a bathroom

is shared, that information is included in our listing.

» The budget category comprises campgrounds and simple hotels where you'll likely share a bathroom. Rates rarely exceed $100 for a double.

» Midrange accommodations, such as most guesthouses, B&Bs, condos/apartments and some hotels, generally offer the best value for money. Expect to pay between $100 and $300 for a comfortable, decent-sized double with a private bathroom.

» Top-end accommodations (more than $300 per double) are mostly resorts that offer an international standard of amenities, including multiple pools, water-sports equipment, fitness and business centers and other upmarket facilities.

| CATEGORY | COST |
| --- | --- |
| Budget ($) | Under $100 |
| Midrange ($$) | $100 to $300 |
| Top End ($$$) | More than $300 |

### Seasons

» Peak season is winter, from mid-December through April, when prices are highest.

» It's best to book ahead during winter, as well as during holidays (see Public Holidays, p233) and major events (see Month by Month, p22), as rooms can be scarce.

» Many properties have three-night minimum stay requirements during peak season.

» Some lodgings close in September, the heart of low season.

### Types of Accommodations

#### B&BS & GUESTHOUSES
» Island B&Bs and guesthouses offer an alternative to the high prices and insularity that come with rooms in

## BOOK YOUR STAY ONLINE

For more accommodations reviews by Lonely Planet authors, check out hotels.lonelyplanet.com/Virgin Islands. You'll find independent reviews, as well as recommendations on the best places to stay. Best of all, you can book online.

resort hotels in the tourist zones.

» The best are distinguished by friendliness and attention to detail from the owners or hosts, who can provide local information, tour bookings and other amenities.

» Standards vary widely, sometimes within a single property. The cheapest rooms tend to be small with few amenities and a shared bathroom. Nicer ones come with added features such as a balconies, fully cooked breakfasts and en suite bathrooms.

» Not all properties accept children.

» Minimum stays (usually three nights) are common.

### CAMPING

» Camping is the most economical approach to a Virgin Islands vacation. Prices run from about $35 for a bare site with no tent to no more than $135 for a deluxe tent that looks like a tree house at Maho Bay Camps.

» Facilities usually include access to drinking water and a shared bathhouse with flush toilets and cold-water showers.

» Campgrounds are sprinkled throughout the islands. St John, St Croix, Water Island, Tortola and Jost Van Dyke all have at least one site.

» Many of the campgrounds, especially in the USVI, are environmentally friendly and use wind and/or solar power.

» Popular campgrounds such as the one at Cinnamon Bay on St John have a 14-night limit during the winter season and require reservations.

» Most sites stay open year-round, with the possible exception of September.

### HOMESTAYS

How do you feel about staying on the couch of a perfect stranger? If it's not a problem, consider joining an organization that arranges homestays. The following groups don't have membership fees, and the stay itself is also free.

**Couch Surfing** (www.couch surfing.com)

**Hospitality Club** (www. hospitalityclub.org)

### HOTELS

» Your best bets for moderately priced hotels are in Charlotte Amalie, Christiansted, Frederiksted, Road Town and Cane Garden Bay. These towns have a number of medium-size, well-tended hotels with pools, air-conditioning, cable TV and rates starting at about $125 per night.

» For the most part, island hotels categorize themselves as 'luxury' or 'deluxe' establishments, and rooms run to more than $250 per night during the high season, unless you have a tour package.

» The Virgin Islands also offer several truly exclusive retreats on private cays like Guana Island and Peter Island, where rates start at $750 per night.

» Hotel rack rates are not written in stone. Call the property and ask about any specials that might apply. Members of AARP (formerly the American Association of Retired Persons) or AAA (the American Automobile Association) might qualify for a 10% discount at hotel chains such as Best Western.

### RENTAL ACCOMMODATIONS

» Condominiums, villas and apartments are widely available throughout the islands.

» Properties are usually located in prime resort areas and offer attractive, well-furnished units with a separate bedroom, kitchen, living space and great views.

» These are ideal if you're traveling with your family or

---

## PRACTICALITIES

» The *VI Daily News* and *St Croix Avis* are the daily papers in the USVI. *St Thomas/St John This Week* and *St Croix This Week* are widely available free magazines, and are published monthly (despite the name).

» The *BVI Beacon* and *StandPoint* are the BVI's main newspapers; they're published weekly. BVI News (www.bvinews.com) offers free daily content online. The free weekly *Limin' Times* has entertainment listings.

» Local TV stations in the USVI include channels 8 (ABC) and 12 (PBS). The BVI has no local equivalent.

» Radio stations include WVGN (107.3 FM), the NPR affiliate in St Thomas; ZBVI (780 AM), island talk and music from Tortola, including BBC broadcasts; and WSTX (970 AM), island tunes and talk from St Croix.

» Both the US and British islands use imperial measurements. Distances are in feet and miles; gasoline is measured in gallons.

» Smoking is banned in all restaurants, bars and other public venues in both the US and British islands.

a large group, because you have room to stretch out, do your own cooking and enjoy plenty of privacy.

» Properties range toward the top-end for costs, though you might find a few one-bedroom places for $250 per night or two-bedroom places for $400 per night. Rentals are usually by the week.

» The following companies rent properties in the Virgins:

**McLaughlin Anderson Luxury Villas** (☎340-776-0635, 800-537-6246; www.mclaughlinanderson.com) Multi-island.

**Purple Pineapple** (☎305-396-1586; www.purplepineapple.com) Multi-island.

**Calypso Realty** (☎340-774-1620; www.calypsorealty.com) St Thomas.

**Carefree Get-Aways** (☎340-779-4070, 888-643-6002; www.carefreegetaways.com) St John.

**Caribbean Villas** (☎340-776-6152, 800-338-0987; www.caribbeanvilla.com) St John and Tortola.

**Catered To** (☎340-776-6641, 800-424-6641; www.cateredto.com) St John.

**CMPI Vacation Rentals** (☎800-496-7379; www.enjoystcroix.com) St Croix.

**Teague Bay Properties** (☎800-237-1959; www.teaguebaypropertiesrentals.com) St Croix.

**Vacation St Croix** (☎340-718-0361; www.vacationstcroix.com) St Croix.

**Areana Villas** (☎284-494-5864; www.areanavillas.com) Tortola.

**Tropical Care Services** (☎284-495-6493; www.tropicalcareservices.com) Virgin Gorda.

## Activities

Diving and snorkeling in the Virgin Islands are so superb we've devoted a whole chapter to it; see p30. Ditto for sailing; see Chartering a Boat, p37. Other resources:

**USVI Game Fishing Club** (www.vigfc.com) Information on local conditions, and regulations in both the USVI and BVI (license required for BVI).

**Skim Caribbean** (www.skimcaribbean.com) Skimboarding hot spots in the Virgins.

**BVI Scuba Organization** (www.bviscuba.org) Links to dive sites and dive shops.

**BVI Charter Yacht Society** (www.bvicrewedyachts.com) Lists BVI companies and prices.

**Virgin Islands Charter Yacht League** (www.vicl.org) Lists USVI companies and prices.

**BVI Mountain Bike Club** Organizes races and social events; search for them on Facebook.

## Business Hours

This list provides 'regular' opening hours for businesses. Reviews throughout this book show specific hours only if they vary from these standards. Be aware, too, that hours can vary from high season to low season. Listings depict peak season (December through April) operating times. Many places are closed on Sunday.

**Banks** 9am-3pm Mon-Thu, to 5pm Fri

**Bars & pubs** noon-midnight

**General office hours** 8am-5pm Mon-Fri

**Restaurants** breakfast 7am-11am, lunch 11am-2pm, dinner 5pm-9pm daily; some open for brunch 10am-2pm Sun

**Shops** 9am-5pm Mon-Sat

## Climate

### St John

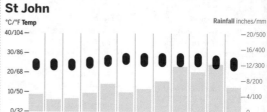

### St Thomas

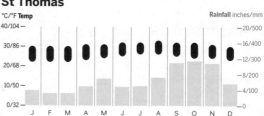

### Tortola

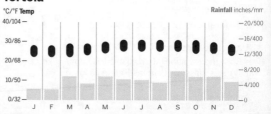

# Customs Regulations

» The USVI and BVI allow a reasonable amount of personal items, including laptop computers and water-sports equipment, to be brought in duty-free.

» Determining what you can take home depends on your country of origin. Check with your country's customs agency for clarification.

» US citizens (including children) can bring home, duty-free, 5 liters of alcohol and $1600 worth of goods total from the Virgin Islands, though at least $800 in items and one of the liters of alcohol must be from the USVI. **US Customs & Border Protection** (www.cbp.gov) has details.

» You do not clear customs entering the USVI if you're coming from the United States.

» You do clear customs entering the BVI, though it is usually a fast and easy process.

» Pets can be brought into the USVI without any special shots or paperwork. For the BVI, you need a permit from the **Department of Agriculture** (☎284-495-2532).

» You cannot take fruits or vegetables out of either the USVI or BVI.

» Save your receipts, as a customs agent may ask to see them along with the items purchased.

## Embassies & Consulates

With the exception of those listed here, there are no foreign embassies or consulates in the Virgin Islands. The closest cache is in nearby San Juan, Puerto Rico.

**Denmark** (☎340-776-0656; www.dkconsulateusvi.com; Scandinavian Center, Havensight Mall, Bldg 3, Charlotte Amalie, St Thomas)

**Sweden** (☎340-774-6845; charlotteamalie@consulateofsweden.org; 1340 Taarneberg, Charlotte Amalie, St Thomas)

## Electricity

110v/60hz

110v/60hz

## Food

Price indicators for eating options in this book denote the cost of a main dish for dinner.

| CATEGORY | COST |
| --- | --- |
| Budget ($) | Under $12 |
| Midrange ($$) | $12 to $30 |
| Top End ($$$) | More than $30 |

## Gay & Lesbian Travelers

» West Indian taboos on the lifestyle are slow to crumble, so while a fair number of islanders are gay, you're not likely to meet many who are 'out,' nor are you likely to see public displays of affection among gay couples.

» The USVI are more open than the BVI. Of all the islands, St Croix is the most gay-friendly, with Frederiksted the center of gay life, but overall there aren't many structured outlets for meeting. One exception is Sand Castle on the Beach, in Frederiksted.

» The following are good resources for gay travel. They include Virgin Islands information, though they are not exclusive to the region.

**Damron** (www.damron.com) Publishes several travel guides, including *Men's Travel Guide, Women's Traveller* and *Damron Accommodations;* gay-friendly tour operators are listed on the website, too.

**Out Traveler** (www.outtraveler.com) Gay travel magazine.

**Purple Roofs** (www.purpleroofs.com) Website listing gay-friendly accommodations, travel agencies and tours worldwide.

## Insurance

Make sure you have adequate travel insurance, whatever the length of your trip. At a minimum, you need coverage for medical emergencies and treatment, including hospital stays and an emergency flight home. See Health Insurance (p242) for further information, including fine print regarding 'dangerous activities' such as diving.

Also consider insurance for luggage theft or loss. If you already have a homeowners or renters policy, check what it will cover and only get supplemental insurance to protect against the rest. If you have prepaid a large portion of your vacation, trip cancellation insurance is worthwhile, especially if you'll be traveling during hurricane season from June through November.

Worldwide travel insurance is available at www.lonelyplanet.com/travel _services. You can buy, extend and claim online at anytime – even if you're already on the road. Also check the following providers:

**Insure.com** (www.insure.com)

**Travelex** (www.travelex.com)

**Travel Guard** (www.travelguard.com)

# Internet Access

» It's easy to find internet access. Internet cafes cluster in the main tourist areas, often near marinas and cruise ship docks. Access generally costs $5 per half hour.

» Wi-fi is widely available. Most lodgings have it in their public areas (though it is less common in-room), as do many restaurants and bars in the main towns. We've identified sleeping, eating and entertainment listings that have wi-fi with a 🛜. We've denoted lodgings that offer internet terminals for guest use with a @.

» Check the regional Information sections throughout the book for suggested facilities where you can get online.

# Legal Matters

## Police

» If you are stopped by the police for any reason, bear in mind that there is no system of paying fines on the spot. Attempting to pay the fine to the officer may compound your troubles by resulting in a charge of bribery.

» For traffic offenses, the police officer will explain your options to you. Should the officer decide that you should pay up front, he or she can take you directly to the magistrate.

» If you are arrested for more serious offenses, you are allowed to remain silent. All persons who are arrested are legally allowed (and given) the right to make one phone call. If you don't have a lawyer or family member to help you, call the nearest embassy. The police will give you the number upon request.

## Drugs & Alcohol

» The blood-alcohol limit in Virgin Islands is 0.08%. Driving under the influence of alcohol is a serious offense, subject to stiff fines and even imprisonment.

» Getting caught smoking or possessing marijuana (or any

---

## GETTING MARRIED IN THE ISLANDS

Say 'I do' in the Virgins, and you sure won't have to travel far for a honeymoon. The islands make it fairly easy to get hitched on their shores.

### USVI

» In the USVI, couples must apply for a marriage license at the Territorial Court in Charlotte Amalie, St Thomas or Christiansted, St Croix. The combined marriage application and license fee is $100, and there is a mandatory eight-day waiting period after the court receives the paperwork. Licenses then must be picked up in person.

» If a judge performs the ceremony, it costs an additional $200. A clergy member also can do the deed, for which costs vary.

» For links to wedding planners, as well as to download marriage applications, see www.visitusvi.com/plan_events.

### BVI

» In the BVI, couples must apply for a license ($110) Monday through Friday at the registrar's office in Road Town, Tortola. The waiting period is three days. The registrar then charges an additional $35 to perform the ceremony at the office, or $100 to marry a couple at a different location. Those who wish to get married in a church must make arrangements for an announcement to appear there for three consecutive Sundays beforehand.

» For details and BVI wedding planner links, see www.bvitourism.com/whattodo/WeddingsandHoneymoons.aspx.

illegal drug) can send you to jail in a hurry.

» Open-container laws do not exist in the Virgin Islands, so you can drink on the streets.

» Servers and police on patrol have the right to ask to see your ID and may refuse service or arrest you if you are drinking without an ID.

## Maps

» Many businesses offer free, fold-out road maps of the various islands and their main towns, which should suffice for driving trips.

» In the USVI, the widely available free tourist magazines St Thomas/St John This Week and St Croix This Week also have maps inside.

» In the BVI, free road maps are available at the airport and ferry terminals.

## Money

» The US and British Virgin Islands both use the US dollar.

» All prices quoted in this book are in US dollars ($), unless stated otherwise.

» See p17 for exchange rates and costs.

### ATMs

You'll find FirstBank, Scotiabank, First Caribbean and Banco Popular in the main towns, with ATMs hooked into worldwide networks (Plus, Cirrus, Exchange etc).

Jost Van Dyke, Anegada and the Out Islands do not have ATMs, so you'll need to cash up beforehand.

### Cash

Though carrying cash is more risky, it's still a good idea to travel with some for the convenience. It's useful for tipping and to pay for taxis. In some cases, cash is necessary to pay for lodgings; inquire in advance to avoid surprises.

## Credit Cards

Major credit cards such as MasterCard and Visa are widely accepted in the Virgin Islands; American Express is less common, especially in the BVI. Without having a piece of plastic you'll find it hard or impossible to rent a car or book a room over the phone. Note that some credit card companies charge a 'transaction fee' (around 3% of whatever you purchased); check with your provider to avoid any unexpected costs.

For lost or stolen cards, these numbers operate 24 hours:

**American Express** (☎866-296-5198; www.american express.com)

**MasterCard** (☎800-307-7309; www.mastercard.com)

**Visa** (☎800-847-2911; www.visa.com)

## Tipping

Tipping is a standard practice but, in restaurants especially, always check your bill to see whether a service charge has already been added.

| RECOMMENDED FOR | TIPPING RATE |
|---|---|
| Restaurant waitstaff | 15% to 20% |
| Hotel bellhop | $1 to $2 per bag |
| Hotel room cleaners | $2 per day |
| Taxis | 10% to 15% |
| Dive boat operators & yacht crews | 10% to 20% |

## Traveler's Checks

Traveler's checks in US dollars are accepted but becoming rather uncommon as people switch to using ATMs for their cash needs.

## Photography

» It is common courtesy to ask people's permission before you photograph them.

» Lonely Planet's Travel Photography book provides tips for shutterbugging like a pro.

## Post

» Postal service is reliable. The US Virgins use the same postal system and mail rates as the United States, while the British Virgins have their own domestic and international service.

» 'Overnight' courier services usually take a couple of days due to the limited number of flights arriving and departing from the islands.

## Public Holidays

### US Virgin Islands

Islanders celebrate US public holidays along with several local holidays. Banks, schools and government offices close on these days.

**New Year's Day** January 1

**Three Kings Day** (Feast of the Epiphany) January 6

**Martin Luther King Jr's Birthday** Third Monday in January

**Presidents' Day** Third Monday in February

**Transfer Day** March 31

**Holy Thursday & Good Friday** Before Easter (in March or April)

**Easter Monday** Day after Easter

**Memorial Day** Last Monday in May

**Emancipation Day** July 3

**Independence Day** (Fourth of July) July 4

**Hurricane Supplication Day** Fourth Monday in July

**Labor Day** First Monday in September

**Columbus Day** Second Monday in October

**Liberty Day** November 1

**Veterans' Day** November 11

**Thanksgiving Day** Fourth Thursday in November

**Christmas Day & Boxing Day** December 25 and 26

## British Virgin Islands

**New Year's Day** January 1

**HL Stoutt's Birthday** First Monday in March

**Commonwealth Day** Second Monday in March

**Good Friday** Friday before Easter (in March or April)

**Easter Monday** Monday after Easter (in March or April)

**Whit Monday** May or June (date varies)

**Sovereign's Birthday** mid-June (date varies)

**Territory Day** July 1

**BVI Festival Days** First Monday to Wednesday in August

**St Ursula's Day** October 21

**Christmas Day & Boxing Day** December 25 & 26

## Telephone

The Virgin Islands' phone system is similar to the US system. In the BVI, be prepared for whopping charges – it is one of the most expensive places in the world for calls.

### Cell Phones

» You should be able to use your cell phone on most islands, but be prepared for exorbitant roaming fees.

» In the USVI, **AT&T** (www.att.com/wireless) and **Sprint** (www.sprint.com) are the islands' main service providers. If you use these companies at home, it's possible you may not have a roaming fee, but definitely check in advance.

» In the BVI, **CCT Global** (www.cctwireless.com), **Lime** (www.time4lime.com) and **Digicel** (www.digicelbvi.com) provide the local service.

» If you have a European, Australian or other type of unlocked GSM phone, buy a local SIM card to reduce costs. They cost about $20, which includes $10 of air time (at roughly $0.30 per minute calling time to the US). This mainly applies in

the BVI, where SIM cards are easy to get at local shops. It's difficult to find them in the USVI.

### Domestic & International Dialing

» All phone numbers in the Virgin Islands consist of a three-digit area code – ☎340 in the USVI, ☎284 in the BVI – followed by a seven-digit local number.

» If you are calling from abroad, dial all 10 digits preceded by ☎1. If you are calling locally, just dial the seven-digit number.

» To call from the islands to the US or Canada (or between the USVI and BVI), dial ☎1 + area code + the seven-digit number.

» For direct international calls, such as to Europe, dial ☎011 + country code + area code + local phone number.

» Many businesses also have toll-free numbers; these begin with 800, 888 or 877 and must be preceded by 1.

### Emergency Numbers

» Dial ☎911 in the USVI, and ☎911 or 999 in the BVI.

### Public Phones

» In the USVI, pay phones are easy to find in commercial areas. Local calls cost $0.25 to $0.35. In the BVI, working pay phones are few and far between.

### Phonecards

» Prepaid phonecards usually offer the best per-minute rates for long-distance and international calling. You can buy them at grocery stores throughout the Virgin Islands.

## Time

The Virgin Islands are on Atlantic Standard Time, which is one hour later than Eastern Standard Time (ie New York, Miami etc) and four hours earlier than Greenwich Mean Time. However, there is no

Daylight Saving Time in the Virgins, which means from mid-March to early November, the time on the islands is the same as in New York and Miami.

**TIME DIFFERENCE BETWEEN CITIES IN WINTER**

| Virgin Islands | noon |
| --- | --- |
| London | 4pm |
| New York City | 11am |
| Los Angeles | 8am |

## Tourist Information

Maps and helpful tourist magazines are available at airports and ferry terminals, as well as at many hotels.

**BVI Tourist Board** (www.bvitourism.com) Official site with comprehensive lodging and activity info.

**USVI Department of Tourism** (www.visitusvi.com) Official tourism site with a 'hot deals' page.

## Travelers with Disabilities

Travel in the Virgin Islands is not easy for those with physical challenges.

» While the Americans with Disabilities Act holds sway in the USVI, facilities are not accessible to the same degree as they are in the US. And facilities are particularly lacking in the BVI. There is little consciousness of the need for curb cuts, wheelchair-accessible taxis and ferries, or rental vehicles for people with disabilities.

» The USVI offers a couple of resources on St Thomas: **Accessible Adventures** (www.accessvi.com) provides island tours on a trolley suitable for visitors in wheelchairs. **Dial-A-Ride** (☎340-776-1277) helps with transportation needs on the island.

» While land travel presents obstacles, cruises are often a

good option for travelers with disabilities in the islands. Many cruise lines can coordinate shore-based excursions in wheelchair-accessible tour buses.

The following groups have general tips on travel for visitors with special needs:

**Access-Able Travel Source** (www.access-able.com) Links to international disability sites, travel newsletters, guidebooks, travel tips and information on cruise operators.

**Mobility International USA** (www.miusa.org) Advises travelers on mobility issues but primarily runs an educational exchange program.

**Society for Accessible Travel & Hospitality** (www.sath.org) Travelers with disabilities share tips and blogs.

## Visas

### USVI

Visitors from most Western countries do not need a visa to enter the USVI if they are staying less than 90 days. This holds true as long as you can present a machine-readable passport and are approved under the **Electronic System for Travel Authorization** (ESTA; www.cbp.gov/esta). Note you must register for ESTA at least 72 hours before arrival, and there's a $14 fee for processing and authorization.

If you do need a visa, contact your local embassy. The **US State Department** (www.travel.state.gov) always has the latest information on admission requirements.

### BVI

Visitors from most Western countries do not need a visa to enter the BVI for stays of 30 days or less. If your home country does not qualify for visa exemption, contact your nearest **British embassy**

(www.ukvisas.gov.uk) or the **BVI Immigration Department** (www.bviimmigration.gov.vg).

## Volunteering

The USVI offers more opportunities for volunteering than the BVI, including archaeological digs, trash clean-ups and turtle counts.

**Friends of Virgin Islands National Park** (www.friendsvinp.org) Volunteer for trail or beach clean-ups on St John. Just show up at the maintenance parking lot (it's well marked) by the park visitors center in Cruz Bay at 8am any Tuesday or Thursday from November through April.

**St Croix Environmental Association** (www.stxenvironmental.org) It has programs (from $35) where you can help count sea turtles.

**Virgin Islands Sustainable Farm Institute** (www.visfi.org) Stay on an organic farm in St Croix's rainforest and work in the fields; lodging is provided from $35 per day.

**Caribbean Volunteer Expeditions** (www.cvexp.org) This US-based organization sends volunteers to work on archaeology and environmental preservation projects in the Caribbean, including St John. Fees typically cost about $800 per week, including accommodations, food and land transportation, but not airfare.

## Women Travelers

It's safe for women to travel solo in the Virgin Islands, though you may attract the occasional catcall or whistle. Just use the same degree of caution you would in a big city at home: be aware of your surroundings and don't walk alone at night in unfamiliar areas. Avoid isolated beaches at any time of day or night.

## Work

### Permits

US citizens can work legally in the USVI without any red tape, but it's difficult for travelers of other nationalities to get legal work in the territory. Foreigners need a work visa, and securing one without a sponsor (meaning an employer) is nearly impossible. Contact your embassy or consulate for more information.

In the BVI, only 'belongers' (naturalized citizens) can work without a permit. The government doesn't issue work permits easily, as it's keen to give jobs to locals. Contact the **BVI Department of Labor** (☎284-494-3451) for more information.

### Finding Work

Generally the best bet for working is to crew with a boat or yacht. As boat-hands aren't usually working on any one island in particular, the work situation is more flexible and it's easier to avoid hassles with immigration. Marinas are a good place to look for jobs on yachts; check the bulletin-board notices, strike up conversations with skippers or ask around at the nearest bar. Marinas in Miami and Fort Lauderdale are considered good places to find crew jobs as people sailing their boats down for the season stop here looking for crew.

You can also look for jobs with a crew placement agency:

**Crewfinders** (www.crewfinders.com) Florida-based group.

**Crewseekers International** (www.crewseekers.net) UK-based group.

# Transportation

## GETTING THERE & AWAY

Flights, tours and rail tickets can be booked online at www.lonelyplanet.com/travel_services.

## Entering the Country

### Passport

#### USVI

US citizens do not need a passport to visit the US Virgin Islands, but all other nationalities do. Entering the territory is straightforward: anyone arriving on a plane from the US mainland or Puerto Rico simply walks off and heads to their destination – there are no immigration procedures – but when departing the USVI, everyone must clear immigration and customs before boarding the plane. Visitors from the US will be asked to show photo identification (such as a driver's license) and proof of US citizenship (such as an official, raised-seal birth certificate).

If traveling to any other Caribbean country (besides Puerto Rico, which, like the USVI, is a US territory), US citizens must have a valid passport to re-enter the US by air. If re-entering via a sea border, US visitors have the option of using a less-expensive passport card. See the **Western Hemisphere Travel Initiative** (www. getyouhome.gov) for further information.

For details on visa requirements, see p235.

#### BVI

Everyone needs a passport to enter the BVI by air. US citizens who enter the BVI by ferry can also opt for using the less-expensive passport card; see the **Western Hemisphere Travel Initiative** (www.getyouhome.gov) for more information. All other nationalities need a passport to enter by ferry.

Whether arriving by air or sea, you'll go through BVI immigration and customs. Officials might ask to see a return ticket and proof of funds, though that's rare. It can take a half hour or so to clear customs. If you're arriving on a ferry, you'll clear through a **customs house** (www.bviports.org) near the dock.

---

## Air

### Airports

St Thomas has the Virgin Islands' main airport. Tortola and St Croix are the region's other gateways. All of the airports are modern, yet small, facilities. Virgin Gorda and Anegada also have airports; they're tiny and used for private charters only.

**Cyril E King Airport, St Thomas** (STT; www.viport.com)

**Henry E Rohlsen Airport, St Croix** (STX; www.viport.com)

**Terrence B Lettsome Airport, Tortola** (EIS; ☎284-494-3701)

---

### CLIMATE CHANGE & TRAVEL

Every form of transport that relies on carbon-based fuel generates $CO_2$, the main cause of human-induced climate change. Modern travel is dependent on aeroplanes, which might use less fuel per kilometer per person than most cars but travel much greater distances. The altitude at which aircraft emit gases (including $CO_2$) and particles also contributes to their climate change impact. Many websites offer 'carbon calculators' that allow people to estimate the carbon emissions generated by their journey and, for those who wish to do so, to offset the impact of the greenhouse gases emitted with contributions to portfolios of climate-friendly initiatives throughout the world. Lonely Planet offsets the carbon footprint of all staff and author travel.

## Airlines

Almost all flights to the Virgin Islands from outside the Caribbean either originate in or transit through the US (including Puerto Rico) on the following airlines. The **BVI Tourism Board** (www. bvitourism.com) provides handy information on the most direct routes to Tortola, depending on your point of origin.

**American Airlines** (www. aa.com) Via Boston, Miami, New York, San Juan.

**Continental Airlines** (www. continental.com) Via Houston, Newark, San Juan.

**Delta** (www.delta.com) Via Atlanta, New York.

**Spirit** (www.spiritair.com) Via Fort Lauderdale.

**United** (www.united.com) Via Charlotte, Chicago.

**US Airways** (www.usairways. com) Via Charlotte.

The following airlines fly to/ from the Virgin Islands from within the Caribbean:

**Air Sunshine** (www.air sunshine.com) Via San Juan.

**American Eagle** (www. aa.com) Via San Juan.

**BVI Airways** (www.gobvi. com) Via St-Martin/Sint Maarten and Dominica.

**Cape Air** (www.flycapeair. com) Via San Juan.

**Liat** (www.liatairline.com) Via Antigua and St-Martin/Sint Maarten.

**WinAir** (www.fly-winair.com) Via Antigua and St-Martin/ Sint Maarten.

## Sea

### Cruise Ship

Cruise ships are big business in the Virgin Islands, especially on St Thomas, which is one of the most popular cruise destinations in the Caribbean. Tortola and St Croix host the other key ports.

#### ST THOMAS

The island has two cruise ship terminals, both of which bustle with taxis and shops. Tenders are not needed to get ashore.

**Havensight** The West Indian Company dock is the busiest of the two terminals, with big ships in every day; it's about a mile east of Charlotte Amalie.

**Crown Bay** The newer, secondary dock; it's about a mile west of Charlotte Amalie.

#### ST CROIX

Ships call on sleepy **Frederiksted** a few times per week. The pier juts out from downtown, so tenders are not needed. The scene here is more sedate than on other islands.

#### ST JOHN

It happens infrequently, but small vessels do call on St John. They anchor offshore in Pillsbury Sound and passengers take a tender in.

#### TORTOLA

Ships call on **Road Town** almost daily during peak season. The dock is downtown, so no tenders are needed – passengers disembark and they're in the heart of the action.

#### Cruise Ship Lines

Cruise ship lines calling on the Virgins Islands:

**Carnival Cruise Lines** (www.carnival.com)

**Celebrity Cruises** (www. celebritycruises.com)

**Costa Cruises** (www. costacruises.com)

**Disney Cruise Line** (www. disneycruise.com)

**Holland America** (www. hollandamerica.com)

**Norwegian Cruise Line** (www.ncl.com)

**Princess Cruises** (www. princess.com)

**Royal Caribbean International** (www.royalcaribbean. com)

**Star Clippers** (www.star clippers.com)

#### Cruise Ship Resources

Good sources for getting a picture of the industry:

**Cruise Critic** (www.cruise critic.com) An in-depth site for people who like to cruise. The message boards are excellent, with detailed critical opinions and information on ships, islands and more.

**Cruise Junkie** (www.cruise junkie.com) An excellent site that provides a well-rounded view of the industry, including safety and environmental issues.

### Yacht

Many visitors arrive by yacht to the Virgin Islands. The main marinas are at the Moorings in Road Town, Tortola, and at American Yacht Harbor in Red Hook, St Thomas. Plenty of others scatter throughout the islands.

» Upon reaching the USVI, you must clear immigration and customs unless you are coming directly from a US port or Puerto Rico. You can clear US customs at Charlotte Amalie (St Thomas), Cruz Bay (St John) or Christiansted or Frederiksted (St Croix).

» To clear customs and immigration in the BVI, you must stop at Great Harbour (Jost Van Dyke), Spanish Town (Virgin Gorda) or Sopers Hole or Road Town (both on Tortola).

» The Virgin Islands' drug-smuggling problem is such that you should anticipate the possibility of being boarded and searched by the US Coast Guard.

» For information about getting a ride as a yacht crew member, see p235.

# GETTING AROUND

Ferries are the primary mode of getting around between islands.

## Air

A few commercial services fly within the Virgins, especially between St Thomas and St Croix. Other than that, you'll need to charter a plane to fly between islands.

**Air Sunshine** (www.air sunshine.com) Commercial carrier with flights between St Croix and Tortola, and St Thomas and Tortola; the latter connects to a free ferry that goes onward to Virgin Gorda.

**Cape Air** (www.flycapeair. com) Commercial service between St Thomas' and St Croix's airports.

**Fly BVI** (www.bviaircharters. com) Charter service, which is especially useful for flying between Tortola and Anegada, though it will go to islands throughout the Caribbean.

**Island Birds** (www.island birds.com) Another charter service that's good for Anegada jaunts, as well as various destinations Caribbean-wide.

**Seaborne Airlines** (www. seaborneairlines.com) Popular commercial service that flies cool floatplanes between wharves at Charlotte Amalie, St Thomas and Christiansted, St Croix. The cost is around $80 each way.

## Bicycle

The lack of shoulder on most roads, the steep hills, the blind curves and the high number of cars on the largest islands conspire to make bike touring risky and not very popular.

Water Island, offshore from St Thomas, is the exception.

## Boat

Frequent and inexpensive public ferries connect the main islands in the Virgins, as well as several of the smaller islands. Locals count on these vessels to get around. See the tables, p239, p240 and p241, for some of the most-used routes.

» For trips between the USVI and BVI, a passport is required.

» Ferries between the USVI and BVI run until about 5pm only. Watch out for scheduling issues if you're trying to get between the two territories early in the morning or in the evening. The one exception is a 9pm ferry between Red Hook, St Thomas and Road Town, Tortola that operates Thursday through Sunday.

» For routes between Road Town and Virgin Gorda, or between Road Town and Charlotte Amalie – ie routes that multiple ferry companies ply – it can be a good idea to just buy a one-way ticket so you're not stuck waiting for a particular company upon return.

» All ferries listed here are for foot-passengers only. The sole car-ferry service operates between Red Hook, St Thomas and Cruz Bay, St John, though most car-rental companies do not allow their vehicles to travel between islands. See p85 for details.

» Despite the convoluted-looking schedule, the ferry service is easy to navigate. The free tourist magazines publish full schedules each month. Good online sources to check are the **BVI Welcome Guide** (www. bviwelcome.com) and **VI Now** (www.vinow.com). Or simply call the companies to get the most current times.

» We've included additional ferry information in the Get-

ting There & Around sections throughout this book.

» If you want to do it yourself, ie operate your own boat, the major islands have marinas where you can charter sailing yachts or powerboats, either bareboat or with a crew. See the Chartering a Boat chapter (p37) for more.

### Ferry Companies

See the ferry tables for the companies' routes.

**Inter-Island** (☑340-776-6597; www.interislandboat services.vi)

**Native Son** (☑284-495-4617; www.nativesonferry.com)

**New Horizon Ferry** (☑284-495-9278)

**North Sound Express** (☑284-495-2138)

**Peter Island Ferry** (☑284-495-2000)

**Road Town Fast Ferry** (☑284-494-2323; www.road townfastferry.com)

**Smith's Ferry** (☑284-494-4454; www.smithsferry.com)

**Speedy's** (☑284-495-5240; www.speedysbvi.com)

**Transportation Services** (☑340-776-6282)

**VI Seatrans** (☑340-776-5494; www.goviseatrans.com)

## Car & Motorcycle

Driving is undoubtedly the most convenient way to get around, as public transportation is limited and taxi fares add up in a hurry. Unlike some Caribbean islands, the

---

### BVI DEPARTURE TAX – BOAT

You must pay a $5 departure tax to leave the BVI by ferry. This is not included in the ticket price, and must be paid separately at the ferry terminal (usually at a window by the departure lounge).

## FERRIES FROM ST THOMAS

### Ferries from Charlotte Amalie

| DESTINATION | DURATION | FARE | FREQUENCY | COMPANY |
| --- | --- | --- | --- | --- |
| Cruz Bay, St John | 45min | $12 one way | 3 daily | Transportation Services |
| Christiansted, St Croix | 90min | $50 one way | 4 days weekly | VI Seatrans |
| Road Town, Tortola | 45min | $30 one way | several times daily | Road Town Fast Ferry, Speedy's, Smith's Ferry, Native Son |
| Spanish Town, Virgin Gorda | 90min | $40 one way | 3 days weekly | Speedy's |

### Ferries from Red Hook

| DESTINATION | DURATION | FARE | FREQUENCY | COMPANY |
| --- | --- | --- | --- | --- |
| Cruz Bay, St John | 20min | $6 one way | hourly | Transportation Services |
| West End, Tortola | 35min | $25-28 one way | 4-5 daily | Smith's Ferry, Native Son |
| Road Town, Tortola | 45min | $35 one way | 9pm night ferry Thu-Sun | Road Town Fast Ferry |
| Jost Van Dyke | 45min | $70 round trip | 2 daily (except none Wed or Thu) | Inter-Island |
| Spanish Town, Virgin Gorda | 75min | $80 round trip | 2 weekly (Thu & Sun) | Inter-Island |

Virgin Islands have no tradition of moped or motorcycle rentals to travelers.

## Automobile Associations

There is no AAA or other emergency road service, but most car-rental agencies will provide service to a customer with a breakdown.

## Driver's License

You can drive in the islands using a valid license from your home country. In the BVI, a temporary license is required if you're staying longer than 30 days; any car-rental agency can provide the paperwork.

## Fuel

Gasoline stations generally stay open until 7pm or so and sell fuel by the gallon. At press time, the price was about $4 per gallon, pretty much on par with the US mainland. You can use credit cards for fuel purchases on some islands but not others (such as St John). Many gas stations still have attendants who pump the fuel.

## Insurance

» Liability insurance is required in the Virgin Islands, but isn't always included in rental contracts as it's assumed drivers are covered under their personal auto insurance. Check carefully.

» A Collision Damage Waiver (CDW), which insures against damage to the car, is usually optional. Some credit cards cover CDW for a certain rental period, if you use the card to pay for the rental, and decline the policy offered by the rental company.

» Always check with your credit card issuer and your personal auto insurance company to see what coverage it offers in the Virgin Islands.

## Rental

To rent a car in the Virgin Islands you generally need to:

» be at least 25 years old

» hold a valid driver's license

» have a major credit card Cars cost between $55 and $85 per day. If you're traveling in peak season, it's wise to reserve a couple months in advance, as supplies are limited. Vehicle types vary:

## FERRIES FROM ST JOHN

### Ferries from Cruz Bay

| DESTINATION | DURATION | FARE | FREQUENCY | COMPANY |
|---|---|---|---|---|
| Red Hook, St Thomas | 20min | $6 one way | hourly | Transportation Services |
| Charlotte Amalie, St Thomas | 45min | $12 one way | 3 daily | Transportation Services |
| West End, Tortola | 30min | $45 round trip | 3 daily | Inter-Island |
| Jost Van Dyke | 45min | $70 round trip | 2 daily (except none Wed or Thu) | Inter-Island |

» On St Thomas and St Croix, most companies offer modern Japanese sedans. A small sedan is perfectly adequate for most conditions; a big car is a liability on the islands' crowded streets and winding roads.

» On St John and in the BVI, companies rent 4WD vehicles, which are better suited to the local terrain and backcountry exploration.

» You can choose between standard (stick shift) or automatic transmission, and vehicles with or without air-con. Standard transmission is preferable because of the constant and sudden gear changes required on the hilly, winding roads.

Major international car-rental companies have branches at the airports and sometimes at ferry terminals.

**Avis** (☎800-437-0358; www. avis.com)

**Budget** (☎800-268-8900; www.budget.com)

**Dollar** (☎800-800-4000; www.dollarcar.com)

**Hertz** (☎800-263-0600; www.hertz.com)

Local car-rental agencies abound. On the smaller islands they'll be your only choice. On the main islands, they sometimes have better deals than the big-name companies. In most cases they will bring the car to you if they're not located by airport or ferry terminal, but always ask. See the individual island chapters' Getting There & Around section for further information on rentals.

### ST THOMAS

**Dependable Car Rentals** (☎800-522-3076; www. dependablecar.com)

**Discount Car Rentals** (☎340-776-4858, 877-478-2833; www.discountcar.vi)

### ST JOHN

**Cool Breeze Jeep/Car Rental** (☎340-776-6588; www.coolbreezecarrental.com)

**Denzil Clyne Car Rental** (☎340-776-6715)

**St John Car Rental** (☎340-776-6103; www.stjohncarrental. com)

### ST CROIX

**Centerline Car Rentals** (☎340-778-0450, 888-288-8755; www.ccrvi.com)

**Olympic** (☎340-773-8000, 888-878-4227; www.olympic stcroix.com)

### TORTOLA

**Itgo Car Rentals** (☎284-494-5150; www.itgobvi.com)

### VIRGIN GORDA

**Mahogany Car Rentals** (☎284-495-5469; www. mahoganycarrentalsbvi.com)

**Speedy's Car Rental** (☎284-495-5240; www .speedysbvi.com)

## Road Conditions

Be prepared for challenging road conditions.

» Steep, winding roads are often the same width as your car, and the potholes can be outrageous.

» Chickens, cows and donkeys dart in and out of the roadway and, oh, did we mention the goats? Keep your eyes peeled for wandering critters.

» Roads can be quite slick after it rains.

» Rush-hour traffic jams occur in urbanized Charlotte Amalie (St Thomas), Christiansted (St Croix) and Road Town (Tortola).

## Road Rules

» Rule number one: drive on the left-hand side of the road.

» Seat belt use is compulsory; children under age five must be in a car seat.

» Proceed clockwise at traffic roundabouts.

» Driving while using a hand-held cell phone is illegal (but ear pieces are permitted).

» The speed limit on most roads is 30mph or less. Road signs and speed-limit signs are rare, but do watch for speed bumps, which are common.

» Note that drivers don't always heed the rules of the road, often stopping dead with no warning in the middle of the road to talk to friends

## Ferries from Road Town

| DESTINATION | DURATION | FARE | FREQUENCY | COMPANY |
|---|---|---|---|---|
| Spanish Town, Virgin Gorda | 30min | $30 round trip | roughly every hour | Speedy's, Smith's Ferry |
| Anegada | 90min | $45 round trip | 3 days weekly (Mon, Wed & Fri) | Road Town Fast Ferry |
| Peter Island | 30min | $20 round trip (free for restaurant customers) | 6 daily | Peter Island Ferry |
| Charlotte Amalie, St Thomas | 45min | $30 one way | several times daily | Road Town Fast Ferry, Speedy's, Smith's Ferry, Native Son |

## Ferries from West End

| DESTINATION | DURATION | FARE | FREQUENCY | COMPANY |
|---|---|---|---|---|
| Jost Van Dyke | 25min | $25 round trip | 5 daily | New Horizon Ferry |
| Red Hook, St Thomas | 35min | $25-28 one way | 4-5 daily | Smith's Ferry, Native Son |
| Cruz Bay, St John | 30min | $45 round trip | 3 daily | Inter-Island |

## Ferries from East End (Trellis Bay)

| DESTINATION | DURATION | FARE | FREQUENCY | COMPANY |
|---|---|---|---|---|
| Spanish Town or North Sound, Virgin Gorda | 15-35min | $40-65 round trip | several times daily (except none Sun) | North Sound Express |

or reversing their cars in the opposite lane of traffic if they've missed their turn.

» A common gesture is the flap: when drivers are about to do something (stop, turn etc), they may extend their arm horizontally out the window and waggle their hand up and down like a flapping bird.

## Hitchhiking

Hitching is never entirely safe in any country and we don't recommend it. That said, hitchhiking is not uncommon on St John, as it is a small island and there are only two main roads connecting Cruz Bay and Coral Bay.

## Local Transportation

### Bus

**Vitran** (fare $1) operates air-conditioned buses over the length of St Thomas, St John and St Croix. Buses run daily between 5:30am and 7:30pm, approximately once per hour.

In St Thomas, 'dollar buses' (aka 'safaris' or 'gypsy cabs') also stop along the routes. These vehicles are open-air pickup trucks that hold around 20 people. They look like taxis, except they're filled with locals instead of sun-burned tourists. Flag them down by flapping your hand, and press the buzzer to stop them when you reach your destination. The fare is $2.

### Taxi

All of the islands have taxis that are easily accessible in the main tourist areas. Most vehicles are vans that carry up to 12 passengers; sometimes they're open-air pickup trucks with bench seats and awnings. Rates are set, with prices listed in the free tourist guides. You can also access rate sheets from **VI Now** (www.vinow.com) and the **BVI Tourist Board** (www.bvitourism.com).

# Health

## BEFORE YOU GO

### Insurance

It's essential to purchase travel health insurance if your regular policy doesn't cover you when you're abroad. Check www.lonely planet.com/travel_services for supplemental insurance information.

Some policies specifically exclude 'dangerous activities' such as scuba diving. If these activities are on your agenda, avoid this sort of policy. You may prefer a policy that pays doctors or hospitals directly rather than making you pay first and claim later. If you have to claim later, keep *all* documentation. Check whether the policy covers ambulance fees or an emergency flight home.

### Medication

Bring medications you may need clearly labeled in their original containers. A signed, dated letter from your physician that describes your medical conditions and medications, including generic names, is also a good idea.

### Recommended Vaccinations

For most foreign visitors, no immunizations are required for entry to the Virgin Islands, though cholera and yellow fever vaccinations may be required of travelers from areas with a history of those diseases. All travelers should be up to date on routine immunizations.

### Medical Checklist

» acetaminophen (eg Tylenol) or aspirin
» anti-inflammatory drugs (eg ibuprofen)
» antihistamines (for hay fever and allergic reactions)
» antibacterial ointment (eg Neosporin) for cuts and abrasions
» steroid cream or cortisone (for poison ivy and other allergic rashes)
» bandages, gauze, gauze rolls
» adhesive or paper tape
» safety pins, tweezers
» thermometer
» DEET-containing insect repellent for the skin

» permethrin-containing insect spray for clothing, tents and bed nets
» sunblock
» motion-sickness medication
» eardrops for swimmer's ear

## Websites

USVI resources:
**USVI Department of Health** (www.healthvi.org)
General resources:
**MD Travel Health** (www.mdtravelhealth.com)
**World Health Organization** (www.who.int)
Government travel-health websites:
**Public Health Agency of Canada** (www.publichealth.gc.ca)
**United Kingdom** (www.nhs.gov/healthcareabroad)
**United States** (www.cdc.gov/travel)

## IN THE US & BRITISH VIRGIN ISLANDS

### Availability & Cost of Health Care

There are no unexpected health dangers on the islands; good medical attention is readily available, and the only real health concern is that a collision with the medical system can cause severe injuries to your finances. St Thomas, St Croix and Tortola have modern hospitals. You will find walk-in clinics on virtually every inhabited island.

In a serious emergency, call ☏911 (in both the USVI and BVI) or ☏999 (in the BVI) for an ambulance to take you to the nearest hospital's emergency room. ER charges are usually incredibly expensive unless you have valid medical insurance.

## ROUTINE IMMUNIZATIONS

| VACCINE | RECOMMENDED FOR | DOSAGE | SIDE EFFECTS |
| --- | --- | --- | --- |
| tetanus-diphtheria | all travelers who haven't had booster within 10 years | one dose lasts 10 years | soreness at injection site |
| measles | travelers born after 1956 who've had only one measles vaccination | one dose | fever, rash, joint pains, allergic reactions |
| chickenpox | travelers who've never had chickenpox | two doses one month apart | fever, mild case of chickenpox |
| influenza | all travelers during flu season (November through March) | one dose | soreness at the injection site, fever |

There are pharmacies on St Thomas, St Croix, St John, Tortola and Virgin Gorda. Pharmacies sometimes run out of medications. If you are dependent on a particular medication be sure to travel with it, and have a copy of your prescription.

# Environmental Hazards

## Food & Water

In the Virgin Islands, standards of cleanliness in places serving food and drink are generally high.

Bottled drinking water, both carbonated and noncarbonated, is widely available on the islands. Tap water is usually OK to drink, but ask locally.

## Motion Sickness

Eating lightly before and during a trip will reduce the chance of motion sickness. If you are prone to motion sickness, try to find a place that minimizes disturbance; for example, near the wing on aircraft or near the center on boats. Fresh air usually helps. Commercial anti-motion sickness preparations, which can cause drowsiness, have to be taken before the trip commences; once you feel sick, it's too late. Ginger, a natural preventative, is available in capsule form from health-food stores.

## Sunburn

Use sunscreen with a high protection factor (SPF) for any parts of your body exposed to the sun.

## Heat Exhaustion

Dehydration is the main contributor. Symptoms include feeling weak, headache, nausea and sweaty skin. Lay the victim flat with their legs raised, apply cool, wet cloths to the skin, and rehydrate.

## Fungal Infections

These infections, which occur with greater frequency in hot weather, are most likely to occur on the scalp, between the toes or fingers (athlete's foot), in the groin (jock itch or crotch rot) and on the body (ringworm). You get ringworm (which is a fungal infection, not a worm) from infected animals or by walking on damp areas such as shower floors.

To prevent fungal infections, wear loose, comfortable clothes, avoid clothing made from artificial fibers, wash frequently and dry carefully. If you do get an infection, wash the infected area daily with a disinfectant or medicated soap and water, and rinse and dry well. Apply an antifungal powder and try to expose the infected area to air or sunlight as much as possible. Change underwear and towels frequently, and wash them often in hot water.

# Infectious Diseases

## Dengue Fever

Dengue fever is a viral infection common throughout the Caribbean. The Virgins and nearby Puerto Rico experience periodic epidemics of it.

A particular species of daytime mosquito spreads the disease. The best way to avoid dengue is to use mosquito repellents liberally, as there is no treatment for the disease once it is in your system. A sudden onset of fever and muscle and joint pains are the first signs of the disease before a rash starts on the trunk of the body and spreads to the limbs and face. Hospitals can treat your symptoms, so by all means seek medical attention if you suspect that you have contracted dengue.

The fever and other symptoms usually begin to subside after a few days. Serious complications are not common, but persisting weakness, returning fever and fits of depression can last a month or more.

## Cuts, Bites & Stings

Skin punctures, such as those caused by coral, can easily become infected in hot climates and heal slowly. Treat any cut by first washing it with soap and fresh water, then cleaning it with an antiseptic such as Betadine. Finally, smear the wound with triple-antibiotic salve to prevent the further introduction of infection. When possible, avoid bandages and Band-Aids, which can keep wounds wet.

The stings of bees and wasps and nonpoisonous spider bites are usually painful rather than dangerous. Calamine lotion will give relief, and ice packs will reduce the pain and swelling. Mosquitoes and no see 'ums (tiny biting insects) can also be a major annoyance. Bring insect repellent.

If you get caught in jellyfish tentacles, peel off the tentacles using paper or a towel to protect your fingers. To alleviate the itchy sting, wash the affected area with salt water or vinegar.

# Glossary

**accra** – a fried mixture of okra, black-eyed peas, pepper and salt

**back time** – a Creole expression meaning 'good old days'

**bareboat** – a sail-it-yourself charter yacht, usually rented by the week or longer

**breadfruit** – an introduced tree common throughout the Caribbean whose round, green fruit is prepared like potatoes

**bush tea** – tea made from the islands' leaves, roots and herbs. Each tea, with names like 'sorrel,' 'tamarind,' 'worry vine,' 'worm grass' and 'Spanish needle'; can cure specific illnesses, such as gas, menstrual pain, colds or insomnia.

**BVI** – British Virgin Islands

**calabeza** – pumpkin soup

**callaloo** – also spelled kallaloo; a soup made with dasheen leaves that resembles a creamy spinach soup.

**calypso** – a popular Caribbean music essential to carnival

**carambola** – star fruit; a green-to-yellow fruit with a star-shaped cross section.

**carnival** – the major Caribbean festival; originally a pre-Lenten festivity blending African and Christian traditions, it is now observed at various times throughout the year.

**cassava** – yucca or manioc; a root used since precolonial times as a staple of island diets, whether steamed, baked or grated into a flour for bread.

**cassareep** – a molasseslike sauce used in local recipes, made of cassava, water, sugar and spices

**cay** – an Arawak word meaning 'small island'

**christophene** – a common pear-shaped vegetable, like a cross between a potato and a cucumber, that is eaten raw in salads or cooked like a squash

**continental** – an individual from the US mainland

**Creole** – a person of mixed black and European ancestry; also the local pidgin language, which is a combination of English (or, elsewhere, French) and African languages; also the local cuisine, characterized by spicy, full-flavored sauces and a heavy use of green peppers and onions

**dasheen** – a type of taro; the leaves are known as *callaloo* and cooked much like spinach or turnip leaves, while the starchy tuberous root is boiled and eaten like a potato.

**Daube meat** – a pot roast seasoned with vinegar, native seasonings, onion, garlic, tomato, thyme, parsley and celery

**dolphin** – both a marine mammal found in Caribbean waters and a common type of white-meat fish (also called mahimahi); the two are not related, and 'dolphin' on any menu always refers to the fish.

**down island** – a Creole expression referring to the islands of the Lesser Antilles south of the Virgins

**duppy** – a ghost or spirit; also called a *jumbie*.

**flying fish** – a gray-meat fish named for its ability to skim above the water

**frangipani** – a small tree with fragrant pink or white flowers called plumeria

**fungi** – a semihard cornmeal pudding similar to Italian polenta, added to soups and used as a side dish; also a Creole name for the music made by local scratch bands.

**gade** – Danish for 'street'

**ground provisions** – roots used for cooking

**gneps** – a fruit the size of a large marble that yields a sweet, orange flesh

**Ital** – a natural style of vegetarian cooking practiced by Rastafarians

**johnnycake** – a cornflour griddle cake (sometimes baked)

**jumbie** – a ghost or spirit; also called a *duppy*.

**jump up** – a nighttime street party that usually involves dancing and plenty of rum drinking

**limin'** – from the Creole verb 'to lime,' meaning to hang out, relax, chill

**mahimahi** – see 'dolphin'

**manchineel** – a tree common to Caribbean beaches whose fruit and sap can cause a severe skin rash

**mash up** – a wreck, a car accident or a street riot

**mauby** – a bittersweet drink made from the bark of the 'mauby' or 'carob' tree, sweetened with sugar and spices

**mocko jumbies** – costumed stilt walkers representing spirits of the dead, seen in carnivals

**native seasoning** – homemade mixtures of salt, ground hot pepper, cloves, garlic, mace, nutmeg, celery and parsley

**obeah** – a system of ancestral worship related to voodoo and rooted in West African religions

**out islands** – islands or cays that lie across the water from the main islands of an island group

**Painkiller** – probably the most popular alcoholic drink in the Virgins, made with two parts rum, one part orange juice, four parts pineapple juice, one part coconut cream and a sprinkle of nutmeg and cinnamon

**pate** – a fried pastry of cassava or plantain dough stuffed with spiced goat, pork, chicken, conch, lobster or fish

**paw paw** – common Caribbean name for papaya

**pepperpot** – a spicy stew made with various meats, accompanied by peppers and cassareep

**pigeon peas** – brown, pea-like seeds of a tropical shrub that are cooked like peas and served mixed with rice

**plantain** – a starchy fruit of the banana family that is usually fried or grilled like a vegetable

**planters punch** – a punch made of rum and fruit juice

**rendezvous diving** – service common to Virgin Island dive operators, where a dive boat picks you up from your chartered yacht and brings you back at the end of the day

**rise and shine tramps** – noisy parades led by reggae bands in the back of a truck starting at 3am during BVI's Emancipation Festival

**roti** – West Indian fast food of flat bread filled with curry (often potatoes and chicken) and rolled up

**scratch band** – a West Indian band that uses homemade percussion instruments such as washboards, ribbed gourds and conch shells to accompany

a singer and melody played on a recorder or flute

**snowbirds** – North Americans, usually retired, who come to the VI for its warm winters

**sorrel juice** – a lightly tart, bright-red tea drink rich in vitamin C, made from the flowers of the sorrel plant

**soursop** – an irregularly shaped fruit with a cottony pulp that is fragrant yet bland or acidic in taste, hinting at guava and pineapple; used for puddings, ice cream, canned drinks and syrups.

**souse** – a dish made of a pickled pig's head and belly, spices and a few vegetables

**steel pan** – also called 'steel drum,' it refers both to a percussion instrument made from oil drums and to the music it produces

**strade** – Danish for 'step street'

**tamarind** – the legumelike pod of a large tropical tree, or the juice made from the seeds

**tannia** – an edible tuber used in soups; also called 'blue taro.'

**USVI** – United States Virgin Islands

**welcoming arms staircase** – a staircase that flares at the base

# behind the scenes

## SEND US YOUR FEEDBACK

We love to hear from travelers – your comments keep us on our toes and help make our books better. Our well-traveled team reads every word on what you loved or loathed about this book. Although we cannot reply individually to postal submissions, we always guarantee that your feedback goes straight to the appropriate authors, in time for the next edition. Each person who sends us information is thanked in the next edition – and the most useful submissions are rewarded with a free book.

Visit **lonelyplanet.com/contact** to submit your updates and suggestions or to ask for help. Our award-winning website also features inspirational travel stories, news and discussions.

Note: we may edit, reproduce and incorporate your comments in Lonely Planet products such as guidebooks, websites and digital products, so let us know if you don't want your comments reproduced or your name acknowledged. For a copy of our privacy policy visit lonelyplanet.com/privacy.

## AUTHOR THANKS

### Karla Zimmerman

Mega-thanks to Lisa Beran and Tamara Beran Robinson for helping research the Painkillers and piña coladas. Thanks the following people for sharing their local knowledge: Casey Mc-Nutt, Don Near, Olasee Davis, Mr Frett, Dmitri at Magens Bay, Matthew Telesford and Bailey at Udder Delite. Extreme gratefulness to Lonely Planeteers Nora Gregory, Bruce Evans, Martine Power and Alison Lyall for advice and extreme patience. Thanks most of all to Eric Markowitz, the world's best partner-for-life and one helluva an eco-camper.

## ACKNOWLEDGMENTS

Climate map data adapted from Peel MC, Finlayson BL & McMahon TA (2007) 'Updated World Map of the Köppen-Geiger Climate Classification', *Hydrology and Earth System Sciences*, 11, 163344.

Cover photograph: Palm trees on a beach, the Baths, Virgin Gorda, Purestock/Photolibrary

Many of the images in this guide are available for licensing from Lonely Planet Images: www.lonelyplanetimages.com.

## THIS BOOK

This guidebook was commissioned in Lonely Planet's Oakland office, and produced by the following:
**Commissioning Editor**
Nora Gregory
**Coordinating Editor**
Martine Power
**Coordinating Cartographer** Ildiko Bogdanovits

**Coordinating Layout Designer** Carol Jackson
**Managing Editors** Bruce Evans, Annelies Mertens
**Managing Cartographers** Shahara Ahmed, Alison Lyall
**Managing Layout Designer** Chris Girdler
**Assisting Editors** Elizabeth Anglin, Beth Hall, Carly Hall, Matty Soccio, Gina Tsarouhas

**Assisting Cartographer** Valeska Cañas
**Cover Research** Naomi Parker
**Internal Image Research** Aude Vauconsant
**Thanks to**
Helen Christinis, Laura Crawford, Melanie Dankel, Anna Metcalfe, Susan Paterson, Averil Robertson, Juan Winata

NOTES

# index

# how to use this book

**These symbols will help you find the listings you want:**

- ◉ Sights
- 🏖 Beaches
- 🏃 Activities
- 🍴 Courses
- 👉 Tours
- 🎉 Festivals & Events
- 🛏 Sleeping
- ✖ Eating
- 🍺 Drinking
- ☆ Entertainment
- 🛍 Shopping
- ℹ Information/Transport

**These symbols give you the vital information for each listing:**

- 📞 Telephone Numbers
- ⊙ Opening Hours
- 🅿 Parking
- ⊝ Nonsmoking
- ❄ Air-Conditioning
- @ Internet Access
- 🛜 Wi-Fi Access
- 🏊 Swimming Pool
- 🥗 Vegetarian Selection
- 📖 English-Language Menu
- 👪 Family-Friendly
- 🐾 Pet-Friendly
- 🚌 Bus
- ⛴ Ferry
- Ⓜ Metro
- Ⓢ Subway
- ⊖ London Tube
- 🚋 Tram
- 🚆 Train

Reviews are organised by author preference.

## Map Legend

### Sights
- ◉ Beach
- ◉ Buddhist
- ◉ Castle
- ◉ Christian
- ◉ Hindu
- ◉ Islamic
- ◉ Jewish
- ◉ Monument
- ◉ Museum/Gallery
- ◉ Ruin
- ◉ Winery/Vineyard
- ◉ Zoo
- ◉ Other Sight

### Activities, Courses & Tours
- ◉ Diving/Snorkelling
- ◉ Canoeing/Kayaking
- ◉ Skiing
- ◉ Surfing
- ◉ Swimming/Pool
- ◉ Walking
- ◉ Windsurfing
- ◉ Other Activity/Course/Tour

### Sleeping
- ◉ Sleeping
- ◉ Camping

### Eating
- ◉ Eating

### Drinking
- ◉ Drinking
- ◉ Cafe

### Entertainment
- ◉ Entertainment

### Shopping
- ◉ Shopping

### Information
- ◉ Post Office
- ◉ Tourist Information

### Transport
- ◉ Airport
- ◉ Border Crossing
- ◉ Bus
- +◉+ Cable Car/Funicular
- -◉- Cycling
- -◉- Ferry
- Ⓜ Metro
- ◉ Monorail
- 🅿 Parking
- Ⓢ S-Bahn
- ◉ Taxi
- +◉+ Train/Railway
- ◉ Tram
- ☺ Tube Station
- Ⓤ U-Bahn
- • Other Transport

### Routes
- Tollway
- Freeway
- Primary
- Secondary
- Tertiary
- Lane
- Unsealed Road
- Plaza/Mall
- Steps
- ⊱ ≡ ⊰ Tunnel
- Pedestrian Overpass
- Walking Tour
- Walking Tour Detour
- Path

### Boundaries
- International
- State/Province
- Disputed
- Regional/Suburb
- Marine Park
- Cliff
- Wall

### Population
- ◉ Capital (National)
- ◉ Capital (State/Province)
- ◉ City/Large Town
- • Town/Village

### Geographic
- ◉ Hut/Shelter
- ◉ Lighthouse
- ◉ Lookout
- ▲ Mountain/Volcano
- ◉ Oasis
- ◉ Park
- )( Pass
- ◉ Picnic Area
- ◉ Waterfall

### Hydrography
- River/Creek
- Intermittent River
- Swamp/Mangrove
- Reef
- Canal
- Water
- Dry/Salt/Intermittent Lake
- Glacier

### Areas
- Beach/Desert
- +++ Cemetery (Christian)
- ××× Cemetery (Other)
- Park/Forest
- Sportsground
- Sight (Building)
- Top Sight (Building)

# OUR STORY

A beat-up old car, a few dollars in the pocket and a sense of adventure. In 1972 that's all Tony and Maureen Wheeler needed for the trip of a lifetime – across Europe and Asia overland to Australia. It took several months, and at the end – broke but inspired – they sat at their kitchen table writing and stapling together their first travel guide, *Across Asia on the Cheap*. Within a week they'd sold 1500 copies. Lonely Planet was born.

Today, Lonely Planet has offices in Melbourne, London and Oakland, with more than 600 staff and writers. We share Tony's belief that 'a great guidebook should do three things: inform, educate and amuse'.

# OUR WRITERS

### Karla Zimmerman

During her island travels, Karla hiked past wild donkeys on St John, ate an embarrassing number of johnnycakes on St Thomas, got splashed by beer-guzzling pigs on St Croix, bashed through the Baths on Virgin Gorda and felt no pain on Jost Van Dyke. She first bounced around the Virgins when she was a kid, and still remembers the awe of seeing the true-blue hue of Magens Bay on that initial visit. Karla is based in Chicago, and writes travel features for newspapers, books, magazines and websites. She has authored or coauthored several Lonely Planet guidebooks covering the USA, Canada, Caribbean and Europe.

Read more about Karla at:
lonelyplanet.com/members/karlazimmerman

**Published by Lonely Planet Publications Pty Ltd**
ABN 36 005 607 983
1st edition – Sep 2011
ISBN 978 1 74104 201 6
© Lonely Planet 2011   Photographs © as indicated 2011
10 9 8 7 6 5 4 3 2 1
Printed in China